Bangkok

Bangkok is one of Asia's most interesting, varied, controversial and challenging cities. It is a city of contradictions, both in its present and its past. This unique book examines the development of the city from its earliest days as the seat of the Thai monarchy to its current position as an infamous contemporary metropolis.

Bangkok: Place, Practice and Representation is an in-depth study of the institutions and the people who shape the Thai metropolis. Adopting insights from anthropology, urban studies and human geography, the book is a powerful account of the city and its dynamic spaces. Marc Askew examines the city's variety, from the inner-city slums to the rural–urban fringe, and gives us a keen insight into the daily life of the city's inhabitants, be they middle-class suburbanites or women sex workers.

Accessibly written and rich in detail, maps and photographs, this is the definitive account of the Thai capital. It should be essential reading for anyone with an interest in urban studies, anthropology or Asian studies, as well as the general reader wanting to learn more about this complex city.

Marc Askew is Senior Lecturer in Asian Studies at Victoria University of Technology, Melbourne.

Asia's Transformations

Edited by Mark Selden
Binghamton University and Cornell University, USA

The books in this series explore the political, social, economic and cultural consequences of Asia's twentieth-century transformations. The series emphasises the tumultuous interplay of local, national, regional and global forces as Asia bids to become the hub of the world economy. While focusing on the contemporary, it also looks back to analyse the antecedents of Asia's contested rise.

This series comprises several strands:

Asia's Transformations aims to address the needs of students and teachers, and the titles will be published in hardback and paperback. Titles include:

Debating Human Rights
Critical essays from the United States and Asia
Edited by Peter Van Ness

Hong Kong's History
State and society under colonial rule
Edited by Tak-Wing Ngo

Japan's Comfort Women
Sexual slavery and prostitution during World War II and the US occupation
Yuki Tanaka

Opium, Empire and the Global Political Economy
Carl A. Trocki

Chinese Society
Change, conflict and resistance
Edited by Elizabeth J. Perry and Mark Selden

Mao's Children in the New China
Voices from the Red Guard generation
Yarong Jiang and David Ashley

Remaking the Chinese State
Strategies, society and security
Edited by Chien-min Chao and Bruce J. Dickson

Korean Society
Civil society, democracy and the State
Edited by Charles K. Armstrong

The Making of Modern Korea
Adrian Buzo

Routledge Studies in Asia's Transformations is a forum for innovative new research intended for a high-level specialist readership, and the titles will be available in hardback only. Titles include:

1 **The American Occupation of Japan and Okinawa***
Literature and memory
Michael Molasky

2 **Koreans in Japan**
Critical voices from the margin
Edited by Sonia Ryang

3 **Internationalizing the Pacific**
The United States, Japan and the Institute of Pacific Relations in War and Peace, 1919–1945
Tomoko Akami

4 **Imperialism in Southeast Asia**
'A fleeting, passing phase'
Nicholas Tarling

*Now available in paperback

Asia's Global Cities is an interdisciplinary series, drawing on the latest thinking in urban studies, cultural geography, anthropology, sociology, history and Asian studies. Each book explores the interaction of the local with the global in the history, development and future of a significant city in Asia. The books are designed to appeal to the general reader seeking a textured portrait of a city as well as students and academics.

Bangkok
Place, practice and representation
Marc Askew

Beijing in the Modern World
David Strand and Madeline Yue Dong

Singapore
Carl Trocki

Shanghai
Global city
Jeff Wasserstorm

Hong Kong
Global city
Stephen Chiu and Tai-Lok Lui

To Dr M.R. Akin Rabibhadana, mentor and friend

Bangkok

Place, practice and representation

Marc Askew

London and New York

First published 2002
by Routledge
11 New Fetter Lane, London EC4P 4EE

Simultaneously published in the USA and Canada
by Routledge
29 West 35th Street, New York, NY 10001

Routledge is an imprint of the Taylor & Francis Group

Typeset in Times by
Florence Production Ltd, Stoodleigh Devon
Printed and bound in Great Britain by
T. J. International Ltd, Padstow, Cornwall

British Library Cataloguing in Publication Data
A catalogue record for this book is available from the British Library

Library of Congress Cataloging in Publication Data
A catalogue record for this book is available from
the Library of Congress

ISBN 0–415–18853–9 (hbk)
ISBN 0–415–18854–7 (pbk)

Contents

Figures

Plates

Tables

Acknowledgements

Many people and institutions have given assistance to me in the long task of research and writing for this book. Above all, I am grateful to the numerous Thai academics, officials, experts, activists and research assistants without whose assistance this work would not have begun, much less been completed. Dr M.R. Akin Rabibhadana has been a constant source of advice and ideas concerning the study of the people of Bangkok – I owe him much. Dr Paritta Chalermpow-Koanantakool, of Thammasat University, has offered valuable advice and insights. Dr Suwattana Thadaniti first welcomed me to the Department of Urban and Regional Planning at Chulalongkorn University in 1990 and has been of great assistance during various research projects ever since. Of my colleagues at the Department of Urban and Regional Planning (where I taught during 1993), particular thanks to Dr Nipan Vichiennoi, Doosadee Thaitakoo, Khwansuwong Athipho and Associate-Professor Kiat Chivakul for their advice and assistance with research materials. Dr Amara Phongsaphich generously allowed me to base my early projects at the Chulalongkorn University Social Research Institute. Professors Pasuk Phongpaichit and Sungsit Phiriyarangsan welcomed me at the Political Economy Centre (Faculty of Economics, Chulalongkorn University) during 1995 when I began my research into the culture of the urban poor in Bangkok. Drs Dhidar Saraya and Sunait Chutintaranond of the Faculty of Letters, Chulalongkorn University, have been a constant source of advice and constructive criticism. Thanks to Dr Banasophit Mekvichai, for inviting me to undertake social research into the Khlong Toei communities under the auspices of the LIFE Programme (UNDP). Professor Srisak Vallibhothama of Sinlapakorn University encouraged my work in its early stages and offered valuable perspectives on local history and cultures in Bangkok. Suchit Wongthes, editor of Sinlapa Watthanatham, gave me insights into the politics of historical memory in Thailand. The support of Professors M.C. Subhadradis Diskul and Kamthon Kulachon was critical to my first entry into research into conservation policy in Bangkok.

At Srinakarinwirote University Dr Plublung Kolchana and Achan Kawee Worrakawin have been stalwart friends who have helped me in numerous ways. For permitting interviews and aiding my research, many thanks to

Dr Uthis Khaothian of the National Economic and Social Development Board, Khun Chaiwat Thirapantu of the Bangkok Forum, Khru Prateep Ungsongtham of the Duang Prateep Foundation, Khun Somchai Chuaykliang of the Training Institute for the Urban Poor and Khun Sompong Patbui of the Grass roots Development Foundation. The indomitable Father Joseph Maier of the Human Development Foundation and his stalwart team of community workers gave much-needed assistance and insights into the complexities and politics of Khlong Toei. Officials and researchers at the National Housing Authority of Thailand generously provided data and helped with a number of field visits to various NHA projects throughout the Bangkok region. The assistance of officials of the community development office of Nonthaburi Province was critical to facilitating my research in Bang Kruai and Bang Buathong, as was the help of my colleague Nirundon Thapachai (Kasetsaert University). To the many Thai graduate students who assisted in various local field surveys many thanks, in particular to Pranee Monthongdaeng, and Orathai Lertjittisuth. Pitch Phongsawat has been a stalwart friend, assistant and sounding board in this research, a remarkable thinker who will one day produce a far more incisive study of Bangkok. Thanks also, Pitch, for the use of your motorbike.

I owe debts of gratitude to numerous people, both inside and outside Thailand, for sharing ideas and providing me with research materials, advice and assistance. Among them are Dr Jacques Amyot of CUSRI (Chulalongkorn University), Dr Douglas Webster, of the Urban Coordination Division, NESDB and Professor Takashi Tomosugi, of the Institute of Oriental Culture, University of Tokyo. Mark Stevenson (Victoria University) and Leif Jonsson (now at Arizona State University) offered ideas and feedback on critical questions of ethnography and interpretation. Chris McConville helped me work through ideas about condominiums in the cities of the Asia-Pacific. The late Dr Larry Sternstein gave valuable perspectives and information on his urban planning experiences in Bangkok in the 1960s. Richard Guitard of Bangkok has encouraged my research from its early beginnings and has introduced me to many remarkable people in the city. Erik White (Cornell University) was always happy to engage in long open-ended discussions about Bangkok. Mike Montesano has been a source of constant moral support. Thanks to Jonathan Rigg, Mark Stevenson and Pitch Phongsawat for reading and commenting on chapter drafts. Mark Selden gave useful comments and sensible advice in the final stages of manuscript preparation. Craig Fowlie of Routledge has been a tolerant, patient and encouraging general editor. Thanks to Chandra Jayasuriya (University of Melbourne) for dealing so cheerfully and professionally with my often complicated cartographic demands, and to the cartographers of the Geography Department of the National University of Singapore and Routledge, London.

Numerous institutions have been vital to the research behind this volume and the various articles and reports on which is based. My thanks to the staff of the National Archives of Thailand, the Thailand Information Centre of Chulalongkorn University, the libraries of the Siam Society (Bangkok), the Echols Collection (Cornell University), the Australian National University, the National University of Singapore, and the Institute of Southeast Asian Studies, Singapore. Particular thanks to Emily Wark and Mark Armstrong-Roper of Footscray Park campus library of Victoria University of Technology. The National Research Council of Thailand allowed me to undertake most of the research which forms the basis for this book.

Earlier versions of a number of chapters have previously appeared as reports or journal articles. Chapter 2 is an extensively revised version of *The Making of Modern Bangkok: State, Market and People in the Shaping of the Thai Metropolis* (Background Report. Bangkok: Thailand Development Research Institute 1993). Chapter 4 develops themes first explored in *The Banglamphu District: A Portrait of Change in Inner Bangkok* (Background Report. Bangkok: Thailand Development Research Institute 1993). An earlier version of Chapter 6 was first published as 'Community-building among the Bangkok middle class'(*Southeast Asia Research* Vol. 7, No. 1, 1999: 93–120). Chapter 9 is based on 'City of women, city of foreign men: working spaces and re-working identities among female sex workers in Bangkok's tourist zone' (*Singapore Journal of Tropical Geography* Vol. 19, No. 2, 1998: 130–50). My thanks to the editors of these journals for permitting me to draw on these previously published articles.

Funding support for research was facilitated by a number of grants from the Australian Research Council (two ARC small grants and one large ARC grant) over the period 1993–7, in addition to supplementary funding from the Faculty of Arts, Victoria University of Technology. Research on the Khlong Toei slum settlements was funded by the LIFE project (UNDP). Supplementary funding for research in Nonthaburi was provided by The Japan International Cooperation Agency (JICA). Additional support for research assistance in Banglamphu was provided by the Thai Development Research Institute. The Faculty of Arts and the Department of Asian and International Studies of Victoria University of Technology kindly granted me the research leave to travel to Thailand for extended periods. Thanks to Professors Rodger Eade, Des Eccles and Stephanie Fahey for supporting my research in Bangkok from its early stages. During my time as teaching fellow at the National University of Singapore during 1997–8 the Southeast Asian Studies Programme kindly permitted me to travel to Thailand to undertake research in Bangkok for various periods. Particular thanks to Dr Richard Chauvel, Head of the Department of Asian and International Studies, VUT, for allowing me the time to complete the manuscript with a bearable teaching load and adding further encouragement with copious supplies of fresh Indonesian coffee and goodwill.

I must extend a special thanks to the ordinary people of Bangkok and region for their vital contribution to the studies which comprise this book. To the people of Ban Dukdin and Trok Bowon-Rangsi, the Sukhumvit area, the Pratchaniwet 2/3 housing estate, the slum communities of Khlong Toei, Bangkapi and Bankum, the *chaosuan* of Bang Khanun and the villages of Tambon Phimonrat in Nonthaburi Province, to all the 'good women of Bangkok', and to the Bangkok traffic police (who did not fine me too much) *khop khun khrap*! The goodwill, generosity, humour and willingness of ordinary Thai people to share with me their thoughts, hopes and fears have been critical to my research. I hope that in the pages of this book I have shown them the consideration and respect that they deserve.

In conclusion, a number of very personal thanks are in order. To Peter McGrady for his constant friendship. To my mother for her undying tolerance. To Arunee Suphason and family who taught me so much about the joys and sorrows of the people of the northeast and their encounters with Bangkok. And to Jane, whose love and understanding made the writing of the final manuscript possible.

Note on transliteration and Thai names

Thais are most commonly identified by their first names and I have therefore followed this practice in the text. I also adhere to Thai convention in listing Thai authors alphabetically by first name in the bibliography. For Thai words in the text I have used a simplified version of the ALA–Library of Congress/Library of Congress transliteration scheme (ALA–LC Romanization Tables, 1997 edn), without the diacritical marks. However, I have followed alternative transliterations of names and places in cases where they are already widely used (e.g. 'Chulalongkorn', rather than 'Chulalongkon', preferred in LA/ALA) or where such variant spellings are already used in English language publications of Thai authors (including books, journals and newspaper articles). In the bibliography, titles in Thai language are first given in transliteration followed by English translations in square parentheses.

Introduction

Interpreting Bangkok: place, practice and representation

On visiting Bangkok in 1923, the English author Somerset Maugham was stimulated to reflect on a perennial question: 'And who can so describe a city as to give a significant picture of it? It is a different place to everyone who lives in it. No one can tell what it is' (Maugham 1995: 151). It is not surprising that the capital city of Thailand (then Siam) should have provoked such a profound reflection for Maugham: for it was an enigma, combining elements of modernity familiar to this urbane Englishman – its busy commercial streets, stately boulevards and European-style buildings – yet throwing up strange juxtapositions with older and indigenous ways of life – glittering temple roofs, serpentine canals and villages. In three succinct sentences Maugham had conveyed much of what postmodern scholars over the past decade have been writing volumes about – that the meanings of cities are variable.

It is in the nature of great cities to provoke powerful responses from visitors and inhabitants alike: they are artefacts which function as metaphors and signs, applied to people, culture and values. Thus Bangkok has generated a variety of responses and images from insiders and outsiders. Since the recent financial crisis, Bangkok's unfinished skyscrapers have been viewed as metaphors for the cupidity of the city's economic elite and a punishment for the overconfidence of the boom decade of the 1980s, when pundits were proclaiming Thailand as the newly arrived 'Fifth Asian Tiger' economy (after Taiwan, Korea, Hong Kong and Singapore). Tourists and scholars alike have marvelled at the ability of this metropolis (with nearly nine million people) to continue to function with its constipating traffic jams and high levels of pollution. Foreign journalists, novelists and scholars gaze at Bangkok as a gaudy world centre of the sex trade – obsessing (like many tourists) on its small number of conspicuous red-light districts geared to western and foreign consumption. These responses, however one-dimensional and simplified, bespeak the tangible reality that Bangkok has become a city of considerable significance in global terms.

Foreigners alone do not fashion the image of Bangkok, although the world media and western academia are myopically self-righteous enough to reproduce simple stereotypes which focus on sin and pollution. From its inception as the Thai royal capital of Krung Thep, this city has stood out from its hinterland as a centre of power and status. In the later nineteenth century, as it emerged as the locus of a commercialised economy and a modernising society, the city generated more complex responses – positive and negative – from ordinary people and intellectuals alike. Distinctions between sophisticated city people (*khon muang*) and simple country 'hicks' (*khon ban nok*) have long been embedded in common forms of Thai discourse, and persist today despite the increasing convergence in values and tastes between the people of Bangkok and those who live outside the capital. As Raymond Williams observed, the persistent force of an oversimplified contrast between 'the city' and 'the countryside' in the contemporary period underlines the fact that this contrast 'is one of the major forms in which we become conscious of a central part of our experience and of the crises of our society' (Williams 1973: 347). By 'experience and crises' Williams was referring to those continuing changes in social and economic relations which have been so intimately tied to processes of capitalism and urbanisation. Early sociologists of the West (whose discipline itself emerged from these transformations) tried to encapsulate these transformations in the concept of 'urbanism', whereby new ways of life, socio-economic relations and even mentalities associated with the city came to increasingly dominate whole societies. As the key site of economic and social change, Bangkok has been represented by Thai moralists as the antithesis of Thai–Buddhist ethics of modesty and self-sufficiency. Others have denounced its degenerate character as a 'second-rate western city'– a foreign import fraught with the contradictions between its plush suburbs and its slums, a denial of the harmonious coexistence between people and their environment which was allegedly a hallmark of the true 'Thai' way of life. Such ideals and constructions ignore that fact that the seeds of modern transformation in Thailand emerged from an earlier history of urbanism based in Thai history and rooted in the social order and functions of its capital city. And however much it is vehemently denied, Bangkok *does* represent Thailand: in an intense, confused and complex way, the capital is shaped by ways of life and power structures which have evolved in Thai society at large.[1]

Bangkok has always been the dominant urban centre of the kingdom in terms of population. By the late twentieth century Bangkok held the highest proportion of its national urban population (56 per cent, according to some sources) of any capital city in the world (United Nations 1991). Thus, in Thailand, the urban experience has been particularly centred in its metropolis. The sociologist Rudiger Korff has aptly noted:

> Bangkok continuously gives birth to new social groups, new meanings and symbols, new institutions and fashions. Even the critique of life in Bangkok and the denunciations of Bangkok society as damaged

> and corrupted is born in the city itself, and can only be understood in reference to the dynamics of change in Bangkok.
>
> (Korff 1989a: 9)

In Thailand over the past decades, Bangkok has been evoked and implicated in debates and commentaries on the question of social, cultural and economic transformation: among intellectuals, academics, leading monks and journalists. A rich and vigorous literature has emerged around the question of the meaning and relevance of the past, whether in terms of Thai values, economy, or of transformations in the material environment. The problems and promises of Bangkok, both as a specific habitat, or as a symbol of urban life, have been a key focus of attention in debate. The varied transformations generated by advanced capitalism and social change have been registered in the emergence of new terms, paradigms and conflicts around the meanings of culture (*watthanatham*) heritage (*moradok*), community (*chumchon*) and development (*kanphatthana*) in the city and beyond.

Manuel Castells has argued that '. . . cities, like all social reality, are historical products, not only in their physical materiality but in their cultural meaning . . .' (Castells 1983: 302). Following this, my aim in this book is to explore the character of Thailand's contemporary metropolis as a dynamic and ongoing product of structural change and broad global processes interacting with history and culture. In the core chapters of this book I study closely the people who live and work in – and otherwise encounter – the metropolis as individuals, groups, neighbourhoods and households. I view them as the key agents in the shaping of this metropolis in all its complexity. This approach is a product of my own encounters with the tangible complexity of Bangkok as a congeries of localities – as experienced not only in my own field research, but also through living and working in this city, exploring its spaces and communities on foot, on motorcycle, on buses and boats, and meeting and talking to countless Thais of all walks of life for the period of over a decade. The core chapters of this book are a set of excursions into a number of sites of the complex social and spatial entity of Bangkok. Through these studies I reflect on the ways that Bangkok is dynamically shaped by the interaction between its people, its inherited structures (physical, social and economic) and new transformations.

The research for the studies comprising this book was conducted largely between 1990–8. The idea to produce this book first emerged in 1992–3 from my involvement in a joint project conducted with Drs M.R. Akin Rabibhadana and Paritta Chalermpow Koanantakool on the question of urban life and change in contemporary Thailand. It reflects much of our concern at that time to integrate a broad study of metropolitan change with detailed data and interpretation of localities in the city (see Askew and Paritta 1992; Paritta and Askew 1993). The book is driven by a cluster of questions directed towards problems of reading, writing and representing Bangkok and the Southeast Asian city in general: to what extent do the spatial and economic transformations taking place in Bangkok suggest a convergence towards an urban form and function seen as common to the contemporary cities throughout the world?; in what ways can global processes be seen to be responsible for key changes in the spatial economic and social character of the Thai metropolis?; and what has been the role of the Thai state in facilitating and mediating these changes? In this book I address these questions in terms of particular sites such as the expanding metropolitan fringe and the changing inner city, as reflected in processes as varied as investment flows, land utilisation and tourism, and in terms of the various agents engaged in this process: the state, the market and people. Another set of questions was generated from a direct study of the specific sites of change in Bangkok: how do we account for the emergence of tourist-related areas in the expanding metropolis?; what is the significance of the growth of the middle classes and how do we characterise life in housing estates, now one of the dominant residential environments in contemporary Bangkok?; how do we account for the persistent rhetoric of community and solidarity used to describe low-income settlements of the metropolis, and how distinct are 'the poor' as a group within the city?; what is the character of life, work and neighbourhood in the older inner areas of the metropolis and how is change mediated and negotiated by ordinary people?; how do the red-light districts of Bangkok function and what is the nature of the interactions and transactions that sustain them? Ultimately these questions, and the field research which has followed them, all address a common question – the meaning of Bangkok as a construct of interacting agents and institutions. My interpretations draw upon a range of theoretical insights into urban form and landscape in the contemporary period; however, the reader will note that I do not opt for any single theoretical model of metropolitan form or social structure to interpret the Thai capital. Rather, I comprehend the making of this metropolis in terms of a number of key themes: *place*, *practice* and *representation*. I should emphasise that I use the term 'Bangkok' to refer not only to the administrative area demarcated by the boundaries of the Bangkok Metropolitan Administration (BMA), but to the whole metropolitan complex which spills well beyond these borders to encompass areas technically known by more specific names.

The approach: ethnography, place, practice and representation

Ethnography

The individual studies that form the core of this book are founded on my basic premise that the urban experience is grounded in sociocultural processes and practices. As such, they need to be explored through detailed locality-focused field research focusing on people in a variety of spaces and environments across the metropolis. I follow here the (much overlooked) anthropologist Anthony Leeds, in his proposal that ethnographic locality-focused studies of urban life should not be seen as presuming that peoples' lives are confined to the horizons of local territories. Rather than imposing the simplistic notion of bounded communities (often a key assumption in microstudies), we need to accept that localities are loci of interaction of various processes, and these loci mediate broader structural forces, such as economic change (Leeds 1994). Studying a variety of localities within the Thai metropolis offers a means to embrace the complexity of the city as it is lived. It offers a way to address a range of economic, cultural and spatial changes as they are manifested and shaped through the mediation of people. At the same time, we should acknowledge the important observation of the anthropologist Ulf Hannerz that, in the contemporary world, the task of understanding the ordering of meaning in particular places is necessarily one that involves interpreting the transnational character of spaces: this is a world where the interconnectedness of global–local economic and cultural flows is central, not merely contextual (Hannerz 1996: 8). That is to say, the everyday lives of people and the meanings that are generated in Bangkok are informed and shaped by images and processes that are not unique to that metropolis alone. Transnational flows of people – particularly tourists – capital, technology, commodities and ideas are continuing to shape life in the metropolis and well beyond.

Ethnography is a research method which involves the intensive study of people through observation, various forms of interview and discussion (both formal and informal) and above all, interaction. It is a methodology central to the practice of anthropologists, despite critical questions that have emerged about its validity and explanatory value in intercultural terms. It aims essentially to generate accounts of culture in terms of social action and meanings, and is characteristically focused on specific localities. There are many problems associated with both ethnographic method and writing, particularly those generated by researchers 'outside' the particular society they study. I cannot claim to have overcome these epistemological and intercultural constraints. In my research I have tried, as much as possible, to follow Clifford Geertz's injunction to explore people's own realities. I have endeavoured to achieve this through a range of anthropological methods, including sharing day-to-day life with people in the localities I have studied across Bangkok over the past decade. I have communicated with people in their own language (Central Thai, or northeastern dialect where appropriate). I have been committed throughout to record what I believe to be people's own understandings of situations and sociocultural reality. My theoretical perspectives have above all been strongly influenced by the work of Thai scholars (at the expense of being academically unfashionable in western terms) and their advice and constructive criticism. Despite its shortcomings, ethnography remains the only way to study directly the people whom one wishes to try to understand. I believe the effort is worthwhile.

Ethnographic inquiry has recently been subject to scrutiny due to questions about the validity of microstudies in a world where specific places no longer constitute the lived worlds of people. It was always a problem in the subdiscipline of the so-called urban anthropology. Most chapters in the second part of this book are based on ethnographic method, combined where appropriate with other forms of locality-based research (such as surveys). My justification for this has been the need to study intensively people in the city, although acknowledging that neither their lives or social horizons are confined within particular localities. There are now arguments by leading anthropologists that the unit of analysis in ethnography should be global and not local, because culture itself needs to be conceptualised as world culture. However, I take my cue here from George Marcus, who had argued that ethnographic practice achieves particularly important insights, and should not abandon its place focus – which is its strength – so much as integrate this with a study of interdependencies with broader systems (Marcus 1998: 50–1). The localities dealt with in this book are not case studies as such – that is, they do not represent all the various types of localities throughout the Thai metropolis. Rather, they are sites and prisms through which I interpret the layered processes that continue to produce the spaces and places that together constitute Thailand's capital (see e.g. Hannerz 1996: 160–71).

Space and place

The language of the social sciences today is replete with spatial metaphors, used with varying degrees of analytical precision and consistency: position, location, site, arena, field and so forth (Silber 1995). The usage of many of these terms will be specific to the topics in the individual chapters in this study, but an outline of some key general terms is appropriate here. Space, as Henri Lefebvre has shown, is not an abstract and neutral void: it is in fact defined by relations between activities, processes and elements in the environment (Lefebvre 1991: 36–46). The spatial dimension, according to its more conventional usage among practitioners of geography and urban studies, refers to various activities, functional clusters, distributions of activities, their interrelations and dimensions at various scales. This is embodied in the concept of region and its various classifications, which is a key framework in economic geography. At a broader scale, space is often characterised in terms of dimensions and functions, such as urban space, social space, public space, symbolic space. However, space is a construct of power relations and as such is intrinsic to the ways societies are structured, and this has considerable importance in understanding the configuration and shaping of social relations and their intimate connection with key processes in the urban context. An allied term which is now employed by some key writers on contemporary cities is landscape – it incorporates the idea that spaces, their uses and symbolisation are produced through powerful processes and institutions, to generate 'landscapes of power' (Zukin 1991). Like space, I have also employed the term landscape in various ways in this discussion (e.g. urban landscape), but the particular application of this term will be obvious from the context of its usage throughout the passages of the book.

As used in this book, the term 'place' has distinct meaning. I have adopted the use of this term from contemporary human geography, and there are essentially two key emphases in its use. First, place is a space made distinct through particular activities; place is the ongoing interaction between people, their activities and territory or space (Certeau 1984: 117; Pred 1984).[2] The second, and related definition, is that place involves the assignment of distinctive meaning to a space by people (e.g. Massey 1995). Thus, the term place–community refers to local societies with particularly strong attachments and associations – usually, historical and cultural or ethnic – to spaces which play a key role in defining the identity of these groups.

Culture and cultural practices

The overriding aim of this study is to understand the ways that people practice their lives and shape space and its meaning through agency. I define this 'agency' as the capacity of people to undertake activities (devise projects or strategies) towards achieving meaningful ends (following Bourdieu 1990: 112–21; Ortner 1995: 187). I aim to investigate people's practice in relation to urbanism (the way people live in and assign meaning to urban life) and the way it relates to the Thai sociocultural system. In contemporary anthropology, most practitioners now deliberately avoid employing the term 'culture' because of its connotations of fixed, bounded and unchanging identities and practices (see Abu-Lughod 1991). This is a product of sensitivities about the danger of anthropology (once the handmaiden of European colonialism) constructing a post-colonial otherness of non-western peoples and expresses a commitment to the postmodern agenda of embracing the importance of pluralities of subjectivity and identities. Culture is resisted as a meaningful analytical concept because it presumes singular national identity among people. Those scholars who embrace the so-called cultural studies approach tend to utilise the term culture as equivalent to ideology (Kahn 1998a: 16–17). I share the concern with presuming the unchanging and unitary nature of meanings in any society by ascribing a fixed frame of meaning denoted as culture. Yet at the same time, and whether we describe it as culture or a system/pattern of meaning, the fact that people in various societies share definable ways of articulating and acting towards each other in the world is an inescapable reality. That questions of cultural/national/ethnic identity are addressed by the state and subject to politically-driven representations should not obscure the fact that people do engage in patterned and meaningful practices and we should attempt to understand this, however flawed and compromised the enterprise.

My view, which follows the work of both Thai and western anthropologists (including Akin 1983; Brummelhuis 1984; Kemp 1984; O'Connor 1983; Sanit 1996), is that Thai culture (or what was once described as the Thai 'sociocultural system') is a frame of idioms and practices which act to structure relationships, define identities and inform the strategies of groups and individuals towards the attainment of power and prestige. These idioms find expression in interaction and are accessible to analysis through the study of the forms in which they are articulated, whether in action – collective or individual – or speech. I refer throughout the chapters of this book to Thai 'cultural' practices and idioms as they are manifest in tendencies to social hierarchy, values of reciprocity, patron–clientage, and pragmatism. This can be applied not only to relations between individuals, but groups and institutions. Such idioms and practices have interacted dynamically with changes in economy and society over time, and often coexist with or contradict other emergent idioms. Thus, factionalism and status rivalry are found within bureaucratic agencies, including the many which have played a part in the shaping of Bangkok. Similarly, patterns of social hierarchy, reciprocity and entourage-building shape interaction, behaviour, decision-making and group formation at an institutional level, from government agencies to the press (see e.g. McCargo 2000: 38–42).

Of course, to speak of a single Thai sociocultural system or set of value orientations one runs the risk of considerable oversimplification. Particularly in relation to Bangkok, we need to acknowledge that within this general matrix that I term Thai there are a plurality of cultural patterns which intersect and coexist: in particular the subculture of the bureaucracy (a particular hybrid of tradition and modernity) and the strength of Chinese patterns of family affiliation and business organisation within the Sino–Thai elites and the middle classes. Over twenty years ago, the prominent Southeast Asianist Benedict Anderson advocated that scholars needed to acknowledge the dynamic nature of the interrelationships between structural and cultural elements in Thai society without privileging one over the other (Anderson 1978: 232). While I may be guilty of doing so in this book, my point is that the cultural factor is not separable from a treatment of the way power is exercised, but is intrinsic to its structuring in Thailand, both across government and non-government agencies (see Kanok 1988). Nor does it stand outside those broad collectivities that writers in the social sciences and humanities define as classes, or (more fashionably) social formations: these groupings are in fact mediated, structured and articulated in particular ways through cultural modes at different levels – ways of organising, interacting and behaving.

In presenting this cultural factor as an essential dimension in interpreting people and their activities, I have drawn upon some of the key concepts utilised by Pierre Bourdieu in his theory of practice. Central to this idea is the notion that social action is characterised by strategies which derive from *habitus*. *Habitus* can be defined as a structuring set of social orientations which set a framework for people's action in the form of strategies. *Habitus*, in a sense, frames the objectives towards which a repertoire of actions are ultimately directed. These strategies aim towards the accumulation of valued symbolic, or cultural capital which is commonly recognised by a group within a given field where the forms of this cultural capital are accepted (Bourdieu 1977: 72, 95).[3] Applying this conceptual scheme to the Thai cultural system, I argue that this cultural capital ultimately takes the form of status and prestige, achieved through various ends, among which are relationships. I utilise these frameworks of *habitus*, and practice in interpreting the actions of people in such diverse contexts as urban slums and orchard districts on the fringes of the metropolis: observable through equally diverse practices aiming towards the accumulation of status, leadership and religious merit. Such culturally-derived strategies are not restricted to interpersonal relations, they also have a tangible impact on the landscape. Importantly, in emphasising the significance of this cultural factor among people of the metropolis, I do not separate it from economic relations and patterns of accumulation and power – rather they are intrinsic to each other and mutually reinforcing (see e.g. O'Connor 1986). It is through this understanding of *habitus* and cultural capital that we can observe the ways that various forms of modernity have been embraced and deployed – and until quite recently concentrated – in Thailand's capital city over the past century or so.

Representation

The term and concept of 'representation' has an important use in this discussion. Drawing on much of the recent theoretical and substantive work on cities in the contemporary period, I argue that Bangkok's spaces can also be seen to be constituted by representation, through symbols, maps and associated icons, of modernity for example. Such representations are derived from powerful ensembles of interests (the state and capitalist institutions) which have a stake in shaping and using urban space for production, consumption and the reproduction of power (Lefebvre 1991). The notion of representation (knowledge) as a form of power also derives from the influence of Michel Foucault, and has been applied in approaches to the study of urban spaces as key sites of power relations (Sharp *et al.* 2000; Westwood and Williams 1997). In this book, I draw on these concepts to show how Bangkok has been fashioned in various periods. Many recent writers on cities have embraced postmodern arguments and portrayed cities as symbolic texts: 'the city' itself is viewed as a construct with an illusory unity (e.g. Barnes and Duncan 1992; Shields 1996). It is important to acknowledge that representations of urban space and meaning are not the exclusive preserve of power regimes – rather there are alternative ways of representing the city and its spaces. In this book I have identified a number of alternative representations of space and territory among subordinate urban groups, and among recent middle-class movements which contest dominant representations of the nature of communities and of history. In Bangkok, as elsewhere throughout the world, the urban has become a critical site where power is contested through representations. There is, indeed, no single entity such as Bangkok, except through representations. Such representations are not free-floating entities; they bespeak power relations and locations of groups, ideologies and practices. Thus, among the numerous intersecting and contrasting representations of the Thai metropolis we find Bangkok represented as a space for private economic accumulation and investment; a space where the state allocates economic and administrative functions through regional and urban planning; a space for tourist spectacle and entertainment; a place of ordinary people for living and survival.

Bangkok can, of course, be represented in essentially empirical terms, through reference to land uses, population settlement, growth and densities and economic functions. In the first part of this volume I have outlined some key indicators of demographic change, economic and settlement characteristics. I highlight some of the problems faced by planners and other specialists in defining the physical boundaries of the Thai metropolis, but I have avoided detailing the more arcane problems debated by demographers and economists. I should note here that I use the term Bangkok in this book not simply to refer to the contemporary administrative territory of the Bangkok Metropolitan Administration (BMA), but to denote the whole metropolis. In this sense Bangkok is used as a metaphor to represent the metropolis as a sociospatial phenomenon.

I also use the term 'representation' throughout this text to refer to the ways that the Thai metropolis and the processes shaping it have been interpreted in terms of various conceptual models by scholars. My concern to explore and query some of these dominant frameworks shapes the character of this book. Each of the chapters in Part II, rather than following a single theoretical focus, presents a debate with some dominant interpretations of the urban process in contemporary cities (in Asia and the world) and scholars' representations of Bangkok in particular.

The structure of the book

The chapters in this book are grouped into two parts. Part I, Krung to global city: the dynamics of transformation, comprises three chapters which function as an interpretative narrative of change and continuity extending from the foundation of Krung Thep as the royal capital of Siam in 1782 to its emergence through the twentieth century as a primate city. These chapters outline the physical and ecological changes which have transformed Bangkok as a living environment in terms of international, national and local trends. They highlight the interplay between the interests of the state, private and foreign capital, historical conditions and the demands and needs of the increasing population of urban dwellers.

Part II, Making Bangkok: studies in place, practice and representation, forms the core of this book. It begins with a study of inner Bangkok, focusing on the Banglamphu district, where I discuss the character of the traditional *yan* of the city. I explore the nature of local neighbourhoods and their evolution, particularly in terms of changes in economic patterns, relations between neighbourhoods and religious institutions and wider transformations such as new retailing patterns in the metropolis. In particular I discuss the emergence of new functions in this inner area as local people respond to the rise in foreign backpacker tourism. In Chapter 5, I interrogate dominant scholarly and NGO (Non-governmental organisations) representations of Bangkok's slums settlements and interpret these representations as an integral element in the overall conflict over urban space and the meaning of the city as a living place. I focus on the dynamics of slum politics in the settlements of Khlong Toei, a slum complex which represents a major paradox in being essentially atypical of Bangkok's informal settlements, yet one which has emerged as a key symbol of the urban poor's claim for a place in the metropolis. I argue that a study of the internal dynamics of slum settlements can highlight some key patterns of social value systems among Thai urban dwellers generally.

Chapter 6 is a study of a middle-class housing estate in northern Bangkok. I argue, through a detailed study of this estate and its people, that forms of neighbourhood identification have emerged among the suburban middle classes, patterns of identification which draw strength from characteristically Thai modes of interaction. In Chapter 7, I present a study of the rural–urban fringe of the metropolitan area, focusing on the gardening districts of western Nonthaburi Province. I portray this changing area in historical perspective and query the dominant model of the 'mega-urban region' in terms of its lack of attention to cultural practices. I attempt to show that patterns of life and labour have always been adaptive in relation to wider socio-economic changes in those provinces formerly bordering the metropolis, but now enmeshed in its processes. Chapter 8 deals with the luxury high-rise condominiums and their surrounding precincts, which emerged in Bangkok as an architectural and social phenomenon from the early 1980s. I discuss the character of the luxury high-rise market and its relation to arguments about a global real estate industry. Focusing on the Sukhumvit area where condominiums have their highest concentration, I consider the extent to which western scholars' arguments about gentrification are applicable to Bangkok's changing inner areas, and find this to be largely inapplicable. I draw attention to the importance of the ecological dimension exemplified in the structure of intersecting tributary *soi* (lanes) and suggest that there are important factors allowing for the persistence of variety and multifunctionality in the face of apparent homogenising tendencies in Bangkok's inner areas.

Chapter 9 shifts attention to the women involved in one of Bangkok's key transnational industries, the tourist-orientated sex trade. In this ethnographic study of Thai women sex workers and their relationship with foreign men, I argue that these women are active agents in the production of place. While this industry is portrayed by most commentators in monolithic terms as an integrated and highly controlled system, I suggest that women's practices in the sex trade can also be viewed from another perspective – as part of their own encounter with difference and modernity in the city and beyond. The final chapter, Contesting urbanisms, departs to some extent from the single-locality focus of most of the preceding chapters and looks at the way that a particular model of the city's history has been promoted by the state in the Rattanakosin conservation plan. Beginning with a treatment of the characteristics of this plan and its key representations of the past, I follow with an account of an emerging and increasingly articulate opposition to paradigms of the city based on models of aestheticised history and urban efficiency among communities and intellectuals. Competing representations of Bangkok's past, urban heritage (*moradok*) and culture (*watthanatham*) are key reflections of concerns and conflicts about the present and future meaning of life in Thailand's metropolis.

Part I

Krung to global city

The dynamics of transformation

1 Cosmology, accumulation and the state

The urbanism of early Bangkok

Introduction: the impress of the past

On the face of it, there seems little in the spectacle of today's sprawling Thai metropolis to suggest the continuing influence of its past. As in other Southeast Asian mega-cities, the visible dynamics and physical landmarks that dominate today's cityscape pronounce a distinctively contemporary logic of spatial form, economic accumulation, consumerism and industry. The lifestyles and occupations of its inhabitants share with those of the bustling cities of the region an engagement with the driving imperatives to survive as well as to accumulate the status symbols of a global age, extending from housing and technology to the fashioning of the modern body. Yet Bangkok's past has not been erased – the very sources of its transformation and its continuing role as a centre of power and status are to be discerned in its history, which has a tangible legacy. The contemporary economic and symbolic functions of Bangkok, its role in the broader sociocultural system and its spatial patterning by institutions and people – in short, its urbanism – articulate in various ways with its origins and the dynamics of its transformation since its foundation as the royal capital over two hundred years ago.

Krung Thep: the palace and the *yan*

Bangkok was founded as the seat of the new Chakkri dynasty in 1782, following the overthrow of King Taksin who had ruled Siam from the city of Thonburi on the western bank of the Chao Phraya River (1768–82). Taksin had begun the task of reconstituting the Siamese state and extending its power following the massive disruption after the fall of the 400-year-old city and polity of Ayutthaya. The early Chakkri monarchs consolidated this process from the new capital of Krung Thep, founded on the site of an old settlement known as *Bang-kok* (the water hamlet of the wild plum tree). Two key points should be emphasised in interpreting the political, symbolic and economic significance of Krung Thep from its foundation. First, by virtue of the nature of Siamese kingship, its Indic-derived ideology of legitimacy (ultimately derived from the ancient polity of Cambodia but with significant Theravada Buddhist accretions) and the urbanistic focus of this legitimacy, this new capital was heir to a tradition which fixed the royal city as a symbolic and structural locus of political power, social hierarchy and religious legitimacy. Second, Krung Thep – like its forebear Ayutthaya – maintained the complementary roles of international port city and a centre for the accumulation and conversion of surplus extracted from a subject peasantry (Evers, Korff and Suparb 1987). It was the centre of wealth in the hands of a commercially-orientated governing elite and a cosmopolitan trading entrepôt which hosted a significant population of traders of diverse ethnic and religious backgrounds.

A number of prominent historians of Thai history have argued that the first king of the Chakkri Dynasty (retrospectively named *Phra Phuttha Yotfa Chulalok*, and later designated Rama I) presided over a period of ideological change. It was expressed in a more explicit Buddhist moral foundation for kingly authority and more secular and cosmopolitan (or bourgeois) attitudes on the part of the elite when compared to the preceding Ayutthayan dynasties (Nithi 1984; Wyatt 1982b). Such changes have been interpreted as flowing from the needs of the new dynasty to demonstrate legitimacy and the necessity of founding the newly consolidated state on a trade-based city. Nonetheless, the foundation of Rama I's city was marked by a concern to re-establish the symbols, spaces and functions of the old capital of Ayutthaya. The new royal capital was given a sanskritised title which signified the transformation of an ordinary space into the consecrated seat of the *chakkravathin* – the world conquering, merit-filled monarch (Wenk 1968: 19). Significantly, the name 'Ayutthaya' was included in the first city title given in 1782. But in 1786, in a second ceremony (coinciding with the year of Rama I's recognition by the emperor of China) the title was changed to:

> The City of Angels, Great City, the Residence of the Emerald Buddha, Capital of the World Endowed with Nine Precious Gems, the Happy City Abounding in Great Royal Palaces which Resemble the Heavenly Abode Wherein Dwell the Reincarnated Gods, A City Given by Indra and Built by Vishnukarn.
>
> (Sternstein 1982: 11)

Notably, the auspicious title (abbreviated hereafter as Krung Thep) still used familiar terms evoking that of Ayutthaya: 'Krung Thep Thewarawadi Sri Ayutthaya' (Dhani 1969). The title evoked a traditional cosmology where Brahmanical and Buddhist elements coexisted.[1] The *muang* of the Thai monarchs took their formal names from the capitals themselves (thus 'Ayutthaya', 'Rattanakosin'), signifying how conceptions of dynasty, capital and polity were inseparable. My use of the term 'Siam' for this early period refers simply to the polity (*muang*) dominated by the Thai-speaking peoples of the Chao Phraya Delta. Since the thirteenth century, Siam (a word probably of Khmer origin) was used in various forms by neighbouring states to refer to the people of the central Thai kingdoms, and later adopted by western powers. But the word was infrequently used by the central Thai and their rulers until the nineteenth century (Chit 1976: 232–5). It was King Mongkut (r. 1851–68) who formally adopted the name Siam (together with a flag of Siam distinctive from his own royal dynastic emblem) in an effort to represent the *muang* as a territorially-defined state recognisable to the west (Thongchai 1994: 171).

Krung Thep was seen to occupy the centre of the *muang* (state, polity) just as Lord Indra occupied the centre of the universe. The most crucial event to be ritually enacted prior to the commencement of construction of the new palace and its citadel was the installation of the *lak muang* (city pillar), which coincided with the establishment of a new dynastic horoscope (Cook 1991: 242–5). Dynasty, capital, *muang* and history were symbolically fused in this pillar and its ritual foundation. Linked with the Indic linga cult associated with the Hindu god Shiva as well as indigenous Tai cults of tutelary deities, *lak muang* were essential to establishing the symbolic centres of polities and assuring the well-being of ruling dynasties and the people of their *muang* (So 1960: 152–4; Terwiel 1978, 1983: 72). King Rama I proclaimed a decree banning popular phallic worship, and on this basis he has been seen as initiating a trend towards the reduction of Brahmanical and animistic influences in the realm; paradoxically, he was anxious to enact a city founding ceremony derived from the same broad tradition. When Prince Mongkut (Rama IV) came to the throne as the fourth incumbent of the dynasty in 1851, he installed a second *lak muang* because his horoscope did not conform to the foundation dates of the earlier pillar (Tambiah 1976: 227). His son and successor Chulalongkorn (Rama V), whose reign has been generally characterised as one of reform and modernisation along western lines, nonetheless reinforced the centrality of Krung Thep's *lak muang* by constructing a new (Khmer-style) pavillion around the pillar and marking its inauguration with a Brahmanic ceremony (Aphar 1982: 14–15).[2]

While the royal chronicles state that Krung Thep was built to resemble the former capital of Ayutthaya, whose past magnificence was still fresh in the memories of its survivors (Wenk 1968: 18), the siting of the new capital (on the eastern side of the Chao Phraya River opposite King Taksin's palace at Thonburi) was dictated more by the practical considerations of defence. Nevertheless the general desire to reproduce the familiar spatial and symbolic signifiers of the royal city as an embodiment of the king-centred polity is clear (for which see Naengnoi *et al.* 1991: 18–19; Terwiel 1983: 72–3). Thus the inner sanctum of the royal palace and its associated royal chapel (Wat Phra Kaeo) with the dynasty's all-important protective palladium (the sacred Emerald Buddha) were sited on the bulge of land formed by a wide loop in the Chao Phraya River, with its eastern perimeter separated from the rest of the *krung* (*krung* is derived from the Khmer word for 'city') by a moat. This privileged core was known as *Ko Rattanakosin* (the Emerald Island of Indra). Within the walled palace (Phraratchawang) which dominated the landscsape of *Ko Rattanakosin* were located the royal throne halls, the chapel royal and residences of the monarch, his immediate relatives and high officials. In this walled complex the *Wang Nai* (or inner palace) was reserved for the king's royal consorts and their dependants. This was the inner sanctum of the monarch's privileged sexuality and symbolic potency. Aside from the women, it was accessible only to the king, following established law and custom. Outside this citadel was the *Wang Na* (the 'Front Palace') of the second king (the *Upharat)* and other princes of the blood, as well as important temples patronised by the dynasty. Attempts were made to replicate the structures of the old capital, but there were numerous deviations from the alignments and distribution of key structures of the earlier capital (*krung kao*).[3]

Krung Thep and its forbear, *Krung Sri Ayutthaya*, were sacred cities, but not in the sense that their plans corresponded in every detail to prevailing Hindu/Buddhist cosmological models of the universe. They were, however, exemplary centres. More than any coordinated system of cosmological spatial orientations, the royal city of Krung Thep was sanctified through the sheer accumulation of symbols. The first Chakkri monarch brought hundreds of revered Buddha images to the capital from old temples throughout the realm and the defeated tributary states, lending legitimacy to his rule as a *Thammarat*, or moral ruler (Akin 1969: 48–9; Suphadradis 1982; Wyatt 1982b: 147). Of supreme importance to the Chakkri dynasty was the Emerald Buddha (*Phra Kaeo*).[4] Popular belief in the sacred power of this palladium was displayed when it was paraded throughout the city as a ritual act of purification during a severe cholera epidemic in the year 1820. Both the socio-political and religious hierarchy symbolised in the royal city were mutually reinforcing and found expression in the organisation of space at different scales: that is, between the spaces in the capital and between the capital and the realm. Beginning in the inner moated precinct, old temples were refurbished and new temples were constructed. These were placed under royal patronage, as distinct from the common temples (many of which predated the foundation of Krung Thep), reinforcing another element of hierarchy in the capital (see Fig. 1.1). The most sacred (*saksit*) of the realm's Buddha images were concentrated there. Ritualistic installation of holy and auspicious objects (*sing saksit*) whether of Buddhist, Brahman or animist origins, gave auspiciousness to the site and protection to the city, the central place of the kingdom's power and potency (Srisaka 1987). The early Chakkri monarchs, with princes of royal blood and prominent nobles, were keen temple-builders: in this they affirmed that wealth and prominence in the profane world reflected a moral hierarchy of Buddhist merit (see Hanks 1962).

The royal city was a space constituted by royal ceremony. From his inauguration as monarch, King Rama I's public life was dominated by state ceremony. Ceremonies ranged in scale and audience from the palace-centred tonsure rites of royal family members to larger scale public rituals such as state cremations, temple inaugurations and the annual *kathin* processions (for the distribution of new robes to monks in the royal temples) (Wenk 1968: 9–15). The early Chakkri monarchs were apparently concerned to strengthen the Buddhist elements of kingship and state ritual (the king as the upholder of the *Thammasat*, or Buddhist law, and the protector of the monkhood) at the expense of the Brahmanical model of the king as *Devarat* (God King) and its connections to the cult of Shiva worship (Akin 1969: 43–4; Tambiah 1976: 227–8; Wales 1931: 242–3). However, Brahmanic-inspired state ceremonies and symbolism invoking the protection of the Hindu gods and the prosperity of the Kingdom persisted throughout the period from the establishment of Krung Thep until the twentieth century (Tambiah 1976: 227; Vella 1978: 13–16).

We may consider the royal citadel of Krung Thep in its collective material and symbolic dimensions as a 'text', or system of signs which aimed to represent and communicate a set of interrelated ideas of kingship, power and social organisation. Following James Duncan's approach to the discursive construction of the capital of the Kandyan kingdom of Sri Lanka under its pre-colonial rulers, we can see this text as constituted by a number of narratives, including the iconic, the linguistic and the ceremonial – complementary dimensions of symbolisation which cumulatively fashioned an ideal landscape (Duncan 1990: 87–94). This ideal landscape, linked to Brahmanic and Buddhist concepts of kingship and authority, served a number of critical functions, even though it belied the considerable economic and political changes surrounding the formation of the Chakkri dynasty and its capital. First, the imperative to 'rebuild Ayutthaya' was a rallying cry for the resurgent Siamese *muang* (Srisaka and Suchit 1982: 64–70). Second, to the new monarch, who could claim no direct descent from the old royal line, the old polity was the only available model: a restored, yet purified system of Ayutthayan law and religion represented both consolidation and legitimacy. This static and ideal 'text' of the royal city (like other ideal models of the state such as those embodied in re-established law codes) hardly corresponded with the dynamic political and socio-economic realities driving Siam during this period (see Wilson 1980). However the ideal of the eternal royal city of culture and religion was critically important. The Chakkri kings saw themselves, and were seen as, the primary protectors and patrons of the symbolic nucleus of social order and culture – the capital. The idea of the monarchy as the defining focus of culture and history has considerable influence in contemporary state representations of the Thai past and Thai identity.

But Krung Thep was more than a royal space defined by ritual and iconography. It was a port city whose trade was a critical base of the wealth and power of the monarchs and the ruling elite. In this, Krung Thep followed the pattern established by the kingdom of Ayutthaya, whose dominance of the region from the sixteenth century had been based on its advantages as a port polity (Dhiravat 1990; Reid 1993: 62–3). Thonburi and its successor capital of Krung Thep were sited much closer to the Gulf of Siam than Ayutthaya, signifying the importance of strategic security from Burmese aggression.[5] Moreover Bang-kok had been the site of a settlement of Chinese traders since the Ayutthaya period and its access to seaborne trade was critically important for the needs of the reconstructed *muang*.

Thai urbanism had long been marked by an orientation to the outside world and a cosmopolitanism in striking contrast to its subject agrarian hinterland. The space of the city was thus not only framed by the presence of the royal palace and its associated hierarchical iconography, but by its trade: its river anchorages, its shipyards, warehouses and trading settlements of foreign merchants. Under King Taksin (who was himself half-Teochiu), Chinese traders of this speech group were encouraged to settle at his capital, many locating along the opposite shore at Bangkok. When Rama I began construction of his new palace, this group was moved south of the new city wall (constructed around the second moat from 1782), in keeping with the Ayutthayan practice which separated the royal centre of power from trading communities (see Fig. 1.1). Named Sampheng, this sprawling settlement extending along the riverbank was the principal focus of the Chinese merchants – whose networks and skills were essential to the kingdom's economy – as well as other groups such as Bengali, Gujarati, Tamil and Malay traders.

The population of the capital (both within and without the walled area with the ruling families and numerous functionaries) was diverse, and its composition reflected not only the cosmopolitanism resulting from commerce, but the needs of the court, the fruits of war and state policies of settling exiled populations. The very diversity of the population of the realm and city was considered an index of the glory and power of the monarch, who graciously extended his royal protection (*Phraboromaphothisomphan*) over people who entered the realm. Krung Thep's population changed over time in response to these factors. Aside from the large communities such as the Mon and the Chinese, others included the *Thawai* (Burmese from Tenassarim), Cambodians, Cham, Hindus and Muslims of the Indian subcontinent, Lao, Malays, Makassarese, Muslims of Persian descent, Portugese and Vietnamese (see e.g. Wyatt 1982b: 145–6). Outside the walled city of the king and court, and beyond the ship anchorages, stretched a patchwork of ordinary settlements, marked by names prefaced with *bang* (literally 'water hamlet') or *ban* (village). Strung out along the Chao Phraya riverside and its maze of dug-canals and river tributaries, these settlements of Thai and Mon and other ethnic communities occupied floating or stilted houses and cultivated the orchards and rice fields which

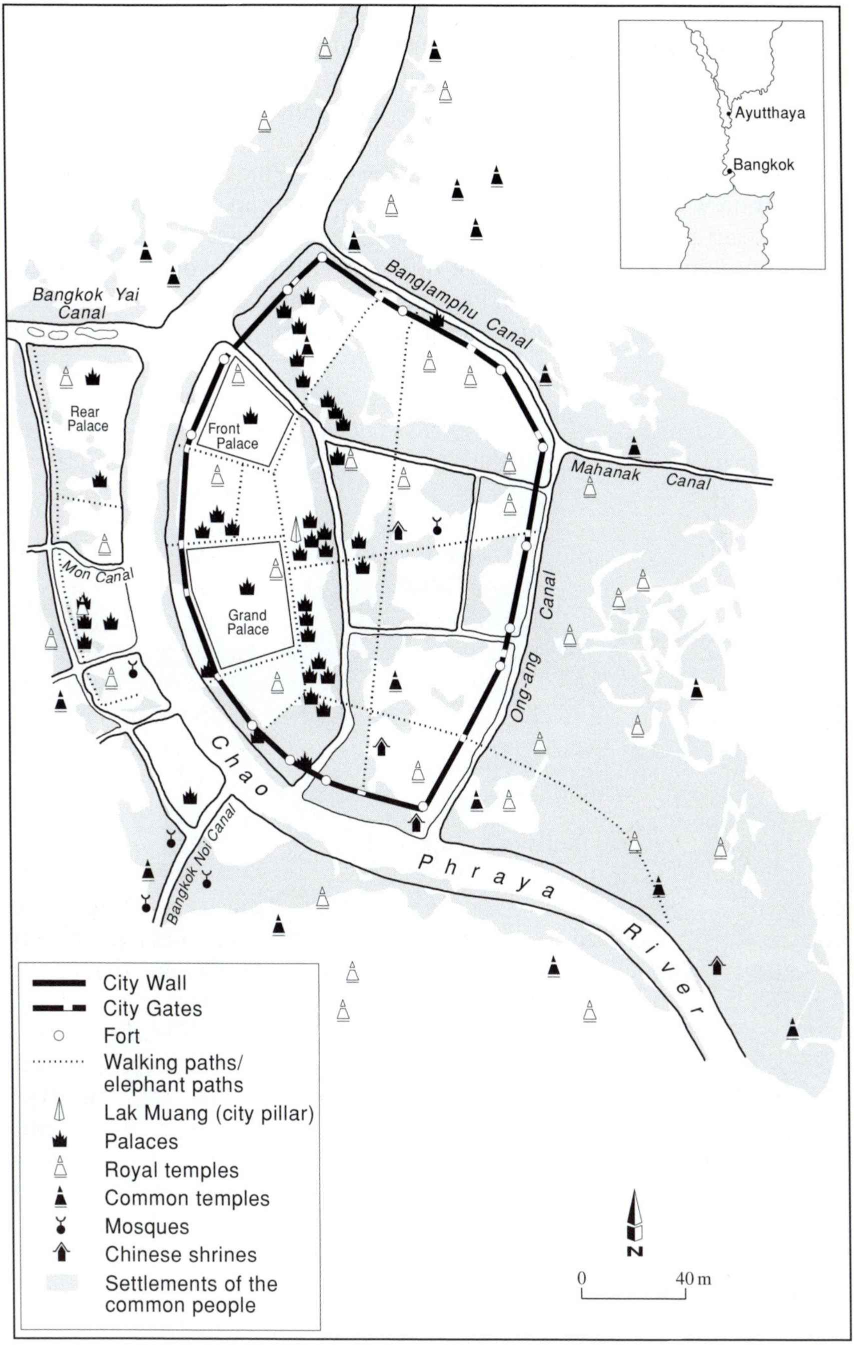

Figure 1.1 Krung Thep *c.* 1820, showing principal settlement areas.

Source: Compiled from Naengnoi *et al.* 1991.

surrounded the small territorial nucleus settled by the elite (see Suchit 1996; Sunait 1998). They formed another dimension of the capital – its common places. They were named according to popular identification, in terms of activities, natural features, or the ethnic character of the settlements (O'Connor 1990: 61).

This diversity of *bang* and *ban* along the Chao Phraya River and its tributary waterways was depicted vividly in the *Nirat* poetry (travel rhymes) of the court poet Sunthon Phu during the second reign. In many of these *Nirat* he described the features of different villages devoted to activities as varied as shrimp-paste making and bowl manufacture (for which see e.g. Terwiel 1989: 23–5; and Department of Fine Arts 1991, especially

Plate 1.1 The aquatic city: houses along a main canal surrounding the walls of Krung Thep (*c.* 1890s). (Photo: Courtesy National Archives of Thailand)

107–17). The neighbourhoods surrounding the palace citadel, and later, those which settled on land, were also known by the Thai word *yan*, which identified places in functional terms, such as Sampheng, sometimes known as *yan kankha khong chin* (the trading place of the Chinese), or simply referred to by name, such as *yan talad Banglamphu* (the place around the Banglamphu market). Like the earlier capital of Ayutthaya, Bangkok was not only an international trading mart, but also a space of small-scale craft production and economic transactions focusing on numerous markets in which common people, particularly women, were central (see Gervaise 1989: 114). Widely dispersed beyond the walled citadel across a terrain of lush tropical vegetation, the population of Bangkok and its surrounds was consistently overestimated by foreign observers. In the mid-nineteenth century, Bangkok was estimated to have boasted only between 50,000–100,000 people (Terwiel 1989: 233).

A notable feature of early Bangkok's urbanism was the coexistence and interaction of the three dimensions comprising the city: the royal citadel, its trading areas, and its mosaic of villages and *yan* connected by canals and river through nodal points of activity, such as floating markets of various sizes and importance. As a functioning city the capital was a space marked by variety and the juxtaposition of contrasting elements, presided over at a distance by an absolute monarch and centred symbolically on the palace. In the royal play *Inao,* attributed to King Rama II (1809–24), an ideal city is described which in virtually all respects was a description of Krung Thep. The verses listed the major landmarks and features of the capital: including the *phae* (floating houses of the common people) the *tuk* (brick and stucco buildings, of the royal palace and the prominent Chinese customs officials), the gilded roofs of the temples and spires of the *chedi* (stupa), the great Shiva swing which identified an urban ritual space, and the moslem mosques which identified the city as a place of ethnic diversity. This diversity was a summation of the city's glory and the king's greatness. Notably trade, and the diverse population which it attracted, was also central to this landscape of greatness:

> Buyers and traders from every place come from many lands,
> Junks are moored in rows with Malay sloops and the sailing ships of the Hollanders,
> Chinese, Cham, Achenese: crowded together here are twelve languages.
> (Authors' translation, from Department of Fine Arts 1963: 5)

The Sakdina State and trade: the foundations of urban dominance

The foundations of contemporary Bangkok's demographic, cultural, political and economic dominance of Thailand were well established by the mid-nineteenth century and were progressively reinforced. This increasing dominance was nurtured by a number of interrelated influences stemming from inherited power structures and more dynamic and novel conditions. First was the pre-eminent role of the royal city and the capital region in the inherited political, social and territorial structure of the Siamese polity. This capital region has been appropriately described as 'the inner core' (Wilson 1970: 51). The traditional Siamese state was essentially a confederation of *muang* (polities) centred on cities. Its territorial organisation was founded on a hierarchical ranking of these centres (*huamuang*) and their subordinate settlements (*muang khun*). They surrounded the capital region, extending from inner to outer rings, and functioned to protect this core. Rulers of these cities were technically appointed by the king (although positions were often in fact hereditary) and enjoyed wide prerogatives over manpower control and taxation. Beyond these *muang* of the realm proper were the vassal states (*muang prathetsarat*) ruled by their own monarchs (Rujaya 1984: 44–5; Wilson 1970: 51–3). In the early Bangkok period, centralisation – political, social, territorial, economic and demographic – developed through the management of this *muang* system based on family politics and patron–clientalism. From the centre of power, patronage and rank were dispensed to the coalition of princes and nobility who controlled the state apparatus (Wilson 1970: 112–36).[6] The centre garnered population to its immediate hinterland and core central provinces by transferring manpower to the capital and its immediate region after victorious wars. There was also a long-standing policy of settling refugees from neighbouring state conflicts in the immediate hinterland, notably the Mon (Akin 1969: 26–7).[7] The demographic dominance of Bangkok and its core region reflected this policy (Sternstein 1966: 69).

Second, the institutionalised political, social and economic system which has come to be known as *sakdina* supported the centralisation of social status and accumulation on Bangkok because of ruling families' command over resources. This occurred despite growing problems associated with traditional controls over labour (through the *phrai* system). The *sakdina* structure (established during the mid-fifteenth century) linked the social ranking and status of a state-appointed nobility (*khunnang*) to a means of control over the labour and economic surplus of commoners (*phrai*) through the *krom* (divisions) and their graded functionaries. The three major ministries of War (*Kalahom*), the Interior (*Mahatthai*) and Finance (*Khlang*) dominated the *krom* system (comprising ministries and divisions) each with military, territorial, legal and tax-raising jurisdictions over the realm. Beneath these and other *krom* of various size were numerous smaller units which were constituted as needed (Akin 1969). While in theory reliant on the king and coordinated from the centre, in practice this system was unstable and segmented, with shifting networks of power and patronage founded on access to *phrai* and economic resources obtained through office-holding in key *krom*. Centralising tendencies operated because the great ministries (controlled by the leading families of the realm) focused wealth and status in the capital by virtue of their control over lucrative taxation and tribute resources and patronage networks.

The *phrai* system (which officially existed in attenuated form until its formal abolition in 1905) was the very basis of what has been called the Siamese 'sakdina state'. Registered under masters (*nai*) for purposes of military service and corvée labour, there were various groupings of *phrai*, whose obligations and circumstances differed (Seksan 1989: 43–4). The *phrai* system was highly segmented among its constituent units and royal control was never direct (Akin 1969). Moreover, it was volatile, since many *phrai* were active in escaping the corvée system and seeking better conditions by simply running away, switching masters, or becoming debt slaves (Seksan 1989: 46–50). Overall, however, the *phrai* system supported the Bangkok-focused accumulation process. Through the collection of *suai* goods (tribute and tax in kind), the *phrai* of the outlying provinces supplied the court and elite of the capital with valuable items used for trade and essential materials (and labour) for the buildings and ceremonies of the royal capital (Rujaya 1984: 66–7).

Third – and ultimately the most powerful influence accounting for Bangkok's dominance as the undisputed urban centre of the realm – was its role as an international trading port. The resurgence of the Bangkok-based state from the late eighteenth century was founded on the goods and money gained through seaborne trade (Seksan 1989: 83–4). Enjoying the duty-free privileges extended by the Chinese emperors to tribute missions, the junk fleets fitted out for the ports of the Middle Kingdom brought back luxuries for the Siamese court (such as silks and eating utensils), components for weaponry (iron), ammunition (saltpetre) and items for general sale in the domestic market (such as cheap porcelain wares) as well as silver bullion (Cushman 1993: 86–7). Goods were resold by the crown and princes to local as well as regional merchants. The court relied on Chinese merchants to conduct this highly commercialised tribute system and also used Chinese seamen. By the beginning of the reign of King Rama III (r. 1824–51) Bangkok had emerged as the most important centre of the Chinese junk trade in the region, a role which persisted for some decades – despite the presence of the new and burgeoning British port colony of Singapore (Cushman 1993: 65–73). Initially, the advent of Singapore stimulated trading activity to the benefit of Bangkok's merchants, aristocrats and their trading fleet. By the 1840s however, western shipping technology and an expanding trading hegemony supported by imperialist conquests (e.g. the Opium War with China) forced the demise of these junk fleets (Sarasin 1977: 238–9).[8]

The internal trends which supported the trade expansion through Bangkok were facilitated by political expansion and the accumulation of manpower. Over the first three reigns, Siam absorbed new territories and incorporated vassal states more directly into its tribute orbit (e.g. northwestern Cambodia and the Lao kingdoms). Thousands of war captives were brought into central Siamese territory, serving to expand the numbers of *phrai* and the quantities of *suai* goods and taxes. Canal construction was motivated primarily by the need for defence, but it furthered Bangkok's economic and administrative hold over its hinterland. Accelerating in the 1820s, it entailed the excavation of lateral canals linking the major rivers of the Chao Phraya delta and major new trunk routes for troop movement to border areas. This Bangkok-focused canal network, financed by a range of new taxes under the third reign, served to channel *suai* goods more effectively from the provinces (Tanabe 1977: 44; Porphant 1994: 25).

Cash and the expanding market economy

The early Chakkri period saw the rise of an exchange economy focused on the central region, particularly the capital. It grew from the combined effects of the expansion of a Chinese entrepreneurial and labouring population, the state's need for money revenue and the progressive reduction of corvée labour pressures on the *phrai*. The rise of the Chakkri dynasty was tied inseparably to trade and the critical need for money income for numerous purposes: the purchase of arms, the hiring of merchants, junk crews and mercenaries, tradable commodities, the payment of the *biawat* (customary annual payments to officials) and maintenance of an expanding royal family (Wilson 1970: 478–82). The Chakkri rulers encouraged the migration of Chinese (merchants, agriculturalists and labourers) whose numbers rapidly increased both in the capital and coastal provinces. Customarily accepted as the principal trading class of the kingdom since Ayutthayan times, Chinese merchants were given preferential rates of port taxes. Granted freedom of movement, they were agents for the crown in purchasing products in the outlying areas to supplement the exportable *suai* items garnered through the royal monopolies. The Chinese expanded commercial pepper cultivation during the 1820s and founded numerous sugar cane plantations and mills in the central provinces. By 1839 sugar had became such a profitable export that it was monopolised by the crown (Cushman 1993: 81; Seksan 1989: 94–5). Non-*phrai* labour became critical to the state, and from the reign of Rama II key public works were contracted to Chinese work gangs who were paid in cash. Chinese craftsmen were also hired to build and decorate temples in the capital (Porphant 1994: 40–1).

From the first Chakkri reign, private trade expanded alongside state-run exporting, and by the early 1820s it overtook royally-sponsored mercantile activity. The number of major export items covered by the royal monopolies had already been reduced by the time King Rama III abolished them and introduced tax farms as a principal cash revenue source (Suehiro 1989: 72; Vella 1957: 23). This system involved the licensing of revenue collection rights to individuals who paid a cash amount based on estimates of the revenue value of key taxable commodities. These farms were leased periodically to businessmen (mainly Chinese) who offered the highest bids. They operated at provincial and district levels and delivered revenues to the various *krom* and their divisions. In this manner, the state transferred the responsibility of administration to private operators but reaped the financial rewards obtaining from the old monopoly rights over goods. The tax-farming system expanded with the exchange economy itself. It was possible both because of the emergence of a class of wealthy Chinese traders able to afford the substantial investment involved in tax farms, as well as the increased capacity of the peasantry of the central region to engage in commodity production and thus acquire cash for tax payments. The numbers of *phrai* able to commute their corvée service by cash payment increased steadily, to the point where income from commutation payments (including cash payments in lieu of *suai* obligations) formed a significant source of revenue for the crown and *khunnang* (Koisumi 1992; Seksan 1989: 387).

The commercial city and its hinterland

By the 1850s, when the monarchy was confronted with the challenge of conceding trading rights to western powers, substantial economic change had already taken place towards an exchange economy, and the role of Bangkok and its hinterland had been central. Under increasing pressure from British trading interests, and acutely aware of the expansion of western colonial power in the immediate region, King Mongkut (Rama IV) signed a commercial treaty with Britain in 1855 (the Bowring Treaty) which was closely followed by similar agreements with other western powers. The treaties reduced import–export duties, abolished customary shipping fees and removed many trading monopolies still in place on export products in the form of the private tax farms. European merchants were allowed to purchase goods directly from suppliers, establish their trading concerns in Bangkok, and be represented through consulates under provisions of extraterritoriality (see Bowring 1857 vol. 2: 212–25). Treaty provisions restricted customary sources of royal income, but they did not destroy the tax farming system and the system of patronage on which its was based. Nor did the treaty restrictions lead to a significant reduction in state revenues, since some tax farms (e.g. opium) did not apply to exports and a range of new tax farms on peasant produce were already in place (Wilson 1970: 621–32). However, they had significant effects which cumulatively transformed the character and functions of Bangkok, the central region and their relation to the outside world. Under the provisions of the treaties and associated constraints of extraterritoriality, Siam became a semi-colony, with its commercialising economy tied to the world trading system (Anderson 1978: 198–200). But the formal sovereignty of its monarchs was preserved, together with the realm's hierarchical structure. It was in this framework of semi-dependency that broad economic forces and a modernising state policy pushed Siam and Bangkok into a period of accelerating change.

Under the treaties the state was impelled to play an active role in encouraging commercialisation by promoting agricultural production and centralising the export economy on Bangkok through transport infrastructure. Through expanding rice production the state aimed to increase domestic food supply as well as expand the base for state revenue through taxation. Farm settlement and land-clearing in the central region were encouraged by incentives such as exempting newly cultivated land from taxation (Ingram 1971: 1975–6; Suehiro 1989: 22–4). Increasing rice prices attracted Thai peasants to specialise in this export crop, and this acted to further erode the *phrai* system. Extensive canal construction aimed to open up new areas for rice cultivation and its transportation to markets. Land grants to royal family members and nobles accompanied some canal projects, and later in the century land concessions were granted to private companies, such as the extensive Rangsit project, north of Bangkok (Ingram 1971: 79–81). From the 1890s, in fact, canal building was driven by private interests, and not the state, such was the intimate connection between rice-growing, transport and land values (Johnston 1975: 52). Large scale landlordism was not a dominant factor stimulating the system of commercialised rice production in the central region. Though landholding inequality in some provinces of the central region was to become marked by the 1930s, this was a product of commercialisation rather than a cause. The transformation of the agricultural economy was achieved largely through the initiative of peasant smallholders attracted by the prospect of increased incomes and their ability to purchase imported consumer goods (Hong 1984: 150). Expansion of rice production was achieved through the intensification of rice farming on traditional lines, not through technological innovations in farming methods. Linked to the world market via Bangkok by Chinese middlemen traders, peasant society and economy in the central region were not radically disrupted by the new capitalist system. The volatility of the commercial rice market and its effects were buffered by strong subsistence traditions (Hong 1984: 152–3).

The Bowring Treaty seems to have given little immediate stimulus to the volume of exports from Bangkok, but the period from the 1870s saw a fundamental change in both the composition and level of Siam's foreign trade. As a proportion of total exports, rice rose from 44 per cent in 1861–5 to 62 per cent by the mid-1870s, reaching over 70 per cent by the time of the world rice boom at the turn of the twentieth century. Other key export commodities in demand in world markets included teak and tin. Together, these three items comprised over 90 per cent of Siam's exports by the early twentieth century (Sompop 1989: 161). Bangkok was the destination of the great proportion of exported goods. In the newly liberalised economy, Bangkok played a key role and experienced considerable change in the process. Together with new western mercantile establishments engaged in exporting and importing came investment in new wharves, warehouses, steam-driven rice mills and saw-milling businesses (Porphant 1994: 48–9; Suehiro 1989: 52–3).

In his study of the emergent capitalist system of Thailand from the 1850s Suehiro identifies three main capitalist groups engaged in investment and accumulation. They were: the European trading houses (the only group reliant on purely private capital); the overseas and local Chinese (including entrepreneur tax farmers); and the Sakdina Group (the royal Privy Purse Bureau, or the king's personal budget) which directed state revenues into investment and loan businesses, including urban land, trade, manufacture and transport infrastructure (Sueiro 1989: 42–105). They were all engaged in investment and business activities which affected (directly or indirectly) the economy, labour market and physical character of the city.

The Chinese

The commercial functions of Bangkok and the activities of its trading population generated a variety of new labour demands, including wage labour for the mills and wharves and clerical work associated with trading. In turn, the growth of the urban population generated consumption needs and new demands for urban space, both residential and business. They fuelled the growth of activities and occupations supporting the city itself, from construction and transport to market gardening and food-vending. Above all, it was the Chinese and the increasing numbers of their Siam-born offspring whose multitude of activities supported the transformation of Bangkok. The Chinese population (almost exclusively male) became a critical resource for the state and a crucial agent of economic change and expansion which flowed from the needs of the state in the post-Bowring economy. There was a steady rise in Chinese immigration to Siam from the late 1860s, because wages for labourers and possibilities for entrepreneurial activities were high. Regular steamship traffic between the south China ports and Singapore facilitated the increased migration flows, which accelerated further from the 1890s (Skinner 1957: 42–3). Expanding entrepreneurial opportunities encouraged Chinese traders to move into the interior and the southern provinces, but large numbers of Chinese continued to settle in Bangkok. At the end of the century, well over half of Siam's total overseas Chinese population resided in and around the capital, and about half of Bangkok's population was of Chinese origin by this time (Porphant 1994: 139–42).

While western firms dominated much of the shipping as well as wholesale imports from Europe and their own colonies, direct control of internal trade and distribution was in the hands of the Chinese (Seksan 1989: 244–7). In terms of its primary role as an exporter of basic commodities, the late nineteenth-century Siamese economy is appropriately described as dependent, or 'peripheral' within the European-centred world capitalist economic order, but the beneficiaries of capitalist accumulation were not only, or even mainly, western capitalists and investors (Hewison 1989: 44–5). Chinese capitalists adapted quickly to the new conditions of the post-Bowring economy. The older group with wealth drawn from tax farming invested in rice trading and rice milling and in fact took control of this sector by the century's close. Business groups outside the networks connected to government profited from trading activities as middlemen in the rice trade and distributors of imported goods to the provinces (Suehiro 1989: 81–3). From rice trading, wealthy merchant dynasties had expanded their interests into banking by the early twentieth century. A host of smaller Chinese business concerns emerged in the capital to fill demands for construction and a myriad of services. They were also active in the emerging urban property rental market.

Well into the twentieth century, revenues derived from the Chinese, particularly the Bangkok Chinese, were indispensable to the state, since income from duties on exports was fixed by the trade treaties and other taxes were insufficient to meet expanding expenditure demands (Seksan 1989: 411–19). During the fifth reign (1868–1910) income from tax farms on the consumer activities of the Chinese (including gambling, opium and prostitution) was the most important source of state revenue (Hong 1984: 127–9; Sompop 1989: 64–5). The lucrative prostitution tax revenues funded the road building projects of Bangkok, under the respectable title of 'the road improvement tax' (Porphant 1994: 138).

The changing urban landscape

Roads and shophouses

The traditional canal and river-based transport infrastructure of Bangkok supported the commercial expansion of the post-Bowring period, serving to link the provinces to the capital and the various districts of the city. This ecology dominated the commerce and everyday lives of Bangkokians well into the twentieth century and formed the grid which determined much of the city's modern road layout. However, beginning in the reign of King Mongut (1851–68), road construction stimulated a number of key changes in the urban system including commodification of land, and initiated the trend towards a land-based city.

King Monkut had paid particular attention to the capital. In 1853 he had a new canal dug (Padung Krung Kasem) to encompass the expanding population outside the old walls of Rattanakosin (Thiphakhorawong 1966 vol. 1: 91–2). At this time the only existing streets were within and immediately bounding the palace. In 1862, Mongkut responded to a petition of European residents and ordered a road to be cut parallel to the river. Named *Charoen Krung* (Prosper the City), and commonly known as 'New Road', it formed the main commercial artery of Bangkok until well into the twentieth century. In following years roads were constructed inside the city walls and nobles and rich Chinese merchants were enjoined to fund the building of bridges where streets crossed canals (Thiphakhorawong 1966 vol. 2: 260–2) (see Fig. 1.2). The announcements accompanying these events stressed both the king's beneficence and his concern to impress western observers with the spectacle of civilisation and progress.[9] Above all, road building in the capital reflected commitment to a wide ranging project of modernisation embraced within sections of the Siamese ruling elite.[10]

Under King Chulalongkorn (r. 1868–1910) road construction in the capital accelerated. During his reign over 120 new roads were built (Porphant 1994: 84). By 1883, when the first postal directory was compiled, there were already 77 streets (*thanon*) and 102 lanes (*trok*) in the capital. Settlement of business enterprises along the key commercial roads by European, Chinese and Indian traders was substantial, but there was also significant settlement among the Thai, particularly within the walled city (Wilson 1989: 52–4). The increase in the construction of new palaces for royal family members stimulated land settlement in the inner areas and encouraged further commercial and residential development. From the beginning, road building aimed to encourage trade and revenues and this was directly facilitated by the construction of shophouses and land-based markets. The colonial cities of Batavia, Singapore, Penang and Calcutta provided the key models for Monkgut and Chulalongkorn (Sternstein 1976: 107). The Privy Purse (formed as the central investment and income-generating organ of the monarchy in 1890) initiated many of these road and shophouse projects (Porphant 1994: 72–8). Princes capitalised on the increasing value of the landholdings surrounding their palaces by constructing shophouses for rental income (Kanchanakhaphan 1977: 17–23; Porphant 1994: 84–5).

The commodification of land

According to ancient laws, the Siamese monarchs were officially the owners of all the land in their realm (expressed in the title *Phrachao Phaendin* – Lord of the Earth), but there had long been a system of de facto land ownership, based on customs of inherited property among both the nobility and the *phrai* population (Seksan 1989: 184–5). Property rights were implicitly recognised by both Mongkut and Chulalongkorn in their own practice of purchasing land, compensating people in cash or in kind if occupied land was used for royal projects, and allowing others to rent land in Krung Thep to foreigners (Department of Fine Arts, n.d.: 95–7; O'Connor 1978: 96; Pasuk and Baker 1995: 17; Wilson 1970: 607). But what was new in the emerging capitalist economic system was the use of land (and in Bangkok, building stock) as a commodity for sale and rental.

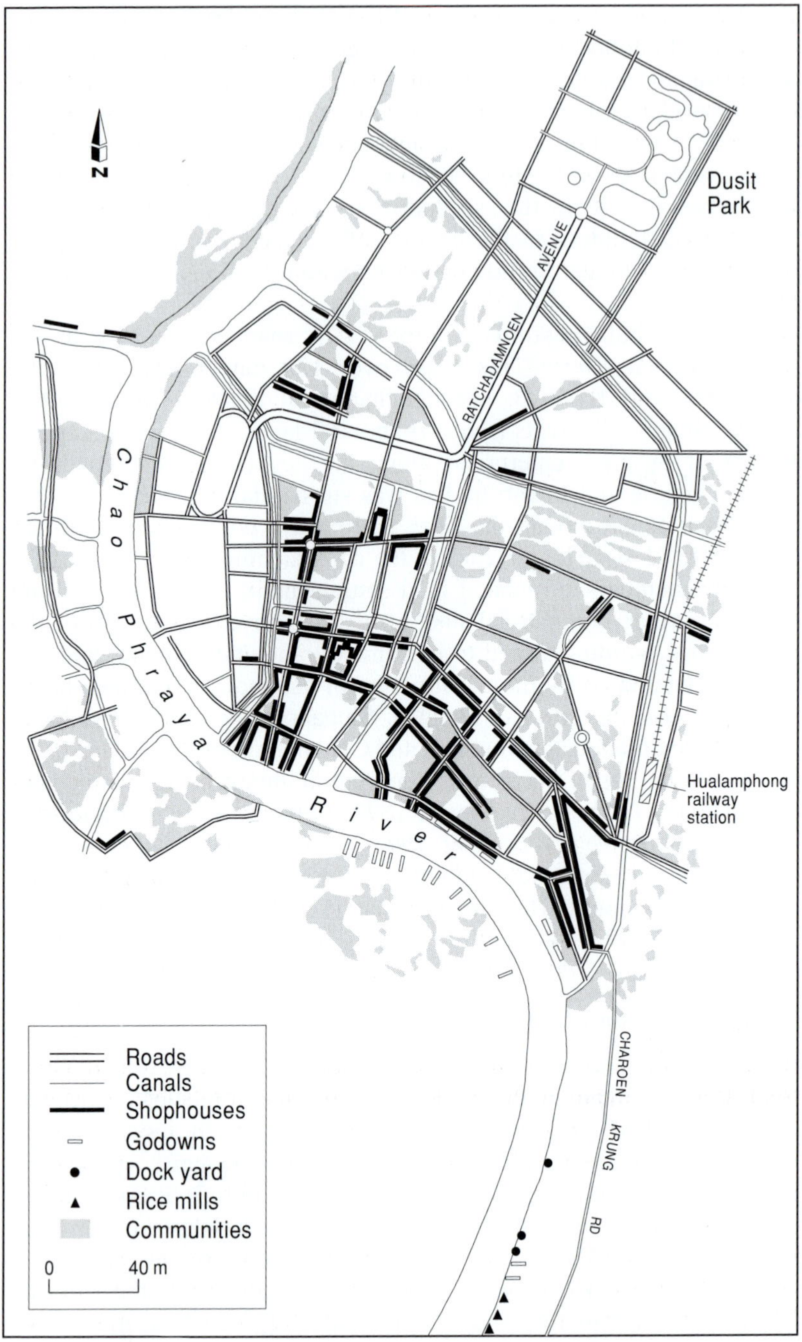

Figure 1.2 Krung Thep *c.* 1910, showing roads and shophouse development.
Source: Compiled from Naengnoi *et al.* 1991.

The monarchy itself was the principal agent in its creation. Road and shop-house construction and the associated demand for a variety of land uses stimulated an urban land market, turning Bangkok into a new field of capital accumulation for the state, the nobility and an emerging group of Thai and Chinese commoners. Women (particularly among the ethnic Thai) emerged as a conspicuous group among the landlords of this new urban rental market (Wilson 1990: 86). The introduction of land titling in the 1890s formalised the developing commodification process. In both Bangkok and its surrounding region, property disputes became common at all levels of the community, reflecting the impact of this commodification process on social relations generally (Tomosugi 1993: Part I). By the end of Chulalongkorn's reign (1910) land ownership was the basis for the wealth of the monarchy and members of the royal family (see Smith 1982: 109).[11]

Modernisation, modernity and monumentality

The fourth and fifth Chakkri reigns are associated with a range of changes generally portrayed under the rubric 'modernisation'. In material, administrative and symbolic terms this process involved the adoption of technologies, methods of government and a diverse iconography drawn from the west towards the objectives of economic advancement, the political integration of the state and the legitimacy of the monarchy. Given the hierarchical character of the traditional Thai social, economic and political order, modernisation was a process which could only be initiated from above (Cohen 1991: 47–55). And, given the urban-centred nature of power and prestige in Siam, Bangkok was the principal site where this process was displayed and generated. A new modern urban text began to displace (or at least subsume) the older text of the sacred city. I use 'modernisation' here to refer to directed change (of which reform is a part). In contrast, 'modernity', as a more multi-sited and diffuse engagement with innovation and new forms, refers to a cultural orientation beyond immediate direction by the state, even though it may be a broad consequence of state policy. In particular, modernity is associated with the consumption and appropriation of new commodities, objects and symbols, and, to paraphrase Marshall Berman, the attempts by people to become the 'subjects' as well as the 'objects' of modernisation (Berman 1988: 5; Frisby 1986: 266–72). In the nineteenth century these objects and symbols were exclusively western, and the west represented the value and process of *siwilai* (a transliteration of the English words – civilised/civilisation). In Siam, the quest for the status of being *siwilai*, in its many dimensions, had begun during the reign of Mongut, but accelerated thereafter (see Thongchai 2000). With Bangkok as the centre, the royal programme of modernisation incorporated new modes and symbols which both transformed and reinforced hierarchical power and status. The capital also developed as a site of new modes of living and values, which became independent of direction from the state because they were tied to the emergence of new groups and a more diffuse circulation of commodities and images through publishing and the marketplace.

Chulalongkorn's reign was marked by a multitude of remarkable changes and reforms. The reforms which he initiated (together with his brothers and progressive supporters) encompassed a restructuring of bureaucratic and military organisation and territorial administration aimed towards the centralisation of royal political power. He oversaw the beginnings of public education and presided over the final dismantling of the *phrai* system and the abolition of debt slavery (Wyatt 1982b: 196–212). Hundreds of foreign advisers were employed to assist in numerous areas ranging from public works, law, revenue, finance and transportation (Terwiel 1983: 274–5). While the progress of many of these initiatives was halting and their results often uneven, one of the cumulative effects was seen in Bangkok's supreme dominance as the power centre of the post-Sakdina monarchy. By the early twentieth century, a new railway system tied the provinces even more closely to Bangkok. A group of salaried civil servants – comprising both nobility and commoners – had grown under the new administrative reforms. They represented the newly emerging urban-centred hierarchy of the modern state, sustained by a status system based, at least in part, on bureaucratic rank and education (Siffin 1966: 111).

Bangkok's emergence as a centre of modernity under Chulalongkorn was a direct result of the monarchy's engagement with the western-dominated cultural and technological order of the nineteenth century. Like his father, Chulalongkorn was acutely conscious of the opinions of western observers in judging his initiatives and achievements, but the changes signified more than this. As both Thai and western scholars have noted, significant transformations and accommodations were taking place in the world-view of the elite as they confronted western science, technology and civilisation. These ranged from perceptions of time, the status of traditional and new knowledge, the body, history and the nature of political space (Atthachak 1995; Peleggi 1997; Thawisak 1997; Thongchai 1994). King Chulalongkorn's fascination with things western is well known. The court became the fulcrum of modern symbolism – from bodily adornment to the adoption of European furniture. In his position as the richest man in the realm, he became the supreme consumer of modern artefacts from the west and a leader of elite fashion, popularising the use of photography, the horse-drawn Landau and the motor car. Aspiring to the role of modern monarch, he aimed to make himself more accessible to his subjects, and in the process generated the cult of kingly personality so dominant in Thailand today (Tambiah 1976: 227). The refashioned image of modern kingship was built around new ceremonial and the presentation of the monarch as the benevolent sponsor of progress (*khwamcharoen*).

Chulalongkorn's architectural and urban projects transformed part of the capital into a space of modernity, the showpiece of a modern monarch.

Plate 1.2 Spectacles of modernity: members of the royal family display their new automobiles in a cavalcade along Ratchadamnoen Avenue (*c.* 1905). (Photo: Courtesy National Archives of Thailand)

His commissioning of European architects to construct western-style buildings in and around the royal palace was a continuation of his father's efforts; however the scale of building and its impact on Bangkok's increasingly terrestrial landscape were much greater. With the construction of buildings such as the Chakkri throne hall and many other structures to house the new ministries and officials, the palace precinct itself may be read as a narrative of stylistic westernisation. Outside the old palace, offices for the new government ministries were constructed, accompanying the introduction of a new bureaucratic work regime involving the separation of senior officials' homes from work places. From 1894, the king donated money for the construction of new iron and concrete bridges across the city's canals to mark his birthday each year (Sirichai 1977: 41–68).

Chulalongkorn's most strikingly monumental achievement in Bangkok was the construction of a new aristocratic suburb (*Dusit*) to the north of the Padung Krung Kasem canal, linked to the old palace by a grand boulevard (*Ratchadamnoen*) and terminating in a royal plaza (*Phra Lan*). These, the most expensive projects of his reign, were stimulated by his visits to western capital cities and monarchs during his 1897 European tour. In a

Plate 1.3 A city of aristocrats: family and servants of Prince Damrong outside his palace (*c.* 1900). (Photo: Courtesy National Archives of Thailand)

succeeding royal tour the king was inspired to add to this monumental ensemble a royal equestrian statue and a new throne hall. Maurizio Peleggi argues that this cluster of projects highlights Chulalongkorn's model of modern kingship. Dusit park and its numerous princely palaces expressed a western-inspired taste for a new residential lifestyle for the aristocracy (a novel lifespace for the privileged), symbolised in the exclusive and planned villa suburb (Peleggi 1997: 87, 95–6). While Dusit was a private royal suburb, other projects embodied expressions of the public meanings of kingship. Ratchdamnoen Avenue (constructed 1899–1903) was the most expensive road project of the reign and its primary role was to host the spectacles of royalty (Porphant 1994: 79–80). The mammoth new Anantha Samakhom throne hall was designed in a baroque basilica style, complete with murals depicting the heroic achievements of the Chakkri rulers. Collectively, these projects suggest how Chulalongkorn had appropriated the symbolic capital of the global urbanism and kingship of his age, and refashioned the public image of Thai kingship in the process (Peleggi 1997: 107–30).

Urban settlement and society from the 1890s to the 1940s

Urban primacy and population dynamics

From the mid-nineteenth century the interacting influences of the expanding capitalist economy and the modernising centralist state generated new dynamics of urban population growth and primacy. Between 1883 and 1913, the population of the capital expanded to over 365,000 people, a growth rate far in excess of average population growth in the kingdom. By 1913 the capital was twelve times the size of the next largest urban centre of Chiang Mai, and gradually increased this level of urban primacy over the following three decades to the point where by 1937, Bangkok was fifteen times larger than the second-largest urban settlement of the country (see Table 1.1). The driving force for population growth to the 1920s was Chinese immigration, drawn by the opportunities for wage labour and trade. Until the late 1920s, Chinese immigrants and the *lukchin* (offspring of their marriages to local women) accounted for perhaps 40 per cent of total population growth (Porphant 1994: 250). The contribution of the Thai to the growth and character of Bangkok's population was not insignificant. The court and the Buddhist Sangkha had always drawn people to the capital, acting as a traditional means of social mobility through patronage and temple-based education (Wyatt 1994a). In the modernising polity of Chulalongkorn, sources of social mobility and status in the capital shifted to education and the opportunities offered by an expanding bureaucracy drew increasing numbers of Thai (children of lesser officials and rich peasants) from outside the capital. Movement of Thai male commoners to the capital seems also have been a factor (albeit undeterminable in quantitative terms) in the expansion of Bangkok's varied settlements. Constraints of the *phrai* system over male population movement had been steadily reducing, and were never absolute. Rural Thai women appear to have been a significant group in this movement, drawn to the capital through marriage contracts with the more settled members of the Chinese urban population (Skinner 1957: 87; Sternstein 1982:

Table 1.1 Estimated population of Bangkok and Thonburi 1883–1937 and urban primacy

Year	*Population*	*Annual average growth (%)*	*Ratio Bangkok/ Chiang Mai*
1883–	169,300	1.90	10:1
1913–	365,492	2.60	12:1
1929/30–	702,544	3.92	14:1
1937	890,453	3.44	15:1

Sources: Porphant 1994: 124; Sternstein 1982: 107.

102–4). But mass rural–urban migration was never a factor in Bangkok's growth in the period to the Second World War. The official abolition of the *phrai* system in 1905 did not unleash a wave of rural–urban migration, because income from rice-farming offered peasants and their families higher average incomes than urban wage-labour into the 1920s. The continued influx of Chinese labour into Bangkok kept urban wages relatively low, providing little incentive for rural people to migrate (Sompop 1989: 164).[12]

Livelihood, ethnicity and status in the city

Bangkok's occupational structure from the turn of the twentieth century to the 1940s was derived from its twin character as a centre of government and international trade, the capital–hinterland relations which were tied to this role, and the expanding demands of its own population. At the most general level, Bangkok's occupational structure has been depicted according to a broad 'Thai'/'Chinese' ethnic specialisation of labour (see Skinner 1957: 91–8). This Thai/Chinese occupational divide was a product of the nineteenth century division of labour fashioned by the *phrai* system, which restricted men of the Thai-speaking ethnic majority to roles in agriculture or various forms of service to the state. With the encouragement of the state, Chinese immigrants availed themselves of expanding opportunities in trade, urban labour and other commercial ventures.

We should note here that by the early twentieth century, many Bangkokians who identified themselves as 'Thai' had some Chinese ancestry, a fact which continues to mark the population of the metropolis today. They were often the children of second-generation *lukchin* fathers who had married Thai women (Skinner 1957: 132). In the nineteenth century 'Thainess' was deemed by the state to be a function of assimilation into the *phrai* system as much as an ethnic label based on cultural assimilation (Kasian 1991). Thus, those men officially identified as 'Chinese' (*chin*) were deemed to be such by virtue of their appearance (pigtails) and their absence of *phrai* tattoos which signified bondage to a master. Another signifier of Thainess was the incorporation of individuals into the nobility (the ranks of *khunnang*) regardless of ethnic origin, and this had occurred throughout the eighteenth and nineteenth centuries and earlier (Skinner 1957: 154). On a broader cultural level, Thainess was a category signifying assimilation of various groups over time (whether Chinese, Mon, or others) into the dominant Thai-speaking ethnic majority. Thainess began to take on racial dimensions only as a consequence of the rise of officially-sponsored nationalism in the early decades of the twentieth century, with the consequence that the Chinese were increasingly identified as an alien and non-Thai minority (Kasian 1991). By this time the process of assimilation into Thai society through intermarriage had slowed, due to the fact that women were conspicuous among the Chinese immigrant groups entering Siam, allowing for endogamy to reinforce group identity and continuity. The rise of cultural institutions (speech group associations and schools) and newspapers associated with strident Chinese nationalism in these years also helped consolidate and distinguish the *chin* in Bangkok society, despite the part-Chinese origins of many of the Thai of the capital (Skinner 1957: 155–71).

The civilian and military bureaucracy was dominated by the Thai, (that is, both the Central Thai of the Chao Phraya Delta and those groups who had become assimilated towards their language and cultural patterns). The importance of the salaried bureaucracy in Bangkok was directly linked to the expansion of the modern state apparatus and the growing administrative ambit of formal government in both kingdom and city from the 1890s. Until the advent of the constitutional monarchy in 1932, the most powerful ministerial positions were monopolised by the royal princes; but a greatly expanded government bureaucracy drew to its middle ranks a significant number of talented and ambitious Thais of non-royal background. They were educated at the new local schools and training institutions, and increasingly trained abroad under royal patronage (Siffin 1966: 56–8; Wyatt 1994b: 243). The salaried bureaucracy included professional positions in the military, judiciary (and new departments such as education), encompassing numerous lesser functionaries dependent on state salaries and status. Government employment (*kharatchakan*) offered both the status of royal service and the security of a pension (however modest) at retirement. Between 1892 and 1899, the number of civil servants doubled, and by 1918 tripled again (Siffin 1966: 94).

At all levels of trade, manufacturing and distribution, the Chinese (both locally and Chinese-born) were the most numerous and dominant group, forming the crucial basis for Bangkok's international trade, the regional economy and the urban domestic market. Chinese business activity encompassed the rice trade and most retail activities through to building, furniture construction and running of pawnshops. The Chinese were to be found at all income levels and statuses throughout the city. They formed the majority among rice-mill labourers (between ten and twenty thousand by the early 1920s), and in Bangkok's small industrial sector. Many others worked as wharf labourers. They engaged in small-scale food vending and repair work, pulled rickshaws, delivered water and worked as street-sweepers (Porphant 1994: 49–50).

The composition of the urban workforce underwent discernible change in the decades after the First World War. Increasing numbers of Thais entered skilled and unskilled wage-work, especially in the tramways and government employment in the state railway workshops (Kanchada 1989: 37–9). The increasing involvement of Thais was directly related to changing economic conditions and government policy. The world economic depression from 1929 saw a sharp drop in Chinese immigration, which was a far more decisive deterrent to the Chinese than the earlier immigration restrictions introduced by Rama VII (Skinner 1957: 176–7). As a result, increasing numbers of Thai men and women entered petty trade and vending occupations. A certain level of rural–urban migration also stimulated this trend. From 1932, under the new military/bureaucratic regime, Thai involvement in the non-agricultural workforce was encouraged through promotion of industries, the application of compulsory employment quotas for manufacturing firms and the banning of ethnic Chinese from vending activity (Kanchada 1989: 43–4).

A portrait of the broad occupational patterns of Bangkok according to the government–private sector and ethnic Thai/Chinese divide tends to oversimplify the nature of Bangkok's pre-Second World War economy and its peoples' livelihoods. The large numbers of people of mixed Chinese–Thai parentage were not a unitary group in terms of cultural or economic orientations. While there was a wide variation in the dynamics and conditions allowing for assimilation, in general, it appears that it was the children of *lukchin* fathers who tended to identify themselves as Thai through language and cultural orientation, while those with Chinese fathers were likely to identify as Chinese and be associated with their business-orientated occupations (Skinner 1957: 132–4). Young men with *lukchin* fathers entered government service and the professions in Bangkok (Sthirakoses 1996), but the status and income rewards of the professions, particularly medicine, were also attractive to the children of Chinese business families (Tomosugi 1993: 157–210). A number of specialised businesses in Bangkok were in the hands of other ethnic groups, such as Indian traders (including Muslims, Hindus and Sikhs) who were conspicuous in cloth importing, the jewellery trade, gem-selling and tailoring. Other Indians occupied menial positions, such as migrants from Uttar Pradesh who, from the early years of the twentieth century, were almost universally employed by businesses across Bangkok as watchmen (Vaid 1982: 296–8; Wood 1965: 14). Although the Malays (descendants of the Pattani war captives) concentrated in rice-growing around the capital, some specialisations were to be found, including goldworking crafts (see Bajunid 1992: 19; Scupin 1981: 171–2).

While Bangkok's growth and the nature of its key economic and occupational changes were tied to its role in the international rice and commodity economy, many of its people lived by supplying the domestic demands of urban dwellers. There was a multiplicity of livelihoods sustained by the various social and economic subsystems of the city, such as the large princely households, temples, markets and local neighbourhoods (see e.g. Kumut 1996: 157). Small-scale market activity had always been primarily in the hands of Thai women, and the age-old practice of selling agricultural and gardening surplus at local Bangkok markets continued. Women were also prominent as vendors of traditional dessert foods along both the canals and streets (Sthirakoses 1992: 58, 103). For ethnic Thais at least, there was no strict bifurcation of life and livelihood among those occupying the modern occupational sector and those continuing in the traditional bazaar sector. In fact, both livelihoods were characteristically pursued at the household level.

The ecology of the capital: duality and continuity

From the 1890s the space of the capital increasingly assumed a dual character, with the small eastern territorial core around the palace spreading over a semi-aquatic landscape dominated by waterways, villages, gardens and ricefields. From 1900 to 1936 the built-up area of the capital expanded from 13 to 43 square kilometres, but was unevenly populated and ecologically diverse. Visiting Bangkok in 1911, the Italian nobleman Salvatore Besso commented on the Thai capital city: 'The Venice of the Far East – the capital still wrapped in mystery, in spite of the thousand efforts of modernism amid its maze of canals' (Cited in Sternstein 1982: 13). The dual character of the settlement geography of the capital and its surrounding mosaic of *ban* and *bang* persisted until at least a decade after the Second World War (and in Thonburi much longer), and this waterway network outside the rings of the old city canals exercised a major influence on the pattern of physical expansion thereafter.

Neither King Chulalongkorn or his successors to the absolute monarchy (Rama VI and VII) translated their fascination with modernism into an overall plan for the metropolis. Nor were the municipal administrations they introduced equipped to control urban development under the impact of economic, social and population change. Until 1892 the capital was administered as a domain of central government in a hybrid arrangement which was a clear legacy of traditional governance. The Ministry of the Palace (*Krom Wang*) controlled policing and other matters in the Rattanakosin area, while the Harbour Department (*Krom Tha*) was responsible for sanitary arrangements and policing around Sampheng and beyond. Under the administrative reforms from 1892, a new Ministry of the Capital (*Krasuang Nakhonban*) was created, with divisions for police, revenue collection, sanitation, construction of roads and the control of public markets (Porphant 1994: 126–8). This development, together with the progressive definition of administrative subareas within the wide expanse of settlements ramifying from the city, all reflected the increasing need to manage a more complex and growing settlement area. Municipal government was essentially an arm of the central state apparatus concerned with maintenance, and there was no public involvement in local government. Other agencies played a greater role in the evolving spaces of the capital. In particular, the Crown Property Bureau – as the greatest landowner in the capital – was responsible for much new commercial development, and other key central government ministries (the ministries for war, education and public works) made decisions which directed new patterns of building.

The monarchs themselves made critical interventions in the landscape through major projects such as Ratchadamnoen Avenue, Dusit, and the construction of institutions.

After Chulalongkorn's death, more amenities and symbols of a modern city continued to be added to the landscape, including hospitals, a new university (Chulalongkorn University, 1917) and Lumpini Park, originally intended as the site for a major international exhibition. A number of functional zones associated with royalty and the state were consolidated. While the old centre of Rattanakosin remained central to key ceremonies of state, the focus of the royal precinct had moved outward, with the king occupying the modern Chitralada Palace in Dusit. Inner Rattanakosin had become the major zone of government offices, a zone which later expanded along outer Ratchadamnoen Avenue. By the reign of King Rama VI, two of Siam's three armies were strategically located in the capital (Chaloeylakana 1988: 160–1). North of Dusit, the main barracks and associated offices of the army housed a military concentration which still dominates this area today (Seidenfaden 1928: 81–6).

In the 1920s western commentators found comfort in finding in Bangkok features resembling other European and colonial cities. They included: the western stores and medical dispensaries of Charoen Krung Road, the hotels (some converted from palaces to serve increasing numbers of affluent western tourists), the leafy western bungalow area expanding from this thoroughfare along Surawong and Silom Roads, the electric tramway system and the French-designed Hualamphong Railway station. One enthusiastic booster went so far as to speculate that the future would see Bangkok as 'a vast well-laid out park-like town intersected with a network of broad shady roads running in all directions . . .' (Seidenfaden 1928: 90). But the settlement patterns taking place in most of the city were less orderly and more indigenous than this portrait allowed. Through initiating and encouraging road building, the monarchy set in train a settlement process which developed its own dynamic. This dynamic was shaped around both old social patterns and evolving economic activities and land uses. The residential precinct of Silom/Suriwong emerged from private land sales and development among the Thai nobility and Chinese businessmen, as did the Wang Burapha commercial area. Key ethnic concentrations were evident, conspicuous particularly in Sampheng/Yawarat (the old trading *yan* of the Chinese) and among the Indians of Phahurat nearby. But the most notable feature of the city was the proliferation of multifunctional working and living areas and the broad dispersal of the Chinese and Sino–Thai among the Thai. One of the most common physical configurations was the *trok* (or lane) settlements of wooden houses (*ban ruan*) surrounded or screened by shophouses (*tuk thaeo*), with Thai communities occupying the former and Chinese traders working and living in the streetside shophouses. The shophouse was the distinctive mark of Chinese presence, although the Thai also occupied these structures as residences.

Aside from these common *ban ruan/tuk thaeo* neighbourhoods, there were other settlements which clustered around the city's many temples on rented land or the subdivided estates of the lesser nobility and their descendants (see e.g. O'Connor 1978: 100–1). The ethnic distinctiveness of some of these neighbourhoods (the Mon, Khmer and Vietnamese for example) faded over time as populations assimilated with the Thai or dispersed, yet others persisted. As in the early Rattanakosin period, ordinary Bangkokians continued to identify the city as a collectivity of *yan*, or districts, identified through the activities or characteristics of neighbourhoods (see O'Connor 1990: 62).

City and society – a site of difference

Bangkok had always stood out from the rest of the kingdom by virtue of its concentration of power, symbols and wealth. In the 1850s Sir John Bowring observed that Krung Thep and its citadel signified visually the dominance of the capital over the kingdom (Bowring 1857 vol. 1: 391). By the twentieth century, images of Bangkok appear to have become more diverse, expressing the nature of change and the distinctiveness of patterns of life among its growing and diverse population. By the close of Chulalongkorn's reign, the capital was more than ever the site of status in the kingdom: associated with the prestige of royalty and the new bureaucracy, together with the architecture and institutions of progress and modernity.

Yet Bangkok was also associated with moral danger, decadence and greed. One English commentator noted trenchantly:

> Those who never go out of Bangkok cannot hope to know the Siamese. Corrupted by the example of Europeans and demoralised by the riff-raff of all nations, the native of the capital must not be held up as a fair sample of his race.
>
> (Thompson 1996: 122)

From the beginning of the twentieth century, accounts of visitors refer to Bangkok's numerous seedy gambling dens and brothels serving foreign sailors, local people (both Thai and Chinese) and aristocrats alike (e.g. Somerville 1897: 86; Thompson 1996: 203). In well-known parts of the city (particularly in Sampheng) there was an underworld of opium-smoking and commercial sex indulged in by a large segment of the urban population (Barmé 1997: 56–8; Sthirakoses 1992: 251–2). Crime, particularly burglary, was frequent, reflecting how the city had become the centre of commodities and luxuries. The Chinese-run pawn shops of the city commonly fenced valuables stolen from the homes of foreign residents and Thai aristocrats (Thompson 1996: 70; Wood 1965: 17–18). Gangs of local toughs (*nakleng*) inhabited many neighbourhoods and often enjoyed the protection of 'influential figures'. They engaged in extortion and banditry, often beyond the reach of police control (O'Connor 1978: 95–6). Stories in the press and novels of young women sold into prostitution by unscrupulous money-lenders and sharks highlight how early this image of Bangkok as a place of evil and exploitation emerged in Thailand (Wilson 1970: 389). Other literary portraits of the city evoked the image of an alien environment with values distinct from traditional rural society, where a distinctive rhythm of time-consciousness connected to the imperatives of commerce, industry and money-making dominated the lives of its inhabitants (Kanchada 1989: 64).

By the early twentieth century, the gamut of changes flowing from Chulalongkorn's modernisaton projects, together with the flow of new images and commodities arriving in the wake of the economic opening to the west, combined to produce a more complex society in Bangkok. The print media had been encouraged in the previous century, and educational and bureaucratic reforms laid the basis for an expanding group of commoners who formed a nascent (although heterogeneous) middling stratum of urban society. By the 1920s this group became engaged with global culture outside the control of the state and traditional aristocracy which had formerly sponsored and patronised the arts, literature and entertainment. A mass commercial culture emerged which soon came to define urban life. It was based on an active publishing and cinema entertainment industry in Bangkok, itself largely generated by entrepreneurs of this diverse middle-stratum of entrepreneurs (Barmé 1997: 40–1). Through these media the new public for popular culture was exposed to alternative images of society, values and sexuality. The new entertainment venues in the city became the hubs of public life and interaction for young people of Bangkok's elite and middle stratum. Ratchdamnoen Avenue became a fashionable promenading area (Kanchanakaphan 1977).

The growth of an urban intelligentsia was part of this broad process of change. Symptomatic of the trend was a group of writers whose novels explored the dilemmas of a generation of overseas-educated Siamese grappling with new questions concerning conflicts between inherited traditions and western values and behaviours, including romance, marriage and gender roles (Emon 1996; Wyatt 1982b: 238–9). However, it was the popular press that most expressed the expanded dimensions of public life and debate in the capital. The period of Rama VI's reign (1910–25) saw an efflorescence of journals and newspapers. Through the press, writers and their readers debated and engaged with new ideas bearing on modernity, 'progress', civilisation, the nature of society, nationhood and the political order (Batson 1984: 71–87; Vella 1978: 251–3). On the eve of the fall of the absolute monarchy in 1932, the nascent middle classes – both within and outside the bureaucracy – together with the popular press, were the driving dynamic both of a volatile public opinion and a commercialised popular culture (Barmé 1997). Ironically, after 1932 the new bureaucratic power elite effectively muzzled the politically insubordinate tendencies of the very press which had helped establish a climate conducive to the demise of the monarchical state. At the same time, however, this elite endorsed with greater thoroughness the drive to modernity in social life generated in the capital.

The 1932 'revolution' and after

In the middle of 1932, within two months of the 150th anniversary celebrations of the Chakkri dynasty and its capital city, the absolute monarchy fell victim to the bureaucratic class to which it had given birth less than two generations earlier. This 'revolution' was in fact a coup led by a small Bangkok-based elite comprising military and civilian bureaucrats, united more by a determination to limit monarchical power and aristocratic government than by any political consensus (Wyatt 1982: 242). Nonetheless the new regime had far reaching impacts and consequences. Notably, it affirmed Bangkok's centrality as a centre of a new national power elite with the capacity to impose its will on the population of the country (Batson 1984: 239). Further, events shortly following the foundation of the new parliamentary arrangements established a pattern of intra-elite rivalry for state power whereby conflicts were resolved by military coups staged in the capital. Under the new regime, patronage resources came under the control of bureaucratic office-holders at the expense of the old aristocracy (Chaloeylakana 1988: 300–1).

The policies of the coup-makers had a number of effects on the society and culture of the city. The influence of formerly important princes was greatly reduced as they lost status as leaders of society and cultural patronage. Some were forced out of the country by the new regime and their palaces were confiscated (Batson 1984: 254–7; Kitthiphongsa n.d.: 92–5).[13] The activities and influence of the monarchy were deliberately reduced by a radical cut in the royal budget (Chaloeylakan 1988: 289). Public ceremonies associated with kingship in Bangkok ceased (Siphanom 1962: 348). After King Prajadhipok's abdication in 1935, his ill-fated successor (the young King Ananda, who died in 1946) spent most of his life in Switzerland. Royalty was virtually absent from Thailand until the arrival of the new king (King Bhumibol Adulyadet, Rama IX) in 1950, but even then the monarch's involvement in public life was deliberately restricted until Field Marshal Sarit Thanarat took power from 1957, and revived the ceremonial functions of the monarchy to bolster his own legitimacy claims (Wyatt 1982b: 245).

Under the first government of Plaek Phibun Songkhram (1938–44), the mystique and symbolism of the monarchy and Chakkri dynasty were transmuted and subsumed within a broader nationalist narrative stressing warrior heroes (*wiraburut*) and their role in the preservation of the nation, which, in 1939, had been renamed Thailand (Terwiel 1983: 342–4). While the

Plate 1.4 Bangkok – centre of political change: the Democracy Monument (completed 1940). (Photo: Courtesy National Archives of Thailand)

political role of the Thai monarchy was sidelined by the new nationalist regime, the monuments and architecture of the citadel city of Rattanakosin were historicised through monument preservation legislation (Askew 1994: 94–7). New urban monuments were constructed in the capital, aiming to proclaim and encourage the ideals of the new elite. The Victory Monument with its neo-realist military heroes and the Democracy Monument on Ratchdamnoen Avenue – a more ambiguous, yet nonetheless powerful icon – were attempts to establish new monumental spaces in the capital of the nation (Nithi 1995b).

In terms of socio-economic change in the country at large and Bangkok in particular, a number of trends and changes were notable. Policies aimed towards nationalising key industries led to the formation of state enterprises in industries such as petroleum and rice-milling. The most important result was the emergence of 'bureaucratic capitalism' whereby Chinese entrepreneurs forged mutually beneficial alliances with state officials. The demise of the aristocrat-led state did not lead to the demise of patron–

clientalism; rather it was reconfigured for the benefit of the new elite (Suehiro 1989: 130–3). Policies intended to reduce the Chinese dominance in the urban workforce led Thais into industry and the informal sector, but the continuing importance of Chinese business families and capital at all levels of the economy remained, albeit disguised under the nationalist titles of the new state enterprises (Kobkua 1995: 148–9; Suehiro 1989: 133–4). Apart from changes within the top echelons of the power elite and their enhanced access to material and status rewards, there was no redistribution of wealth – no fundamental change to the socio-economic structure of the countryside or the city flowed from the revolution. The landholdings of most of the old nobility in the city and its hinterland (and most of the crown's land) remained intact (Batson, 1984: 238–9; Chaloeylakan 1988: 289–96).

Few substantial physical changes occurred in Bangkok during the years of the first Phibun government (1938–44), even though Bangkok's population was fast increasing (at 6 per cent annual growth over the national average of 3.5 per cent) (Sternstein 1982: 94). Notably, most of the city's modern infrastructure – the airport, the electricity supply, the railway system, and the two bridges linking Thonburi to Bangkok – had been established prior to the revolution. Some road building occurred, with the construction of a northern highway (Pahonyothin Road) and the commencement of a southeastern route (later known as Sukhumvit) out of the city. In 1933, the two transriver municipalities of Krung Thep and Thonburi were created as part of a new system of municipal government that allowed for some increase in participation in local government. But these municipalities were largely concerned with maintenance, not policy, and they were subordinate to central government. During the years of Japanese occupation, Phibun proposed building a new capital city in the north at Phetchabun. This suggested that he had little interest in further developing Bangkok (Thak 1979: 4–5).[14] In fact Phibun resigned his premiership in 1944 following a parliamentary vote against his proposal to shift the capital. The idea of creating a new administrative capital away from Bangkok has since become a recurring fantasy for national leaders. Despite the confident rhetoric which accompanied Phibun's policies of national economic development – spurred by the confidence born of the ending of foreign extraterritoriality in 1938 – Thailand's economy by the close of the Second World War still relied overwhelmingly on agricultural commodity exports. Bangkok remained a service-dominated commercial city tied to the world system and the vicissitudes of its markets.

2 The transformation of Krung Thep

Introduction: state, capital and people

During the bicentennial celebrations of the founding of Krung Thep in 1982, the governor of the Bangkok Metropolitan Administration (Admiral Tiam Makarananda) set forth in official tones the significance of Thailand's capital city:

> In no other capital city are the ideals of a people so concentrated, and no other capital city so determines the ideals of a people as does Bangkok.
>
> (cited in Sternstein 1982: preface)

By 1982, over two decades of national development planning and economic transformation had reinforced the administrative, economic and symbolic dominance of the capital over the nation as never before. The Thai administrative title of the BMA capital region – Krung Thep Mahanakhon – recalled the old royal name of the city, but notwithstanding the state-sponsored historical evocation of the Rattanakosin precinct in these years, the city's significance was rooted in its status as a capital of a modern nation state and the focus of economic accumulation and social advancement. The landscape of the city itself was a register of the major forces and contradictions marking the uneven development of previous decades. The burgeoning slums belied the dreams of technocrats to forge a uniformly modern social and economic space. The governor of Bangkok's affirmative proclamation obscured the more complex realities of the metropolis and the ways it was experienced by ordinary people. At around the same time, the writer Wanich Jarunggidanan exposed a different image of the city in his short-story '*Muang Luang*' (The Capital). Set in a Bangkok bus in the middle of a traffic jam, the story evokes the indifference of the crowded city – a place of alienation, grief and loss. The main character bemoans his fraught urban existence as an office clerk, dreaming of the simple and happy village life he forsook so long ago in search of advancement in the city. In the climax of the story, a labourer from Isan (the north east) spontaneously breaks into a traditional folk song about romance and loss, tears rolling down his face (Wanich 1985). The city is here defined as an oppressive, dehumanising force, a place to be endured, not lived. It is a story about the new urban dwellers – the migrants to the city – who now outnumbered the old-style Bangkokians who were born and bred in Krung Thep and its surrounds. Wanich was only one of numerous writers who depicted Bangkok as a place of alienation, commercialism and moral decadence at this time (see e.g. Lockard 1998: 178–83). In the decades after the Second World War Bangkok became an increasingly complex space, generated by the intersection of local transformations and transnational forces. Contrasting and varied images of the metropolis were a reflection of the ways Bangkok was experienced and encountered by its varied population.

This chapter incorporates within a narrative of change the key agents that have shaped the sociospatial complex of Thailand's contemporary metropolis since the Second World War. These agents can be broadly summarised as the state, capital (domestic and foreign) and ordinary people who have actively created the metropolis in their search for livelihood and status. Their dynamic interaction has developed in relation to forces of change at national, regional and global levels. Over the period of three decades from the late 1950s Thailand underwent transformations of massive proportions, transformations in which the capital city functioned as the key fulcrum and beneficiary, and – from a less sanguine perspective – their victim. In economic terms the period saw a transition towards an export-orientated industrial economy and the commercialisation of the agricultural sector. It was fuelled by overseas development aid and technical assistance, facilitated by a development-orientated state, and embraced enthusiastically by an overwhelmingly urban-based financial and entrepreneurial elite. In demographic and social terms, Bangkok expanded rapidly into a major metropolis by world standards, drawing waves of migrants from all over the country in search of profit, education, employment and survival. The nature and trajectory of Bangkok's physical, social and economic transformations were tied to historical legacies, but intimately bound with the wider world economy. As used here, the term 'Bangkok' refers to the whole metropolitan complex, not merely the territory delimited by the municipal administration of the BMA. But beyond this, we need to acknowledge that many 'Bangkoks' emerged from the transformative processes in the post-war period, defined variously in terms of state representation and policy, urban functions, settlement patterns, ecologies and ways of life. Bangkok's existing functions as a centre of government and prestige were considerably enhanced, but new dimensions also emerged as economic change articulated with space and society – Bangkok became simultaneously a key industrial city, a city of the poor, a city of the middle classes and a tourist city.

Within a broad chronological frame, I here link a number of usually separate perspectives of urban change, including: (a) a functional perspective of the metropolis in relation to general economic forces and the national urban hierarchy; (b) an ecological perspective on the metropolis as a dynamic and evolving spatial complex; and (c) a perspective which treats the metropolis as a site for the emergence, interaction and conflict between key groups. The periodisation used here is applied simply to frame in general terms the emergence of key trends, which in some cases correspond with political regimes, development plans or economic phases. They are not used to strictly demarcate the many overlapping levels and spans of change. A key dimension informing this narrative is an emphasis on the significance of a complex of Thai behavioural–institutional practices which I define broadly as a culture of power and informality.[1] They are critical to comprehending the networks of influence and key relations between groups, institutions and people which continue to shape the metropolis and explain its evolution as a site of accumulation and power at all levels.

Post-war expansion: 1945–58

The post-war world and Bangkok-centred development

Thailand entered the post-war period with an economic structure that was unchanged from the pre-war years. The economy relied overwhelmingly on the export of basic commodities (primarily rice, but also rubber) produced by a society of rural smallholders who lived and worked in villages largely isolated from the metropolis. Bangkok remained utterly distinct from the rest of the country over which its elites presided. In 1947 the capital dwarfed all other urban centres of the nation (being 20 times the size of the second-largest centre of Chiang Mai), even though the municipalities of Bangkok and Thonburi housed only 781,662 people, representing just over 4 per cent of Thailand's population (Donner, 1978: 792). Bangkok maintained its traditional hold on trade, with the overwhelming majority of imported and exported goods being processed, handled and distributed through the city, principally via Sino–Thai business concerns.

In the early 1950s, the commodities export boom induced by the Korean War boosted Thailand's economy, and particularly Bangkok. American economic assistance to Thailand beginning in 1950 (and supplemented by increasing government expenditure) became significant to growth. Aid was directed towards development projects aiming at resuscitating Bangkok's war-damaged infrastructure (particularly roads and power supply) and expanding and diversifying national economic production. In the context of emerging Cold War hostilities, the second Phibun military-led government (1947–57) enjoyed increasing support from the USA, whose leaders were intent on building Thailand as 'a bastion of freedom in Southeast Asia' (cited in Kobkua 1995: 281). The formal US–Thai alliance, together with Thailand's strategic early entry into the United Nations, gave Thai government agencies access to World Bank and UN assistance. Large numbers of young Thais destined for work in high levels of national administration received university training overseas (Girling 1981: 96; Muscat 1994: 49–54).

Government expenditure programmes during the second Phibun-led government were directed to improving national income and social welfare in a broad array of areas, from urban housing to irrigation (Kobkua 1995: 150–1). Generally uncoordinated, the programmes implicitly favoured centralisation, having the cumulative effect of consolidating Bangkok's urban primacy and benefiting key economic actors in the capital and urban consumers generally (Muscat 1994: 52). Significantly, the first major infrastructure project benefiting from international loans was the development of a new port at Khlong Toei, five miles downriver from the central city. Mooted from the mid-1930s, dredging of the river to create this port area was completed in 1954, significantly enhancing the international import–export capabilities of Bangkok (Porphant 1994: 210–11). In 1955 the government introduced a premium on rice exports (levied on exporters) in order to enhance government revenues and stabilise domestic rice prices and provided the government with windfall revenues due to high world commodity prices. The premium allowed the state and private employers to keep salaries and wages low by acting as an income subsidy. In the process, it exacerbated rural–urban income disparities. It operated at the expense of rural households because merchants passed on the costs in the form of lower farm-gate purchase prices (Pawadee 1987: 186–90). Combined with the stagnating wage effects of an increasing labour supply in Bangkok, the rice premium (only abolished in the mid-1980s) enhanced the profitability of investment in urban-based manufacturing and service industries, which grew significantly in the following decade (Muscat 1994: 75–7; Porphant 1994: 194–8).

The centre of accumulation and consumption

During Phibun's administration, economic nationalism had provided the policy and ideological framework for the wide-ranging involvement of the state in economic affairs. By the post-war years a large number of manufacturing and trading enterprises in both urban and rural areas had been taken over or penetrated by the state. However, the achievements of official goals to retrieve capital from 'aliens' (particularly the Chinese) and enhance self-sufficiency were limited. Notably, many enterprises were still managed by ethnic Chinese who had become Thai citizens. Moreover, articles produced by the enterprises (paper and gunny sacks, for example) did not reduce demands for imports of essential industrial items (such as machinery). The state enterprises (as well as many private concerns) were run as fiefdoms by government departments and powerful office-holders

(Muscat 1994: 54–62). This rent-seeking pattern of behaviour – also described as a 'patrimonial economy' – of state institutions was essentially a reproduction of the older tribute system of the sakdina state, but paradoxically, such behaviours coexisted together with an increasing professionalism and corporate identification based on meritocracy which had increased after the 1932 revolution (Girling 1981: 78; Jacobs 1971: 15–16; Evers and Silcock 1967). The eminently practical Chinese business elite adapted to this system by developing client relations with influential figures (Girling 1981: 78–9; Pasuk 1980: 42–3; Skinner 1957: 360–1).

Between 1951–6 imports into Thailand (both luxury and capital goods) almost doubled, with the renewed trading activity boosting the wealth of Bangkok's business groups.[2] Throughout the 1950s and into the next decade economic growth was led by services (such as trading and banking), not exports, as had formerly been the pattern (Chatthip 1968: 40–2). At the same time, consumer goods imports were steadily rising, largely serving the as-yet-small urban elite and middle classes, whose consumption levels increased throughout the decade (Ingram 1971: 226). For example, between the years 1947 and 1957 the number of private cars in the municipalities of Bangkok and Thonburi increased by over 650 per cent, representing 87 per cent of all private cars in Thailand (Manop 1973: 17).

The period of war and Japanese occupation weakened the traditional hold of the European trading houses and banks in Thailand. In their absence, largely Bangkok-based Chinese entrepreneurs diversified their fields from trade to commercial banking and insurance, so that by the end of the war these commercial banks had formed an independent business base for financial dealings and investment (Suehiro 1989: 154–7). Another trend influencing economic activity in Bangkok was the tendency for Chinese Thais – after the 1949 communist takeover of China – to retain their savings in Thailand. This provided a pool of local capital for business development (Keyes 1987: 152–3) The European firms which set up in the post-war period concentrated on importing, specialising as agents for items such as automobiles, or they maintained engineering divisions for the servicing and installation of capital works (Suehiro 1989: 174–7).

National development and the reshaping of a metropolis: 1958–71

The Sarit regime and 'Phatthana'

The great spur to state-coordinated economic development policy came in 1957 with the accession to power of Field Marshall Sarit Thanarat through his coup and his assumption of personal executive power in the following year. His 'revolutionary' dictatorial regime avowed a commitment to a programme of economic and social development (*phatthana*), which aimed to unify the nation against the dangers of communism and to advance modernisation. Notably corrupt, Sarit nevertheless engineered considerable change in the bureaucracy by promoting a more thoroughgoing commitment to economic efficiency and national development policy management. Economic nationalism was dropped in favour of an open-door economic policy, and the oppressive parasitism of the state enterprises and their cronies was eased with a more accommodating treatment of Chinese business elites and private domestic capital (Darling 1965: 194). While individuals in the ruling elite continued their connections with business, the state withdrew from direct control of commerce and industry – as a result, the private sector grew (Girling 1981: 79–80; Muscat 1994: 113–14).

Following the US strategy to cultivate Thailand as a bastion of anti-communism in the region, and in response to persistent requests by Sarit's government for more aid, technical support and military and development funding to Thailand increased (Darling 1965: 206–9; Pasuk and Baker 1995: 276–7). Receptive to a World Bank Mission report of 1958, Sarit established the National Economic Development Board (NEDB) and the Board of Investment (BOI) to boost industrial growth, foreign investment and diversification in the national economy (Keyes 1987: 151–3; Suehiro 1989: 178–9; Ingram 1971: 231–2). Western-trained technocrats were brought in to assume leading advisory roles and the NEDB and key institutions such as the Bank of Thailand were staffed by new western-trained Thai technocrats committed to management and efficiency. These technocrats came to form a significant professionalised subculture within the bureaucracy (Evers and Silcock 1967: 103–4). They filled a critical mediating role with international agencies and were part of the regime's project to establish a climate conducive to increased overseas aid and private investment. While the actual capacity of the NEDB and its technocrats (later renamed the NESDB – National Economic and Social Development Board) to implement programmes was limited and hampered by persistent rivalries and inefficiencies of government line agencies, this period saw the advent of a new rhetoric of development planning and a growing capacity among state agencies to monitor the economy and map its people through statistical measurements. Bangkok was one of the first objects of planning, and the failure of this planning serves to highlight the dominance of more powerful forces shaping space and society in the metropolis.

The fantasy of city planning

Sarit's understanding of national development was basic and unsophisticated. *Phatthana* was expressed in terms of his paternalistic concern for social happiness and the promotion of modern ways (Thak 1974: 327). Direct intervention in the urban process included his decree of 1959 banning the three-wheeled *samlor* (pedicabs) from the streets of Bangkok (because they were 'unsightly' and unfit to be seen in a modern city), the clearance of some major slums, a welfare programme aiming to reduce street begging, and a vain effort to send an increasing flood of rural–urban migrants back to the countryside (Thak 1979: 164). Aside from these heavy-handed efforts, policy formulation as such was left to overseas consultants and the Thai technocrats. These included a development plan for the metropolis. The *Greater Bangkok Plan 2533*, developed by the American consultant team Litchfield and Associates in 1960, aimed to establish land-use zoning and directions for urban growth for the next three decades (Sternstein 1982: 109).

By the time of the commencement of the Litchfield study, Bangkok had already made the transition to an automobile and road-based city in place of its old canal-based infrastructure. Certainly the two transport modes coexisted at that time and across the river in Thonburi, the canals were to remain principal arteries of transport for at least another two decades. By 1960 a large number of both minor and major canals had already been filled in and roads constructed in their place. While the Litchfield consultants acknowledged the significance of the *khlong* as drains for storm water, fire protection, disposal of sewage and even bathing, their plan was predicated on the model of a modern Western city (Litchfield *et al.* 1960: 21–2). Despite its growing redundancy, the canal system would determine much of the pattern of future urban development, with ribbon-type growth extending parallel to older water routes. In 1960 land values tended to be high along the major east–west canals, a reflection of anticipated road development and older high-status residential concentrations.

In the late 1950s Bangkok was still a relatively compact city. In 1947 the Bangkok and Thonburi municipalities (formed in 1936) housed well under a million people in an area of between 60 to 67 square kilometres (Donner 1978: 792). By 1960, under the impact of population and settlement growth, Bangkok's built-up area had increased to some 90 square kilometres. By that year the population of Bangkok–Thonburi had reached over 2 million (Donner 1978: 791). As was typical of Western observations of Bangkok and other cities of Southeast Asia, Litchfield's report emphasised the lack of clear zonal organisation, with minimal separation of industrial, commercial and residential uses. The most noticeable departure from this predominantly pre-war configuration was the cluster of industries that had located close to the newly excavated river-port of Khlong Toei and a predominantly middle-class suburban strip which had developed along Sukhumvit Road.

The *Greater Bangkok Plan 2533* produced by the Litchfield team in 1960 was never implemented. In 1963 Cyrus Nims, the USOM (United States Overseas Mission) city planning adviser to the Thai government, noted that effective implementation of the plan required adequate enforcement powers and an effective planning authority for a capital district encompassing Bangkok, Thonburi and surrounding provinces. Above all, the task required coordination between numerous agencies in national government. Nim's evaluation was pessimistic – coordination among agencies was not evident, a new city planning office languished as a minor section of the Ministry of the Interior, and the national government was choosing to ignore the plan's recommendations (Nims 1963: 104). He was also prophetic, because the Litchfield Plan was never implemented. By 1971 an amended master plan was produced by the Department of Town and Country Planning, which acknowledged the dramatic level of population growth by revising the population estimate for 1990 upwards to 6.5 million. Two years earlier, a *Greater Bangkok Plan* BE *2543* (CE 2000) was produced by the City Planning Division of the Municipality of Bangkok, despite the fact that this office was not officially authorised to develop general plans. Neither of these plans had statutory force – for a decade they floated in a bureaucratic limbo and were then virtually forgotten (Sternstein 1982: 111; Kammeier 1984: 20). Their failure illustrates much about the various power holders in the city, the inability of state agencies to coordinate and cooperate, and the dominance of property interests in the rapidly growing city.

It is a mistake to assume, as some have done, that Litchfield's plan imposed a prescriptive western urban model onto a pristine indigenous city (see e.g. Bello, Cunningham and Li 1998: 97). First, the 'automobile city' was already emerging with the tacit support of government, industry and the urban middle classes. Second, there was no legal framework or political will to impose comprehensively the planning ideals of the Americans. By the 1990s land use maps would play a broad role in contests over land prices (a Bangkok Master Plan was finally adopted in 1992), but generally the commitment to comprehensive planning was a symbolic exercise. Increasing numbers of western-educated Thai planning professionals and national technocrats cherished the dream of a manageable and comprehensible metropolitan space. But as Nims had feared, master plans were to function mainly to 'decorate the wall' (Nims 1963: 105). For the next three decades planners would be kept busy monitoring and mapping the dynamic spaces of the metropolis on paper: their functions were restricted to 'painting the colours' (*rabai si*) of the land uses they could not control. The power to shape the city lay elsewhere.

Engineering Bangkok's primacy – transport infrastructure and unbalanced growth

While expanding economic activities, consumer demand and accelerating population settlement were the principal forces fuelling Bangkok's growth, state agencies did play a significant role in setting a framework (intended and unintended) conducive to change and urban growth. The development programmes set in place from the First National Development Plan (1961–6) directed government expenditures and development aid principally towards energy and transport infrastructure (Pasuk 1980: 64). They had the cumulative effect of reinforcing the capital's economic dominance, exacerbating regional inequalities and accelerating the transition towards a road-based city. Under the impetus of US advice, aid and loan funding, highway construction received considerable attention. Many provincial road projects were aimed primarily at enhancing military security in the northeast (towards the Lao border) but they had a catalysing effect on trade and transport flows (Muscat 1990: 313; Porphant 1994: 289). Major highways built in the late 1950s such as Sukhumvit (linking Bangkok to the Cambodian border) and the Friendship Highway (connecting the capital to Nong Khai in the northeast) had the almost immediate effect of stimulating road traffic (Muscat 1994: 120; Porphant 1994: 300–1). The new highways and associated secondary road network not only stimulated economic activity (which was an explicit NEDB objective) but also facilitated the movement of people to the capital, particularly from the impoverished north-east, a distinctive regional flow which accelerated from this time.

Within the city itself a number of key roads were widened and new routes were built. The advent of the Khlong Toei Port necessitated further construction of new roads, such was its impact on economic activity and transport patterns. For the first time, the western settlement of Thonburi received attention, and by the early 1970s three new bridges spanned the Chao Phraya River. Traffic congestion became so severe in the city that existing highways leading from the city to the provinces needed widening. Numerous Bangkok canals had fallen into disuse prior to this period, but during the 1960s many more were filled in or were reduced to functioning as small roadside drains (Porphant 1994: 212–13, 226–8). Road expansion both stimulated and followed the spread of settlement and construction activity. By 1970 the built area of the city had expanded to 184 square kilometres (Sternstein 1976: 108).

Thailand comes to Bangkok

From the early 1950s Bangkok's population grew at a strikingly faster rate than the country and other growing urban centres in Thailand (London 1980: 32–5). The key factors reinforcing Bangkok's primacy were both demographic and economic in character. Differentials between farm incomes and urban wage rates had been minimal prior to the Second World War, largely due to the availability of rural land, demand for agricultural labour in the highly productive central region and a relatively low population growth rate. These conditions changed in the post-war period. An accelerating population growth (from 1.9 per cent per annum 1937 to 3.2 per cent per annum 1947–60) put pressure on rural farm incomes, leading to increasing tenancy, indebtedness and reduction in farmholding sizes. Significant disparities emerged between wage rates for unskilled labour in the burgeoning urban economy and the countryside. Bangkok benefited disproportionately from Thailand's post-war economic growth. By 1960

Plate 2.1 New shophouse construction along a main road: the spearhead of Bangkok's characteristic 'ribbon' development. (Photo: Author)

the per capita regional GDP of Bangkok was nearly twice that of the central region and over five times that of the northeast (Thai University Research Associates 1976: 330–1). Bangkok was the key destination for those in hope of better incomes.

In the first post-war decade rural–urban migration became the driving force of Bangkok's expansion (accounting for up to 50 per cent of its population growth to 1960) and continued to be the major contributor to population growth into the 1970s (Kritaya 1988: 8). Government restrictions on Chinese immigration from 1947 played a role in increasing the demand for urban labour. The majority of migrants were from the central region provinces, but there was a significant and increasing flow from the northeast. It was a process linked to expanding opportunities for social mobility among a range of groups, and was not restricted to the poor. However, the rural peasantry were the most visible new group in the urban landscape. Robert Textor's study of the Lao-speaking *samlor* (pedicab) drivers from Isan was one of the first to explore the values and experiences of this new group of peasants in the city who found a niche in the expanding urban services economy of low-cost transportation. A vanguard of an increasing northeastern peasant presence in the city, they engaged in a Bangkok subculture marked by consumption-orientated expectations and opportunistic behaviours. While apparently changed by these experiences, they retained loyalties and aspirations informed by their rural family ties (Textor 1961: 32–46). In the 1950s Thailand literally came to Bangkok. Communications made Bangkok increasingly accessible to the rest of the country, while also rendering the countryside more open to flows of images and commodities signifying status and modernity. In this way, Bangkok – acting as a conduit of new urban aspirations – also came to Thailand (Paitoon 1962).

The middle classes

The urban middle classes were the greatest beneficiary of the economic boom generated in the Sarit years, and the growth of this heterogeneous social formation was one of the more striking developments in the post-war period (Pasuk 1980: 19). Bangkok became the centre of consumption for a growing Thai and Sino–Thai middle stratum and the focus of social mobility and status acquisition. Expansion saw growth and diversification across a spectrum of occupations in the private sector, including small-scale trade, technical, manufacturing and service sectors. These groups comprised a broad petty bourgeoisie whose opportunities grew with the burgeoning urban domestic economy, a professional and white collar stratum which spanned both government services and business, and an entrepreneurial bourgeoisie whose fortunes were linked more directly to overseas capital (Anderson 1977).

Tertiary and technical education was one of the key forces underlying the growth of key groupings within this socio-economic formation. The state's education expansion programme of the later 1950s, boosted by overseas scholarship schemes, produced an educated and well-paid professional stratum. In 1970, by virtue of the concentration of administration and business in Bangkok, three quarters of Thailand's university graduates resided in the metropolis (Thai University Research Associates 1976: 256). This also concentrated consumption power in the metropolis. The growing disparity in per capita income between the Bangkok and the provinces was a clear indication of this trend. Between 1960 and 1970 per capita income in the Bangkok–Thonburi area grew at a rate higher than the nation's average, with income for the metropolis averaging 11,234 baht in 1970 compared with 3,849 baht for Thailand as a whole (Keyes 1989: 159; Prasert 1987: 286).

Industrialising Bangkok

Investment in manufacturing from the early 1960s, particularly from overseas, expanded Bangkok's manufacturing base and stimulated industrial development, which sprawled into adjacent provinces (Kammeier 1984: 21). Of the four administrative areas comprising the so-called Greater Bangkok Area, the municipality of Bangkok held 54 per cent of industrial establishments, Thonburi municipality 20 per cent, Samut Prakan province

20 per cent and Nonthaburi province (later to become a dormitory residential district) less than 4 per cent (Donner 1978: 827).

In 1960 the characteristic manufacturing unit in Bangkok was small, with an average employment of just 8.5 people. The largest employers were in older sectors such as hardware, printing, saw milling, rice milling and weaving. At the end of this decade, however, new factories were established under the government's incentive programmes for joint venture schemes and the average size of the manufacturing units grew. Between 1963 and 1970 the proportion of manufacturing establishments employing over 100 people expanded from 47 per cent to 72 per cent. New industries were stimulated by the Board of Investment schemes, including car assembly, textiles, electrical appliances and food processing. Most grew in response to the existing policy of import substitution, which offered protection against foreign competition through import tariffs (Suehiro 1989: 178–86). The regional GDP for 1972 showed that Bangkok and its adjacent provinces were responsible for nearly 60 per cent of GDP in the nation's manufacturing sector (Thai University Research Associates 1976: 268).

Bangkok as a third-world city: housing crisis and slum growth

The rapid increase in the urban population during the decade 1960–70 was not matched by expansion in housing supply. Neither private sector housing construction nor existing public housing agencies were equipped to meet the needs of thousands of low-income earners, many of them migrants from the provinces in search of work (Thai University Research Associates 1976: 111–15). In 1960 there were an estimated 740,000 people living in overcrowded areas in Bangkok. Such areas, however, did not warrant the title of slums – they incorporated established residential areas of very mixed income levels and reflected the general densification of inner city settlement since the Second World War (Litchfield *et al.* 1960: 53, 84). The trend was for migrants to Bangkok to move into the central, crowded areas, while older residents moved away to suburban locations (Sternstein 1971: 14). The older slums of Bangkok were generally small in size; they were well-established low-income neighbourhoods with strong links to local economies and employers and most residents were either born in the area or long-term residents (Akin 1978: 10–11). By contrast, the newer squatter slums were composed almost entirely of rural–urban migrants and were, in some notable cases, extremely large. The Khlong Toei slum comprised over 25,000 people (79 per cent of whom were born outside Bangkok) and covered 325 acres of land. Its development was tied to the labour demands of the Khlong Toei port and the chronic shortage of affordable shelter. Most squatter settlements occupied land in the inner and middle ring areas of the city, because of such critical factors as accessibility to work and the fact that much of the unused land controlled by government departments was located there. Others were formed on private land plots (rented with agreements with landlords) or on areas unsuitable for building, such as the banks of the canals (Sopon 1985). Levels of tenure security depended on a range of factors relating to the value of the land and the type of land owners (government, private or institutional, e.g. temples). Whatever the type of ownership and tenure, the slum settlements were located in poorly drained, unsanitary and flood-prone areas. The ecology of urban settlement in Bangkok at this time revealed much about the principal inequalities which had developed in the city – income and access to land and housing.

Bangkok and the world

The international city

In the post-war years Bangkok emerged as an international city by virtue of developments in world trade, communications and the Cold War. From 1947 the American and British legations were upgraded to embassies and other countries soon followed, underlining Thailand's new importance in the emerging geopolitics of the Cold War (MacDonald 1949: 212–13; Stanton 1956: 202–3). Thailand was one of the foundation members of SEATO and from 1955 its headquarters was stationed in Bangkok, together with other key international organisations, including the United Nations Educational, Scientific and Cultural Organisation (UNESCO), the Economic and Social Commission for the Far East (ESCAF, later ESCAP) and the Food and Agriculture Organisation (FAO). Bangkok functioned as an important link in international aviation routes: regular international Pan American services began in 1948 and throughout the 1960s a growing volume of air traffic led to the upgrading of Don Muang airport. Increasing numbers of foreign advisers, journalists, diplomats and businessmen expanded the expatriate foreign community and, from the early 1960s, US military personnel added to their numbers. The residential rental market for foreigners boomed, with the Sukhumvit district developing as a major foreign expatriate zone.

Tourism

International tourism to Bangkok was a money-earner in the period when sea travel was dominant, but it was small in scale. Developments in international air transport enhanced this function for Bangkok, where in 1957 tourists were already spending 120 million baht. In 1959 the new Tourist Organisation of Thailand was established and began to promote Bangkok as a destination, with an emphasis on its exotic temples and markets. Under the First Development Plan (1961–6) a new runway was built at Don Muang Airport to cater for new jet aircraft. By 1962 tourists were spending 310 million baht in the country, largely in Bangkok (NIDA 1967: 4; TAT 1990: 3).

The expansion of tourism during the 1960s fuelled substantial growth in the services sector of the capital's economy, despite the lack of direct coordination by government. Bangkok's entertainment precinct had tended to concentrate in the area around New Road, south of the old city, along the river, or along Ratchadamnoen Road. By the late 1950s it had spread north and north-east, with new hotels and tourist services clustering along Silom Road and the Ploenchit area around the Erawan Hotel, built in 1956–7 (Litchfield *et al.* 1960: 45–6). During the 1960s local entrepreneurs and joint venture enterprises capitalised on the influx of tourists, businessmen and R&R troops, consolidating these entertainment and hotel precincts and expanding into Sukhumvit. The number of hotel rooms in Bangkok increased from 2,041 in 1964 to 8,763 by 1970, giving rise to claims that there were too many hotels in the city (Donner 1978: 836).

During the period of direct US engagement in the Vietnam conflict, American military personnel, especially those on R & R leave, boosted the hotel and entertainment sector, generating the infrastructure for the later expansion of tourism, and sex-related tourism in particular. Over half of the 652 bars, nightclubs and massage parlours opened in Thailand from 1966 were located in Bangkok (Boonkong 1974: 50). The famous red-light district of Pat Pong Road was a product of this period – this formerly shophouse-lined soi between Sathorn and Silom roads became a lucrative investment for its owner, Udom Patpong (Dawson 1988: 38–41). The New Phetchaburi Road extension was a precinct of clubs and bars relying on the custom of American servicemen. Overseas tourism was also booming during these years – with tourists outnumbering R & R servicemen by 10 to 1 in 1970 – although servicemen (14 per cent of all visitors) on average spent three times the amount of non-military vacationers (Boonkong 1974: 46; Economist Intelligence Unit 1974: 19–21). The R & R wave declined from 1972, but there was a 28 per cent increase in tourist arrivals (NESDB 1975: 36).

Metropolitan expansion and transformation: 1971–81

Metropolitan growth

The decade 1971–81 was eventful for both capital and nation. Economically, its early years were overshadowed by a slump caused by the international oil crisis, the rise in commodity prices and the withdrawal of American personnel and military aid. Violence and political unrest framed the brief democratic experiment of the 1973–6 period (Anderson 1977; Morell and Chai-anan 1981). Despite these disruptions, the trend of urban expansion and change continued.

In 1971 Bangkok's population exceeded three million people and the urban area had doubled its size of the previous decade. The problems facing the growing metropolis were manifold. The early years of the decade saw

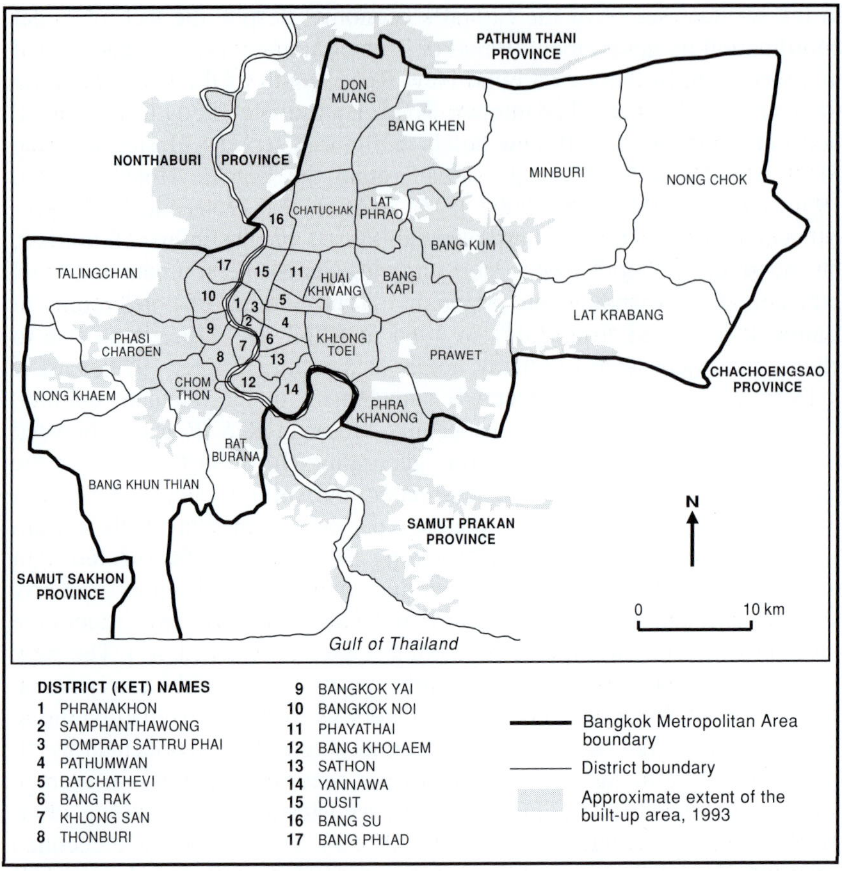

Figure 2.1 The Bangkok Metropolitan Area and surrounding provinces, showing built-up area, 1993.

the formation of the single metro-wide Bangkok Metropolitan Administration (BMA) (1972) to replace the former Bangkok municipality (founded in 1971 from the administrative unification of Bangkok and Thonburi) (see Fig. 2.1). The National Housing Authority was established to coordinate public housing provision (1973), and other agencies were created, such as the Expressway and Mass Transit Authority (ETA) to develop transport and communication infrastructure. It was not until the period of the Fourth Plan (1977–81) that the question of unbalanced regional growth – and Bangkok's disproportionate benefits from national development planning – were addressed. Planners urged the adoption of an urban decentralisation policy and a polycentric model of metropolitan development (Manop 1973, 1985). But metropolitan growth patterns continued to be determined by market and demographic forces. The BMA added to the agencies engaged in urban planning and management, but it was only one among a plethora of official bodies with an interest in and impact on the capital.[3] City planning – incorporating spatial strategies and mapping of use zones – remained a highly symbolic modernistic ritual for sections of the western-educated municipal and state-level bureaucracy, but it was effectively impotent as policy (see e.g. Suchitra 1985). For much of the decade the metropolis was under the control of officials appointed by the Ministry of the Interior. A brief period of elected BMA assemblies and mayors in 1975–6 gave way again to central government control, as the generals who assumed power feared that elected officials could become a base for political opposition (Ruland and Bansoon 1997: 36–7).

Colonising the urban frontier

Land markets and settlement

Private landownership and the dynamics of the urban land market were the key influence on settlement patterns and land use in Bangkok. The paradoxical permissiveness of the Thai administrative system – together with the fragmented and competing jurisdictions of government agencies – allowed the urban environment to deteriorate further under the pressure of increasing traffic congestion and pollution. While regulations controlled building heights in some districts and building standards existed, there was no regulation of plot sizes in the city, so private subdivision could proceed at the desire of developers and landowners. Moreover, without enforcible land use controls, planners could not hope to channel or forecast traffic flows in the expanding city (Kammeier 1984: 27).

By the early 1970s the broad pattern of urban expansion followed the trends of the previous decade, but it proceeded at an accelerated pace. This was due to a number of central factors: the growth of a real estate and development industry financed from profits in the commercial sector; a reorientation of the building industry to housing estate development following a drop in investment in infrastructure projects; and micro-speculation by the middle classes of the city (Durand-Lasserve 1980: 12–14). The highest concentration of commercial and residential development took place to the southeast in the Bankapi/Phrakhanong area forming a corridor some 15 kilometres in length. Mixed development also stretched north along the main northern route of Phahonyothin Road and southwest along the Phetkasem highway (see Fig. 2.2).

Unregulated land use helped to duplicate the pattern of mixed economic functions in new areas. Large pockets of land between the major roads were under-utilised – some still being farmed, some lying vacant. Other land pockets were gradually occupied by the urban poor whose tenure would be dependent on the economic decisions of the private landowners who controlled most of the land in the newly expanding districts to the north, northeast and east (Chatchai 1986: 37, 77–81).

A wave of new housing: the private and public sectors

The *mubanchatsan* (housing subdivision/estate), now the dominant feature of Bangkok's suburbs, was a product of changes in the building industry during the 1970s and increased land prices in the inner city and older suburban areas. Increasingly accessible through the expanding road network, land parcels in the cheaper farmland of the urban fringe were purchased by developers and subdivided into small blocks for ready-made housing (PADCO 1987, vol II: 104–5) (see Fig. 2.2). Boosted by the increased availability of financing at attractive terms through commercial banks and finance houses, many new companies took to the housing estate idea with zeal, responding to the demand for accommodation in the growing city. In 1974 the number of developer-built housing projects amounted to 60 and by the following year the number had increased to 154 projects, with the majority located in the north and northeast (Nipan 1982: 152–4; Sangad 1986: 197).

In demographic and social terms, the new suburban landscape of ready-made housing estates was above all a product of new household formation within the middle classes of Bangkok and the movement of these households away from parental homes in the inner urban areas. The largest number of buyers of estate units during the 1970s were aged between 25 and 35 years and were from Bangkok. Comprising many newly-married couples, the major motive for suburban settlement among this group was independence from the parental household. A smaller proportion of buyers were from outside Bangkok, with the highest proportion of these purchasing homes for their children who were studying in the city (Nipan 1982: 172–6). The planned housing estates emerged as a distinctively new ecology for living in Bangkok, designed essentially for nuclear families in contrast to the older forms of compound housing which had formerly dominated the older residential spaces of the city. This ecological transformation was one dimension of a broader transformation in ways of life, which incorporated the commuting experience and the decline of the extended family as a domestic unit (Bundit 1983: 209–15).

Building activity was also strong in the public sector. The formation of the NHA in 1973 signalled a more coordinated state response to housing demand, with projects aimed at provision for both the poor and lower-middle-income groups. The NHA's optimistic production targets were scaled down within a few years to account for fund shortages and unanticipated delays (Chiu 1985: 112–26). By 1978 the NHA had abandoned its exclusive reliance on subsidised housing provision due to lack of state funding and adopted a multiple strategies approach which incorporated slum upgrading and sites-and-services projects on slum sites. The NHA

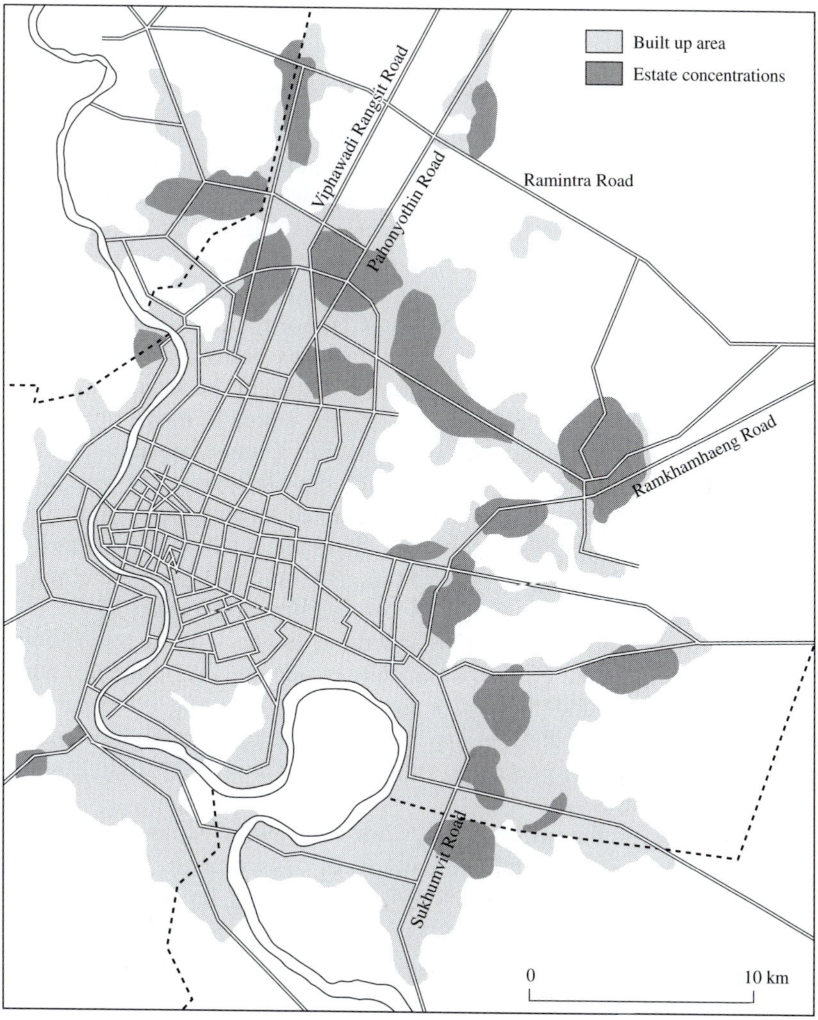

Figure 2.2 Housing estate development and the built-up area, Bangkok 1970–80.
Source: After Bundit 1983.

fulfilled a dual role: it provided hire-purchase housing estates for middle-income-earners (particularly civil servants) and undertook resettlement and flat-building for the poor. One scholar judged that NHA policy had amounted to a campaign to push the urban working class to the under-serviced periphery of the metropolis. The NHA's forced abandonment of the high-subsidy approach to low-income housing hardly suggests such a conspiracy, but it did reflect the state's capitulation to the forces of the urban land market in locating estates on the suburban periphery where land was cheaper (Chiu 1985: 129–31; Durand-Lasserve 1980: 21).

Food and retailing, transformations and continuities

Retailing patterns in Bangkok underwent substantial change during the 1970s, reflecting cumulative transformations in production patterns as well as consumer tastes. The department stores, which first appeared in the 1930s, expanded considerably after the Second World War in response to western retailing patterns as well as the increasing purchasing power of those urban consumers with tastes for imported products. The first stores, located at Yawarat, were introduced by Chinese merchants. This location was then the principal retailing centre and was convenient for the consumers of modern goods and appliances residing in the nearby European quarter, but the trend of the 1950s was for the stores to move towards the Suriwong/Silom area. By the mid-1960s another group of stores were established in the Ratchprasong and New Petch area following the developing distribution of retail areas. The large modern department store model was pioneered by well-capitalised business dynasties, such as the Chirathivat family (the Central Group) and the Sarasins (Daimaru), who were able to take advantage of foreign capital and connections (Hewison 1989: 151). The new growth phase of the 1970s saw the emergence of the trade centres such as the Indra Trade Centre, Ploenchit Arcade and Siam Square, which focused activity around the nodes formed by hotels and other services. These centres, following American models, were deliberately designed to draw consumers by providing a variety of attractions, including supermarkets and theatres.

The increase of the white-collar work force with expanding incomes encouraged changes in traditional patterns of consumption, while changes in the rhythm of urban life and the development of the suburbs encouraged the trend towards ‘convenience’ or ‘one-stop’ shopping. From the late 1970s the shopping complexes, comprising department stores, supermarkets, offices and restaurants, expanded in number. But most of the largest stores and complexes date from the early 1980s, including the larger branches of Central and Robinsons, New World Department Store in Banglamphu and the Maboon Khrong Centre. While the major stores multiplied their branches in the existing retailing districts, a clear trend from around 1983 was for branches to expand into the suburbs following the growth of new concentrations of consumers generated by infrastructure-driven suburban growth. Thus, to the west of the Chao Phraya River – on the formerly thinly settled Thonburi shore – large branches of chains such as Welco, Merry King and Central sprang up along the main transport corridor of Phetkasem Road. Growing inter-firm competition stimulated a system of price-slashing campaigns which only the highly capitalised retailing conglomerates could easily afford. Seasonal sales (as well as

Plate 2.2 '*Pak soi*': the entrances of Bangkok's *soi* retain their importance for daily food purchases. (Photo: Author)

incentives such as raffles and gifts – *khong thaem*) became an established part of retailing strategy and shopping culture (Kanithar 1991).

By the late 1970s fast-food outlets had become popular, particularly among teenagers of the city. First appearing with the arrival of the American troops and growth of the expatriate community, foreign franchises such as Kentucky Fried Chicken and Dunkin' Donuts were making incursions into the Thai food consumer market. More than simply changing tastes in food, the fast food phenomenon represented an increasing engagement with modernity among consumers. As one report on new business and consumption trends emphasised: 'a combination of air-conditioning, pop music, bright decor, fast service and western favourites like hamburgers, pizza and doughnuts, definitely has appeal in this city . . .' (Bangkok Bank 1983: 410–11).

In Bangkok the old hierarchy of markets, both food and goods, underwent change. In the old Banglamphu and Phrakhanong market areas, ready-made clothing (as well as mass-produced jewellery) took over as the major commodity of sale. But in some important respects the markets retained their key functions for many ordinary Bangkok people. Food markets (*talat sot*) multiplied and dispersed following population growth and settlement trends. In 1980 the distribution of the city's 203 private markets reflected population concentrations, with the exception of the old

Phra nakhon and Sampanthawong districts, which hosted some of the most established and specialised market places (such as Pak Khlong Talat, which specialised in flower sales). For a number of reasons – not least because of the established patterns of household food buying, the need for easy and regular access by lower income groups, and the relative ease of access into petty trading occupations – markets persisted and continued to act as focal points of activity in Bangkok's neighbourhoods, helping to preserve older forms of public life. Despite the advent of supermarkets which became a preferred source of essential goods for the expanding middle classes in Bangkok, the traditional buying and selling space of *pak soi* (the mouth of the lane) retained their function in the transforming city (see Chira *et al.* 1986).

Bangkok on the run – readjustment and the export boom: 1982–91

The restructuring of the economy and the Bangkok mega-urban region

Thailand entered the 1980s with an export economy still largely reliant on agricultural commodities and a domestic-orientated manufacturing sector enjoying high rates of tariff protection. However, by the mid-1980s the economy was experiencing strains, leading ultimately to fundamental structural change. Macroeconomic policy played a key role in facilitating this transformation, yet it was ultimately driven by global and regional events. The second oil crisis of 1979–80 plunged the balance of payments into deficit, leading to major World Bank loans. Exports suffered from a rising baht (pegged to the US dollar) and in 1981 the currency was devalued twice. Initially, the government sought an easy way out by promoting international tourism and exporting labour to the oil-rich Middle East (Pasuk and Baker 1995: 143–6). In the face of increasing bankruptcies and imminent recession, the government again devalued the baht (1984) and, under pressure from the NESDB, introduced tax and foreign ownership concessions to encourage export-based manufacturing.

Fortuitously for Thailand, the Japanese yen rose in value, providing favourable conditions for industrial expansion as Japan, the leading economy in the region, sought ways of reducing production costs. From the mid-1980s a massive relocation of manufacturing plants from Japan, then Taiwan and Korea, to Southeast Asia and China occurred as firms sought to benefit from low labour and production costs (MacIntyre 1993: 261–5). In Thailand, as with Malaysia and Indonesia, there was a surge in foreign direct investment from the East Asian economies, with Japan taking the lead.[4] Demand for labour in manufacturing, construction and the expanding service industries of the metropolis drew workers from the rural areas where farmland had reached its limit of expansion. Until the early

1990s, the relatively low wages of this labour pool gave Thailand a competitive advantage in world markets in key areas of manufacture (textiles and electronic circuitry, for example) and food-processing. Such was the impressive surge in exports, economic growth and income levels in Thailand that politicians, technocrats and the popular and academic press alike began touting the country as the next NIC (Newly-industrialised country) (Janssen 1988; Voravidh 1991). Thailand's story became part of the 'East Asian Miracle'(World Bank 1993: 138–42). Predictions that Thailand would reach the condition of economies such as South Korea and Taiwan flew in the face of the reality that the country's manufacturing was heavily dependent on foreign technology and expertise, that the most sophisticated export products (such as electronic and computer components) were generated by companies relying on foreign capital, and that there was a chronic shortage of skilled workers and qualified professionals able to support sophisticated manufacturing.

In 1980 the BMA's population topped 5 million people. The built-up area of the sprawling metropolitan complex had grown 30 per cent over the preceding decade to reach 239 square kilometres and it continued to expand. In 1980 the population of the capital was fifty-one times the size of the second-largest city Chiang Mai. By 1991 the BMA population (over 5.5 million) people was forty-one times the size of the next-largest urban centre (now Nakhon Ratchasima). Some demographers have noted a slight reduction in metropolitan primacy over the decade to the early 1990s, due to the expansion of provincial centres such as Hat Yai in the south, Nakhon Ratchasima in the northeast and the expanding Eastern seaboard conglomeration (Chet, Jones and Chanpen 1996). But the capital was still overwhelmingly predominant in the urban system. The built area of the metropolis and its population spilt well over the borders of the five adjacent provinces to comprise a total population of over 8 million people, representing some 41 per cent of the country's urban population (NESDB 1986: 50; Rimmer 1995: 189). Decentralising urbanisation had become the priority for planners, linked to the concern to address the chronic imbalance between rural and urban incomes. But new manufacturing plants – both foreign and locally capitalised – were overwhelmingly concentrated in the metropolitan area, and the state's favouring of capital-intensive investment projects contradicted the official decentralisation goal (Fuchs and Pernia 1987: 88–108; Medhi 1996: 312–13).

Through the 1980s economic, regional and urban planners were compelled to reconceptualise the metropolis to acknowledge the spatial dynamics of the economy, labour force activity and land-use change. The urban space governed by the Bangkok Metropolitan Administration was only part of a more complex economic, territorial and demographic configuration. The term Bangkok Metropolitan Region (BMR) gained currency to refer to the BMA and the five adjacent provinces into which the commercial and residential built area and industries had sprawled. Even this was

Plate 2.3 The factories meet the village in the mega-urban region. View from Bang Chan in Bangkok's Minburi District, once considered by American anthropologists of the 1950s to represent a 'typical' central Thai village. (Photo: Author)

a limited spatial framework. It gave way to the terms 'Mega-urban Region' or 'Extended Bangkok Metropolitan Region' (EBMR) among the NESDB planners. The new terms reflected the influence of geographers' reconceptualisations of new urban spaces in Asia under the economic restructuring processes of the late twentieth century. This was pictured as a 'megalopolis' of interacting functional zones and nodes stretching north to Ayutthaya, east to Chachoengsao Province and along the coast to Rayong (Nophakhun 1993; Utis 1995) (see Fig. 2.3). Under continuing boom conditions driven by the metropolis, the imperative was not to restrict the growth of this complex, but to harness its vital dynamism (see Table 2.1). With appropriate spatial and sector-based planning, the Bangkok megalopolis was to act as the strategic hub for Thailand in the Southeast Asian regional economy, competing for global profits (in trade and services) with rivals such as Singapore (Phisit 1988: 79–97).[5]

The NIC capital and its workers

In the 1980s Thailand's export economy experienced a fundamental shift, with manufactured products reaching 68 per cent of exports by 1989. From 1987, foreign direct investment in Thailand boomed, with Japan taking over from the USA as the major FDI source (Bangkok Bank 1985–9).

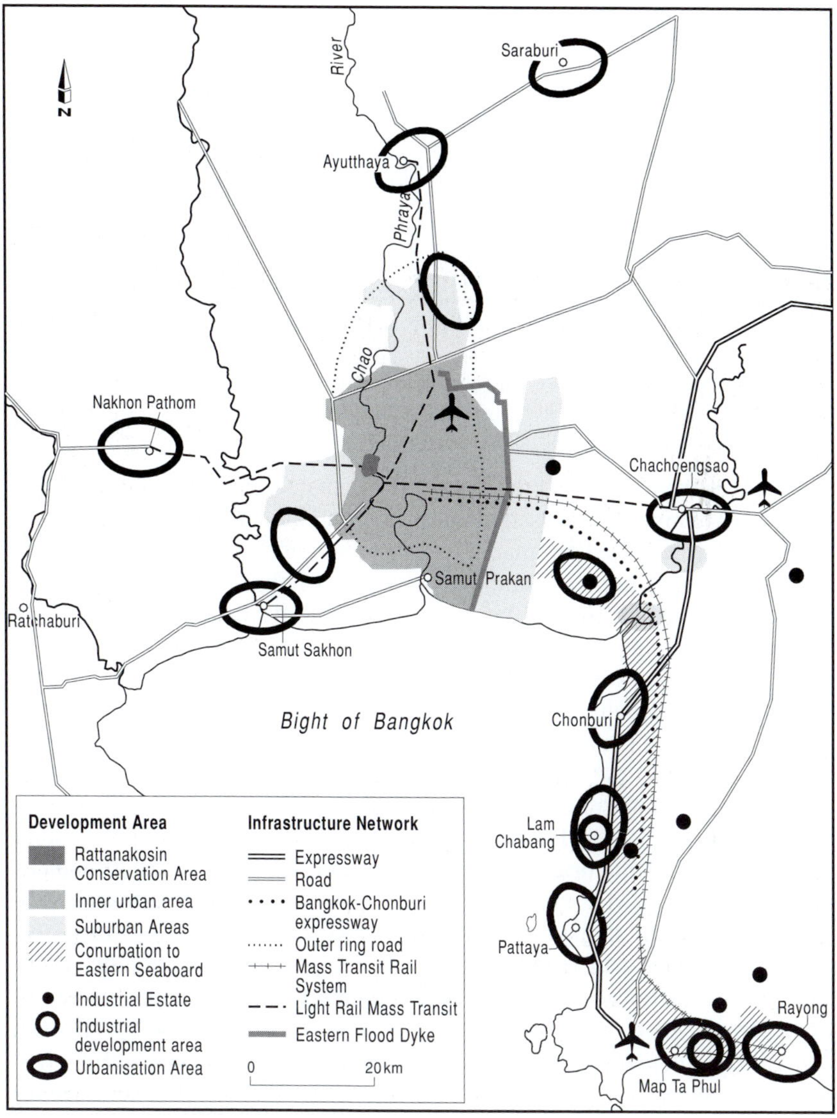

Figure 2.3 The Bangkok megalopolis as represented by the NESDB as a functional system, 1992.

Source: Based on Utis 1995.

Table 2.1 Regional distribution of GDP in Thailand, 1986–95

Distribution of GDP (%)	*1986*	*1990*	*1995*
Bangkok and vicinity	46.8	52.6	51.5
Central*	4.1	4.0	4.4
East	9.3	8.2	9.8
West	5.3	4.4	4.2
North	11.7	10.0	9.1
Northeast	13.4	12.0	12.0
South	9.4	8.7	9.0
Total	100.0	100.0	100.0

Source: Office of the National Economic and Social Development Board, statistical data bank.

Note

* Excludes Bangkok and vicinity provinces of Nakhon Pathom, Nonthaburi, Pathum Thani, Samut Prakan and Samut Sakhon.

Much investment was directed to export-orientated manufacturing and this was overwhelmingly focused on the metropolitan region, where annual economic growth (led by manufacturing and services) was almost three percentage points higher than the country as a whole (10.63 per cent). New industries generated by FDI continued to locate near those services most important for supply and export, despite the BOI's attempts to decentralise industry through extra-metropolitan zone-based incentives. Policy played little part in influencing manufacturing firm's location decisions (Banasopit *et al.* 1990: 75–88: Parnwell and Luxmon 1997).

Thailand, with the BMR as its core, emerged as an assembly and processing base integrated with the NICs of East Asia (Asian-Pacific Center 1996: 10–11, 47). The BMA itself accounted for around 60 per cent of newly registered factories between 1986 and 1991. The five provinces surrounding the BMA experienced the highest growth rates in manufacturing employment in the country (Charit 1993: 115–23; Charit *et al.* 1986). Distinct precincts had emerged in the BMR provinces of Pathum Thani and Nonthaburi to add to the existing pattern of concentration in Samut Prakan, with many large foreign-backed firms locating in the private and government industrial estates. Although larger factories concentrated in these provinces, we should note that household-based enterprises, small and medium sized factories actually dominated the BMR in terms of numbers (Banasopit 1990: 69–70). In 1989 some 25 per cent of the economically active workforce were employed in manufacturing in the BMA alone. Women outnumbered men in those sectors directly connected with the export industry, such as textiles (a ratio of almost two in every three workers) (NSO 1980, 1990a).

Work opportunities had progressively drawn young women from rural areas to the Bangkok employment market from the 1960s, but the profile of their employment opportunities changed as industrialisation proceeded.

Formerly in demand as housemaids and service workers, by the 1980s they began filling the demand for a semi-skilled factory workforce for the labour intensive low-end manufacturing (textiles, food-processing, electronic equipment assembly) which drove the export surge. Women were an essential agent in Thailand's manufacturing export boom, accounting for 80 per cent of employment in the ten leading export sectors (Bell 1997). For young village women, factory work was far superior (in income and status) to the demeaning status and restrictive conditions of domestic service (Mills 1999: 116). Outnumbering men in the migration flows into Bangkok, a high proportion of females (nearly 50 per cent) were in the 10–19 year age groups – the majority were from the poorest of Thailand's provinces in the northeast (ESCAP 1988: 29–31).

The progressive engagement of rural people in urban labour was enabled by characteristic village cultural modes, whereby new arrivals were advised and assisted by friends and neighbours already working in the city (Fuller, Peerasit and Lightfoot 1990). Labour conditions and workplaces varied considerably, from the small shophouse workshops of Thonburi to large international firms in Samut Prakan. Similarly, the experience of housing was varied. Factories often supplied specialised dormitory accommodation, while other workers lived outside factories in rented apartments and slum houses. Experience in the urban and industrial workforce was shaped by the dynamics of the life cycle and the enduring connection of people with their natal villages. We might describe the movement patterns as both 'circular migration' and 'oscillation', with the former describing regular sojourns in the city and the latter highlighting short-term and irregular patterns of movement between city and village. Typically from the ages of 15 or 16 years, young women entered the industrial and service workforce of the capital or provincial towns, but they regularly returned to visit parents on key festival days and irregularly at times of family emergency. Marriage (whether to village men or suitors encountered in the city) and childbearing brought women back to their natal homes, although many returned to the city to take up work again. Parents and grandparents played a critical function in taking care of children, allowing women to continue to seek wage work in a wide variety of fields, whether in the capital, provincial towns or overseas.

Throughout the working lives of men and women change of employers was frequent, as they sought better or more suitable work. The option of returning home (*klap ban*) for wage-earning men and women remained ever-present as a coping mechanism in times of stress or difficulty, but in reality rural villages could not support their populations. It has been suggested that these persistent cultural characteristics have ensured that Thailand's industrial workforce has never been completely proletarianised in terms of consciousness or attitudes to industrial work experience (Odhnoff, McFarlane and Limqueco 1983: 66).[6] On the other hand, engagement with urban life had become so common as to be an accepted part of

Plate 2.4 Young factory workers from Bangkok visiting a friend on the occasion of his ordination as a monk in their home village (Khon Kaen Province). (Photo: Author)

existence. It was driven both by necessity to support parents, younger siblings and children, demands for conspicuous consumption items in the villages, and a shared desire to participate in the modernity of consumerism and self fashioning (Mills 1999: 1–23). The transformation of the metropolis into an industrial centre was a process which was built on the backs of village households, and the rural world was also changed in the process. City and country were mutually dependent.

The informal economy

As in other cities of the region, economic modernisation did not lead to a decline of the so-called 'informal sector' – that domain of microbusiness operation and employment distinguished by an absence of contractual relations, formal training, education and licensing. This sector became increasingly important, both as an employment source and a mechanism ensuring the functioning of the burgeoning city and its economy (see ESCAP 1993: 3–22). Recent definitions of informal sector employment promoted by the International Labour Office have been broadened to include industrial workers who receive lower-than-award wages and those unprotected by formal social security arrangements. In 1990, according to this ILO definition, Bangkok's informal sector encompassed 58 per cent of its total workforce (ILO-ARTEP 1991: 2). Notably, studies in the late 1980s found that even within the formal sector and among large firms (of over 50 employees) a significant proportion of workers (23 per cent) were hired on a daily basis with no job security (Chalongphob 1987: 36). Researchers who limited their definition of 'informal sector' to small-scale enterprises estimated that it encompassed some 45 per cent of the employed labour force in Bangkok, including operators and unpaid family helpers (Teera and Yaruma 1989).[7] The occupational subgroups in this sector include transport services, food vending, small-scale manufacturing and subcontracting to formal sector businesses, waste recycling, and – according to some writers – prostitution (Forbes 1996: 58).

During the 1980s, increasing numbers of people entered Bangkok's informal sector. Between 1980–90, the number of food vendors in the BMA grew at a faster rate than the employed population (Chomlada 1991: 38; NSO 1980, 1990a). Food vendors are active in the burgeoning business districts, attracting considerable custom from office workers, who save money by buying cheap food (Achara 1994). In a city bedevilled by traffic jams (*rot tit*) and long commuting hours, people rely on take-home food purchased from these vendors (Malee 1990). Similarly, motorcycle taxis are an essential means for many people to reach work and home in the traffic-clogged city. While a large proportion of those engaged in micro-enterprises are poor, this is not exclusively the case – indeed in some subsectors they offer a significant means for accumulation. While the informal sector seems to function to allow rural–urban migrants access into the urban economy, most entrants to small business enterprises (even food vending) are long-term residents of Bangkok, a point which confirms the importance of investment capacity among small-scale entrepreneurs (Pasuk *et al.* 1988: 19). The main characteristics of the informal sector are diversity, fluidity and flexibility, reflecting much about the creativity with which the less-educated (who form the bulk of informal sector operators) negotiate the possibilities of the urban economy and its spaces (Nanthana 1991; Romijn 1993: 1–3). The informal sector has been the target of intermittent attempts by the metropolitan authorities to regulate their activities and occupation of space. By the 1990s vendors in particular were more prone to demonstrate publicly their opposition to official efforts to relocate them away from certain areas. In any case, the banning of vendors in certain locations simply led to them shifting to other areas in the city – it has not reduced their numbers.

New landscapes of living

By the mid-1980s the dispersal of housing had reached a limit imposed by travelling times, infrastructure and transport costs. However, fuelled by economic recovery in 1986–7 and stimulated by new road construction,

Plate 2.5 The motorcycle taxi, a key informal sector service in Bangkok. (Photo: Author)

suburban development surged outward again, spearheaded by the *muban-chatsan*. The resurgence of private housing estate construction was primarily due to fundamental changes in the finance sector and government policy, with both of these responding to improved economic conditions, higher middle-class savings and pent-up housing demand. In the previous decades the commercial banks had given home mortgage-lending a low priority. But from the mid-1980s these banks – now flushed with funds – were drawn into housing finance with the encouragement of the Bank of Thailand (which lifted restrictions on bank credit expansion) and in competition with the restructured Government Housing Bank. Further reforms in the finance sector allowed insurance companies to tap overseas loans and lend to house-buyers and builders. Housing finance became an integral part of the increasingly complex Thai financial system centred on Bangkok, reaping massive profits for an expanding finance-based bourgeoisie (Sidhijai 1993: 4–8; Sakchai 1993: 11–12).

The housing estate industry burgeoned. It was led by a few large companies, such as Land and House, Quality House and Bangkok Land, but numerous smaller operators were drawn into the field in search of profit (Borisut and Chantharaphen 1995). Competition soon became fierce as supply surged ahead of demand. It required aggressive marketing, a focus

Plate 2.6 Urban dreams: the modern Thai nuclear family represented with its new home in the suburbs. (Photo: From a housing estate advertising brochure)

on location, facilities and icons of exclusivity. Magazines and manuals for practitioners and consumers proliferated to support this boom (see e.g. Borisut *et al.* 1990). The new *mubanchatsan* swamped the landscape. They varied in size and design, but shared the characteristics of the middle classes' engagement with the commodity-driven imaginary of modernity. Designs covered the gamut of neoclassical (*Sa-tai Ro-man*), Tudor and Californian–Spanish styles, with a plethora of hybrids. The more expensive estates incorporated leisure and fitness facilities. The naming of the estates expressed the obsession with prestige, from the quaint 'Floraville' to the unashamedly crass *Muban Yingkwa Ruai* ('Village of the even Richer') (see e.g. Pathomawan 1996).

Another trend in the housing pattern was an increase in apartments and condominiums at the expense of detached houses. This accounted for increased population densities in some inner-city areas. The proportion of households residing in apartments increased from 2.6 per cent to 6.2 per cent between 1970 and 1980, and by 1990 this had further increased to 9.7 per cent. More dramatically, the use of townhouses (a popular housing form on mid-priced housing estates) increased from just 2.5 per cent to 9.3 per cent over the same decade (NSO 1970, 1980, 1990a). Soaring suburban land prices influenced the trend to more concentrated patterns of subdivision. Multi-storey condominium blocks began supplying the middle-income market. From the mid-1980s low-cost townhouses appeared on the market. Following new legislation in 1979, condominiums emerged as a conspicuous mode of inner city accommodation, particularly among the expanding numbers of European and Asian expatriate professionals. Early luxury condominiums were concentrated around Sathorn, Pathumwan, Ploenchit and the *soi* of Sukhumvit Road (Bundit 1983: 176–7; Sakchai 1993: 9–11). Bangkok-based developers of condominiums and luxury residential complexes expanded their investments into the provinces, as far afield as Hua Hin in the south and the city of Chiangmai in the north, in order to meet the demand of the Bangkok bourgeoisie for weekend retreats (Hamilton 1994: 162–4; Lubeigt 1994: 123).

In the later 1980s developers had built cheap housing on the urban fringe, but after 1991, soaring land prices reduced options for cheap housing. Developers moved to these areas for high income housing projects so as to offset price spirals in the inner city (Sakchai 1993: 15–16). One specialist estimated that whereas in 1991 some 50 per cent of households could afford to purchase a new housing unit, by 1993 the proportion would be reduced to 40 per cent (Sopon 1992: 48–9). The increase in employer-provided accommodation, near or on work sites, was a symptom of economic and work force changes, particularly in the BMA's outer districts and adjacent five provinces. By 1990 households living in private sector employer-provided accommodation outnumbered government accommodation by over 10,000 (NSO Population and Housing Census 1980, 1990a). The outer districts were housing the greater number of factory workers in dormitories on, or near, work sites (De Wandeler and Areepan 1992: 124–6; Prapasri 1993: 144–9).

The landscape of the extending metropolis comprised not only manufacturing and residential components, but also a leisure industry in the form of golf courses. Reflecting international trends (especially in the societies of East Asia), golf emerged in Thailand as a recreational form with important social and status display functions. By the mid-1980s, membership of the prestigious exclusive clubs was expensive but critical for aspirants to elite status. The subsequent explosion of golf course development both in resort centres and the metropolis reflected the increasing affluence of the business elites and the expansion of international tourism. In the period 1990–2 alone, forty-six new golf courses were opened or planned, while seventy-eight were under construction. The largest number were located within the BMR and its fringes (Banasophit *et al.* 1990: 38–9;

Cohen 1995: 4–5). Golf course construction was a key driving force of real estate development on the urban fringe, and many of the largest courses were huge projects funded through joint venture enterprises, largely with Japanese backing (Cohen 1995: 10–12).

Bangkok: city of the poor

For the least-privileged groups of the population, the early 1980s were grim. Severe floods in 1983 prompted state agencies to introduce flood control measures, which involved clearing many informal settlements located along these waterways (Roovers *et al.* 1989). In the inner city, both state and private sector development pressures had a critical impact. Between 1984–8, a quarter of all inner city slums disappeared, yet the total number of informal settlements increased, with most being formed in the rapidly industrialising fringe areas such as Pathum Thani and Samut Prakan (Yap 1992: 40–4). In 1992 the NHA estimated a total of 1,744 slums in Bangkok and three contiguous provinces, housing 16.2 per cent of the population and constituting 80 per cent of all slums in the country (Sungsidh and Somchai 1996: 31). Optimistic claims by some specialists that Bangkok's private housing market was responding to the needs of low-income earners were based on the observation that the proportion of slum housing to overall housing stock has fallen (Dowall 1989). Others suggested that there had actually been a significant 'densification' of housing in existing settlements and that other forms of substandard housing (such as worker accommodation on city building sites) had not been counted (Akin 1991). Alternative estimates including small settlements of the poor (including those under bridges) suggested that by 1990 a greater share of the metropolitan population were living in slums than ever before (Setchell 1991: 12–13).

By the mid-1980s the relationship between rural–urban migration in the generation of slums was much less clear than earlier decades. One researcher argued that migration from the provinces played a negligible role in slum growth, citing survey results showing that two-thirds of slum-dwellers were born in Bangkok. Notably, however, nearly 60 per cent of household heads (the older generation of settlers) had been born outside Bangkok (Sopon 1987). Rural–urban migration was not entirely negligible in the process of slum formation – it had simply become another contributor in a complex dynamic. Nevertheless, NGO leaders continued to argue that rural–urban disparities were a continuing stimulus for Bangkok's slum growth (e.g. Prateep 1986; *Siam Rath* 26 December 1988). In the 1970s, officials renamed slums 'crowded communities' (*chumchon ae-at*) to remove the stigmatic title 'slums' from official discourse: it was part of a programme to refashion state policy towards Bangkok's poor as development policy. By the mid 1980s, eviction pressures in the capital had stimulated greater levels of organisation and coordination within and between slum-dwellers, aided by local and overseas NGOs. Encouraged by world movements championing the cause of habitat rights and the poor, a new and assertive rhetoric developed among these organisations. Habitat became the focus of more strident claims for the urban poor, and the contest for a place in the city was the critical symbol of its struggle.

Bangkok as tourist capital

By the year of the Rattanakosin celebrations in 1982, tourist arrivals to Thailand numbered over 2 million (compared to around 600,000 ten years earlier), and foreign tourists were contributing nearly 24 million baht annually to the national revenue (TAT 1990). By 1982 tourism became the country's largest revenue source in the Thai economy (overtaking income from rice exports) and the services sector became increasingly geared to this industry (Economist Intelligence Unit 1984: 17). Recognising the significance of foreign tourism for foreign exchange and employment growth, the government promoted tourism more vigorously through the Tourist Authority of Thailand, Thai Airways and other agencies. By 1987, the official 'Visit Thailand Year', annual tourist arrivals had increased to over four million, reaching over five million by the end of the decade (Muscat 1994: 196–8; Pasuk and Samart 1993: 163–4). Thailand's tourist infrastructure and attractions expanded into the provinces, with conspicuous growth in the holiday resort centres of Pattaya and Phuket and the southern city of Hat Yai. Despite the introduction of direct flights to the two latter centres, Bangkok continued to reap the benefits of tourist expansion in the 1980s, since over 90 per cent of tourists by air entered the country through its airport (Economist Intelligence Unit 1984: 25). Although the average length of stay of tourists in Bangkok was lower than other key destinations (e.g. Chiang Mai, Phuket and Pattaya), the number of tourists staying in the city was over four times the number at any other single place in the country (Alpha Research 1994: 121).

Besides its key logistical role, the capital offered its own attractions. The TAT promoted the country as 'Exotic Thailand', a place of traditional culture, gracious people and, increasingly, a place of pageantry connected with Thai royalty. As for Bangkok, the city had long been touted as an alluring blend of the ancient and the modern, with its temples juxtaposed with modern shopping centres and other cosmopolitan features. As one French tourist handbook remarked, without being too explicit: 'Bangkok is all things to all men' (Papineau 1980: 337). Tourist attractions in and around Bangkok had multiplied, with emphasis ranging from pure entertainment to cultural heritage in various commodified forms. Thus the Rose Garden west of the city featured staged elephant battles and other demonstrations. A standard destination promoted for tourists was the largely artificial floating market of Damnoen Saduak Canal in Samut Sakhon. In the city itself, temple tours were standard. By the late 1970s the historical

Park 'Ancient City' (*Muang Boran*) was opened in Samut Prakan, with replicas of key monuments in Thailand, as well as a village, and floating market (Pradai 1979). Developed by a Sino–Thai millionaire who proclaimed his own mission to remind Thais of their heritage in art and architecture, the park became appropriated into package-tour itineraries along with other spectacles such as crocodile farms. As Erik Cohen has stressed, the attractions and images of Thailand – and Bangkok – can be described in terms of the dual themes of 'the exotic' and 'the erotic' (Cohen 1996: 2–3). These themes were already pervasive in the 1970s, but they were reinforced as tourism boomed. The fame of the city's red-light districts (conspicuously Pat Pong but also other areas) was well established. It is thus hardly a coincidence that of foreign tourists to the country, men formed the majority (71.6 per cent in 1985 and 65.4 per cent in 1991) (TAT 1990).

The tourist population of Bangkok was diverse, in terms of country of origin and age-groups. An important group among the increased tourist numbers were visitors from the booming Asian economies of the region. As well as the Japanese (who had been the largest group among all tourists since the early 1980s) they included Taiwanese, Korean and Chinese tourists. Venues and precincts within Bangkok developed in response to this mix. Thus, a new street in the Pat Pong red-light district (Tanaya) was devoted exclusively to Japanese customers, as were numerous 'member clubs' and karaoke bars. The hotels of Sampeng/Yawarat (or Chinatown) hosted Chinese visitors. The small area of *Soi* Nana North had become an enclave for middle eastern Muslims. There had been a spectacular expansion in so-called 'backpacker tourism' among young men and women, particularly from the west. Bangkok functioned as a travel hub for young adventurers in Southeast Asia and beyond – their increasing numbers and importance in the tourist economy helped spawn a growing concentration of cheap guest houses in the Banglamphu area. Bangkok was also a popular centre for international conventions, where delegates combined business with tourist activities. While the number of these conventions declined towards the close of the decade (due, it seems to Bangkok's worsening environment and traffic conditions), Bangkok's large luxury hotels (over 130 by 1990) continued to host the overwhelming majority of conventions held in the country (roughly two hundred per year) (Alpha Research 1994: 119).

The hybrid city: urban form and ecologies

Bangkok's hybrid spaces reflected the complex and multilevel engagements between the state, global and local capital, land and people. A number of dominant settlement and land use trends were clear during the first years of the economic boom. First, there was a progressive movement of population towards the outer areas (beyond 10 kilometres of the notional city centre), spearheaded by road construction, industrial and residential growth. The spatial pattern was one of dispersal of growing activities such as commerce, retailing and government (NESDB 1986: Annex 2–4; Kidokoro 1992: 80–4). Second, the polycentrism of earlier decades was in fact exacerbated, but over a wider territory. By the 1980s Bangkok's emerging form and settlements suggested that there was (at a general level, at least) a tendency towards the formation of certain homogeneous zones responding to both local and international forces. This was seen in the transformation of the inner commercial areas of Sathon, Silom and Sukhumvit-Ploenchit to high-density, high rise precincts, the burgeoning swathe of housing-estate suburbs in the middle and fringe areas, and a certain concentration of large manufacturing concerns on the rural–urban fringe. But these concentrations developed in the context of a more complex spatial pattern.

Bangkok's sprawling outer landscape was characterised above all by an intense mixing of activities. Beyond the roads and highways which formed dense corridors of commercial and industrial development, the newly-settled areas of former rice land hosted old village settlements, industry, and new housing and recreational spaces (notably golf courses) in a confusing mosaic. On the fringes of this landscape, households occupying villages were abandoning agriculture as a livelihood, a trend already noted in earlier decades (Banasopit *et al.* 1990: 40–66; Thiravet 1979). Focusing on strategic new transport intersections, huge mall complexes served an expanding middle-class population whose lifestyle patterns depended on the automobile and conspicuous consumption. Yet these complexes also draw to their environs the ordinary people of surrounding low-income communities – particularly youth (Edler 1996: 84). Promenading the malls in the Bangna area (to Bangkok's Southeast) became a favourite weekend pastime among young girls in the factory workforce of Samut Prakan. The juggernaut of capitalist land development seemed to presage the sprawling and fragmented postmodern landscape of late capitalism typified by Los Angeles, a city described by the prominent American urbanist Edward Soja as the new contemporary paradigm of the 'post-metropolis' (Soja 1996: 21–2; Webster 1995).

Despite the existence of discernable concentrations of residential or manufacturing activity, the ecologies of most middle and inner districts were in fact characterised by internal diversity. One analysis of building and activity distribution proposed the simple relationship between proximity to main roads, building types and land uses in determining ecology. Thus in locations close to main roads shophouses dominated, followed in sequence by housing estates, unplanned housing areas and then slums (Tsukasa 1992: 4–6). While this is a simplistic general schema, it does point to the relation between use and access in determining distributions of activity spaces. So, for example, slums that remained in their old locations were those which were marginal to the uses of developers by virtue of poor access and undesirable location.

The traditional ethnic division of housing preferences – with the Chinese occupying shophouses and the Thais free-standing homes – has, to an extent, been reproduced in contemporary Bangkok (Santi 1978). The shophouse form (albeit with more modern adaptations for car space) with its dual business and residential utility, continued to be popular among the Sino–Thai and was reproduced by the building industry throughout the metropolis (Kammeier 1992: 15–16). In 1990, 56 per cent of households occupying shophouses in the metropolis still utilised them for business (NSO 1990a). Among better-off Sino-Thai households, separation of home from shophouse workplace was occurring as families moved into housing estates in the suburbs (Kitti 1994). Established social networks had formerly sustained many old shophouse precincts as discernible 'neighbourhoods' (Litchfield *et al.* 1960: 39), and local identities were never completely eroded. Despite the dispersion of some older neighbourhoods of traders, the mixed uses of shophouse clusters still supported considerable diversity. While shophouses have been turned to a variety of uses, most old and new trading zones and pockets of the Sino–Thai are still dominated by this characteristic space of living and working. At the micro level of the local *soi*, both continuity and change were evident. In many areas shophouses (new and old) also function as cheap rental accommodation, while others host small-scale family-based manufacturing and services. Shophouse-based general stores still continue to serve local neighbourhood populations. The *soi* in Bangkok vary according to their location and length, yet many are still characterised by a persistent variety – comprising apartments, free-standing modern homes and old compound houses, as well as slums.

Infrastructure and the impress of the State

The Thai State – that congeries of competing agencies charged with devising and implementing policy and projects – was a key actor influencing ecological and spatial change in the metropolis, despite its ill-coordinated activities and legal impotence in enforcing land-use controls. This occurred principally through transport infrastructure, which served to direct patterns of expansion and ultimately determined land values and use zones. New clusters of private commercial and residential development followed the routes of new roads across, into and out of the sprawl. Proximity to new highways leading into the city and bypassing traffic bottlenecks were the main selling points for *mubanchatsan*. At the same time, these major projects exacerbated uneven concentration of land development, due to a chronic lack of smaller distributor roads which private developers were loath to provide (Halcrow Fox and Associates 1991: 21).

By the 1990s overpasses, elevated highways and private tollways snaked through the metropolis, dividing once-contiguous community settlements, displacing slums, fragmenting the scale of the urban landscape and transforming everyday experience in the city. They were a product of efforts to solve Bangkok's chronic traffic congestion, acknowledged by 1993 as a 'national crisis', due to its negative effects on trade, overseas investment and the quality of life (EIT 1993). As with other cities of the region, such projects created a two-tiered transport system reflecting class differences in the population and the dominance of elite and middle-class transport preferences in policy considerations (see e.g. Tadiar 1995). New land-expropriation legislation in 1987 was a result of the increasing demand to build new roads and to acquire land (usually at the expense of the urban poor and to a lesser extent middle-class inhabitants) for large-scale transport infrastructure projects (Pitch 1995: 13). It was much easier for governments to promote these large and expensive road projects than to tackle the inadequacy of land-use planning and the sovereignty of property speculation which lay at the heart of Bangkok's traffic and infrastructure problems. Moreover, such projects offered lucrative kick-backs for cabinet members and their cronies in the construction industry and handsome profits for overseas investors. Notably, a major World Bank-funded study warned in 1991 that further increase in expressways and tollways in the metropolis (beyond five already approved) would be 'entirely counter-productive' (Halcrow Fox and Associates 1991: 18).

The capital of everything

By the late 1980s Bangkok was the undisputed focal point of Thailand's burgeoning economy. The metropolitan region was the engine of a resurgent export-drive, the centre of finance, prosperity and consumption. The double-digit growth flowing from the East Asian industrial investment and relocation boom of the late 1980s led foreign economists to pronounce Thailand an example of laudable policy management (Warr 1993). In macro terms, the state may indeed be regarded as the principal fulcrum of Thailand's growth experience. But it was also clear that such growth had been uneven at the expense of the provinces and the rural population. All social and economic indicators pointed towards the benefits enjoyed by the metropolis over the rest of the country, whether in terms of the number of schools, universities, hospitals, medical practitioners, wages or salaries (Alpha Research 1994). For over three decades the Bangkok-based state had framed macroeconomic, finance and investment policies which served to generate the growth which disproportionately favoured the capital. From the 1970s the NESDB attempted to offset the diseconomies and imbalances induced by its earlier national economic plans, but it was unable to effectively reorientate the Bangkok-centred trend of development. The state had only ever managed to frame the broad trends of change, allowing economic elites to provide the driving force for economic transformation. And despite the significant growth of provincial business, Bangkok's financial, commercial and industrial elites retained an overwhelming influence on state policy (Christensen 1993).

As for the metropolis itself, state agencies were unable to meet the manifold challenges posed by urban growth. In Bangkok the rhetoric of rational problem-solving dominated the discourse of town and regional planners in district offices and universities alike. This was reinforced regularly by the impressive volumes of international consultant agencies' blueprints for traffic management, road construction and land use regulation. But on the ground, intervention in the urban process was haphazard and uncoordinated. Bangkok's spaces were, in fact, being made by a range of groups, not only state agencies and large property owners, but also the middle classes and the urban poor. Demands for – and conflict and compromises over – space and its use had produced a metropolis that in many ways encapsulated some of the key relationships and struggles within Thai society as a whole.

3 The 1990s – a global city in a global age

Introduction: Bangkok as a 'global city'

Urban centres have long been recognised as key nodal points in the world economy. In the 1980s John Friedmann advanced a model – the 'World City hypothesis' – which proposed that there existed a hierarchy of urban centres worldwide, with key cities (London, Tokyo and New York) exercising a 'headquarters' function in global corporate activities and decision-making, and others functioning in subordinate roles in particular regions, which formed their own related subsytems. In this schema, Bangkok was identified as a secondary city in the urban network of a semi-periphery zone of the world system, with Singapore acting as a core city of this subregion (Friedmann 1986: 72) (see Fig. 3.1). The world city model attracted considerable discussion, and while indices for measuring such rankings of cities differ, and new centres have since achieved greater prominence within the proposed network (such as Shanghai), the general framework of a world urban system is accepted among economic geographers (Thrift 1989). Within the context of increasing economic globalisation – associated with transnational manufacturing and advanced services dispersal from core centres (especially Japan) and intensified flows of deregulated financial capital – many of these urban centres became increasingly important. In the transforming geography of world capitalism, East Asia had become a major zone of accumulation and production, with its expanding and increasingly interconnected urban regions acting as critical nodal points of this new geography (Yeung and Lo 1996: 17–47).

A related concept of 'global cities' was advanced by Saskia Sassen-Koob, who argued that London, New York and Tokyo were characterised by distinctive economies and occupational structures (especially in advanced services) and marked by major contradictions between high technology services and low-paid informal sector work (Sassen-Koob 1986). More recently, this scholar has expanded the label of 'global' to other major cities throughout the world, signalling a convergence between her framework and that of the 'world city' proponents. Against arguments that the new global economy of electronic capital flows overrides older space economies and boundaries, Sassen argues that 'global cities' (including Bangkok) have been central, not marginal, to the emerging global space economy. This economy requires to be reproduced, serviced and financed by a wide range of specialised functions: 'Global cities, with their complex networks of highly specialized service firms and labor markets are strategic sites for the production of these specialized functions' (Sassen 2000: 49).

For scholars and policy-makers alike in the 1990s, Bangkok seemed to suit the designation of 'world' or 'global' city. Bangkok was an important regional and international hub for passenger traffic, air freight and shipping cargoes. While Khlong Toei as a river port had a limited capacity due to its insufficient depth, it was the second-ranked port in East Asia next to Singapore. As the central air traffic hub, Bangkok was still the entry point of most tourists to Thailand. The Thai metropolis was also developing as a centre of telecommunications and media technology in mainland Southeast Asia (Rimmer 1995: 190–1). The city was fast becoming computerised, facilitating rapid business transactions and international communication. Bangkokians eagerly embraced the new internet technology which was sweeping through Asia (Scroggins 1992; Sopon 1992: 47–9). Thai cultural influence was expanding as a result of media and communications entrepreneurship in the region, with Thai TV programmes beaming into Laos and Cambodia and businesses securing lucrative opportunities beyond Thailand's borders (in hotels, telecommunications and construction). The launch of the first national satellites (THAICOM 1, 2 and 3) in 1993 added to the confidence that Thailand was becoming a regional leader (Lewis 1996: 10–15).

Yet intensifying competition within the urban hierarchy of Pacific Asia (including Jakarta, Kuala Lumpur, Hong Kong, Taipei, Shanghai and Singapore) for trade, investment and tourism made it critical that the metropolis be positioned to advantage (Gregory 1995; Mehdi 1996: 332; O'Flahertie 1995). Numerous major projects aimed towards this end, including the much-delayed Eastern Seaboard project (first launched in 1981), the Laem Chabang deep water port, a new international airport in Chachoengsao Province, a fast train project and an inland air freight terminal in the outer suburbs. In addition to the NESDB and numerous ministries, the BMA administration was also engaged in this planning, envisaging the central city as an efficient internationalised business centre with a new stock exchange and finance precinct. The draft plans prepared by international consultants – as always – looked wonderful, but they were based on a scenario that presumed that the existing culture of power among the multitude of relevant state agencies was capable of working to produce such a systematically organised global centre (see e.g. MIT Consulting Team 1996). In effect, the implementation of projects was halting and impossible to coordinate. The new airport project was delayed, cancelled by the Chavalit government in 1995, then revived (Bandit and Dharani 1995; *Bangkok Post* 6 February 1997; Chatrudee Theparat and Amornrat

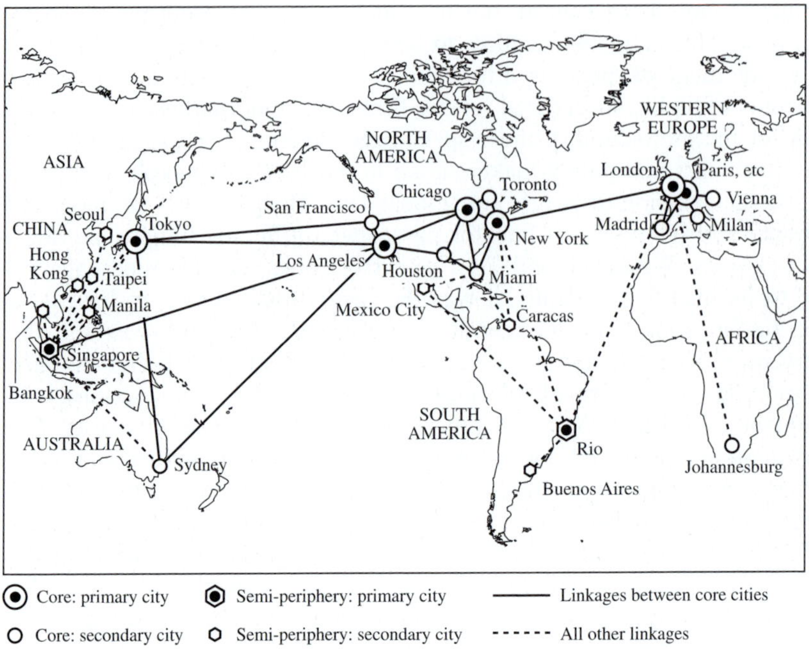

Figure 3.1 The 'Hierarchy of World Cities' according to J. Friedmann.
Source: Based on Friedmann 1986.

Mahitiruk 1998). Powerful officials clung to the lucrative sinecure of Khlong Toei as the deep-water port project slowed. New road and mass transit programmes were delayed as ministries fought over their jurisdictions, and contracts between government and companies were disputed (Unger 1998: 139–66). By 1999 only one of the mass transit schemes planned in mid-decade, the BTS skytrain project, had been opened.

Forms of spatial restructuring were taking place under the pressure of global imperatives, largely driven by the sheer force of private business and the market, and shaped – to some degree – by the Thai State. Thus, a new business precinct emerged along Ratchdaphisek Road through the building of the Queen Sirikit Conference Centre on redundant Tobacco Monopoly land. Further south, in the formerly undeveloped area of Yannawa, the Rama III road extension attracted a sprawl of business and upscale residential development, quickly publicised by the BMA as 'a new CBD of highest international stature' comparable to the London Docklands (BMA n.d.). By the mid-1990s new elevated passenger systems had commenced. Projects such as these, while often fraught with delays, were a product of more concerted efforts of NESDB technocrats to implement long-term goals and a BMA governorship which was both more professionalised and responsive to growing demands of the middle-class Bangkok

Plate 3.1 Flooding in a Bangkok street: an annual hazard. (Photo: Author)

electoral constituency for improved amenities. For an invigorated BMA, there was also international tourism to consider as a key motive for organising the city centre, particularly since the average duration of visitor stays in Bangkok were falling as the city's environment worsened (Crispin and Goad 1999).

Despite the trends which indicated a steady (if uneven) restructuring of city form and function towards the model of a dynamic second-tier city in the global space economy, Bangkok was fraught with contradictions. While the City of Angels boasted a high-tech stock exchange and new elevated expressways, traffic lights were operated manually by the metropolitan traffic police. Confident rhetoric about a modern capital notwithstanding, Bangkok suffered a chronic shortage of telephone lines – it was a critical problem offset only by the timely advent of the mobile phone. While skyscrapers were rising, the city was literally sinking, due to the unregulated pumping of groundwater. The annual monsoon rains and seasonal tides brought floods which regularly paralysed the city (notably severe in 1983 and 1995) (Ross and Suwattana 1995: 279–80).[1] Royalty and visiting dignitaries were the only people travelling through the city with convenience, and then only through the time-honoured system of police-regulated cavalcades.

These contrasts and contradictions accompanying Bangkok's emergence as a regional centre in a competitive world economy were also matched by new dimensions of polarisation in the workforce and population, noted by Sassen as key elements of the economic restructuring accompanying the rise of global cities (Sassen-Koob 1986). Notably, Thailand was still an exporter of labour (primarily male) to the high income countries of the middle east, (to Singapore, Brunei, and to a lesser extent, Japan), but it also became an importer of labour. This was evident in the increasing migration of illegal workers from Thailand's poorer neighbours. Men and women from Burma, Cambodia and Laos flocked to the metropolitan region to take the lowest-paid and most onerous jobs – men worked in rice mills and on construction sites, and women entered domestic service (Prema-Chandra-Athukorala and Manning 1999: 178–9). Also, with fewer girls from the northern Thai provinces turning to prostitution in the later 1990s, increasing numbers of young women from the cross-border areas of Burma entered Thailand's domestic sex trade (see Anjira 1997b; Bussarawan 1997). The Khmer and Burmese were also prominent among Bangkok's increasing population of beggars (Sanitsuda 1996; Tunya 1996).

The city's dependence on the world was expressed above all in the importance of maintaining a positive image for business and tourism. Thus, modernity and progress were the critical themes emphasised during the 1991 World Bank meeting in Bangkok. Notably, the appointment of the interim technocrat prime minister Anand Panyarachun by the military coup-makers of 1991 expressed the primacy of the need to assure foreign investors that it was business as usual in Thailand. Managing the international image of the nation (the 'Land of Smiles') and Bangkok (the exotic city of contrast) has been essential to preserving tourism in the context of a globalised and highly competitive travel industry (tourist city). In the wake of the escalating AIDS pandemic of the late 1980s, adverse exposure of sex-tourism, and recurring accidents (e.g. a disastrous LPG gas truck explosion in Phetchaburi Road and the Khlong Toei chemical container explosion of 1991, the Kader Industrial fire in Nakhon Pathom in 1993) government agencies and officials have been constantly engaged in managing the image of Thailand to protect both the nation's honour (especially Thai womanhood) as well as inflows of crucial foreign currency through tourism and investment (Cohen 1996: 325–45; Nattaporn 1998: 76–8).

The fall of the global city of angels

It is hardly surprising that Thailand's economic boom has been portrayed by commentators as a Bangkok-based boom (Bello, Cunningham and Li 1998: 24; Clad 1989: 96–8). As the powerhouse of Thailand's industrial export surge, the centre of its key financial institutions and the conspicuous site of new wealth, Bangkok was the critical base of the emergent financial globalisation trends. The expanding middle classes of the metropolis were the boom's major beneficiaries, both directly and indirectly. When the financial crisis came in mid-1997, it hit Bangkok hard, exposing

Plate 3.2 The tourist gaze: western tourists visiting a temple. (Photo: Khwansuwong Athipho)

more than just the vulnerability of the city's financial sector, but decades of unsustainable, shallow and dependent economic development. Its greatest victims were thousands of labourers of rural origin who had benefited the least from the prosperity.

The principal feature of contemporary economic globalisation – financial liberalisation – had in fact been emerging since the mid-1970s in the wake of the world oil price crises. As noted already, Thailand's technocrats and leading financial institutions had been forced to adjust policy accordingly and fortuitously positioned the economy to benefit from East Asian industrial restructuring and competitive price advantages. By the 1990s globalisation pressures intensified – symbolised by the GATT agreements – and generated a range of financial liberalisation measures in Thailand. A key aim of the Bank of Thailand (BOT) was to create the conditions for Bangkok to become a regional financial centre (Sopon 1992: 15). To attract overseas bank capital and portfolio investment, the government began deregulating the financial system in 1993 by establishing the Bangkok International Banking Facility (BIBF) which permitted institutions to borrow cheap funds offshore. Other measures allowed for bond and equity markets to flourish, while a shift in credit assessment criteria by the BOT made it easy for finance institutions and small banks to borrow.

Massive flows of foreign capital were now directed into Bangkok's formerly small-scale and highly-regulated stock exchange. The competition for lending became intense, with a large proportion of funds directed to property lending and consumer credit expansion rather than industry. The financial system was increasingly vulnerable, since much capital inflow was short term; moreover, borrowing was based on the inflated value of property collateral in an urban land market already suffering from a domestic building glut (Montes 1998: 10–13). Foreign investors' confidence relied on the assessments of international credit-rating agencies, and these ratings were founded on the Bank of Thailand's record of conservative macroeconomic policy and general projections of continued economic growth. But by the 1990s the Bank of Thailand was not in a position to control the forces unleashed through financial sector liberalisation. Its remaining powers (control over domestic interests rates and a pegged baht) ultimately exacerbated the economy's vulnerability to currency speculation, capital flight and erosion of foreign reserves (Warr 1998: 323). Non-bank private sector foreign debt expanded with little restraint and under the new financial regime, foreign exchange speculation soared (Sirilaksana 2000: 37–8).

The final collapse of Thailand's 'vulnerable miracle' at the hands of the international economy which had given it birth was a result of two converging trends: export slowdown and financial crisis. The vulnerability of low-end labour-intensive manufacturing was already exposed during 1991–3 when these exports slumped in response to world economic slowdown. However, export recovery in 1994 restored confidence in growth, despite a continuing decline in FDI. In the metropolis, over-building of housing estates and condominiums in advance of demand by the early 1990s suggested signs of trouble, but this neither slowed investment in property nor bothered economic analysts too much (Bank of Thailand 1994: 23–6). Early in 1996, a slump in textile, garment and electronics exports took place due to declining price competitiveness, exposing the effects of increased domestic wages and the entrance of cheaper competitors in the region. The falling Japanese currency reduced exports to this key trading partner (Warr 1998: 327–9). Three years earlier, manufacturing companies had begun cutting costs by laying off workers in favour of subcontracting, but by 1996 lay-offs in Bangkok's factories began in earnest (Chitraporn 1996). Thailand's increasing external debt and stagnating exports panicked offshore investors, and prices plunged on Bangkok's artificially-inflated stock exchange as they withdrew funds. Compounding this negative scenario was a glut in the property market which had attracted much of the lending from BIBF finance companies. The BOT restricted loans to finance companies while increasing interest rates to keep foreign capital flowing, leading to a rash of bankruptcies and non-performing loans which became too conspicuous to conceal from the global marketplace (Bello, Cunningham and Li 1998: 25–36). By mid-1997 the vulnerability of the economy to global forces was fully exposed when the Thai baht (still pegged to the US dollar) collapsed under the onslaught of speculation. The subsequent currency float by the BOT saw the baht plummet in value within a few days, wiping out paper fortunes. The global market, once celebrated as an avenue of wealth-making, had turned into a demon of destruction. By late 1997 the Thai government called on the IMF for a currency bail-out and was compelled to accept stringent restructuring requirements (Pasuk and Baker 1998: 122–5).

From the time of the publicising of the spectacular bankruptcies of the Finance One company and Bangkok Bank of Commerce in 1996, government investigators and press sleuths progressively exposed the business–government cronyism underlying loan transactions and fraud in the financial sector (Pasuk and Baker 1998: 103–10). This was hardly a new phenomenon, but never had it been so fatal in its wider effects. It reflected the persistence of the strong cartel networks in Sino–Thai business and their overlapping personal alliances with bureaucrats and elected politicians (see e.g. Clad 1989: 106–7; Chatrudee and Krissana 2000). Also, the persistent culture of reciprocity underlying the tradition of the patrimonial economy had been reflected in demands on the government by business in 1996 to bail-out the crippled property sector and the ailing stock market. From mid-1997 the flush of bankruptcies among the Bangkok bourgeoisie, both large and small, was one conspicuous result of the crash, as was the halt to high-rise building projects which scarred the city skyline into the next century (Crispin 2000). The mass auction of repossessed luxury cars in the fashionable *Soi* Tonglo gave some comfort to ordinary people that the plutocrats and the middle classes were meeting their just rewards for conspicuous consumption. A palpable decline in Bangkok's traffic congestion was another sign.

Yet it was the ordinary people who suffered disproportionately from the hubris of the Bangkok business elites' engagement with global finance markets. Dismissals from finance companies and particularly factories was an immediate consequence. Workers in the industries concerned with textiles, garments and electronics were particularly hard hit, as well as construction workers. At the end of 1997 official estimates numbered unemployed factory labourers at over 300,000 (7.4 per cent of factory workers), construction workers at over 100,000 (5.1 per cent) and private sector white-collar workers at nearly 180,000 (5 per cent), with numbers rising (Thai Farmers Bank 1997). By mid-1998 over 1,300 factories had been closed. Industrial areas such as Rangsit were particularly affected by the mass lay-offs; notably, women formed a higher proportion among these laid-off workers in low-end manufacturing (*Bangkok Post* 31 July 1998; Sanitsuda 1998; Wichai 1997). The traditional recourse of returning to home villages was adopted by many labourers, who attempted to eke out a living on family rice farms. For many workers this was only a temporary expedient, since rural households typically relied on cash from wage-earning members (Crispin and Wang 1999; Thai Farmers Bank 1998). Reports that the 'rural northeast' registered the highest unemployment rates actually reflected this dependence on Bangkok and other urban-based employment sources. By the end of the decade, the effects of the company closures and lay-offs was still profound, with at least 1.6 million people still unemployed (*Bangkok Post* 27 March 2000).

To some extent, a deepening of the manufacturing sector towards more sustainable high-technology exports was evident by the late 1990s, however recovery in exports was fundamentally based on the same basic industries that sustained the original export boom. One official short-term solution to the crisis was to capitalise on the plummeting currency by promoting tourism – particularly shopping in Bangkok – under the rubric of 'Amazing Thailand', a campaign which drew record numbers of international visitors (*Bangkok Post* 16 October 1998). But the crisis did vindicate the earlier misgivings of technocrats concerning unsustainable and thinly based growth. It strengthened their arguments for greater state direction of economic restructuring and regional equity. Ironically, this task required greater reliance on the global economy and institutions than ever before – through encouraging FDI into high technology industry and seeking international assistance for rural employment and human resource development (Mehotra 1999). For policy-makers and their advisers, further integration into the global order was the only solution (Amnuay 1998; Sprague 2000).

Domestically, one immediate reaction to the crash and the cupidity which had been its main cause was a renewed emphasis on traditional Thai–Buddhist values of humility. There was a denigration of the materialistic values associated with the city in much of the public commentary of intellectuals and some journalists. This lent some strength to earlier moral jeremiads against materialism and sharpening inequalities – outcries which had been largely muted in popular media discourse by boom optimism. It was spurred significantly by King Bumibhol's proposal for a return to 'traditional' subsistence ethics. Among intellectuals the varied forms of globalisation and its consequences had been subject to debate some years earlier (Reynolds 1998: 127–41). With the 1997 crisis these issues were simplified by the popular news media in its portrayal of the IMF as a personification of the evils of globalisation and a threat to Thai sovereignty. As a result, the characterisation of Thailand's crisis in terms of the 'Age of the IMF' (*Yuk IMF*) became common among ordinary people of the metropolis. Yet another, and more profound consequence of the crisis was the acceleration of conflicts and debates which had been building since the 1992 political confrontations and the events surrounding the framing of the new national constitution. The disproportionate impact of the crisis on the poor highlighted the necessity for political reform, access to resources, 'people-centred' government and better leadership (Arsa and Chira 1999). Paradoxically, the claims for the participation and representation of marginalised people in the emergent public politics of the decade were framed within a globalised rhetoric of human rights and democratisation (Atiya 1997; Mydans 1999). In turn, this impacted on the way Bangkok functioned as Thailand's political centre.

Bangkok as a political space

Bangkok functions as both a centre of state power and of key national-level conflicts. The capital continues to dominate the nation as a centre of power by virtue of bureaucratic centralisation. This nexus between the city and the modernising centralised state apparatus was furthered by the coup of the military/bureaucratic elite in 1932 and reinforced by the subsequent military-led regimes which dominated the country's administration almost continuously to 1988. Thus, as Rudiger Korff argues, the modern Thai state has been essentially urban (Korff 1989b). It was only from the mid-1990s (as a result of the forces unleashed by the May 1992 events) that decentralisation was seriously commenced and the all-powerful Ministry of the Interior began to loosen its grip over provincial administration, particularly as decentralisation commitments were linked to issues of democracy and representation through the new constitution. Until the recent retreat of the military from national leadership ambitions after 1992, regime change in Thailand though *coup d'état* was always relatively easy, because capturing the city was tantamount to capturing state power and neutralising critical centres of opposition.

While the central function of Bangkok as a state power centre is changing, it remains the most critical site for politics, viewed here in a broad sense as encompassing control and contestation over resources, prestige and – most recently – ideologies of legitimisation. Structural social and economic change has meant that the origins and stakes of such contests have been generated outside the capital itself. However, such is the level of Bangkok-based concentration of communications, public media and state agencies in the capital that control over the capital has meant control over the nation. Political contestation can no longer be said to take place within a small and contained Bangkok elite (if that description was ever applicable, even in 1932). The rise of provincial elites, parliamentary politics and the entry into the political arena of extra parliamentary groups such as farmers and students (from the early 1970s) broadened considerably the forums and sites of debate and contestation (see e.g. Pasuk and Baker 1997).

Bangkok remains the principal stage on which national political and ideological dramas are played out. These have been etched on popular memory by the powerful images of the violence accompanying the dramatic political–military confrontations of 1973, 1976 and 1992. As a result, key spaces and symbols in the city have undergone a transformation in political meaning over time, representing struggles at a national level. Most notably this can be seen in the transformation of meanings associated with

Plate 3.3 New meanings for urban spaces: demonstrators at the Democracy Monument, May 1992. (Photo: Courtesy Matichon)

the Democracy Monument on Ratchadamnoen Avenue. Constructed by the 1932 coup-makers as a celebration of the achievement of constitutional government, the monument was never infused with any force through rituals of legitimacy in the surrounding space itself, and the meaning of *pratchathipatai* (democracy) was, from the time of its popularisation by a small and faction-ridden elite, particularly ambiguous (Nithi 1995b: 114–18). Events from the 1970s began to generate new associations with the space of this monument, but none more so than the mass protests in this precinct during the Black May demonstrations of 1992 against the government of General Suchinda Kraprayun. Originally a monument to a small coup-making elite, by the 1990s this space and its centrepiece came to be viewed as emblematic of mass political action and the martyrdom of ordinary people in the cause of popular democracy (Nalini 1998).

Bangkok also retains its political importance in Thailand because it is through symbolic action in the capital that broader conflicts are dramatised by the national and international media. This transformation of the uses of the city has emerged with the development of new extraparliamentary alliances and a new public politics. Protest marches of rural people on Bangkok began in 1992 with the campaign against forced eviction from forest lands. But the most dramatic expression of the new protest mode has been the activities of the network-based 'Forum of the Poor'.

Comprising aggrieved rural producers and slum-dwellers coordinated by NGO allies, the Forum of the Poor besieged parliament in 1996 in a non-violent demonstration lasting 99 days. This new coalition politics uniting different groups exposed problems facing both the rural and urban poor through the tactical uses of public embarrassment of officials, confrontation through delegations and press coverage (Baker 1999). The Bangkok-based press was an essential instrument of image dissemination, highlighting the strategic political uses of the city as a national centre of influence over public opinion in the new politics of an emerging civil society (Ockey 1997). Public demonstrations in Bangkok were not entirely new, but the more open political climate of post-1992 saw a notable increase. In organisational and ideological terms such events can be seen as a reflection of what Ulrich Beck depicts as 'the new globality' of politics and civil society, harnessing the rhetoric of a global political community through middle-class NGOs for causes which are both local and worldwide (Beck 2000: 64–108). Many staged events dramatically (and often festively) expose the contradictions in the state's development orientation. They ranged from anti-World Bank forums and slum-dweller's anti-eviction demonstrations in Ratchadamnoen Avenue, to parades of elephants and their mahouts protesting exclusion from the city's streets by the BMA and the loss of income opportunities in rural areas (see e.g. Poona 2000).

Whereas conflicts and politicised issues dramatised in Bangkok are commonly co-extensive with extra-metropolitan struggles, the capital may nevertheless be depicted as distinctive. Thailand's electoral politics has been portrayed in terms of a rural–urban divide, with money politics and vote-buying dominating rural areas, in contrast to Bangkok, where these practices are notably less widespread, and loudly criticised. From the 1970s, the expansion of the intelligentsia and the educated middle classes in the capital – with a corresponding growth of liberal and anti-authoritarian attitudes – generated a political culture increasingly critical of military authoritarianism and the corruption accompanying the rise of civilian governments. This has not rid the country of the characteristic cupidity of party politics and official corruption, since only 10 per cent of the national parliament are returned by the Bangkok electorate.[2] Nor has the growth of a critical urban electorate transformed significantly the dominant pattern of non-ideological parties and voting for personalities. This can be seen in the rising popularity of Taksin Shinawatra in the capital – qualified in middle-class eyes for leadership through his business success – and his formation of a new *Thai-Rak-Thai* party (Vatikiotis 1995). However, it has given rise to a pattern whereby governments win power through rural votes but fall as a result of opposition from Bangkok-based criticism, allied to the power of the urban media (Anek 1996).

For decades, with the exception of a few short periods, municipal-level electoral politics in Bangkok were muzzled by military-led regimes.

But from 1985, during the semi-democratic rule of General Prem Tinsulanond, the BMA governorship became elective, and a distinctive urban politics emerged in the capital. Notably, the decisive victory of Chamlong Srimuang (former army general turned ascetic Buddhist) was won by an appeal for clean and morally-upright urban government, sympathy for ordinary people – he wore a simple blue peasant shirt to highlight this identification – and attention to the urgent environmental problems of the metropolis. The support of the press was critical to his campaign (McCargo 1997: 113–15). Chamlong's mercurial rise to national political prominence during 1991–2 as leader of the democracy movement tells us much of the importance of an urban base for reform-orientated politics in Thailand, but his experience was atypical of municipal-level politicians. Nevertheless his two terms of office as BMA governor were significant in establishing the importance of the office (see e.g. Ruland and Bhansoon 1996: 41–3). Since Chamlong's governorship (1985–92), the nature of campaigning and the policies of successive gubernatorial incumbents reveal much about the expectations of the middle-class Bangkok electorate and new attitudes to both urban governance and urban life. Top-down administration still prevails in a city where traditions of local government are absent, but new attention to amenities and public participation have emerged through the influence of a wide spectrum of groups and advocates in the city. However, despite the advent of elective BMA governorships and the emergence of party politics in the metropolis, the powerful Ministry of the Interior continued to assert its prerogatives over governing the capital through its command over funds and claims on leading administrative appointments. This has led to recurrent tussles between governors and this key arm of the centralised state apparatus (McCargo 1997: 140; Ruland and Bhansoon 1996: 37–8).

The BMA is only one of a range of institutional actors influencing urban-related policy, and it does not delimit the sphere of urban politics in the metropolis. The impact of the policies and decisions of numerous national-level agencies on urban life and resources (largely in the form of urban land and living and working space) is considerable, and has generated increasing opposition from both the poor and the middle classes in the metropolis. These agencies include national cabinets, the Expressway and Rapid Transit Authority, the State Railways and the Crown Property Bureau. 'Politics', as defined here, requires the mobilising of support from varied sources, and the playing of competing individuals and institutional actors against one another to delay, change or cancel projects. During the 1980s new middle-class organisations advocating urban environmental improvement (such as Khunying Chotchoi's Magic Eyes group) needed to develop sophisticated lobbying and publicity skills to contest the transport infrastructure projects of various ministries and initiate public campaigns to clean the metropolis (Quigley 1996: 10–15). A new high-profile advocacy network formed in the 1990s was the Bangkok Forum, with a broader agenda to redefine urban life and conservation (see Chapter10). Included within this sphere of contestation and advocacy within the city are the numerous groups representing slum-dwellers and other marginalised populations in the capital. Characteristically these groups rely on alliances and networks which overlap business and government connections as well as university academics and the press.

Power and culture

Contestation and competition in Bangkok has been portrayed in terms of a power structure shaped by key 'strategic groups' formed around competition for appropriation of surplus. This model (first developed by Hans-Dieter Evers and adapted in an analysis of Bangkok and Thailand by Rudiger Korff) depicts strategic groups as emergent classes: they are not fully developed in the Marxist sense because of factors such as the predominance of state agencies in the extraction of economic surplus and weak levels of group consolidation around an economic base underpinned by control over industrial production. They comprise: capital (two groups: monopoly capital and competitive capital); the State (two groups: higher civil servants and middle-ranking civil servants); landowners (two groups: large and middle-sized landowners); and professionals (incorporating professionals who are employees, civil servants and self-employed). At an abstract level, the depiction makes sense, although it simplifies the intersection between metropolitan and extra-metropolitan groups in focusing on an assumed internal power structure particular to the metropolis. Another critical issue is how to conceptualise the way that the emerging middle strata and labouring classes (for want of a better term) fit within this essentially elite-focused model of power distribution in the city. Posited as a 'scientific community', the professional group (essentially a fraction of the middle classes) are said to influence the normative system through their expertise and the media. But this is a particularly idealistic view of one small group within a highly fragmented social formation deriving resources from private and public sector accumulation. Similarly, portrayal of the lower classes as the 'urban insecure' – essentially referring to slum-dwellers – oversimplifies the varied life experiences and life-chances of a diverse population of ordinary wage earners and self-employed people (Korff 1986b). Despite its shortcomings, this structural approach – like the political economy approach which more confidently identifies class formation and conflicts in both city and nation – highlights how the process of competition for power over resources in the city constitutes the power structure and both shapes and is configured by key institutions.

Clearly the metropolis is a key site for speculation, profit and accumulation. It can be conceived as comprising numerous fields of accumulation for dominant groups. Interestingly, however, the almost exclusive focus on the economic base of this dominance in structuralist models misses the central cultural dimension of power accumulation and its exercise both in the city and outside. The explanation of Thai power structure in terms of cultural dynamics has been bypassed by many political scientists because anthropological portraits of Thai society – built around models of person-to-person relationships and a complex of hierarchical entourages – seemed to downplay groups and corporate actors in the power structure as well as essentialise Thai culture as 'unchanging' (Anderson 1978: 231–2; Korff 1989b: 44–5). The corporate reality of the Thai State has been periodically expressed in repressive actions, when usually fragmented agencies temporarily cohere to preserve the broad structure of power when it is perceived to be threatened. But the Thai State is also a constellation of competing groups whose internal structure is informed by enduring cultural patterns. 'Culture' does not stand outside structures of power: culture itself – as a system of behaviours and norms – is embedded in these structures.

Key behaviours and values prevalent among bureaucrats, interest groups and other political actors are institutionalised in practices informed by individualism, factionalism, personal relations, networks, entourages and hierarchies, despite the legal, procedural and normative frameworks that define their jurisdictions, internal hierarchies and legitimacy. As such, they can only be defined as cultural. These institutionalised practices are seen in the entourage-building that takes place within agencies such as ministries and state enterprises (see e.g. Morell and Chai-anan 1981: 16). They are seen in such specific cases as frequent competition over tendering and the looseness of government contracts, which have led to constant disputation and delay in major urban project implementation (Patcharee and Haller 1994). Prevailing tendencies of factionalism and fragmentation around *phuyai* (big men of renown) in bureaucracies have often stymied the policies of technocrats. Paradoxically, these obstacles have only been overcome by technocrats (in the NESB, for example) through a complementary mode of informal influence and persuasion (Thinapan 1990: 44–7). As noted above, there are varied modes and sites expressing such practices, from the Sino–Thai family system underlying monopoly capital (in the key banks, for example), to the subculture of vertically integrated bureaucratic agencies. Family connections and personal relations between key elite groups (state managers and capitalists) in fact constitute the dynamic cultural dimension which gives Thai capitalism its distinctive character (Hewison 1989: 211–13). While mutual dependencies through reciprocity may bind groups, such relations are also marked by pragmatism and self-interest, albeit often expressed in cultural idioms of benevolence and respect. This is clearly seen in the public associations between politicians, bankers and prominent godfathers (*chao pho*) of the criminal underworld in Bangkok and the provinces (Ockey 1998; 39–44).

While these cultural practices – informed by pragmatism, self-interest and discretionary use of power and privilege – underlie systems of corruption and illegal accumulation (gambling and prostitution organisations, for example), paradoxically, the idiom of personalism and hierarchy also facilitates positive outcomes in causes of social justice. Thus, the slum activist Prateep Ungsongtham was able to effectively battle against the eviction of Khlong Toei squatters precisely because of her astute cultivation of people of power and repute in the capital (for which see Chapter 5). In the metropolis, the customary rent-seeking behaviour of the bureaucracy, notably the police, is territorialised at the level of the district, the highway and the street. Vendors, motorcycle taxi riders and ordinary drivers are commonly required to make payments to policemen, who channel payments upwards through the ranks of the superiors who are their benefactors. Brothels, bars and gambling dens operate under the direction, or conditional protection, of certain police groups. Yet at the same time there is a mutual reciprocity that marks relations between arbiters of power in the city and Bangkokians at the micro level. It is common at New Year for motorists to give gifts to local traffic police, in thanks for past and continued favours. Bangkokians participate in this system by accepting the discretionary relationships forged through such exchanges. For example, government employees (including university professors) can easily avoid traffic fines if they show their identity cards to police. For a wide variety of purposes, payments are used to *yot namman* (oil the wheels) of administrative processes at all levels. Personal contacts are used for a spectrum of purposes (often with expected recompense), from the enrolment of school children to the collection of rubbish in private housing estates. A system of pragmatic cultural practices marked by discretionary favours and personalism thus informs the exercise of power and its negotiation at all levels in the city. In many ways it subverts the process of 'rule-by-law' embraced by activists in the broad movement towards civil society and good governance in Thailand. It perpetuates inequalities and exploitation, but it also leads to creative solutions to conflict and confrontation.

Contemporary Bangkok: the permanent space of modernity

Bangkok still functions as the pre-eminent symbol of modernity in Thai society – the crucible where 'the new' is embraced, synthesised and projected. It may be argued that the metropolis no longer functions as a centre of difference in relation to a tradition-bound rural society. Clearly, rural society has been transformed by fundamental changes towards a commercialised economic structure characterised by wage-labour and geographical mobility with lifestyles and values shaped increasingly by consumerism and commodification. The 'boundaries' between the Thai capital and the countryside, it has been argued, have been dissolved by a new space economy of regional and global markets (Rigg 1997: 258–68). Rural society's embrace of global media images (even though generated by a popular media machine concentrated in the Thai metropolis) make it questionable now to locate 'Bangkok' so easily as a centre of modernity's diffusion, since the market and consumption forces are 'everywhere' (Reynolds 1998: 115–16). The circulation, transformation and mass market for new sexually provocative renderings of *Lukthung* folk songs is one case illustrating this problem of locating a 'centre' for the generation and consumption of images. Modernity, expressed in images of assertive female sexuality, is consumed everywhere (Amporn 1999). Where, for example, is northeastern culture produced and located? Conservative promoters of 'Isan Tradition' vehemently denounce the commercial transformation of new renderings of Lao '*lam*' ballads and music, but rural communities enthusiastically hire 'Mo Lam Sing' troupes (invariably based in Bangkok or other cities) to present performances of amplified northeastern music accompanied by explicit sexual lyrics and scantily-clad female dancers.

Nonetheless, the metropolis still stands out as a central site of difference in Thai society. Bangkok is implicated in all the central conflicts (over cultural and political meanings) in Thailand (Korff 1989a: 9). Thus, an old (arguably redundant) dichotomy between Bangkok and countryside still prevails in the arguments of public moralists such as Sulak Sivaraksa who identifies Bangkok as 'a second-rate western city', responsible for the introduction of alien cultural values and a consequent moral degeneration in Thai society (Sulak 1990: 177–9).[3] Popular central Thai and northeastern ballads and folk songs (*Mo Lam* and *Luk Thung*) still bewail the abduction of young women to the morally dangerous metropolis, or evoke the seductive lure of the glittering metropolis for womenfolk as a place for work or adventure (see e.g. Amporn 1999: 15; Pasuk and Baker 1995: 76–80). City–county contrasts are also perpetuated in Bangkok's media representations. In fact, Nithi Aeuosrivongse has argued that the wide coverage of the Forum of the Poor by the Bangkok-based national media was stimulated by the novel spectacle of a peasant congress in the city. But the press's fascination with the exotic and rustic peasant 'other' wore off as the protest prolonged its stay in Bangkok (Nithi 1999). Bangkok is presented by advocates of alternative development as a threat to wholesome rural community culture and an enemy to agrarian self-sufficiency in its persistent role as a magnet for the peasantry (Sanitsuda 1990: 31–9). Feature films and serialised television dramas, commonly focusing on the lives and domestic spaces of Bangkok's wealthy bourgeois families, invariably portray the countryside as a peaceful haven from the busy and status-ridden city – the antithesis of modernity and a crucial imagined space for the urban bourgeoisie (Hamilton 1992: 265–6). Yet the dichotomy is not only a product of these discursive representations – whether of consumer imaginaries or political ideologies. The distinction is established in popular self-and-other ascriptions in the Thai language which contrast *khon ban nok* ('rural-dweller'/'hick' – connoting simplicity, naivety and ignorance) with *khon muang* (city dweller – sophisticated, intelligent, streetwise). Opinion surveys in the capital show that these contrasting stereotypes of Bangkok and *ban nok* personality traits persist, while increasing press commentary and debate on 'urban society' (*sangkhom muang*) reinforce these distinctions (e.g. Korff 1993: 245; Sermsin 1997). The national press and other mass media – concentrated in the capital – continue to shape perceptions that it is in the city that the most important public affairs are centred, thereby constructing differences between urbanity and rurality. As a recent study of the Thai newspaper industry comments: 'Beyond Bangkok is a kind of hinterland, where nothing of much significance is deemed to occur' (McCargo 2000: 4).

It has been argued that the continuing prominence of Bangkok in the national imaginary reflects the intrinsically urban-centred focus of Thai society. Richard O'Connor proposes that Thai society is informed by the complementary cultural idioms of community (horizontal–familial bonds) and hierarchy (vertical structures of prestige ranking) centring on the *muang* (city-based polity) in general, but particularly the capital city (*Muang Luang*). These have endured – albeit in transmuted form – into the contemporary period, where the once royal-centred image of Bangkok has been subsumed within a hierarchy of status markers associated with modernity (see Chapter 10). This modernity was once the prerogative of a narrowly-based elite, but an urban-centred bourgeoisie and state bureaucracy have arrogated these associations to themselves (O'Connor 1990). The association of royalty with modernity and its link with progress and cosmopolitanism has never been lost. In fact, it was heightened from the

Plate 3.4 High-rise luxury apartments: icons of an urban life of sophistication and prestige. (Photo: Author)

prosperous years of the last two decades, and expressed most conspicuously in the cult of the equestrian statue of King Chulalongkorn in Bangkok and the widespread popularity of commemorative coins, amulets and images of this most famous of Thailand's monarchs (Sanitsuda 1997). From its inception, Krung Thep was the site for the accumulation of the cultural capital of global modernity (represented first by China, then by the west), where new objects, artefacts and styles (from architecture to bodily adornment) were appropriated by an expanding group of consumers for practical and symbolic purposes. In many ways, then, this concentration of consumption in Bangkok, and the power of the capital to legitimise new syntheses of status markers, reflects a persistent historical pattern in Thai society (Barme 1997; Peleggi 1997; Reynolds 1998: 120–3).

Space and society – Bangkok as a postmodern crucible

Within the broader spaces of a transforming Thai society, Bangkok attracts attention and definition as a distinctive site. Scholars from a variety of disciplines are still drawn to focusing on the Thai capital as the centre for the production of meanings and new movements. It is a 'capital of desire', a space where a discernable 'Bangkok culture' is reproduced through the continued consumption and production of meanings generated around modernity or postmodernity (Lewis 1998: 239–41; Van Esterik 2000: 122–3). The hybridity which is claimed to be the characteristic of postmodernity is most evident perhaps in those organisations and new spaces which have become a mark of middle-class life. For example, the new Thammakai Buddhist sect, with its emphasis on individualism and prosperity through ascetisicm, has been seen as a quintessential urban and middle-class movement, focusing particularly on its main temple in the north of the metropolis in Pathum Thani (Jackson 1989). Thammakai is, however, only one element in a religious marketplace of sub sects and cults which also echo old Buddhist and popular religious forms (e.g. the tradition of the wandering Buddhist monks) while serving new material and individual needs (Jackson 1999; O'Connor 1993; Paritta 1999). In this context, new sacred places (such as shrines and temples) – local and pan-local – have developed while old ones are revived, generated by (and also generate) cults of various sizes and followings. The cult of Rama V drew adherents from far beyond the capital, but had a special focus at the site of that king's equestrian statue in the royal plaza in Bangkok. This cult emerged during the prosperous early 1990s, but one prominent cultural analyst suggested that it drew strongest support in Bangkok among the lower middle classes whose livelihoods were uncertain (Nithi 1993). The statue of King Taksin, on the Thonburi side of the river, also drew devotees, particularly during the onset of the economic crisis, because it was seen to symbolise victory over adversity. Humbler sites were also given attention: in Phrakhanong, a small shrine dedicated to Mae Nak, the leading character of a long-standing popular ghost myth, received increasing attention during the 1990s, perhaps due to growing publicity of this legend through books and a major film.

Other sites have emerged in connection with the central activities of the mundane world. The massive shopping malls of the metropolis function as sites for sociability based around consumption, display and refashioning of identities (Edler 1996: 17–30; Van Esterick 2000: 123). The shopping malls represent one of the conspicuous 'non-place' realms characteristic of late capitalism and its product, the so-called 'postmodern city'. They are invented commercialised fantasy lands divorced from older locality-based identities generated by history and memory (Auge 1995: 94). The new is juxtaposed with older forms of life, representations and commodifications. Bangkok's stunning variety of contemporary commercial, domestic and leisure architecture is one conspicuous example of the promiscuous visual juxtaposition of past and present characterising the postmodern urban landscape and symbolisation. In many ways, however, this juxtaposition – which extends to contrasting patterns of life and ecology – has always been a feature of Bangkok as a cosmopolitan cultural crucible, expressing more intensely than anywhere else in the country the appropriation and mediation of new forms and meanings characteristic of Thai cultural orientations (see e.g. Reynolds 1998: 120–4).

Arguments about the postmodern intersect with models of globalisation and its impact on space and experience. Manuel Castells argues that globalisation is reflected in the dominance of electronic communications and images in the economy and people's lives (the 'space of flows'), and that as a result 'place' – in the sense of locality-bound communities – is largely redundant. Place, to Castells, is now only meaningful and functional to marginalised groups. In the information age, new cultural communes actually develop though virtual interaction rather than literal proximity between people (Castells 1997: 60–7). To an extent, we can see this approach vindicated when we consider the way that middle-class Bangkokians create virtual communities across the metropolis and beyond through the radio, mobile phone and internet (Cate 1999: 32–3). As in cities in the west and across Asia, we find the familiar lament that the city has become less and less the environment of place-based communities, and that new fragmented spaces have emerged through the actions of both the state and the market (Korff 1993: 248). Yet at the same time, place itself has been renegotiated and constructed by practices of people in the city at both micro levels and across the city itself. For example, it is not necessarily the case that the traffic jam or the housing estate have generated permanent alienation. Social interaction and identity have been forged through people's interaction in new electronic spaces and neighbourhoods, phenomena which throw doubt on assumptions of the homogenising force of global culture and the alienation of social existence generated by modernity (see e.g. Soraj 1998; Yok 1997). At the same time the past and old urban places have been resurrected by various agents as both commodities and symbols of continuity. This has been a result both of deliberate state policy and of contestation among groups in urban society claiming alternative meanings for Bangkok as a site and as a 'place'. Modernity necessitates the invention of the past, and this has been the case among all groups, not only state agencies (Askew 1994).

The new emphasis on 'hybridities' and 'difference' now entering Thai studies (and writings on Bangkok in particular) reflect the postmodern turn in the social sciences. 'The city' now attracts attention among scholars as a site for the production of numerous texts and narratives generated by a multitude of agencies and actors (see e.g. King 1996; Watson and Gibson 1995). This has legitimised a multilevel approach to understanding the production of meaning and space in the city, at the same time making it much more difficult to offer a simple portrait of what 'the city' is. How then do we characterise Bangkok? In this chapter I have portrayed Bangkok as a historical and dynamic entity shaped by economic processes at the global and regional levels, a centre whose dominance at the level of the national urban system has expanded with the power of its key elite groups. It can thus be seen as a field for the reproduction of elites through accumulation, a site where the state has attempted to regulate change through mediating the global economic processes on which Thailand has always been dependent. At a more proximate level, Bangkok has been a site where symbolic capital is accumulated and displayed at all levels of urban life, expressed most conspicuously in the rising middle classes. It is marked by social and economic inequalities which have been conspicuously revealed in conflict over land resources between the state, landowners and those who lack formal means of access to this critical survival resource. Yet the Thai metropolis is not only an economic artefact: narrowly conceived economic processes cannot explain the ongoing configuration of Thailand's metropolis, its spaces and its society. The ways that status resources are utilised, the modes of competition that have developed over such resources, and group formation and identity itself, have been informed by a complex of cultural traits characteristic of Thai society. I have argued here that these are not static, but have rather interacted dynamically with the evolving social and economic order. The theme of economic, spatial and cultural relations informs the following chapters of this book.

Part II

Making Bangkok

Studies in place, practice and representation

4 Banglamphu

Change and persistence in the *yan*

Introduction: the complexities of a locality

Of the many changes occurring in contemporary Bangkok, the transformation of the old inner city *yan* is a conspicuous part of the process. The Thai term *yan* can be roughly translated as 'district', but it is a popular word, not an administrative one; it recalls a premodern identification of the city as a conglomeration of centres of particular activities or people, often both (see Chapter 1). In the Banglamphu district, we see vividly the complex interconnections between local history and the ecological legacy of premodern settlement (for example, in mixed economic and residential functions) and contemporary forces of change on a broader scale (in the shape of state planning and international tourism). Until the 1970s the locality of Banglamphu was known and frequented only by Bangkokians. It was famous for its market and a number of key products and specialist shops (traditional medicines, for example). By the late 1980s Banglamphu was described by the Lonely Planet guide as a 'World Traveller Centre' (Cummings 1987: 73). Viewed from tourist web sites, Banglamphu today (and particularly its now-famous Khaosan Road) is widely represented as an international space, a gathering place for young budget travellers with all the facilities they need: restaurants, internet cafes, travel agencies, trinkets and accommodation. Together with Katmandu in Nepal and Kuta Beach in Bali, it functions as an international junction for young travellers through Asia (Mydans 2001). But viewed from the local spaces shaped by its web of old lanes (*trok*) and their neighbourhoods, the Banglamphu district is a multilayered locality, revealing people adapting to changes in livelihood opportunities and still embracing patterns of neighbourhood identification characteristic of an earlier form of urbanism, despite such change. While Bangkok's old *yan* are seen by some Thai conservation advocates as a key to conserving an indigenous mode of urban life, we need to acknowledge that these *yan* have always been a product of adaptation and change in the metropolis since its foundation. While threats of extinction are certainly real, survival of the *yan*, as seen in the case of Banglamphu, may only be possible through forms of transformation and new modes of coexistence between people, and between global and local connections.

The 'inner city' has received particular attention in the study of western cities, giving rise to models of change summarised in concepts such as 'gentrification' – a sociospatial process whereby lower-income 'place-communities' are displaced by the transformative dynamics of the capitalist land market and the state, a process transforming downtown areas into 'bourgeois playgrounds' (Smith 1996: 28). The situation in Bangkok's old inner areas is somewhat different, due to historical legacies of settlement, ecology and multiple land tenures. But as with contemporary western cities, the state and economic processes have been key agents generating new patterns of transformation in Bangkok's inner areas. The much-publicised resistance of Muslim residents of the village of Ban Khrua in the face of the Expressway Authority's determination to built a freeway bypass in central Bangkok has shown vividly how the few remaining old *yan* of the city are in danger of being sacrificed to make way for urban 'development' in the guise of infrastructure efficiency (see Chapter 10). Physical change, imposed not only by land development pressures but also infrastructure imperatives, will persist as the metropolis continues to grow, and as planning bodies generate representations of the city as a system of traffic flows and efficient infrastructure. The anthropologist Richard O'Connor argues that it is this process of state-sponsored modernisation which threatens to overwhelm Bangkok's once-distinct place-based neighbourhoods and promote a more homogenised landscape, eroding distinctiveness and differences (O'Connor 1990: 70–1). The state (at both national and metropolitan levels) has played a key role in shaping Banglamphu, framing the environment within which economic and physical patterns persist and change. This can be seen at a number of levels. The BMA plans a number of street extensions through local neighbourhoods which will impact on local ecology. The Rattanakosin Conservation Master Plan restricted high-rise building in this area to preserve vistas of the palace precinct and banned industrial development (see Chapter 10). At the same time, this opened the way for the construction of new low-rise guest houses which catered for the surging flows of budget tourists, whose arrival was itself partly a result of the publicity given to Thailand as a tourist destination. But it is not only the state which impinges upon localities, but new, more instrumental, relations between key institutions and people which have emerged around the uses of urban land. This is manifested particularly in the way that urban monasteries – key landowners and traditionally the focal points of long-term rental settlements – now utilise their land for profit generation or institutional expansion at the expense of the neighbourhoods which have coexisted with them for generations.

These are not the only factors underlying inner Bangkok's transformation. Since the mid-1970s Bangkok has become an important tourist city within a world and regional network of leisure and travel nodes (see e.g.

Mullins 1999). With an important sector of its services economy geared increasingly towards tourist-generated earnings, the landscape and workforce of the Thai metropolis have changed accordingly.[1] The rapid expansion of a particular form of international tourism – backpacker travel – has had a major impact on the ecology of a section of Banglamphu, and local entrepreneurial activity has interacted with this global phenomenon in generating a distinctive tourist-orientated enclave in this small but multilayered inner district. Ordinary people in the *trok* neighbourhoods (alleyway neighbourhoods) now manage their lives in terms of the new urban functions which have emerged around them.

Inner Bangkok

Bangkok has been characterised by municipal and planning authorities as comprising three concentric rings of settlement: the inner, the middle and the outer districts (NESDB 1986: 20). This is a simplistic portrayal, based largely on population densities, but it does outline some broad characteristics. Of these, the inner *khet* (districts) of Bangkok are probably the most diverse in their individual characteristics. A common demographic feature of these areas is their overall population decline both in absolute terms and as a proportion of the total population of the Bangkok Metropolitan Area. It is an indication of the pace of urban growth that today, most of the *khet* regarded as comprising inner Bangkok were located on the outer fringe of the built-up area forty years ago. At the close of the Second World War the built-up area extended only as far north as Dusit, east to Pathumwan and west to Thonburi. Driven by both internal structural changes and foreign aid-driven development programmes, the old Bangkok gave way to an expanded city based on the economic and transport characteristics of western cities.

The physical, functional and social characteristics of the old Bangkok were moulded by historical processes of a kind distinct from those which transformed the city in the post-Second World War era. It was a city characterised by an administrative and palace core, surrounded by precincts, or *yan*, which were distinctive by virtue of the activities of their various populations. Until the post-Second World War era, Bangkok still retained many physical and sociospatial characteristics of a non-Western city: much of its population still lived in the same location as its work places, and the common mode of transport was by canal rather than road. With barely a million people at the first post-war census of 1947, Bangkok was still a dual city: both terrestrial and water based (Litchfield *et al.* 1960).

For the purposes of this chapter, 'Inner Bangkok' refers to the administrative area covered by today's *khet* (districts) of Phranakhon, as well as Pomprap and Samphanthawong. Although much has changed over the past three decades, these areas maintain distinct features. At its centre is Rattanakosin Island – comprising the old palace, temples and fortifications which formed the symbolic heart and focus of the city. Beyond Khlong Lot – the inner canal which encircles this royal precinct – are the more differentiated districts bounded by the first canal – the city moat known as Khlong Ong-ang in the west and the south, and Khlong Banglamphu in the north. The third canal, constructed during the early years of the reign of King Rama IV, encompasses the areas of Dusit and Thewet in the north and Sampheng (or Chinatown) in the south (see Fig. 4.1).

The different land uses of these *khet* (see Table 4.1) indicate something of the distinctive characteristics of the area. A comparison of the different concentrations of uses such as commerce, government offices and education shows the diversity of inner Bangkok, encompassing special districts, such as the palace area around which many government institutions focus and the old commercial district of Sampheng (in *Khet* Samphanthawong). It also highlights the multifunctional character of the area as residential, commercial and institutional. This concentration is an inheritance of Bangkok's earlier urbanism. These *khet* did not fully participate in Bangkok's building boom from the mid 1980s, largely because they are already fully built-up. In the case of Phranakhon, much of the district was subject to building restrictions due to the ordinances which followed the Rattanakosin Conservation Plan during the early 1980s. In fact, over the past five years Phranakhon has registered the second or third lowest level of construction activity in the whole BMA (BMA 1993). Yet another characteristic of the area is the large number of markets still existing, many of them in their original locations. In 1982 *Khet* Phranakhon boasted twelve markets, (the fifth largest number in the BMA), and the site of the greatest number of market stalls of all the *khet* in the BMA (Kiat *et al.* 1982).[2] The total area of commercial and private residential space in the Phranakhon district is substantially restricted because of the high level of institutional structures and uses. Within the old city space bounded by the

Table 4.1 Selected land use, inner *khet* (districts), 1986

Land use	Khet			
	Phranakhon	*Pomprap*	*Samphanthawong*	*BMA*
Residential	21.18	29.02	18.37	11.54
Commercial	12.38	19.02	31.34	1.14
Industrial	1.09	2.61	0.86	1.42
Warehouse	0.43	1.20	7.35	0.44
Government office	19.89	5.61	1.38	2.66
Education	5.46	3.24	1.82	0.84
Roads	14.30	19.49	9.06	2.45
Unused	0.03	5.93	1.94	39.77
Waterways	10.73	2.66	5.81	3.45

Source: BMA Planning Division 1986.

Table 4.2 Population change in the Banglamphu area, by *khwaeng* (subdistrict), 1982–90

Khwaeng	*1982*			*1990*		
	M	*F*	*Total*	*M*	*F*	*Total*
Ban Panthom	6,993	6,613	13,606	5,893	5,543	11,436
Bowoniwet	6,099	6,250	12,349	4,262	4,405	8,667
Chana Songkhram	3,051	2,698	5,749	1,957	2,064	4,021
Talat Yot	3,761	4,254	8,015	2,528	2,805	5,333
Total	19,904	19,815	39,719	14,640	14,817	29,457

Source: House Registration Data, Khet Phranakhon office.

Banglamphu/Ong-ang canal, commercial activities are largely concentrated to the north in the Banglamphu district, and to the south at Wang Burapha. Both of these areas have developed from earlier origins as market and trading *yan* of the old city.

Although Phranakhon and its adjacent *khet* were a focus of steady population growth in the pre- and post-Second World War years, a key demographic feature of the inner areas has been a continuing trend of population decline. This has been a characteristic at least since the late 1950s relative to outer areas of Bangkok, and certainly in absolute terms since the 1960s. Between 1980 and 1990 the population of Phranakhon fell by 6.6 per cent (from 111,199 to 103,835). In addition, from the early 1980s this district has had a lower than average proportion of younger people in the age groups 0–9 years and 20–9 years, and a higher proportion aged 40 years and above (NSO, Population and Housing Census 1980, 1990).

The Banglamphu area

Characterisics of the Banglamphu area

Banglamphu lies in the northern section of *Khet* Phranakhon (see Fig. 4.1), the boundaries of which encompass the old heart of Bangkok. Richard O'Connor has characterised the popular image of Bangkok – the image of its ordinary people – as 'a patchwork of named places', arguing that Bangkok's traditional urbanism persists in the ways that people in the settlements of the inner city identify themselves with their surrounding neighbourhoods and their associated functions (O'Connor 1990: 61). While the connections between people's movement patterns and livelihoods and these areas are now often more attentuated than in earlier generations, the legacy of this identification is still apparent in the language that people use to map their city and its environment. It is a language that does not follow the bureaucratic divisions and namings of city districts. Naming and identification of city areas can be very specific. Strictly speaking, in

Figure 4.1
The Banglamphu area, showing land uses and guesthouses, 1992.

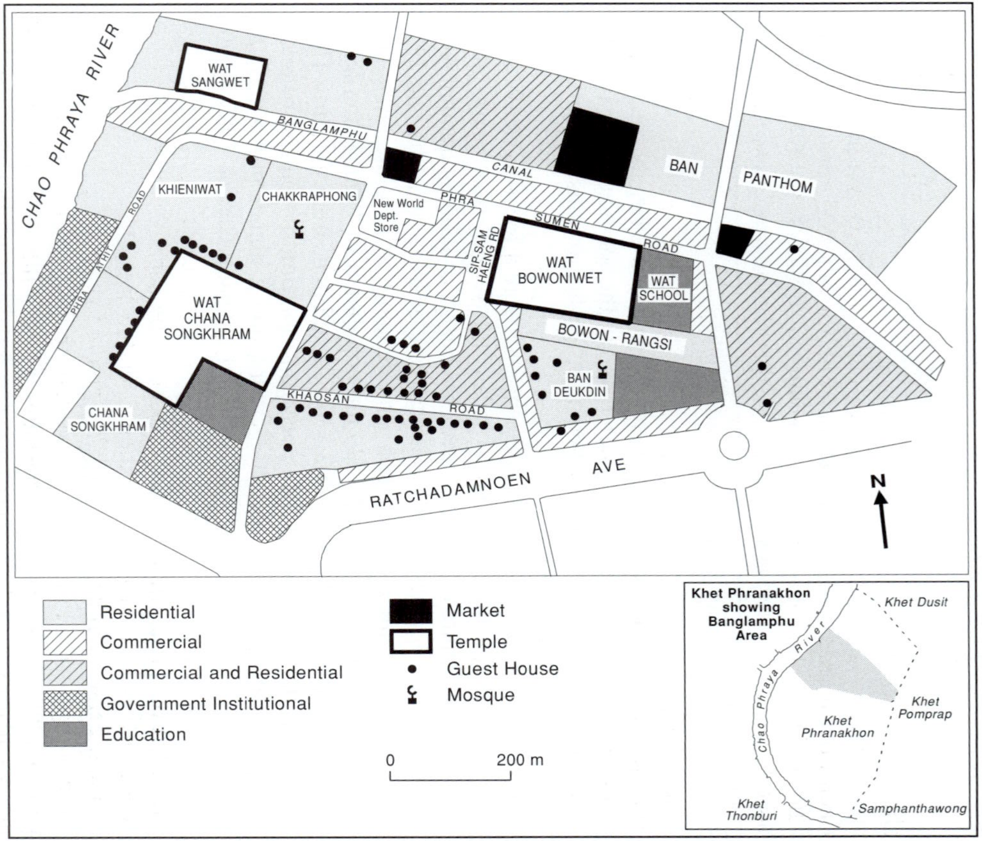

fact, many of the people who were interviewed in this study would not identify themselves as belonging to Banglamphu as such. To them, Banglamphu is that small area focusing around the New World Department Store, formerly the famous Talat Yot of Bangkok, a market well-known for its fresh food. Their named places are more proximate, with the *trok* (alleyways) known by old village names (e.g. Ban Phanthom) or institutions (e.g. Surao Chakkraphong and the vicinity of Wat Bowoniwet) around which their homes focus. I choose the name for this study area simply to indicate that the old market area – together with the canal from which it takes its name – is the physical centre of this settlement cluster. In administrative terms this settlement area comprises the four subdistricts (*khwaeng*) of *Khet* Phranakhon named Talat Yot, Bowoniwet, Chana Songkhram and Ban Panthom.[3] A characteristic of these subdistricts is high population density and a mixing of commercial, institutional and residential functions. Despite the high population density, all the subareas of the district are experiencing continual population decline (Table 4.2).

No single area of inner Bangkok can be claimed to be typical of the inner city in general, given the varied histories and characteristics of settlements. Nevertheless one can claim to be dealing with some elementary features of its old forms in Banglamphu. When introducing a case study of Banglamphu in a wider study of settlement in Thailand nearly forty years ago, Larry Sternstein made a claim for the typicality of this area. This was made on the basis of characteristic elements, including the market and its characteristic building forms of shophouse, wooden homes (*ban reuan*), as well as institutional and office constructions and the mixed area functions so characteristic of Bangkok (Sternstein 1964: 154). However, since Sternstein's study a number of inner districts have undergone important transformations in various ways which have led to considerable differentiation. The Silom Road district is perhaps the most dramatic instance of inner area transformation over the last three decades of the twentieth century. With a considerable amount of large, privately-owned land holdings, and close to the old western trading precinct, Silom developed into a new international business centre with a significant tourist entertainment and high-rise residential component (see Nopporn 1992). The area of Sampheng/Yawarat – the traditional centre of Chinese trade and community – experienced less comprehensive physical restructuring, due to the continuing importance of its varied business functions, its tenure patterns and small size of property holdings (distributed between small private owners and the Crown Property Bureau). Nonetheless this precinct has experienced a decline of residential population and an outmovement of larger business and financial concerns. Inner areas of Bangkok have developed new or complementary specialised functions. Such an evolution needs to be understood not only in terms of the changing urban economy and its relationship to regional and world processes, but also in its relationship to the specific histories, functions and characteristics of these areas. The experience of the Banglamphu area reflects these interactions and the continuing multilayered nature of inner city settlements.

Among Bangkokians, the name Banglamphu is identified with its functions as a place of buying and selling. However, the clustering of retail activies around the old site of Talat Yot – now replaced by the New World Department Store – is not in itself an adequate summation of the surrounding two-square kilometre area wedged between Ratchadamnoen Avenue, Khlong Banglamphu and the Chao Phraya River. A closer view of the area, walking from the Chao Phraya River landing place under the Pin Klao bridge, along Phra Athit Road to Khlong Banglamphu, will encompass a view of an old residential precinct of the nobility, some now defunct riverside industries, as well as shophouse-based commercial functions. Walking through some of the narrow *trok* we see large two-storey wooden houses in various conditions. Depending on the route taken, we emerge at Wat Chana Songkhram, Surao (mosque) Chakkraphong, or the busy road after which that mosque is named. Another turn takes us to the modern New World Department Store. These views encompass the variety of urban functional elements combining to form the landscape and functional ecology of the Bangplamphu area. Not all of its elements interact. Indeed, the area should be seen as a collection of coexisting neighbourhoods and areas with their own histories and characteristics. Historically this northern sector of Rattanakosin has functioned as a residential area for government servants and their retainers whose settlements clustered around the temples, along the minor canals and the small lanes (*trok*). The market which moved onto the land from its position near the mouth of Khlong Banglamphu was a response to changes occurring across the growing city generally in the late nineteenth century, just as the development of the palaces along Phra Athit Road reflected a trend of suburbanisation among the nobility. Some historians would argue that the changes to Banglamphu are a clear expression of the impact of an expanding capitalist market economy on a local urban area. The emergent settlement patterns of the latter decades of the nineteenth century are still evident in the built landscape, but the separate areas and activities that comprise this district were once more clearly articulated through different socio-economic bases and a far lower population density. Bangkok was comprised of an agglomeration of semi-independent communities focused around markets, institutional and religious nodal points. This pattern no longer informs the basic urbanism of modern Bangkok: however, one can argue that the surviving small-scale societies of the inner city – such as Banglamphu – may still be viable if certain pressures are eased. The following discussion is an attempt to explain some of these pressures in the context of change in this area.

***The evolution of the* yan**

The Banglamphu area was settled well before the establishment of Krung Rattanakosin by King Phra Puttha Yotfa. There were three *wat* already existing in the immediate vicinity when the new Khlong Banglamphu was being dug by Khmer prisoners of war during the reign of King Taksin (1769–82). There was Wat Klang Na (later named Wat Chana Songkhram to celebrate victory over the Burmese), then immediately to the north Wat Samchin, so named because of its association with three Chinese patrons who built the temple to make merit. It became known as Wat Banglamphu and then Wat Sangwet when it was created a royal *wat* by King Rama I (there was also Wat Rangsi which was built on a site to the east of the present Wat Bowoniwet). The latter – and subsequently far more famous – *wat*, was constructed in 1822 on land next to Wat Rangsi, which eventually fell out of use. Except for the name of a group of monks' *kutthi* in the grounds of Wat Bowoniwet, there is nothing left to signify the existence of the earlier temple, except the name of the *trok* (Bowon-Rangsi) which runs behind the temple and which gives its name to a small neighbourhood which formerly comprised middle and low-ranking civil servants. The area first gained importance as the vicinity of Wat Bowoniwet (constructed during the reign of Rama III). It was here that Prince Monkut was Abbot for some 14 years (from 1837–51) before he assumed the throne. During that time Wat Bowoniwet became renowned as a leading centre of Buddhist scholarship and the home of the new Thammayut order of monks (this new order followed the more rigid strictures associated with Mon Theravada Buddhism) (Moffat 1961: 15–16).

From the beginning of its resettlement under the first Chakkri king, the Banglamphu area was marked by ethnic variety and a diversity of settlement functions. In this respect it was a microcosm of the city itself. Mon soldiers and their families settled around Wat Chana Songkhram after their return from the Burmese campaigns in the late eighteenth century. The Thai Muslims of the area can claim a history of continuous settlement since the foundation of Krung Thep. They decended from Muslims of Ayutthaya, and pre-dated the later settlement of the Pattani Malay war captives who were largely settled in outlying areas of the city and the central provinces.[4] They formed two groups, one located near the present day Surao Chakkraphong and another at Surao Ban Dukdin, close to their patron who was a Muslim naval commander favoured by King Rama I (Naengnoi 1991: 341–50). In the 1880s the single largest group of people living in the area were settled along the Banglamphu canal outside the city walls. Many of them were traders in food and other goods. Precursors to the land-based market established in the twentieth century, they lived on floating or stilted houses set into the canal banks. People living along the Banglamphu canal made up about a quarter of the whole population of this area of northern Rattanakosin. At this time, the people settled on the land in this largely amphibious city were clustered in groups linked together by small lanes and waterways. They were grouped around the households of the *nai*, near the temples, or along the *krok*, (another term for *trok*) – which had evolved from the pathways between the minor khlongs which interlaced the area. By this time even the Chinese – who were free of the *sakdina* system of servitude to superiors and the state – were operating small shops along various *trok*, including a section of what evolved into Khaosan Road ('the road of hulled rice') and along Sipsam Haeng, a street opposite Wat Bowoniwet. The Chinese comprised about a quarter of all household heads in the Banglamphu area. Lower level workers for administrative departments of the king (mainly at the level of *luang*) lived in wooden houses on land rented from Wat Chana Songkhram and Wat Bowoniwet. Muslim gold-leaf makers were prominent and lived close to the present day location of the two mosques (Surao Chakkraphong and Surao Ban Dukdin) of the area (Bangkok Postal Department 1883).

From the last decade of the nineteenth century Banglamphu began to undergo a transformation. Following settlement trends initiated by King Chulalongkorn in building palaces for his sons to the north of the old city wall in the new Dusit district, a number of the nobility established their palaces along today's Phra-Athit Road. This road followed the path just inside the dilapidated old city wall (parallel to the Chao Phraya River), turning at the decayed Phra Sumen fort to follow the route of the Banglamphu Canal. Parallel to Phra-Athit Road, Chakkraphong Road was built northwards as a continuation of the new Ratchdamnoen Nai, part of King Chulalongkorn's great project of building a royal thoroughfare from the palace to Dusit. As part of the same project, the wide avenue of Ratchdamnoen Klang separated the districts around Wat Chana Songkhram, Wat Bowoniwet and the Banglamphu market from Saochingcha (the area of the old Shiva swing). By 1910 Wat Bowoniwet had added its own contribution to urban change by building rows of income-generating shophouses along Tanao and Dinso Roads. This followed a general pattern in Bangkok whereby the urban *wat* used their land to enhance revenue, thus actively participating in urbanisation. At the centre of the changes was the expansion of the market area. In 1902, a private market was specially constructed on land just to the south of Phra Sumen Road by one of the nobility, an action which accelerated an existing trend for trading activities to move onto land. Banglamphu's three markets, Talat Yot, Talat Nana and Talat Turian became famous fresh produce markets in the city from that time.[5]

The boundaries of the neighbourhood settlements became more clearly defined by the new roads which began to enclose and screen the older *ban* settlements (except Ban Dukdin, which was cut in half by Ratchadamnoen Avenue later in the 1890s). From 1902–10 more shophouses – this time on royal land – were built at the corner of Phra Athit and Phra Sumen Roads parallel to the Chao Phraya riverline. They curved around the

Plate 4.1 The *trok* neighbourhood: shophouses screen a cluster of Thai wooden houses in Phra Athit Road. From an aerial photograph, 1946. (Photo: Courtesy National Archives of Thailand)

wooden houses of the Mon neighourhoods of Trok Kaechae and Trok Khieniwat. Notably, very few of these new masonry rowhouses were used as shops – they were occupied as residences by government servants, presumably because this area, close to new princely palaces, did not generate as much traffic and trade as anticipated. The process of urbanisation created another level of physical differentiation, between the brick shophouse (*tuk thaeo*) and the wooden home (*ban ruan*) and an entirely new configuration – the enclosed *trok* neighbourhood. This pattern has persisted until the present day, and is particularly evident in many of Bangkok's old inner districts. This process of 'enclosure' did not impose exclusion or segregation on the settlements – it was simply a physical pattern which tended to define more clearly pre-existing micro-zones of different activities and different groups of people.

Transformations

The market

As a trading site, a market area is more liable to experience outside influences and changes than predominantly residential settlements. Over the last fifty years changes in methods of selling have had a fundamental impact in the market area of Banglamphu. The first department stores of Banglamphu were small and did not really displace the small specialist shops at all. But gradually, the character of the shopping area did change. By 1960 gold shops were a major feature of the area, possibly linked to the gold craftmen of the neighbouring communities, but more clearly connected to the expansion of prominent branches of the Chinese gold businesses of Sampheng into this area of growing population. In the apparel business, more shops began selling ready-made clothes, formerly restricted to other markets in Bangkok and, conspicuously, the number of food vendors increased. This was partly due to the twin impacts of rural–urban migration and the growth of an informal sector of employment in the city as a whole. Already a landmark area of the metropolis with a name for general goods, fresh food and special home-made sweets (*khanom*), the Banglamphu market area attracted new entrepreneurs.

It was the building of the New World Department Store in 1982 that altered the face of Banglamphu as a market *yan* permanently. Not only did it attract more people to this area, but it displaced the fresh-market (*Talat sot*) traders, driving many to areas outside Banglamphu. Part of the old fresh market survives in an old market building opposite the New World Department Store, near the Nanarat Bridge, formerly a building devoted to *Like* performances. It is a paradox that a department store, symbol and institution of modern consumption and selling patterns, should bring about an expansion in the informal sector of vendors in Banglamphu, but this has in fact been the case. Expansion in the number of vendors in Banglamphu has taken place since about 1984, corresponding with the opening of the store and the resulting expansion in numbers of people attracted to the area for shopping (Yongthanit 1989: 64). This expansion also changed the composition of the vendors, who, before 1984, were primarily residents of the neighbouring areas. Talat Yot, the old covered market with some 150 stalls, had been surrounded by various vending enterprises for many years (Kiat *et al.* 1982: 411; Sternstein 1964: 156–8). Indeed, shoppers often preferred to buy their goods from the vendors directly outside the market because of the congestion inside. The New World Department store, located directly on this old site, has replicated this pattern, with vendors surrounding the building along Chakkraphong, Phra Sumen and Sipsam Haeng Roads. Recent studies show that there are around 850 vendors selling from stalls in the immediate area of the store. Some 65 per cent sell garments and 20 per cent sell food (Chomlada 1991:

Plate 4.2 The New World Department Store, located on the site of the old Talat Yot. (Photo: Author)

63–4). The store was completed and opened in the same year that building height restrictions were announced following the Rattanakosin Island Conservation Project. It took another ten years for the BMA to force the store to begin demolishing five of its top storeys in conformity with ministerial decrees. Overall, however, the advent of New World did not displace the earlier pattern of small-scale selling in the area.

Living places

The period after the Second World War marked a turning point in the history of the Banglamphu area, as it did for many settlements in Bangkok. After the war the population rose dramatically, while wealthier people moved away from the area. Local people identify this time as the years of the coming of the 'strangers' (*khon plaek na*) to their neighbourhoods, referring particularly to the people who moved from the countryside to find work in the city and rent rooms and houses in neighbourhoods. The close of the Second World War marked the beginning of irreversible changes to the lives of these people.

Until the 1960s, Ban Phanthom was still distinctive for the craftsmen and women who made bowls. The official *khet* name still reflects the persistence of this *yan* identity, which, like so many parts of Bangkok, was identifiable by the livelihoods of its inhabitants. Ban Phanthom covers the area between Chakkraphong Road on the west to Ratchdamnoen Nok on the east along the northern rim of the Banglamphu Canal (see Fig. 4.1.). The processes which eroded the former functional identity of Ban Phanthom are the same as those that account for the decline of the *ban* and *bang* of the old city generally – they are both economic and social and physical in character. In the post-Second World War years the advent of machinery and materials to produce cheaper metal drinking-bowls undercut the livelihood of the families of the area. By this time the production of bowls took place in workshops attached to the homes of families who followed a variety of occupations, but particulary the highly-favoured government service. The process of social mobility among the households of the workshop owners thus differentiated the population of the area. While the competition from the automated factories (in other areas of the city such as Thonburi and Sampheng/Yawarat) reduced the number of workshops in Ban Panthom, other pressures were affecting the craftspeople. Reduced in number and suffering because of contracting income, these people were increasingly forced to leave the area as land changed hands. Many of the workers rented their homes from the workshop owners and were vulnerable when the owners left Ban Phanthom. This was increasingly the case in the post Second World War period, when families of the old *phaya* and *luang* moved away, selling the old Turian gardens and banana plantations for the attractions of the expanding northern or eastern suburbs.

Some of the members of the old local elite still remain in the area, however. An example is the family of Khun Sa-ang Chawee, who lives in her 100-year old brick house built in the classical style by her great grandfather Chao Phraya Khuan Phetsena. The land faces Klong Banglamphu. Before this mansion was erected her grandfather lived in a teak Thai house which still stands in one corner of the large compound, which has another three houses for relatives. Yet the family now has no relationship with the surrounding neighbourhood. The new mass-produced manufacturing of cheap metal bowls for the consumer market undercut the economic nexus on which the patron–client ties of this locality were based. More expensive and exclusive bowls continued to be produced for an elite market. However, although the few remaining shops producing these luxury items owe their origins to local craftspeople, they provide little local employment in the area and they have no relationship to the Ban Panthom neighbourhoods. The occupations of most of the households in Ban Panthom are related to labouring, government service and small-scale services.

In what ways does the experience of Ban Phanthom compare with the other trok neighbourhoods? Consider, for example, the change occurring in Trok Bowon-Rangsi. Until the 1950s this area comprised relatively traditional wooden houses with Thai families of long standing. Most of the male household heads worked for the government in some capacity. The land was rented from Wat Bowoniwet on long leases, but the houses themselves were built by the the first leaseholders. Changes in the *trok* began occurring after the Second World War when numbers of older and better-off residents moved away to the growing suburbs and let their homes to tenants from up-country. Increasingly – and with the *wat* showing little concern – the area became congested. New wooden homes were built by leaseholders to house immigrants from the country, especially the north-east. But as long as the tenure pattern persisted, this neighbourhood could survive – even in its altered state – because many of the older residents still remained. They were either the poorer ones who could not afford to move their homes elsewhere, or they simply preferred to stay in the area where they had grown up. For example, Pa Daeng (now 68 years old) came as a child from Ayutthaya to live with her grandfather (a civil servant) who had built a compound house in Trok Bowon-Rangsi on land rented from the *wat*. The house was passed on to her when her grandfather died, but the land was still rented from the *wat* on a rolling lease. The lower floor of this old stilted Thai-style house was closed in by new cement walls to accommodate Pa Daeng's granddaughter. People asked Pa Daeng many times to rent the house from her in order to sublet rooms to workers – owners could receive as much as 1000 baht in rent per month – but she did not want to leave the neighbourhood.

Changes in institutional attitudes have affected the customary security of tenure, which was based not on contract, but on common understandings between the *wat* and the community. However circumstances in the changing environment of Bangkok are rendering these older understandings obsolete. Land is now too precious for many of Bangkok's *wat*, and demands for the uses of that land are gradually placing increasing pressure on older communities. In 1991 a fire broke out in Trok Bowon-Rangsi, destroying over 20 houses and leaving many people without homes, including Pa Daeng. The Wat Bowoniwet management seized this opportunity to prevent the rebuilding of houses (invoking BMA regulations applied to squatting and slum settlements). The management planned to wait for existing lease agreements to lapse; they would then implement a project to extend the sports grounds of the prestigious secondary school administered in connection with the *wat*. Residents were dumbfounded by this move, which undercut their security completely. By this time homeowners comprised the minority of dwellers in Bowon-Rangsi (only nine resident owners), and they were thus in a weak bargaining position because the renters were prepared to move to other areas in search of rental housing.

Residents faced a severe economic predicament because their houses were, in most cases, their only capital asset. Houses had been impossible to insure against fire hazards because of the crowded and fire-prone conditions of the neighbourhood. The *trok* was so narrow that when the fire broke out, the fire trucks could not enter. Pa Daeng, like her neighbours, lost everything. With their houses and other belongings destroyed, former homeowners could not accept the offer from the *khet* office for alternative accommodation at housing estates in Lat Krabang (30,000 baht down payment with monthly repayments of 780 baht for 15 years) or Thonburi (NHA houses for 483,000 baht). This neighbourhood, earmarked by the *wat*'s plan for demolition and the extension of the temple school, was destined to disappear, including the people and buildings in the *trok* whose land is owned by the *wat*. Five years after the fire the *wat* had still not implemented its project, and the residents who remained there, like Pa Daeng, rented homes from people in neighbouring lanes. Most left the area.

The monks of Wat Bowoniwet, who pass through Trok Bowon-Rangsi for alms every morning, showed no apparent interest in the peoples' plight. They probably knew little of the dire plight of the local people, some of whom were angry at the *wat* for its apparent indifference. For others it was difficult to be angry at such an entity, because it is a religious institution and the monks are respected. Nobody suggested organising a delegation to see the abbot of the *wat*, who also happens to be the Grand Patriarch of the Sangkha of Thailand. Wat Bowoniwet is not a local wat, it is a national centre of the Thammayut order and a place of scholarship and strict Buddhist practice since the days of King Mongkut. Rents are collected and finances managed by a special foundation, not an officer of the wat, a practice which has bureaucratised the relationship between *wat* and neighbourhood. Indeed there seems to be no close relation between the community and the *wat*. Some people make merit, i.e. make offerings to monks, at Wat Bowoniwet, but others go to other *wat* outside the area where they know particular monks; this is common practice among Thai Buddhists. Urban *wat* and their surrounding neighourhoods often contrast with rural Thai temple communities. In the former, the kin connection between monks and communitites is characteristically weak or non-existent because of the large number of monks who are outsiders to the local community. There is also a distinction to be made in the case of highly prestigious royal temples, such as Wat Bowoniwet, where local laity involvement is usually minimal (O'Connor 1978: 100–4). In the urban environment the connection between *wat* and community has been founded on a more basic and pragmatic coexistence: local people rented the *wat* land and the *wat* derived a nominal income. In the common case where *wat* land has been tenanted for many generations, there is a tacit expectation that residence will continue indefinitely. However, over the past few decades these understandings have changed. Tension between the *wat* and neighbouring tenant settlements have increasingly emerged over issues of land use as the *wat* administrations begin to treat their land as a valued commodity. The wat–neighbourhood relationship, formerly a key foundation of Bangkok's earlier urbanism of coexistence, is rapidly being eroded.

Ban Dukdin abuts the neighbourhood of Trok Bowon-Rangsi. Formerly a separate village, it now forms a contiguous settlement accessed through the appropriately-named Trok Dukdin, which was once a small canal. It has been made even more narrow by the settlement of squatters on one side of the *trok*. This is a Muslim settlement established during the reign of King Rama I. Ban Dukdin was once well-known for its goldsmiths and gold-leaf makers; today only two male household heads carry on this craft, while an elderly woman carries on the production of gold-leaf on a part-time basis. Younger members of these families are in professions or businesses unconnected with gold crafts. Nevertheless, neighbourhood bonds are strong due to continuity of residence, kinship ties and a common religious identity focused on the local mosque. Yet there is no strong sense of social division between the Muslims of Ban Dukdin, and the Thai Buddhists of Bowon-Rangsi. *Phi-nong kan* is the common expression used to characterise the cordial relations between the neighbourhood groups. There has been a history of intermarriage between the Buddhists and Muslims of the adjacent neighbourhoods which highlights close levels of inter-neighbourhood interaction over past and present generations.

In contrast with Trok Bowon-Rangsi, the land of Ban Dukdin is privately-owned by its Muslim residents. This has assured the persistence of the original neighbourhood's territory. Like Bowon-Rangsi, the *trok* is completely filled with houses, and very congested. In the late 1980s a fire destroyed over fifty of Ban Dukdin's old wooden houses. The owners – supported by the Islamic communities of Bangkok – were able to recover financially and rebuild their homes, most of them now in brick. Unlike the Trok Bowon-Rangsi neighbourhood, which lacked a leadership structure, the people of Ban Dukdin enjoyed a high level of organisation through their mosque and its Imam. The experience of the fire helped to galvanise the community of Ban Dukdin, whereas the later fire at Bowon-Rangsi demoralised the latters' residents. In Ban Dukdin, local people express a strong feeling of solidarity derived from the new awareness that they have been able to help themselves in a common crisis. The *Kammakan Ban* (chairman of the community committee) believes that Ban Dukdin is a better place to live in since the fire, both because of the security afforded by new brick buildings and the general confidence: 'The government had never helped us – we help ourselves', he states. Security of tenure in addition to communal coherence through religious traditions underly the persistence of Ban Dukdin as a 'place-based' community. Although the economic base of households has become diversified through occupational change, there is still a tendency for residents to stay in the area if they can. Locals say that residents who have moved away from close friends and relatives tell them stories of being particularly homesick, or *mai sabai chai*.

Ownership of land and a proven ability in self-help are not enough to resist the pressures of change in the urban environment. The BMA plans to cut a bypass connecting Dinso Road with Tanao Road and thence to

Khaosan Road, on land which the BMA owns or will soon purchase. Local people fear that this project will destroy the seclusion of the mosque and the community. The original Ban Dukdin was cut in half by Ratchdamnoen Avenue in the name of modernisation one hundred years ago and now the remains of that old *ban* settlement will again be carved up, this time in the name of bureaucratic efficiency. When I asked the *kammakan* and a group of his neighbours 'what should the authorities do for the community?', the response was unanimous: 'leave us alone'.

A study of the *trok* neighbourhoods highlights the importance of understanding the relationship between the city and the provinces. These urban communities did not exist in isolation but derived identity and nourishment from social networks which connected the people to the countryside. The membership of the Islamic communities of Ban Dukdin and Surao Chakkraphong were renewed through immigration and intermarriage with Islamic communities from the southern provinces and the Muslim settlements of Pathum Thani, north of Bangkok. In Bowon-Rangsi, the long-standing residents were linked to families in the central provinces. Some of the elderly women of that neighbourhood, like Pa Daeng, first came to the area as young girls from the central provinces, sent to live in the households of Bangkok-based relatives. The Thai and Mon *trok* communities' links with the provinces have disappeared with the aging of people and the movement of the population. The Muslim households of the Banglamphu area are still strongly connected with other communities through their continuing religious affiliations and intermarriage.

In Trok Khieniwat, the neighbourhood owed its origin to a group of Mon families who first settled there during the reign of Rama I. A generation ago there were some twenty households; now there are just seven families in this *trok* who can claim a Mon heritage, but only the older women can speak and understand the Mon language. Unlike some other Mon communities, the one settled at Trok Khieniwat was not linked to a handicraft or trade as in other parts of Bangkok. The original Mon were soldiers or sailors in the service of Rama I. The settlement of one neighbourhood of Mon was founded by a group of soldiers who were invited to live in the vicinity of the nearby Wat Chana Songkhram by their commander, the brother of Rama I, after the successful war against Burma. Another group comprised the retainers and relatives of a Mon admiral in the service of the king. In addition to the community in the immediate vicinity of Wat Chana Songkhram, another settled along today's Trok Khieniwat, Trok Phraya Woraphong and Trok Kaechae, in addition to households along Khaosan Road. The persistence of Mon ethnic identity has relied on the maintenance of the Mon language, customs of spirit worship and particular rituals and modes of Buddhist practice. But these were ultimately insufficient to prevent assimilation with the broader Thai Buddhist community. The households of Khieniwat maintained a special link with Wat Chana Songkhram through the Mon monks. Boys from Mon communities in other provinces came to this *wat* for ordination. Contacts between the Khieniwat community and the wider Mon group were maintained through contact at times of festivals and rituals, particularly Loi Krathong and Songkhran. These were times of reunion and contact between families. Through this process family linkages were maintained with the 'mother communities' outside Bangkok – in this case with the Pakret Mons. Connection with Pak Kret was crucial for continuity in the identity of this community through intermarriage and shared participation in religious rites. However the Mon identity of Trok Khieniwat is only a small remnant, with just one woman now keeping on the traditional practices of respecting the family *phi* (associated with totemic animal spirits). With occupations in the civil service and continued connection with Thai people, the Mon families intermingled with the Thai and in some cases the Sino–Thai. They lacked that strong underpinning of a distinct craft or family livelihood which reinforced identity with locality. Over a period of time the connections of the present neighbourhood with Pak Kret became distant, and with a high level of geographical mobility out of the area, the critical number of families necessary to ensure the level of ethnic coherence was reduced. For most of the families of the *trok* today, the fact of their Mon heritage is purely a curiosity; they consider themselves to be Thai. Nevertheless when Pa Net's elderly mother died two years ago, she made sure that all rites and rituals would be conducted according to the old Mon custom, with Mon monks, Mon music, and Mon dancing at the ceremony.

In contrast to the pressures on tenure which undermined the continuity of the Thai neighbourhods of Ban Phanthom and Trok Bowon-Rangsi, insecurity of tenure has never been a problem for Trok Khieniwat residents. Their land is crown land which their families have rented for generations and which they and their families have customary rights to occupy, and they remain in the area because it is convenient for them. Although the *trok* is crowded with very little space between the houses, the family homes are large and relatively spacious two-storey timber structures. Most households are supported by family members who work in government service. As in other communities of the area, younger family members move away on marriage or entry into the workforce, leaving behind them a progressively aging neighbourhood. Nevertheless, children frequently visit their families in the *trok* and there is a high level of interaction between neighbouring families. Small, family-run food stalls encourage a high degree of public sociability which is enhanced by a shared social and occupational background where there is no family which is either very poor or extremely wealthy.

Work and neighbourhood

The majority of residents in the neighbourhoods of the Banglamphu district were born outside Bangkok, with the greater number of these coming from the central provinces, but a substantial minority (over a third of all adults) were born in the area. While Banglamphu was a site for the settlement of up-country migrants in the post-Second World War years, most neighbourhoods today are places of long-term residents (mostly of over ten years standing), regardless of provincial birthplace. In occupational terms there is a wide distribution, encompassing the self-employed (mainly vendors) clerical workers, lower-level civil servants, soldiers and policemen. This occupational pattern indicates a notable level of continuity with earlier patterns in the area, although the decline of local craft workers (gold-leaf makers, jewellers and bowl-makers) is conspicuous. The largest single group of residents (over a third) are small-scale self-employed workers in the informal sector, engaged in shopkeeping in the *trok* or vending in the Banglamphu area. Most householders describe themselves as *khon thammada*, neither poor nor wealthy, and their occupational and income patterns bear this out.[6] The social hierarchy which once marked the area in pre-Second World War days is not so clearly discernible, and most residents (certain homeowners) tend to share broadly similar social status due to the considerable out-movement of the local well-to-do a generation earlier.

For the great majority of the self-employed (over 90 per cent) and over half of the unskilled workers who live in the surrounding neighbourhoods, the Banglamphu area is the focus of livelihood. Almost two-thirds of all householders in employment work in the Banglamphu area or a few kilometres beyond. This includes those residents (mainly men) who work as *kharatchakan* (civil servants) in the various government departments nearby. The home is often used as both a work place and living place, largely because women – who dominate among the district's vendors – use their homes for the preparation of the food they sell. Food-selling occurs both at the *trok* level and beyond, at the mouths of the alleyways and along the streets of the busy area around the market district. The district is an ideal location for maintaining a regular income from small-scale business. Along the *trok* branching from the international backpacker tourist thoroughfare of Khaosan Road, local vendors have adapted to a new market of foreigners. Many alternate between selling their standard Thai breakfast fare to residents in the early morning, then switching to selling items more palatable to young tourists such as fruit and less spicy food from early morning to afternoon.

Many residents of Banglamphu's neighbourhoods believe that there has been an increased population in their immediate living area over the past decade. This perception of increased crowding – set against the demographic reality that the population of the area is in fact declining – points to a process of 'densification' of individual settlements and uses. This is due to a number of factors, including: pressure on land by institutions for expanded functions; the increasing use of older residential building stock for tourist accommodation by owners of larger homes and the consequent increase in pedestrian movement through the *trok*; the emergence of small

Plate 4.3 Vendors selling food outside the New World Department Store. (Photo: Author)

informal settlements of the urban poor on vacant land and along the Banglamphu canal; and increasing use of some areas for cheap rental accommodation by outsiders. The building stock along these *trok* is generally old, with most of the timber homes built over twenty years ago and some much older, many of them in poor repair. In addition, there is a constant fear of fires breaking out in the narrow lanes of timber homes.

Yet what amounts to a sense of overcrowding and degeneration of the environment does not seem to overshadow local people's generally positive attitudes to the quality of social life in the *trok*. Notably, the majority of longer-resident household heads affirmed the importance of friendship networks as a key feature of their immediate environments, expressed in tangible practices of mutual help and sociability. This is most strongly expressed in the Muslim settlements clustering around Surao Chakkraphong and Ban Dukdin behind the Sino–Thai operated shophouses of the area's key thoroughfares, but it is also evident in *trok* such as Khieniwat, which have a strong continuity of residence. Long-resident local families also lend to some of these *trok* neighbours a strong sense of continuity and identity. So for example near Wat Sangwet, the Duriapanit family of musicians and their music school (which is conducted in the family home) forms a hub of local activity, linking other families who trace their lineage to performers of *Like*, for which the Banglamphu area was once renowned. Ritual also brings people together at the neighbourhood level. The annual custom of *thambun soi* (the laneway merit-making ceremony) is one such collective activity. Among the many Sino–Thai of the area, annual ceremonies in honour of market deities are also conducted near the site of the old Banglamphu Talat Sot. Here a temporary shrine was erected, and later a new one built, following displacement through the construction of the New World Department Store. To the north an annual ceremony still takes place near the site of the former Talat Nana which pays homage to a spirit of this old Chinese marketplace (the spirit of a Thai nobleman said to have drowned in the canal last century). Such ceremonies affirm the significance of place-connected social networks throughout the area.

We have viewed the Banglamphu district here from the perspective of the *trok* and the character of its functions as a *yan*, largely in relation to economic and social changes within the metropolis. However, the neighbourhoods of Banglamphu have become increasingly tied into broader changes affecting the Thai capital – notably the surge in overseas budget tourism. It is to this topic that we now turn.

Backpackers, local entrepreneurs and Khaosan Road

The hippie trail and Banglamphu: the end of the frontier

While the level of trading activity has increased in Banglamphu in response to urban population growth and economic diversification, the area has also taken on new functions in response to the changing relations of Bangkok with the outside world, notably through international tourism. In the mid-1970s the first westerners started to venture into the Banglamphu area in large numbers, in part because the Vieng Thai hotel, first established in 1962 for businessmen, was becoming known as an affordable hotel for budget travellers. Some adventurous local householders in the lanes off Khaosan Road offered cheap food and lodging to groups of young travellers, and the trend of development progressively escalated through the late 1970s, driven by word-of-mouth networks (Pimpaka 2000). Bangkok became an established stop on the expanding 'hippie route' extending from Afghanistan (Kabul) Nepal (Kathmandu) and India (Goa) through into Southeast Asia. From Bangkok these earliest budget adventure travellers could proceed to the as-yet undeveloped Thai islands of the Andaman sea (such as Phi Phi) or the Thai Gulf (Ko Samui).

The growth in importance of backpacker tourism in Bangkok was registered in the expansion of the guest house trade of the city, which offered cheap, no-frills accommodation. Guest houses were established near the Silom Area (Soi Ngam Du Phli) as well as Pratunam and Sukhumvit. By 1990 the trend of concentration was clear – around 70 per cent of all tourist-orientated guest houses in Bangkok were to be found in Banglamphu, particularly along Khaosan Road and its immediate vicinity, extending northwards into Thewet (Wilai 1991). Khaosan and its environs offered clear advantages to budget travellers: the rooms were cheap, and the accommodation was close to a number of central cultural attractions – for example, the royal palace – as well as the Chao Phraya River and its water ferry services. Ancilliary facilities attached to, or close by the guest houses – such as restaurants serving western food – were another advantage. Above all it was the pace at which an infrastructure of services evolved and the sheer concentration of backpacker travellers that gave the Khaosan precinct its attractiveness. The development of a budget travel industry in the west, complete with publications and accommodation guides (such as the Lonely Planet series), reinforced knowledge of the Khaosan area among the growing numbers of students and other young people seeking adventure in Asia.

By the 1980s Banglamphu and Khaosan were the acknowledged base of an increasingly important group of tourists in Asia. Classified in the tourist industry as backpacker tourists, they generally called themselves 'travellers' to distinguish their adventurous approach to travel from other tourists associated with package tours and luxury. Thus the author of the 1987 edition of the *Lonely Planet Guide to Thailand*, clearly identifying with these young travellers (as distinct from tourists), felt confident in denigrating other foreign accommodation precincts of Bangkok, such as Sukhumvit and Ngam Du Phli, as ghettoes, distinct from Banglamphu, which was apparently less invasive or offensive (perhaps because young travellers on budgets were not identified with sex-tourism) (Cummings 1987: 73). Yet even by this time, the core area of Khaosan Road, its character and the nature of its attractions contradicted this distinction. The pioneers of the hippie trail who had put Khaosan on the map were no longer its principal visitors. International youth travel had become a highly commercialised, and generally predictable, form of tourism with established routes, infrastructure and services. The facilities and environment of Khaosan developed to a point where it stood apart from its local Thai urban surroundings as a haven of a global youth culture with a social life of its own, one which was standardised and highly commercialised. It was a far cry from the frontier of an earlier generation of hippies in search of authenticity. Kane, a backpacker from Australia, highlighted this paradox to me one day:

> People insulate themselves in Khaosan Road, they drink iced coffee and pancakes and talk about Thailand and Thais as if they're across the other side of the world, but they *are* in Thailand . . . it's weird: we travel to go somewhere different, but end up somewhere the same.
>
> (interview with Kane Macintyre, backpacker, December 2000)

He was echoing the thoughts of the main character in the recent film *The Beach*, where, in an early scene set in Khaosan Road, Leonardo De Caprio

Plate 4.4 Khaosan Road: the backpacker thoroughfare with all conveniences. (Photo: Pitch Pongsawat)

bemoans the end of the travellers' frontier: '. . . everyone's got the same idea – we all travel thousands of miles just to watch TV and check into somewhere with all the comforts of home' (*The Beach*, 1999). Banglamphu, centring on Khaosan road, has become another foreign ghettho in Bangkok. The tie-died shirts, sandals and strange hair of young backpackers, far from being a cry of rebellion, are in one journalists' recent portrayal, simply 'the gray flannel suit of the budget traveller'. Similarly, the standardised features of this western comfort zone reflect the fact that the hippie 'Age of Discovery' has ended: 'all roads have been traveled and the words "remote" and "exotic" have all but lost their meaning' (Mydans 2001).

Banglamphu had developed outside the formal system of official Thai tourist promotion, which was geared to expensive package tours and established hotel and resort chains. It was only in the early 1990s that the Tourist Authority of Thailand began to monitor the budget tourist accommodation sector and commissioned studies began to acknowledge the economic importance of backpacker spending to the industry in Bangkok and well beyond (Thitinan and Fahn 1993). Other, less positive, aspects of Khaosan's impact were also gaining notice, particularly narcotics use among young travellers. While the area provokes varied responses from foreign and Thai commentators, the precinct centring on Khaosan Road is now an established feature of the city's landscape, and officialdom, in the guise of the TAT and BMA, have appropriated it into new programmes (such as the Songkhran, the Thai New Year festival) to enliven city life for both tourists and Bangkokians (Sirinya 2000). Paradoxically, this precinct has become a spectacle for Thais in their own country. Backpackers themselves describe Khaosan Road as 'the Zoo', highlighting how they have become an object of the Thai gaze.

Khaosan Road was already ripe for change by the mid-1970s, when the first hippies came to stay in the area. By the 1960s Khaosan had changed considerably from the time when it comprised a few wooden row houses and noodle shops with large homes of government officials and nobility. The number of restaurants had multiplied along the street, a response, no doubt, to the increasing population in the area as well as the location of the government departments along Ratchdamnoen Avenue which supplied the food shops with customers. In addition, characteristic businesses in Khaosan were tailoring and dressmaking shops (Sternstein 1964: 151–6). Yet, as old residents remark today, it was then an ordinary local street (*soi thammada*) with the usual services for a local area: some druggists, a doctor's surgery, and a barber's shop. Shops tended to face the street and residences (mostly wooden, or old brick free-standing dwellings of former well-to-do public servants) were accessible at the rear by means of the narrow *trok*. Older residents remaining in Khaosan Road reminisce that the area was once a quiet street of middle-class Thai educated families. Although the area was changing in the post-Second World War years, with wooden row houses being torn down for masonry shophouses, it could still maintain a neighbourhood character – today that is clearly no longer the case. Many old residents are not happy. They once shared a common occupational background in their work for the government service, and were connected through strong friendship ties and cooperation among families. When property began changing hands after the Second World War, the beginnings of new functions in the street were apparent, but it was not until the guest house and tourist business arrived that the street became truly transformed. Many people in the neighbourhood left their houses in Khaosan Road because of the increasing noise and traffic consequent on increased business activity drawn to the area by the young tourists. There are still many homes behind the shops that line Khaosan Road, but they are increasingly converted to guest houses or tourist-related businesses.

Khaosan Road is known to Bangkokians as *Thanon Farang Khaosan* (literally 'Khaosan, the street of Foreigners'). It is today identified directly with young foreign backpacker tourists, offering all the services that this group requires – including long-distance telephone calls, travel services, tailoring and a wide variety of international food. Guest houses, souvenir shops, trinket sellers, currency exchanges and accessory shops are dominant activities in the street. There is nothing Thai about the character of

Khaosan Road: everything is for the foreign backpackers – from the clothing to the jewellery to the food. Most local residents in surrounding neighbourhoods tend to keep the road at an arms length and do not claim a close identification with it, as they do with the nearby shopping area and New World Department store. However, the development of Khaosan Road and its vicinity as a distinctive foreign enclave has been very much a product of local entreprenuers. The guest house business they built forms the core of the infrastructure that supports the most significant foreign backpacker enclave in Southeast Asia. The following section investigates the characteristics of these operators and their businesses.

The guest houses of Banglamphu

The guest houses of Banglamphu represent both an important agent and a response to changes in the Banglamphu area and Bangkok generally. They are both a symptom of adaptive entrepreneurial activity among people within the locality as well as outside. From the later 1980s the guest-house precinct, once confined to Khaosan Road, expanded further north across Khlong Banglamphu, as well as eastward behind Ratchamnoen Avenue and west around Wat Chana Songkhram to encompass the area of Trok Kaichae and Trok Khieniwat. Guest houses are now a conspicuous feature of the local ecology and foreigners are a feature of daily life for local people in these lanes. A TAT survey of 1991 revealed that there were eighty-three guest houses with over 1,700 rooms in Banglamphu. It was estimated at this time that each year between 230,000 and 250,000 tourists came to stay in the area of Khaosan Road (Hobbs 1992; TAT 1991). By the end of the decade the number of guest houses in the street and its vicinity had increased to around one hundred (Surath 1999).

The following data are the results of a survey of fifty guest houses in the Banglamphu area. This survey aimed to ascertain the extent to which these enterprises constitute a development from within the locality itself, or a process stimulated by entrepreneurs from outside the locality. It also

Table 4.3 Guest house types and years in operation, Banglamphu

Type of structure	*Years in operation*				
	1–2	*3–5*	*5–10*	*> 10*	*T*
Wooden house	6	3	5	1	15
Shophouse	11	8	3	—	22
Specially built	2	6	—	—	8
Other buildings*	3	1	—	—	4
Total	22	18	8	1	49

Source: Author's survey 1991.

Note
* Commercial buildings or detached brick houses.

Table 4.4 Number of rooms and employees by type of guest house proprietor

Type of proprietor	*Total employees*	*Average no. of employees*	*Number of rooms*	*Average no. of rooms*	*Total guest houses*
ERes	88	4	333	15	22
NRes	52	4–5	323	29	11
N	55	4	332	24	14

Notes
ERes = Established resident of Banglamphu (over 5 yrs) living in GH.
NRes = New resident of Banglamphu (less than 5 yrs) living in GH.
N = Non-resident proprietor (living other premises and/or outside Banglamphu).

attempts to determine the scale and characteristics of the guest houses as enterprises and their role in providing opportunities for local householders.

Most of the earliest guest house proprietors were residents and home-owners before establishing their businesses. They converted their own wooden homes by upgrading and creating new rooms for guests. In general, the earliest guest houses maintained only a small number of rooms, but more recently arrived proprietors in the district tend to operate larger establishments. It appears that the majority of the older established residents who began a guest house business use it as their sole source of income. More than half of the proprietors who have lived in the district five years or less have other incomes in addition to the guest houses. This may be because they are younger in contrast to the longer-serving residents, some of whom were already retired when they commenced business; but it may be due to a more entrepreneurial attitude, and reflect the second phase of the guest house industry in Banglamphu.

While some guest houses surveyed began operation from the early 1980s, the majority were established in the later years of that decade. This is a clear expression of the pace of change in the Banglamphu area and the significant expansion of international backpacker tourism. The second wave of guest house proprietors (mid to late 1980s) utilised shophouses as well as private houses, while the third phase (late 1980s–early 1990s) signalled the beginning of investment from people outside the Banglamphu area, including a number of partnership arrangements among young professional people. Larger-scale investment enabled the construction of larger, multi-storeyed guest houses with better dining and leisure facilities for guests. While recently opened guest houses are generally larger, the number of employees does not seem to grow substantially with the increase in size of the guest houses. Direct employment in guest house businesses has evidently not greatly increased employment opportunities in the area. The small guest houses rely primarily on family labour. However the expansion of services – in both formal and informal sectors – which cater to the needs of young backpackers has been notable. As well as the restaurants, trinket shops, travel agencies and photo shops, internet cafes have grown rapidly from 1997 onwards. Khaosan Road itself has now reached the limits of its capacity.

Competition among guest houses and other businesses in Khaosan Road has increased markedly over the last few years. The greater number of proprietors interviewed in 1991 admitted to feeling that there were already too many guest houses in Banglamphu. Competition is high in the peak months of October to February, when most of the foreign tourists come to Bangkok. By the end of the decade there were even more establishments and competition among them was fierce. The glut in guest houses is a phenomenon typical of the patterns of tourist infrastructure development in Bangkok, where conformity and duplication dominate investment decision-making. It can be seen in other subsectors ranging from luxury hotels to dancing bars. Even the most recent initiative of internet cafes has succumbed to this trend. Various strategies have been adopted to meet the increasing challenges of competition. Establishments providing multiple facilities often have an advantage over the more basic 'Ma and Pa' establishments. Yet again, backpackers preferences differ, and some prefer the small and quiet establishments further away from Khaosan Road. A large number of the guest house operators report that they rely on regular customers, highlighting one advantage of smaller-scale enterprises and the importance of personal involvement in the business by the proprietors.

The development of *Thanon Farang Khaosan* and its environs of Banglamphu is a phenomenon of local peoples' adaptation in the changing economic environment of the city. Well over half the owners of Banglamphu guest houses lived locally before establishing their businesses, which shows that the impression that guest house owners are outsiders is wrong. Running guest houses is often a supplementary income earner for owners, whose family members help to operate the establishment after their regular work hours. However, the increasing competetiveness is forcing many owners to become more entrepreneurial and invest more money into upgrading facilities. In the early 1990s there were reports that some businesses were becoming too large and demanding for single families to manage, leading to more corporate involvement in these enterprises. The evidence, however, does not support this view of wholesale transformation towards large-scale businesses, perhaps with the exception of Khaosan Road itself. Behind Khaosan Road, which has become a 'sea of neon signs and aluminium facades', small family businesses continue to survive (Hobbs 1992). Since the 1980s, the growth of the guest house business has moved far beyond Khaosan Road itself, leading to a differentiation of tourist-related areas. This differentiation through growth can be monitored in the Lonely Planet budget tourist guides. In 1987 the entry for guest houses highlighted Khaosan Road, Phra Athit Road and a few neighbouring *trok*, in addition to some guest houses scattered in Samsen to the north. Ten years later, however, the growth in guest house accommodation was such that the author had to subdivide the area into north, south, west and east Banglamphu in addition to its northern extension towards Thewet (Cummings 1987: 75–7; Cummings 1997: 199–206). Khaosan Road functions as the key thoroughfare and service centre of a widely dispersed district, yet its garish commercialism is not representative of the many quieter *trok* where guest houses operate and offer a more homely environment for tourists.

The Banglamphu area represents the process of differentation in the tourist spaces of Bangkok. The age and income profile of the tourists who flock to this much-acclaimed budget-priced mecca is distinct from that of the foreign tourists who reside in the higher-priced areas of Silom and Sukhumvit. Eighty-two per cent of these tourists are between the ages of 15 and 34 years, and they spend an average of 580 baht per day, which is half the average spending of foreign tourists to Thailand. The Banglamphu area is also distinct from precincts such as Sukhumit, because foreign prostitution and sex-orientated entertainment is absent. The sexual activities that take place involve foreign tourists, and Thai visitors are explicitly barred from guest-house rooms. Khaosan and its environs reflect the mores of a modern international youth culture, focusing on parties and often involving drug use. It is a place for networking and recreation among a highly mobile young population who use it as a base for travels to other destinations in Thailand and the region. As a leisure precinct it has undergone considerable change towards commercialisation, with specialist pubs and music bars emerging on Khaosan Road. This reflects the increasing disposable income of the average backpacker. Local residents and those who work in Khaosan show an ambivalent attitude towards these foreigners. On the one hand there are Thais who disapprove of young tourists' informal and strange dress, weird hairstyles and often assertive manners, but there is a degree of relaxed and easy interaction among Thai staff and their clients in the guest houses and shops of the area. To some observers this small precinct appears to be a cultural travesty – an introspective Farang comfort zone in a Thai city. One Thai journalist recently offered this comment:

> Is Khaosan an idyllic community of Asia voyagers or a traveler's dystopia . . . it's been nearly twenty years since Khaosan Road was – if actually it ever was – a community of young Thais and foreign travelers, looking out for and learning from each other. Today, Khaosan is a caricature.
>
> (Ling 2000: 29)

Negative portraits of Khaosan Road as a cultural travesty abound, but for many it is a new and positive space. A recent trend has been for young Thai professionals and students to frequent the area to sample the relaxed lifestyle and amenities, or to meet young foreigners and practice the English language in an informal social setting. For many young Thais in contemporary Bangkok, Banglamphu and Khaosan Road represent a cosmopolitan zone ('a permanent exhibition of alternative world society'), where they can escape temporarily from their own cultural environment (Smith and Anusorn 1999). George, an English backpacker, commented positively on this cosmopolitan character, observing: 'Where else but Khaosan Road could you see an Italian teaching the Australian Didgeridoo to a Thai university student' (Interview with George Harvey, backpacker, December, 2000).

Conclusion

The experience of Banglamphu dicussed in this chapter shows that processes of change in the inner city are influenced by local, historical and international dynamics. Despite considerable change in the economy and spaces of the city, the inner areas of Bangkok still host a mix of groups who have inherited various tenures and locations. The degree to which they are pushed out by eviction or changing trends of land use, or pulled by the attractions of less congested living in the outer districts, depends on the mix of opportunities and benefits deriving from incomes and environments. The coexistence among groups and institutions which was a major characteristic of the old Bangkok is becoming precarious in the face of varied pressures on land and the changing demands on inner-city areas. However, some local neighbourhoods still manage to persist, finding viable livelihood opportunities to support households, while at the same time maintaining significant social networks and enjoying security of tenure. Together with this pattern of local life, Banglamphu's traditional role as a famous market centre continues, drawing shoppers to its well-known specialist stores and in search of bargains. In the 1970s Banglamphu's location, character and householders were favourably positioned to benefit from an increasingly important segment of international tourists – young budget travellers. Today, the Khaosan Road precinct in the Banglamphu area hosts a young foreign tourist subculture that is distinctive from other tourist areas in Bangkok. Ironically, this distinctive precinct (now nearly thirty years old) has become another of Bangkok's patchwork of named places, coexisting within an inner city area still marked by multiple and multilayered functions, albeit in transmuted form.

5 Genealogy of the slum

Pragmatism, politics and locality

Introduction: representing the slum

In September 1991, Bangkok played host to the World Bank/International Monetary Fund Conference. The venue was the newly-built Queen Sirikit Conference Centre in downtown Ratchadaphisek Road. As the prospering centre of the newly-dubbed 'Fifth Tiger' of the Asian economies, Bangkok was to be displayed to the world as the quintessential contemporary city (Bello, Cunningham and Li 1998: 43). A key measure in choreographing this display of modernity was to hide the slums which abutted the convention centre. The Sirikit Centre had been constructed on government land abutting the squatter slum settlement of Duang Phitak, which the authorities had been unable to evict in time for the conference. Across the wide new road which had sliced this settlement in half six years earlier, the Phaisingto slum also remained. Unable to clear the surroundings of the centre completely before the conference commenced, the authorities compromised with a makeshift strategy – new walls were constructed to obscure these unsightly habitats of the poor. Local and visiting foreign journalists were quick to report this ironic contrast between the sumptuous conference venue and the surrounding ecology of poverty (Pilger 1992: 210). In protest against this effort to negate their presence, Phaisingto residents painted the walls with brightly-coloured murals. Conference organisers hid the murals with lines of buses (*Nation* 3 October 1993: 21). In another affront to the doctrines of market-led development, an alternative Peoples' Forum was held at Chulalongkorn university, featuring foreign and local NGOs and community representatives who spoke on the contrasting goals of communities as against the market-driven logic of state-led development projects (Vitoon 1991).

These events in Bangkok symbolised a decade of change which saw the emergence of an assertive and broadly-based 'peoples movement', charged with the ideology to support the claims of the poor to development on their own terms. In the urban arena, the number of NGOs had expanded, drawing on local and international donors to develop a wide range of community-based organisations (or CBOs) in Bangkok's slums, aiming to foster self-help and solidarity. Such developments were derived from global networks of NGOs. Assertive representations of the urban poor, and slum-dwellers in particular, have been a necessary ideological tool in the intensifying conflicts over urban land in a booming metropolis. But do they correspond with the realities of slum-dweller's lives? Akin Rabibhadana has demonstrated how the extensive literature and public discourse on slums in Bangkok has generated a range of representations which have simplified a complex and varied social formation (Akin 1999: 305–19). The grass roots development discourse presents a portrait of cooperative and equally poor low-income households joined together in the task of collective and sustained betterment for income and environmental improvement, joined by NGO partners in the task of advocacy for securing a durable tenure. In this view a community can be 'built'. It can also be 'broken', but generally by outside forces and enemies of 'the people', such as corrupt community leaders. Specialists on low-income housing settlements have been disappointed when slum-dwellers have made pragmatic and individual decisions to sell their housing plots and return to congested settlements in the inner city. This gives rise to another definition of slum-dwellers, as individualistic opportunists, who, like their urban middle-class counterparts, buy and sell land resources for profit in the marketplace (Yap and Angel 1992: 69–70). Yet another long-held stereotype (in literature on slums in the Asian region as well as Thailand) is that of the tightly integrated 'face-to-face' society, characterised by bonds of kinship, mutual friendship and close emotional links to a local area (e.g. Jocano 1975; Nithet 1987; Thai University Research Associates 1976: 129). This representation of the 'community of the poor' is a standard image employed by organisations such as the Duang Prateep Foundation of Khlong Toei and media allies in efforts to galvanise public support (in Thailand and internationally) to oppose slum eviction.

In this chapter I take up Akin's suggestion that it is more appropriate to study slum-dweller's practices than to attempt to reduce them to the simple classifications: communities or not-communities (Akin 1999: 306). Poverty in the contemporary Thai metropolis takes a range of forms, and arguably a focus on slums excludes the most desperate of the urban poor – particularly rising numbers of 'street children' (see e.g. Somphong 1997). Nonetheless, the slums are a particularly conspicuous reflection of inequality in Bangkok and its surrounding urban region. I present an interpretation of the slums of the metropolis as multilayered economic, social and spatial formations, spaces of survival, accumulation, status and inequality. I draw the general themes together by focusing on the 'slum' of Khlong Toei, highlighting its paradoxical role in contemporary Bangkok: as the least typical settlement of the urban poor (a 'rich' slum), yet the source and lynchpin of the assertive and politicised slum movement – a site of conflict and factionalism which expresses much about the political economy of urban space in contemporary Bangkok.

Economy of the slum – economy of the city

As elsewhere in Southeast Asia, the slums of Bangkok have been defined by the state, planning agencies and housing specialists in ecological, environmental and legal terms as congested settlements located on poorly serviced land with insecure tenure. Their functions and process of growth are, however, better encompassed in the broader term 'informal settlements', which highlights the processes of their growth through the occupation of space and its negotiation. Slum growth in Bangkok has been fuelled by the persistent imbalance between urban and rural sectors, the inability of the state and market to provide affordable shelter for low-income groups, and the reliance of the urban economy on cheap unorganised labour and services. This statement may suffice as a broad portrait, however it is unrealistic to equate the slums completely with the urban poor, or with the informal sector which is typically associated with their livelihoods. Nor can slum growth be attributed simply to rural–urban migration. In 1991 there was a population of one million people living in congested settlements in the BMR, yet less than 208,000 people were estimated to be living below the official poverty line (TDRI 1991: 91–1). Estimates of 'poor' households in the slums range between proportions of twenty to forty-three per cent (NESDB 1986: 21; Sopon 1992: 68). A significant proportion of slum households earn incomes in ranges comparable with averages for households living outside the slums (see Nanak and Medhi 1996).

In slums there is a spectrum of economic status, including households struggling to meet bare subsistence needs, those who are relatively more secure (or 'relatively poor') and those who are clearly well-to-do (see, e.g. Orathai and Kusol 1994: 41). Income averages and distributions vary considerably between slums of different sizes, ages and locations. A large proportion of slum households are marked by lack of education and unskilled, vulnerable occupations which are an ongoing product of structured inequalities in Thai society (Douglass and Zoghlin 1994: 171–3). While not exclusively settlements of the most marginal of the urban poor, the slums host a substantial group of the city's low-income earners.

Studies of the urban occupations of slum-dwellers and their income sources show a high level of diversity. In some settlements government or semi-government authority workers comprise well over 10 per cent of all male household heads (Nibhon *et al.* 1983: 65; Sopon 1985: 43). General labouring work in the private sector (or *rap chang*) is the most common occupation, with between fifty to sixty per cent of male slum household heads following this type of semi-skilled and unskilled employment (Sopon 1985: 43; Sungsit and Somchai 1996: 98; TDRI 1991: 109). It is common to find that wage-earning occupations in the formal sector are related to work places in nearby localities (Askew 1998: 12; Igel 1992: 9, 20). Slum households generate income from a wide range of micro-enterprises now commonly referred to as 'informal sector' enterprises, defined as economic enterprises established outside the legal framework of registration, involving few formal skills and qualifications, and primarily maintained by family labour. The role of the informal sector in generating employment among the urban poor has been widely noted, but only relatively recently has the integral connection between the urban informal sector and its important contribution to the urban economy been emphasised in relation to urban consumption, production and recycling of goods (ESCAP 1993: 5-5; Romijn 1993; Sungsidh and Somchai 1996: 102–6). Occupations in informal sector enterprises span the sectors of services (particularly transportation and rubbish recycling), trade in food, and manufacturing (including subcontracting of piece-work) and repair. Most informal enterprises are directed towards the urban consumer market outside slum communities, either in the immediate localities surrounding settlements or further afield.

Slum households commonly combine involvement in both informal and formal sectors, which offer complementary sources of income in an overall strategy of survival. Income from wage work often funds investment in informal sector activities, while informal sector work can also be a part-time activity of household wage-earners. Barbara Igel's study of three slums in different districts of Bangkok showed that 54.8 per cent of households earned incomes from both sources, while Rudiger Korff's research in Khlong Toei concluded that 53 per cent of households combined both

Plate 5.1 Making do in the city: a home in a slum settlement, Bangkum district (northeast Bangkok). (Photo: Author)

modes of income generation (Igel 1992: 10; Korff 1986a: 282–3). The slum settlements themselves are also the sites of entrepreneurial activities (TDRI 1991: 113–14). The slums can therefore be characterised both as key locations for households engaged in the urban economy generally as well as spaces of economic transactions, or consumer micro-markets. They are more than simply residential quarters. Considered in terms of the livelihoods of their households, they are products of the strategies of low-income groups to position themselves in the labour, consumption and production sectors of the metropolis and the neighbourhood surrounding them. The slums are also sites of income generation linked to internal social and economic resources. Even if informal sector workers sell their goods outside the slums, the home itself constitutes an important site of production, or preparation, in the case of food selling. More than this, social resources and networks play an important role in supporting family enterprises, not only in the provision of labour assistance and work contacts for casual labourers, but for forms of supplementary income and informal sources of credit. The multiple advantages of the home and neighbourhood in the pursuit of livelihood is the reason for the persistent reluctance of slum-dwellers to live in the flats and housing estates offered by housing agencies (see, e.g. Thai University Research Associates 1976: 126).

Accumulation, inequality and dependence

If the slums constitute a space of social reproduction in the urban economy, they are also spaces of accumulation and inequality. From their earliest period, slums have been diverse social formations marked by internal differentiation. This reality led Rudiger Korff to modify his definition of the Bangkok slum as the 'worker's quarters' of the city to the description: 'the living area of the lower to lower-middle class in the city' (Korff 1986a: 232). Well-located slums offer agglomeration economies for both better-off and poor households in terms of multiple income sources, benefits that are less available (and certainly more expensive) in other parts of the city. There is a common distinction between houseowners and house renters. For slum-dwellers with large enough homes, renting space to others was an important means to gain increased income. There are also large landlords who have become enriched by accumulating the homes of indebted and impoverished neighbours. Yet the characterisation of slum social systems as exploitative (Sopon 1992) may well be oversimplified.

Slums are spaces of accumulation. One of the key bases of this accumulation is the valuation and use of housing rights as a commodity which, in turn, is a fundamental source of inequality within slum settlements. As others have noted, settlement in slums, even squatting slums, is never free (Berner 1997: 69). Slum-dwellers occupy homes on the basis of purchasing housing rights (*kammasit*, or *sit*) in an invisible real-estate

Plate 5.2 The beginnings of an informal land market: concrete posts mark the claims of the first arrivals for housing rights in a new slum. (Photo: Author)

system regardless of the legal tenure status of individual settlements. This exists as a system of space allocation in newly settled slums, but at its heart is a commodity valuation which allows assets (however humble) to be accumulated and sold for income generation (Smart 1986). In small slums housing rights cost around 30,000 baht, but in large settlements housing rights now cost up to 500,000 baht. This mode of allocation is defined by one researcher as a 'popular form of allocation' (Nopadon 1995: 79–81) which only holds as a definition because it denotes a system accepted by popular custom, not because resources are commonly distributed or shared. In fact, there is really little to distinguish this system from capitalist modes in terms of valuations of settlement space, since they are both commodified with prices sensitive to market availability.[1]

Sociability and reciprocity

If pragmatic strategies of survival and accumulation inform the value which slum-dwellers assign to their settlement space, they are not the only valuations. People rarely entered the slums as individuals, nor do their households exist in isolation. A significant proportion (particularly women) came to join, or accompanied their families to these settlements (see e.g. Chira *et al.* 1971: 71; Nibhon *et al.* 1983: 31). In both small and large settlements, networks of relations of varying kinds establish a social space. In this space, the imperatives of sustaining livelihood and patterns of sociability are often mutually reinforcing. Social networks are built around a range of activities, including mutual cooperation in tasks of home-building, assistance in finding work, the borrowing of money, the taking care of children and the watching of houses (*fao ban*) (Korff 1986a; Nopadon 1995: 220–5; Sharhand, Tekie and Weber 1986: 74–5). These networks and relations, patterned over time, are often expressed by slum-dwellers to describe their neighbourhoods in positive terms such as closeness (*phukphankan*), cooperation (*mi kanruammu*), helping (*kanchuaikan*), or togetherness (*mi khwamsammakkhi*). The positive social valuation of slum space as a locus of mutuality and identification between households is primarily due to the sociability and activities of women. Daily patterns of social interaction are dominated by the women of the slums, whose dominant roles in childcare and domestic maintenance (cooking, cleaning) are based in their own neighbourhoods. So too are many of the income-generating activities which women carry on to either fully support or supplement the incomes of their households through work and loan circles (Sharhand, Teckie and Weber 1986: 9). Generalising from her own research experience in Khlong Toei, Susanne Thorbeck argues that women in fact produce a distinctive slum culture which derives from their multiple patterns of interaction (Thorbeck 1987: 152).

Although intense patterns of interaction and mutuality are a significant feature of slum life, it does not follow that such sociability incorporates whole settlements. The fragility of these relationships is in fact a feature often remarked on by slum people themselves. Slum-dwellers will often use the expression *tang khon tang yu* 'everyone for themselves' to describe the privatised attitudes of themselves and their neighbours in these settlements. As with the assumption of homogeneity of material status, the assumption of communality as applied to slum societies is an oversimplification.

The contingency of community – locality and bargaining for space

In a recent study of slum mobilisation in Manila, Erhard Berner proposes 'the locality' as a key framework to understand the sociospatial relationships underlying group identity among the urban poor. Localities, he argues, are 'socially defined and created spatial entities'. In defining localities as emerging from social practice (everyday life strategies), Berner suggests a fruitful way of understanding the dynamic relation between the way of life of the urban poor and their environment, one which emphasises their agency in making and claiming places in the city. A key dimension of localities, in this definition, is that they are products of collective agency in the guise of locally-based organisations (Berner 1997: 57–8).

His argument has also been applied to Bangkok (Berner and Korff 1995: 217–19). It is not specific communities, but the span of organisational activity across urban space which gives to groups a collective identity. However, there is a danger that this definition simply replaces one essentialism (the natural slum community) with another (the organised locality), while reproducing the myth of resistance and its basis in collective consciousness.

In Bangkok the emergence of slums as organised localities, has developed through the increasing intervention of the state as well as a reformist middle class – in the guise of academics, specialists and NGOs – in response to concerns for social, environmental and housing conditions in the slums. Prompted first by the prominent social reformer and acknowledged father of the NGO movement in Thailand, Dr Puey Unkpakorn, the Faculty of Social Administration of Thammassat University conducted surveys in some of Bangkok's largest slums, drawing attention to the education and health needs of slum children (Chira *et al.* 1971: xv–xvi; Suthy 1995: 99–100). Funding and publicity from international organisations such as UNICEF spurred local agencies to establish health centres and created an environment where slum-dwellers' needs for basic services such as water and electricity could be addressed officially. By the late 1970s a new system of temporary house registration allowed increasing numbers of slum children to enter government schools. During the brief period of parliamentary democracy (1973–6) more concerted and sympathetic attention to housing and welfare issues led to the BMA introducing a system of slum community committees which could act as intermediaries between households and agencies for basic services such as water and electricity supply. Some settlements such as Khlong Toei had already developed a system of committees earlier in the decade to fight eviction; in contrast, the BMA system was principally an administrative mechanism. By 1982, the BMA and National Housing Authority (NHA), formalised and extended this system by establishing regulations for committee elections (Nalini *et al.* 1998: 52). With UN funding, the NHA began a programme of slum upgrading, involving repair and improvement of walkways in slums. From 1980 the inauguration of local parliamentarians' development funds enabled the establishment of facilities such as day care centres and local health clinics in a number of slums. As a result of these trends, the appearance of slums began to change, albeit unevenly and in the context of continuing tenure insecurity. The increasing formalisation of slum management and availability of services sustained a greater confidence in some of the larger slum settlements, and laid the foundations for more concerted bargaining in the future. Paradoxically, emerging state initiatives for the provision of facilities, basic infrastructure and resettlement were set against an increasing trend towards slum eviction in the inner city (Somsook 1983).

The significant change by the mid-1980s was a new institutional environment within which slum-dwellers (sometimes collectively, but mainly at the level of the household) negotiated the city as survival space. In this context slum households were not passive, and they exploited whatever opportunities emerged to translate resources to immediate advantage. They often ignored calls to participate if local upgrading projects had no immediate bearing on their quest for security and livelihood. NHA alternative urban housing projects were utilised by slum households in ways that officials and the increasing numbers of housing specialists had not foreseen. Thus, new flats constructed for low-income groups quickly changed hands as the poor sold occupation rights to better-off Bangkokians (with the clandestine cooperation of NHA officials). Resettlement sites suffered the same fate.[2] Land-sharing achieved a degree of popularity in planning circles from the late 1970s and formed the basis of several successful efforts among slum settlements to collectively bargain for space. In most cases, while they had revealed a considerable organisational capacity on the part of local community committees, the projects also exposed divisions among residents and the different interests of renters, owners and squatters (Jensen 1989b). Moreover, after land sharing, many original owners sold their rights and moved away.[3] Many of the realities about slum life were bound to disappoint idealists.

The critical change from the mid-1980s was the expansion of NGO activities in community development and anti-eviction activities, accompanied by more concerted and organised forms of lobbying and publicity of slum-dwellers' problems. A number of key trends had a tangible influence in slums in this period. Depicted variously as the emergence of slum solidarity, localities and new weapons of the weak, these changes hinged upon the cultivation of slum leaders and the encouragement of community-based organisations (CBOs). They have been depicted as critical transformations in the consciousness of the urban poor, both in ideology and organisation (Ockey 1996, 1997). But the process has been more complex than this. While there have indeed been fundamental changes in the slums attributable to the NGO presence, they need to be viewed more as the appropriation by slum-dwellers of a new rhetoric and set of methods towards forwarding pragmatic goals of acquiring land, security and status than a transformation in consciousness towards NGO ideals of local democratisation and sustainable development.

In the 1980s a number of NGOs emerged whose approach to working in slums was distinguished by an emphasis on participatory development, empowerment and network building as opposed to the welfare-based approaches of earlier NGOs and international agencies. The Human Settlements Foundation (HSF) was a key group in defining this new approach. In Bangkok the HSF focused on fostering community-based organisations and empowerment through self-reliance and sustainable local development (Somchai 1987: 33; Pratt 1993: 41). Notably, the first projects of the HSF involved working with slum settlements under threat of eviction through assisting them in bargaining for higher compensation from landowners. A key strategy was to establish savings groups which channelled funds towards the purchase of new land, chosen through the assistance of the NHA. By the 1990s, the idea of savings groups and housing cooperatives was widely accepted.[4]

Thai writers on the Bangkok slums have pronounced the last decade as one of '*kansuanruam*' (togetherness/cooperation) within slum settlements due to the grass roots methods of NGOs (Nalini *et al.* 1998). The question as to whether NGOs such as HSF and a number of its successors have been able to catalyse an enduring community-conscious grass roots leadership and foster autonomy has been raised by recent studies. Some have pointed to the role of NGOs as necessary and permanent intermediary institutions between low-income communities and the state, in contrast to the radical ideal that NGOs are empowering agencies which will eventually wither away (see e.g. Lee 1998). The existence of strong, weak, united or divided communities is tied to circumstances and settlement histories, but the more important question here is how the slums (as social formations) and slum-dwellers (as agents) have incorporated the ideals and methods and language introduced by NGOs.

One evident outcome of the slum–NGO encounter has been that group identification, when it is mobilised, is ultimately tied to leadership. It is clear that the principle of elected communities and a formalised division of labour among community members has actually been incorporated into

Plate 5.3 NGO workers assist at a savings group meeting at the Sammakkhi Phatthana slum. (Photo: Author)

the internal social organisation of these societies. While evidence shows the emergence of organisation and the important role of local slum leadership in advancing claims of people to survival space and legitimacy, it is worth noting that the majority of slum settlements (an estimated 61 per cent) do not in fact have elected committees, and thus many households have still not gained the housing registration which facilitates access to the basic facilities of public water and electricity supply (NHA 1990: 51). NGO involvement and local organisation in the slums of Bangkok and its region is thus very uneven.

The strategies of NGOs and slum-dwellers both meet and diverge in the process of local development. In 1996 and 1997 I studied a number of Thai NGOs and their activities in both small and large slums in Bangkok, observing and interviewing ordinary slum residents and their interaction with NGO activists. The outstanding feature of the NGO workers was their commitment to listening to people and focusing on practical issues of concern to initiate projects. NGO workers have a keen understanding that slum people only respond to projects of immediate and practical concern, and therein lies the success in the relationship and a vindication of the Thai radical tradition of social development work born in the 1970s. For example, in the span of a two-year relationship between the Training Centre for the Urban Poor (TCUP) (run by a former leader of the HSF) and the people of Chumchon Sammakkhi Phatthana, the community gained house registration, concreted their walkways, built a meeting shelter, acquired funding for a day-care centre for children and established a savings group.

To some extent the TCUP could claim continuing success: it had nurtured a committed local leadership, and the language of *kanphatthana* (development) and *kanruammu* (cooperation) had entered the daily vocabulary of all committee members. But here the convergence of interests seemed to end. The broader goals of the NGO to foster democracy and social change through consciousness-raising and networking faltered in the face a number of enduring behavioural and attitudinal patterns among people in the slum. The NGO leader summarised these in his own work diary and labelled them as 'Personality characteristics of slum people which are obstacles to development work' (Somchai 1997). The key points included:

- A persistent belief in *wenkam* (personal fate) to explain misfortune
- An acceptance of government authority and respect for officials
- An acceptance of *phuyai* and *phunoi* (hierarchy) and *lukphi/luknong* (patron–client) relations
- People don't listen to those of equal or lower status than themselves
- Love of independence (*rak issaraseri*) and fun (*sanuk*), don't have discipline
- They want freedom but don't like working in groups or teamwork

- Forgive and forget easily
- Have extravagant tastes and compete in displaying possessions
- Like to build personal influence and honour.

This inventory of individual and collective traits was, in fact, nothing short of an outline of broader cultural characteristics of Thai society focusing around personal networks and the accumulation of material and symbolic capital. Notably, these very characteristics were seen as constraints against the more egalitarian and transformative ambitions of radical NGOs. They could be observed in the ways that slum-dwellers perceived the achievements of their projects and how NGO workers were incorporated into a system of face-to-face networks of patronage.

This was demonstrated in the Sammakkhi Phatthana community when the time came to receive the prized house-registration certificates from the local district office. At this ceremony, held in front of the newly built childcare centre, government officials were given pride of place at a table where the certificates were ceremonially handed to individual householders from a gold cup. It was an expression of the achievement of a new status for these slum householders. As others have also noted, the ordinary slum householders evaluate NGOs and their own leaders on the basis of immediate achievements enhancing survival and access to survival resources and living space, in contrast to 'grass roots' NGO indicators of success which stress the wider aims of self-reliant activity management, networking with other communities and consciousness of structured social inequalities (Pratt 1993: 70). Just as notable in this ceremony were the attempts of community leaders to show respect and honour to the NGO leader. Already addressed with the respectful term of *achan* (teacher, an appellation with which he was uncomfortable) he was embarrassed when invited to sit in the front row of visitors to view the ceremony (he sat at the rear), an act that would visibly display a notion of hierarchy which he had been working to discourage. In this ceremonial arena, both officials, as representatives of the state, and NGOs were acknowledged in a customary idiom as patrons in the task of assisting households to achieve a legitimate place in the city. As also found in recent studies of slum settlements in Manila, Bangkok slum-dwellers' perceptions of their environment, lives and actions are marked by the cultural categories prevailing in the broader society, and they work through these to achieve socially valued goals (e.g. Berner 1997: 194; Pinches 1991). Attempts by slum advocates, NGOs and academics to represent the patterns of resistance and local organisations of the urban poor as class-based social movements mobilised against capitalist property relations founder in the face of these basic cultural and social realities.

The right to the city: networks, anti-eviction and new tactics

The fact that slum-dwellers' goals are inherently limited does not mean that they are politically apathetic or uninterested in wider action. Events from the mid-1980s set in train a process of expansion in the tactics of groups to claim the right to coexistence in the city. These changes involved more concerted forms of lobbying, public demonstrations, the use of media, the organisation of umbrella networks covering slum settlements and the emergence of specialist leadership cadres among individual slums. James Ockey has argued that it represents the birth of new forms of resistance, or 'weapons of the urban weak', involving a transition in the mode of slum leadership, from 'traditional' forms, relying on local gangsters (*nakleng*) and patronage networks within slums, to 'modern' forms, centring on more educated leaders who facilitate access to basic needs through formal NGO networks, lobbying and the media (Ockey 1996). Clearly, slum-dwellers have added to their arsenal of techniques to forward their claims since the mid-1980s. However it is far less clear that these claims can be characterised as resistance in the class terms that he suggests (Ockey 1996: 49). Moreover, patronage, hierarchy and internal dependency relations so characteristic of dominant Thai cultural patterns can be seen to be largely reproduced in the most successful cases of slum mobilisation (see Green 1990: 195–6).

The objectives of slum-dwellers and their leaders has been to negotiate a better position, rather than confront the social and political order, notwithstanding the stridency of confrontational rhetoric of the rights of the urban poor. This was well expressed in the banner of the Phaisingtho community when it camped outside the BMA offices: 'We don't mind eviction, but we want the authorities to help us' (Jamnong 1987: 12). Notably, key public figures in slum advocacy reflect slum-dwellers' own practices in stressing that compromise and conflict avoidance is itself a distinctively Thai approach to managing differences. In this sense it can be argued that the assertion of 'rights' is the assertion of the right to coexistence and compromise. In the urban context, formal mechanisms have supplemented traditional informal patterns of compromise (Prateep 1986: 43–5; Somsook *et al.* 1988: 28). The struggle over urban land has been dramatised by notable cases of conflict. But slum-dwellers do not question capitalist property relations, as implied by class-based portrayals of their public struggles – they simply want a place in the city and aspire to landownership, legality and status.[5] These are the objectives towards which their collective and individual strategies ultimately aim.

By the 1990s the slums were increasingly tied into the political structures of Bangkok and wider civil society–state confrontations. The predicament of slum-dwellers and the nature of their societies were subject to ideological discourses of resistance which gained increasing authority from global alternative development paradigms and rhetoric. Scholars suggested that these changes signalled a transformation in consciousness and organisation. It was clear that slum-dwellers negotiated their survival in a more complex environment, but the fundamental pragmatism of their aims persisted. Patronage within slums has not declined, rather its forms have diversified. The NGOs do not stand outside the politics of the slums, but are in fact part of the multilayered conflicts that have emerged between groups, especially in larger slums. In the following section of this chapter I consider the case of Khlong Toei (the largest agglomeration of low-income settlements in Bangkok) and show how it has emerged as a key site of contestation and conflict: it is not only a survival territory of the poor and a field of social work for NGOs, but a space where individuals, local and city-wide interest groups compete for resources, status and influence.

Khlong Toei and the politics of locality

The massive squatter slum of Khlong Toei and its long-running battle with the Port Authority of Thailand has dominated representations of slum issues and the nature of the slum 'community' in urban Thailand, particularly among western researchers and development workers (see e.g. Drakakis-Smith 1981: 70–7; Korff 1986a: 308–9). There are understandable reasons for this, despite the fact that this slum is quite atypical. The settlements comprising this extensive slum developed as a direct result of the demand for cheap labour in the new port of Bangkok in the 1950s. The largest squatter slum in the city, it dramatised the contradictions of uneven development. One scholar remarked of this settlement:

> Viewed from the air Khlong Toei appears as a sprawling mass of tin roofs in a swamp, its houses built on stilts over waist-deep water, with narrow, precarious plank walkways linking the shacks to the dirt roads. Khlong Toei has become a symbol of the larger problem of squatter slums which are developing throughout the city.
>
> (Goldstein 1971: 38–9)

However appropriate as a symbol of the contradictions of the Asian city, as a Bangkok slum Khlong Toei stands out as a specific and special case – in terms of its socio-economic structure, its history of successful mobilisation against eviction, the critical role of its NGOs and the identity of its people and key advocates. Notably, many Khlong Toei people identify their settlement as unique. Local slum-dwellers humorously refer to it as *Nakhon Khlong Toei* (the city of Khlong Toei), or *Thawip Khlong Toei* (the continent of Khlong Toei). It reflects an identification with a locality having a particular political history and role in the city. Why, then, is it appropriate to explore this slum yet again? First, because its symbolic status is itself a product of an unusually successful defence of territory using a variety of tactics; second, this defence of territory highlights much about the characteristics of power relations within Thai society, notwithstanding the influence of global and local change in organisation and representation of conflict. Third, it is an opportunity to investigate how the pragmatic strategies (the informality) of ordinary slum-dwellers have become entwined within these relations and events.

Despite a broadly-based popular identification with Khlong Toei and the political evocation of a single slum community (*chumchon Khlong Toei*) by leading NGO advocates and local slum leaders, there is not one settlement, but many (see Fig. 5.1). With a population estimated at 73,634 people and 24,931 households (as of 1994), Khlong Toei Slum actually comprises twenty-one settlements marked by considerable variation in history, size and socio-economic status. The only grounds for considering these varied settlements as a single unit is that they are located on land officially owned (or partly-owned) by the Port Authority of Thailand (Community Development Office, BMA 1994: 42–3). They range from ramshackle settlements strung out along railway lines and canals, or hemmed in between company warehouses, to blocks of NHA flats and the officially laid-out subdivision of 70 Rai community. The tenure status of residents and the security of settlements also differs (Askew 1998: 9–10). The political evolution of Khlong Toei as a 'locality' has been a complex and uneven process, emerging from – but in continual tension with – the

Plate 5.4 A slum settlement of Khlong Toei (Wat Khlong Toei Nai 2). (Photo: Author)

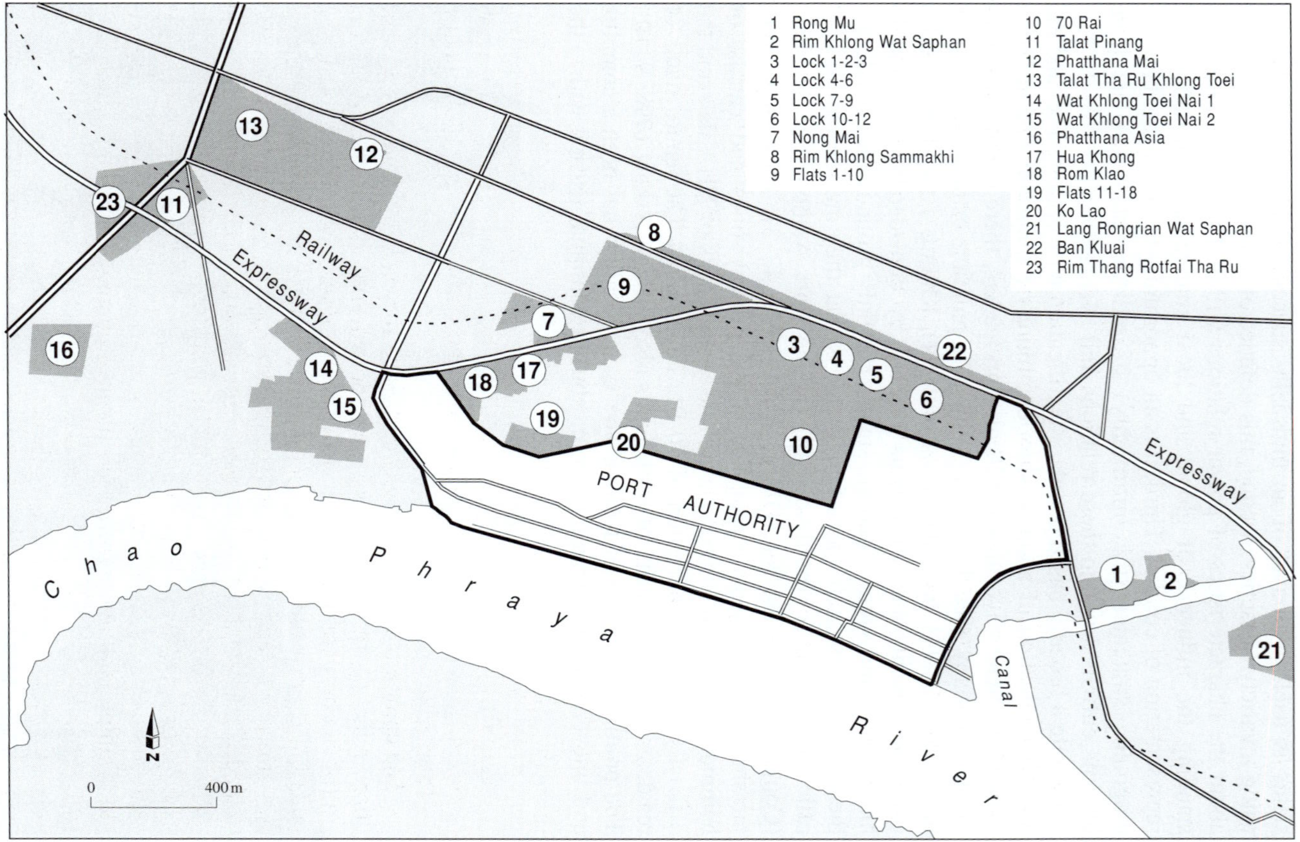
1 Rong Mu
2 Rim Khlong Wat Saphan
3 Lock 1-2-3
4 Lock 4-6
5 Lock 7-9
6 Lock 10-12
7 Nong Mai
8 Rim Khlong Sammakhi
9 Flats 1-10
10 70 Rai
11 Talat Pinang
12 Phatthana Mai
13 Talat Tha Ru Khlong Toei
14 Wat Khlong Toei Nai 1
15 Wat Khlong Toei Nai 2
16 Phatthana Asia
17 Hua Khong
18 Rom Klao
19 Flats 11-18
20 Ko Lao
21 Lang Rongrian Wat Saphan
22 Ban Kluai
23 Rim Thang Rotfai Tha Ru
Railway
Expressway
Expressway
PORT AUTHORITY
Chao Phraya River
Canal
N
0
400 m

Figure 5.1 The Khlong Toei slum settlements.

dynamic and varied experience of these diverse settlements and the survival strategies of their inhabitants.

Struggle and identity

The dominant representation of Khlong Toei as a united and integrated community with the capacity for self-reliant community development has its source in a thirty-year history of conflict with the Port Authority of Thailand (PAT). A consideration of this struggle highlights the role of common experience and popular mobilisation. More than this, it demonstrates the significance of key individuals, pressure groups and the particular nature of the Thai bureaucracy, culture and power structure in enabling the success of such place-making strategies, however temporary and tenuous.

From the time of the port's first opening the early 1950s, labourers had been actively encouraged by the PAT to come and work at the river port of Khlong Toei (Interviews Locks 1–3, Khlong Toei Nai 1996). They settled in the low-lying arc of land surrounding the port area or along the nearby Hualamphong and Phrakhanong canals. Progressive eviction of slums in the city and the eviction of settlers to make way for expanded port facilities led to an increasing population and density of settlement, so that by 1971 over 25,000 people lived in the area (Chira *et al.* 1971: 4). The first overt conflict between slum-dwellers and the port authorities occurred in 1970, when PAT officers, supported by police, began to forcibly evict settlers of Lock 12. The difference this time was an increasing level of organisation among groups of slum-dwellers aided by sympathetic academics, who helped publicise both the conditions and the economic role of Khlong Toei slum-dwellers.

The common pressure of eviction helped forge a high degree of cooperation, resulting in committees being formed and leaders chosen to direct anti-eviction activities. A key actor in this drama was Prateep Ungsongtham, a 19-year-old Khlong Toei-born student teacher who had established an informal school. When attempts to negotiate a settlement with the PAT failed, Prateep and her supporters demonstrated at the office of the Prime Minister, Field Marshall Thanom Kittichachon, and then appealed to the king. Pressured by public opinion and adverse publicity, the PAT finally agreed that Lock 12 residents could stay for seven years if they relocated to swampy land away from their planned container terminal (Somsook *et al.* 1988: 10–11). The result of these experiences was an increased level of organisation within the settlements. Although organisation did not encompass all communities, and was unable to prevent further forcible relocations into the increasingly crowded swamp land, it gave rise to a central local leadership focused on the relocated Lock 12, now renamed *Muban Phatthana* ('The Development Village') (Sompong 1986: 10–12). It was these communities located directly behind the port on the former swamp land that formed what may be described as the core territory of this emerging locality, both in terms of organisation and spatial concentration (see Fig. 5.1).

The period after the first anti-eviction campaign saw a range of activities that led, incrementally, to a more permanent settlement in the core territory. The democratic period of 1973–6 encouraged mobilisation on a number of levels. The early interventions of Thammasat University academics were followed by student volunteers engaged in a range of projects focusing on education and social welfare. A new youth group encouraged a variety of activities and seemed to displace older *nakleng*-based patron–client networks as a focus of loyalty for local teenagers (Somsook *et al.* 1988: 17; Korff 1986a: 311). With the encouragement of the new NHA, from 1977 local committees (based on earlier informal networks in Lock 12 and nearby settlements) assumed responsibilities for basic services such as house registration, water and electricity supply and children's school enrolment. Increasing publicity about Khlong Toei acted as a magnet for a range of international aid programmes and agencies.

Much of the attention and public sympathy accorded to the Khlong Toei slums focused on children's welfare. Prateep's 'One Baht School' for local children, formed at her family's home in 1968, had been a meeting place for the first anti-eviction groups in Lock 12, and acted as a symbolic focus for the surrounding neighbourhoods in later years. In 1978 Prateep's standing was boosted considerably when she won the prestigious Mangsasay Award for community service. She used the funds to establish the Duang Prateep Foundation (DPF) which began by funding a wide range of children-focused activities such as a kindergarten, school lunches and scholarships (Cheang 1988). In the following year her tenacity in defending the school was vindicated when, after a long battle with the Bangkok municipal authorities, it was officially recognised as legal. The publicity accompanying these activities attracted both international and local support, and played a critical role in enhancing positive publicity for the growing slum settlements in Khlong Toei (Hata 1996 43–5).

In founding the DPF, Prateep exercised considerable skill by offering key honorary positions to patrons (such as the then-Prime Minister General Kriangsak Chomanan and former Police-General Pao Sarasin) whose influence and reputation would both enhance the legitimacy of her current activities and provide a moral counterweight to the power of the PAT in eviction actions. However, Prateep's activities were not restricted to her school and the foundation. By virtue of her organising skills and reputation in the local slums, she was constantly called upon to participate more widely in promoting local development. Through these activities she developed important connections with a wide range of professionals and administrators (Hata 1996: 41; Prateep 1986: 43). The expansion of sympathisers among the wider public, which included members of the royal family, provided an important local funding base for the DPF. In the early

1980s, when the PAT launched its second major attempt to clear the slums of Khlong Toei, Prateep mobilised her personal networks to good effect.

In 1981 the PAT proposed a scheme for developing an export-processing zone on its Khlong Toei land. It was argued that this necessitated the eviction of all slum households in the immediate area behind the port, an eviction involving hundreds of families. The committees of Locks 1 to 12 had anticipated a further eviction move, and a sophisticated plan was already in place for coordinating protest, reflecting a keen awareness of the changing institutional and political environment. The strategy was three-pronged, involving the assistance of a wide range of groups outside the slums. The first element was to publicise local community activities to show that slum-dwellers were able to help themselves: in short, to announce the existence of a well-regulated community. To this end, the Khlong Toei Slum Federation was formed as a coordinating body and mouthpiece for eighteen community committees. The second was to demonstrate through specialists' research that the proposed scale of port expansion was unnecessary and inconsistent with the Fifth National Development Plan objective to develop a deep-water port on the eastern seaboard. Enlisting support from allies in the NHA, Prateep and other slum leaders advocated land-sharing as an appropriate option to accommodate both parties on PAT land. The third component was to publicise the history of evictions in the settlements and their destructive effects on slum-dwellers' livelihoods (Somsook *et al.* 1988: 18–19).

The result of this multilevel campaign between 1980–2 was a land-sharing agreement between the NHA and the PAT. This saw the PAT occupy a third of the former squatting settlement to build its container terminal, with an area of 70 rai (28 acres) leased to the NHA for a twenty-year period, subdivided into regular sites-and-services blocks and rented to residents. This was accompanied by an NHA master plan to upgrade surrounding settlements on the same principle in the future. The plan was acclaimed as a victory for housing rights for squatters and a vindication of community organisation. The compromise was also seen as a boost for the status of the NHA and those among its staff who advocated land-sharing as the best solution to the land question (Sanitsuda 1987). Several years after the final relocation of Muban Phatthana to the new location in 1985, NGO leaders affirmed that Khlong Toei was a model for demonstrating that once tenure security was achieved, grass roots community development in slums could flourish. In the new subdivision, owners constructed good quality two-storey homes as evidence of this new confidence: 'For Khlong Toei itself, the era of "eviction" will from now on be replaced by the new future of "housing development"' (Somsook *et al.* 1988: 14).

Publicy proclaimed as a success, the shift from the old Muban Phatthana location to the new subdivision (named '70 Rai') was actually fraught with difficulties. The experience of managing the project and the long-term outcomes exposed many of the inequalities at the heart of slum communities and slum-dwellers' strategies of accumulation. One internal report by a member of the DPF noted how the first local committee charged with surveying eligible housing right-holders in 1982–3 colluded with NHA officials to secure more blocks in the new subdivision. As a result, two NHA officials were dismissed and the community committee was dissolved, to be replaced by a committee of outsiders. Based on a count of right-holders settled since 1971, the land-sharing scheme excluded many households who had arrived after that year. Families who rented could not participate, and special housing needed to be constructed for them in another part of the slum. Prateep herself publicly acknowledged the shortcomings of the project, noting that the poorest of the poor did not benefit (Prateep 1986: 43). Further, a number of families found that the cost of rebuilding was too much. Indebted, they eventually sold their rights and became renters (Askew 1998: 28). Such had been the level of turnover – often due to debt incurred by the first families – that ten years after the move, only 21 per cent of the original owners of 70 Rai plots remained (Nopadon 1995: 175).

Through the anti-eviction campaign Prateep and her colleagues had secured part of the slum complex as a survival territory for its inhabitants, but they were unable to transform slum-dwellers into the community that they envisioned. To those NGOs working closest to the poorest people of the settlements (such as the Human Development Foundation) the day-to-day struggles of many households, and the multiple forces affecting them, were too intractable to allow the luxury of these ideals (Maier 1993; Sanitsuda 1987). From the mid-1980s, however, the narrative of the 'community born of struggle' would be a necessary and often a persuasive image to be used in the defence of locality. The struggle had consolidated the core territory of five communities centred around 70 Rai. This was the territory on which the symbolic institutions (the DPF school and headquarters, the Human Development Foundation and others) focused, and the organisations around which groups would form, including an increasing number of NGOs who founded headquarters in and around 70 Rai. The other squatting settlements located on PAT land were linked into this core through various committee representatives and shared activities. However, most Khlong Toei settlements had not gained from the land-sharing arrangement or gained any security from the NHA master plan. For example, most residents of Chumchon Phatthana Mai never gained house registration. Again, it was the DPF which attempted to bridge this gap by establishing services such as a mobile library.

Forces for solidarity

In Khlong Toei, broadly based horizontal solidarity across communities, when it emerged, was a response to immediate threats, and often died away just as quickly (see e.g. Drucker 1987). However, external forces and recurring problems affecting the growing settlements preserved some unity of sentiment. While the land-sharing deal gave a new sense of security to residents of the inner core areas, it did not protect the smaller outlying settlements from eviction threats. In the 1980s and 1990s these settlements (*chumchon rop nok*) came under increasing pressure as the PAT took advantage of their isolation to issue eviction threats under various pretexts. Notably, it was the DPF with its growing corps of full-time staff which acted to assist these communities (not always successfully). By contrast, the Khlong Toei Slum Federation came under increasing criticism for its lack of support for the outlying communities (Khlong Toei Slum Federation 1993: 3–4). This lack of organisational effectiveness casts doubt on recent portrayals of the Khlong Toei slums as a unified defended territory of the poor (e.g. Korff, 1996).

A more broadly-shared problem emerged in 1989 when the Interior Ministry of the newly-elected Chatichai government announced a plan to relocate all households to a new settlement in the province of Prachinburi, over 100 km to the north east. Flamboyantly announced as the 'New Life Project', the programme was a hastily-devised strategy to eliminate the Khlong Toei problem once and for all. Households were to be given farmland and trained to work the land, with facilities supplied by the BMA. The announcement created panic in Khlong Toei, and once more Prateep was called upon to persuade the government that this was an established urban community (*Matichon Raiwan* 8, 14 March 1989). Another event promoting unity through adversity was a major fire in 1990 caused by a chemical explosion in the PAT's warehouses next to Ko Lao. It wiped out housing and caused long-term health problems for many residents. While the PAT accepted responsibility for inadequate safety precautions, compensation to families was slow and their buildings were not replaced. In fact, the homeless were accommodated in the new sports field near 70 Rai. Ostensibly a temporary measure, the PAT ignored all appeals to allow homeless residents to return to their old site. Events such as these continued to reinforce a widely-shared view among residents that the Khlong Toei slums were a neglected part of the city (a *luk mia noi* status – child of a second wife).

The initiatives and support underlying community organisation were in the hands of a committed cadre of full-time workers for the DPF, the Human Development Foundation, and a core group of local residents and active community committees, including a youth group. They were joined in 1990 by the Grass Roots Development Foundation, founded by Sompong Patbui, formerly of the DPF. The locally-based Japanese agency SVA (Sotoshu Volunteer Association) added further support by funding youth and educational activities. They formed the interface between the community and the increasing amount of aid being directed towards Khlong Toei by Thai and international NGOs and politicians. The physical environment of the core territory saw improvement as parliamentary development funds were directed towards upgrading of walkways and the establishment of local facilities such as health centres and libraries. In the 1980s Prateep had forged an alliance with Chamrong Srimuang, the new Governor of Bangkok and leader of the Phalang Tham Party; this generated further improvements, such as the establishment of the sports ground and more efficient rubbish collection (author's interview with Prateep Ungsongtam, 3 July 1997).

Collective events to encourage participation and local identity were staged such as sporting events, 'community clean-ups' and new-year festivals. Efforts to encourage local peoples' organisations bore fruit with the foundation of housewives groups (*klum maeban*), savings groups and cooperative rice stores. The constant hazard of fires was addressed with the formation of a committee to coordinate aid to fire victims. A local fire station, complete with fire trucks and volunteers, was founded with outside funding. By the late 1980s the presence of these organisations and activities was used by Prateep and other local activists to bolster claims to the legitimacy of settlement and recognition from national leaders and the broader public (*Matichon Raiwan* 7 March 1989).

Social structure and power relations

While the slums of Khlong Toei have been presented to the broader public as a united, self-reliant community and an exemplar of NGO–people partnerships, its social system and internal power structure are complex. The new organisations formed throughout the 1980s did not replace informal networks or the enduring patron–client relations which were founded both on neighbourhood relations as well as unequal access to resources (Nopadon 1995: 297–9). Arguments that the experience of resistance against eviction transformed Khlong Toei communities towards a more egalitarian model tend to downplay the persistence of these patterns (e.g. Korff 1986a: 314–15). Interviews among residents in the slums show that community committees are often staffed by local influential residents (*phu mi itthiphon*) who have little communication with their neighbourhoods. Of the twenty-eight-member committee of Lock 1–3, only two or three are active, and meetings are rarely held. At Wat Khlong Toei Nai, an inactive committee chairman of ten years was replaced by householders only when rebuilding after a destructive fire demanded decisive action and organising skills (author's interview with Chairman, Chumchon Wat Khlong Toei Nai, 14 November 1996).

Committee membership enhanced leaders' status, but active work was delegated to their *luknong*, or clients. Resources gained through office (such as annual funds from the BMA Community Development Office) were distributed to bolster support (Interviews Lock 1–3, 1996). In Lock 1–3 a prominent member was feared by locals because of his connections with the police, who had protected his son from prosecution after he murdered a neighbour (Interviews Locks 1–3, 1996). People were linked into a pattern of dependency relations with local leaders who were often money lenders and landlords. This meant that they were unwilling to openly criticise these leaders for involvement in illegal income-generating activities such as drug-dealing or gambling. Committee membership could be used as a cover to protect private interests. It is widely known that some committee chairmen reported success in the periodic community drug-free zone campaigns simply to keep the DPF happy and protect their domains. Some leaders involved in gambling dens and drug dealing could be readily accepted and admired if they also exercised benevolence and were seen to be engaged in public activities benefiting their neighbourhoods (Nopadon 1995: 300). As events in 1996 were to show, it was only when influential figures overstepped the mark and were perceived to be advantaging themselves disproportionately that rumour and common knowledge were transmuted into public denunciation.

The sheer size of the population of the Khlong Toei settlements and their location in a hub of activities generated by the port and Khlong Toei market (the largest in Bangkok) makes the district a significant political constituency and source of extra-legal resources for competing interests. Slum-dwellers are linked through these interests and the resources they offer to broader power structures in Bangkok. In the 1970s an increasing number of slum-dwellers gained housing registration which qualified them to vote, and political parties began to draw on them for support. At the collective level, support for individual politicians delivered tangible benefits for communities in the shape of new facilities and development funds. Groups such as the DPF attempted to foster a united voice for single parties in garnering community development benefits, but slum-dwellers often made their own choices according to the immediate benefits to be gained. The economic boom from the late 1980s gave increasing resources for funding local campaigns and purchasing votes to political parties. Local slum leaders were the prime targets for local candidates. Tied into a political patronage system, influential local leaders with a large entourage of clients reaped rich rewards, while subordinate neighbourhood campaign managers received payments of up to 3,000 baht. Votes were bought for an average of 200 baht per head (author's interview with Somphop Witthabun 29 August, 1996 and Chairman, Chumchon Wat Khlong Toei Nai, 14 November 1996). During the fiercely-contested 1992 elections, the leadership of the Khlong Toei Slum Federation (composed of community committee chairmen) split into warring factions over the spoils of campaigning, much to the embarrassment of local grass roots development activists (Khlong Toei Slum Federation 1993: 1).

The port of Khlong Toei is well-known as the lucrative fiefdom of the Ministry of Communications, a prize eagerly sought after in the ministerial allocations accompanying the notoriously frequent change of national governments. Benefits from corruption and extra-legal port transactions are immense and take place at all levels, involving port officials and employees, police of all ranks, slum gangsters and ordinary slum-dwellers alike. In the port itself, there is an established system of kickbacks (or tea money) paid to employees and their superiors which derive from storage and handling fees. This is so systematised that it is accepted by local and international customs and forwarding agents (*Bangkok Post* 14 January, 10 February 1999). The police (who are directly paid by the Port Authority) derive extra income from protection rackets focusing on the markets of the district and payments from the owners of local gambling dens, for whom they also serve as guards in their time off (author's interview with chairman, Khlong Toei Market Committee 16 September 1996; Ampha 1996; *Bangkok Post* 15 April 1999). Police customarily receive protection payments from the drug dealers of the slum (who are generally the gambling den owners, or part of their 'mafia'). Large numbers of ordinary slum people have given up calling the police to arrest drug dealers, because they know that the two groups are well-connected and they fear reprisals and intimidation (author's interviews with residents, Chumchon Rim Rot Fai, 1997).

But the corruption which prevails in Khlong Toei as a source of oppression is also accepted by ordinary slum-dwellers as a source of enrichment and a routine part of life. The benefits accruing to port work for regular employees of the Port Authority are accepted, and the most lucrative positions (such as crane and forklift operating) are much sought after and admired as occupations which will bring income and status to families. So too, local people who work for customs agents are much admired and envied because of the extra discretionary income they enjoy (Korff 1986a: 321–3; author's interview with Somphop Witthabun 29 August 1996). Among householders who transfer or purchase housing rights, payment to BMA and NHA officials is an accepted practice which accompanies these illegal transactions. There are, of course, different scales of corruption and extra-legal practices, and to slum-dwellers there is a considerable difference between widely-shared routine payments which facilitate access to basic needs and those which impact negatively on their lives and advantage already powerful groups.

By the 1990s, it was increasingly clear to many slum people that, in addition to the day-to-day battle that marked the life of the settlements' worse-off residents, the enemy was both inside and outside the community. The powerful interests which were using Khlong Toei as a site of accumulation through drug-pushing, gambling and protection rackets both endangered the aims of local community development workers and limited the capacity of ordinary residents to mobilise against emerging eviction threats. Khlong Toei was a far more diverse settlement than it had been a decade earlier. While the poor remained, there was a substantial group of households who had better incomes and resources at their disposal (30 per cent with monthly incomes between 10,000 and 15,000 baht) (Askew 1998: 13). Most of these were concentrated in the core settlements around 70 Rai which had benefited most from the funding and facilities delivered by NGOs. The demanding tasks of maintaining community development work and responding to frequent crises as they emerged (including eviction threats to the outlying settlements and fire disasters) still remained in the hands of an active corps of professional and volunteer workers attached to the local NGOs (the DPF, the Grass Roots Development Foundation and the Human Development Foundation). In 1997 Father Joseph Maier, the long-serving director of the HDF, advanced the depressing but acute observation that: 'If it wasn't for Prateep, the HDF and about twelve other people, Khlong Toei would be dead in the water' (author's interview with Fr J. Maier 30 June 1997). In every community there were local people, often women, who supported community-based savings groups, anti-drug campaigns and neighbourhood patrolling. But the obstacles to local development seemed overwhelming in the face of persistent social problems symbolised by debt, drug taking and HIV/AIDS (*Phuchatkan Raiwan* 4 October 1996). These conditions underlay responses to the next major eviction threat, which exposed major divisions in Khlong Toei.

In 1993 the news broke that the PAT had rescinded its agreement with the NHA for further land-sharing, and planned to develop the Khlong Toei market site as a commercial complex and the neighbouring slum areas as a container and parking zone. This involved the relocation of over 5,000 families from the ten settlements comprising the inner core of the slum area, including 70 Rai (*Nangsuphim Nisit Naksuksa* 1993). Local NGOs swung into action to mobilise a comprehensive campaign against this threat, but the climate was now different. The PAT's argument that the new complex would contribute to developing the inner city was accepted by the NESDB, which supported the logic that the soaring value of inner city land outweighed any arguments about preserving a low-income community, most of whose residents lived in single-storey housing. The land was simply too valuable. The rational use of urban space was the key principle among NESDB planners (author's interview with Dr Uthis Kaothian 1997). This time the plan developed by the PAT was more difficult to combat with the argument that the institution was acting irresponsibly, even though it was clear that it was essentially the income-generating exercise of a powerful bureaucratic fiefdom. Coordinating with the NHA, the PAT offered residents the choice of moving to two large resettlement zones on the urban periphery, or shifting into new flats nearby. Compensation was offered and cheap loans provided by the Government Housing Bank to support resettled families. Special bus routes were to be established linking the new relocation settlements to places of employment in the inner city and Khlong Toei Port. All this was designed to counter the now-familiar arguments of slum-dwellers against relocation to the outer suburbs (Amornrat 1997).

On the face of it, there appeared to be a unanimous opposition to this threat of eviction. The Khlong Toei Slum Federation (1993: 1–2) was charged with the responsibility of encouraging a united front among residents to support a movement to persuade the authorities that there were more than only two options for their future. A third existed: for the settlement to remain. There were opportunities for effective opposition and delaying tactics. First, the Port Authority plan threatened not only the slums but the market, which had a highly organised management committee of Sino–Thai business operators. The issue was thus wider than slum eviction alone, because the market was a popular institution in the city. Further, an even larger group of specialists and academics were now available to add to the pressure applied to government to delay the implementation of the plan. Since the use of the land was partly for non-port-related uses, it was necessary for the PAT to obtain cabinet approval, and before this could be obtained, it had to be demonstrated that this plan was in the public interest. This allowed the broad coalition of opponents to organise. The DPF commissioned an American researcher to demonstrate the important role of the Khlong Toei market in the city and its links to local communities, and the results were published in the press.

Political conditions were also favourable, because the frequent change of coalition governments in 1993–5 delayed cabinet considerations of the PAT's plan. The election of Pichit Rattakul to the BMA governorship was of critical importance. Pichit's electoral success was largely attributable to his campaign for comprehensive environmental improvement to Bangkok. Harnessing the support of middle-class environmentalists and urban activists, he had proposed a new vision for the city with a flexible and responsive administration based on expert advisers and community consultation. This offered another important point of leverage for Khlong Toei slum leaders. Sompong Patbui was recruited to serve Pichit as an adviser, together with a number of progressive planners and environmentalists with important links to United Nations funding agencies. A further study of the Khlong Toei slum was commissioned, revealing that the great majority of all income groups in the slum settlements (82 per cent) were unwilling to leave (Askew 1998: 22).

While Khlong Toei-based NGOs and community organisations made strong efforts to generate united opposition around the historical identity of the locality, events from 1995 exposed differences of interest among slum-dwellers based on existing inequalities and internal power structures. Even before formal cabinet approval was given for the planned commercial complex, the PAT conducted seminars and garnered the support of a number of key community chairman for relocation to one of the new outer-suburban sites (Soi Watcharaphon). By early 1996, housing-right holders in the Locks 7–12 began to sign up to move. By September nearly one hundred of the eligible 541 families had built homes in the new subdivision, located forty kilometres from the central city, and by mid-

1997 this number had doubled (Askew, field notes 1997). Why was this occurring? To Prateep, and her supporters for a united community, divisions were being created by outside forces. It was rumoured that the PAT was engaging in a new tactic of 'buying-off' local leaders in order to split the community. In Locks 7–10, the households that refused to move argued that leaders were receiving extra land blocks and cash payments as rewards for persuading households to relocate (Interviews, Locks 7–12, 16 September 1996). Yet the process was not so simple. Relocation was embraced as a viable option by those families who could afford to rebuild, and the process was very similar to the earlier relocation to 70 Rai. Those who stayed were the poorest families, and the renters. The most prominent community leader promoting the move (Kamol Loy-Taley) had certainly gained advantages from the shift, but the relocation would have been impossible unless his neighbours shared similar aspirations.

In Khlong Toei, rumours were rife about the corruption of the leaders who cooperated with the PAT and the exploitation prevailing in the new settlement at Soi Watcharaphon. There were known cases of indebted households selling their rights to move to other slums (HDF Focus Group transcripts 1997). Yet research conducted by the Human Development Foundation (HDF) in 1997 at the Watcharaphon resettlement site showed that the people who had moved and built there were united behind Kamol. He himself was adamant that the new settlement represented a vast improvement to people – there were no drug problems or gambling, and people could start a new life, as long as they worked hard to repay their loans to the Government Housing Bank. Neighbours agreed that this settlement was not to become a 'slum' (HDF Focus Group transcripts 1997). Watcharaphon was linked to Khlong Toei by a new bus service funded by the PAT. As Prateep noted, there was every likelihood that Kamol was receiving kick-backs for supporting this company (author's interview with Prateep Ungsongtham, 3 July 1997). Yet corruption accusations notwithstanding, Kamol was simply benefiting from the expected perquisites of his leadership, and there was no evidence that he was resented by the residents at Watcharaphon. He was acting out the important role of patron and protector in an accepted mode of reciprocity, and in this he reflected the leader–entourage system prevalent in the slums and the broader society.[6]

The mobilisation and conflicts surrounding the PAT plan from 1995–7 created an environment where competing power groups in Khlong Toei were brought into the open. With the advent of the Banharn Silpa-archa government in 1995, a notable increase in drug trafficking took place in Thailand. Among the pickings offered to his political clients were transfers for senior-ranking police to the lucrative Khlong Toei district. In the period 1994–5 Khlong Toei strengthened its position as the central distribution point for illegal narcotics as police teamed up with gambling and drug organisations. Profits from the drug trade in Khlong Toei alone during 1995–6 were said to be as high as 20–30 million baht (Onnucha 1997b).

Plate 5.5 Houses in the new settlement at *Soi* Watcharaphon. (Photo: Author)

At the level of the streets and alleys of the slums, the impact was seen in the increasing numbers of heroin and amphetamine addicts, while indebted householders were often required to sell drugs to meet obligations to drug-operator landlords and creditors. As the DPF and its support groups continued their efforts in community development and self-help through anti-drug campaigning, increasing conflict with the local gambling and drug lords exposed the complexity of power networks linking the slums to wider interests.

In late 1996, frustrated by the resurgence of drug dealing despite a number of promising community-based campaigns, Prateep publicly denounced the gambling and drug networks in Khlong Toei. Members of the Khlong Toei Slum Federation – long suspected of links with the lucrative gambling and drug underworld – accused Prateep of tarnishing the image of the community with her announcement. As a defensive tactic, this strategy misfired. It provoked representatives of thirteen communities to rally to Prateep and tell the press that there were ten big gambling dens in the slum, protected by thugs and policemen. They withdrew their communities from the twenty-four-member Federation (Ampha 1996). Information formerly kept within the slum was now public knowledge. Tension mounted when a large police operation was conducted in Khlong Toei and the homes of Federation leaders were raided. Prateep was widely thought to have pressured the police into this action. A symbolic gesture of farcical proportions – the raid including the use of helicopters – yielded the arrest of just one lowly police warrant-officer, and was clearly known of in advance (*Bangkok Post* 26 February 1997; Onnucha 1997b).

The botched police raid generated more public exposures about the drug and gambling interests in the slum, pointing to the secretary of the Khlong Toei Slum Federation (Olarn Pisutkorakul) as a major figure (*Bangkok Post* 27 February 1997). In an effort to clear himself and his supporters, Olarn responded with a charge that Prateep was misusing the funds of the DPF and exaggerating drug problems to further her own status (*Phuchatkan Raiwan* 28 January 1997). It became clear that for years the Slum Federation has been used as a front to protect gambling and drug interests and that Olarn was also protected by a network of police and politicians. Amidst the mounting polarisation surrounding this publicity, women residents of Olarn's own community pointed out that it was strange that he was extraordinarily wealthy, despite his humble occupation as a *tuk-tuk* driver. These issues were also intimately bound to the PAT project, and it became known that Olarn's group were each receiving 20,000 baht monthly from the Port Authority to persuade residents to leave (Mongkol 1997; Onnucha 1997b). But Olarn was never indicted, instead his networks exerted pressure in characteristically informal ways through death threats and intimidation. Prateep's stand against the local mafia generated strong support from community leaders, but in her March 1997 community anti-drug campaign most of them received death threats and were too afraid to expose the gangs any further (Thaksina 1997).

In early 1997, the PAT project implementation was successfully stalled by a multi-front campaign which harnessed the influence of the new national-level popular lobby, the 'Forum of the Poor' (*Samacha Khon Chon*) and the Governor of Bangkok. In early 1997 the FOP successfully pressured the government to force the PAT to donate land for a sports field at Khlong Toei, which acted as a symbolic claim over permanent space for the community (*Bangkok Post* 1, 26 February 1997). The NESDB arranged a public hearing where officials proposed turning Khlong Toei into a version of the London Docklands, featuring high-rise low-income housing, shopping complexes and offices. It was opposed by community representatives (author's interview with Dr Uthis Kaothian 1997). However, it was the onset of the mid-1997 financial crisis that put an end to the PAT's ambitions for a decisive transformation of Khlong Toei. Without the crisis, large scale eviction and relocation would almost certainly have taken place.

Nonetheless, the divisive events of early 1997 showed how Prateep became a rallying point as local leaders distanced themselves from gangsters. This did not reduce the economic power of the drug lords in Khlong Toei, but it did signal how, more than ever, Prateep symbolised the identity of Khlong Toei as a community committed to development. Her wider influence and prestige, enhanced by her involvement in the democracy movement, were strong enough to withstand any of the charges that she was building her own personal empire.[7] This, of itself, had not prevented households from leaving Khlong Toei as they embraced new opportunities to improve their livelihoods. But a core group of local supporters forming the backbone of local organisations – largely comprising long-term residents and large numbers of people whom the DPF had assisted over many years – had stayed and made efforts to persuade other residents that in unity was better bargaining power.

In the ongoing struggle for urban space and the related emergence of locality-based identity among slums in Bangkok, the history of Khlong Toei reveals some common experiences and many of the features of other slum settlements. We have seen this particularly in the ways that new forms of organisation have been utilised by individual householders and that, rather than replacing earlier forms, such as patron–client networks, these have been combined in the quest for security and advancement. Perhaps more than any other slum, Khlong Toei has been pronounced an exemplar of the success of peoples' organisations and participatory development. These organisations are less than all-embracing, and reflect how persistent patterns of inequality and the day-to-day struggle for survival limit the ability of the very poorest groups to participate. Not only have many communities been dependent on outside agencies to establish organisations, but these community organisations are often structured into a hierarchical system whereby leaders appropriate status. If the poorest lack networks to gain access to assistance, they often remain marginalised (Nopadon 1995: 288–9).

In the case of Khlong Toei, the emergence of 'locality' (defined as a pattern of organisation together with commitment to the defence of living places) has been a contingent process tied to struggles for power and access in the city. Khlong Toei is in this sense atypical of other slums, in that it has so far succeeded in preserving a survival space in the city. This success has been based on its sheer size and location, its historical relationship to advocacy groups and emerging NGOs, its access to international aid, and in particular its leadership and focus based on Prateep Ungsongtham as a popular rallying point.[8] Her ability to exploit opportunities created by the fragmented power structure of Bangkok and to draw on traditional Thai and modern idioms of community, and above all to sustain simultaneously a role both as a prominent public figure and a neighbourhood-level patron, help to explain much of her effectiveness (Hata 1996: 115–23). Prateep has always been anxious to attribute the achievements of the Khlong Toei slums to the ordinary people, but it is significant that her very traditional role of patroness and protector is expressed by the way local people almost universally address her by the respectful term *Mae* (mother).[9] In this lies one of the keys to understanding the social system of the slums and the leadership which has informed the emergence of place identity and locality in the complex society of Khlong Toei.

Conclusion

The essentially simplistic representations of slum communities generated by academics, government agencies and NGOs are a product of the ideological contexts and conflicts which have accompanied the conspicuous growth of inequalities in the metropolis. The slum-dwellers themselves cannot be separated from these contexts, since as social–economic settings and political sites, the slums have been shaped by and interacted with the institutional, economic, social and ideological changes around them. The people of the slums are pragmatic and individualistic, but they are also linked in locally-based social networks within which they fashion relationships and status. In this they reflect the characteristics of Thai culture. The growing bureaucratic and ideological environment which has entered their lives – including the significant NGO presence – has afforded them a new language and a strategic framework within which to advance both individual and collective claims to resources – including land, capital and status. But the meanings they assign to concepts and strategies may not conform to the often idealistic aims of the institutions and groups which sponsor them. It is in this layered and dynamic framework that they attach importance to the relationships and spaces around them, and in doing so, negotiate and make the city.

6 A place in the suburbs

Making a neighbourhood in the middle-class housing estate

Introduction: the suburban landscape

In the 1990s, the burgeoning housing estates of Asia's sprawling urban areas were the most dramatic physical symbol of the rise to prominence of the middle classes, along with the associated consumption and status icons of the private car, the mobile phone and the shopping mall (Chua and Tan 1999: 145–9). Consumerism has been identified as the leitmotif of the Asian middle classes, attached prominently to material and emotional investments in the home and the housing estate (Young 1999: 67–9). In Bangkok, from the 1960s, the provision of housing and the process of suburbanisation became a critical dimension in urban growth and change. Arguably, the most significant socio-ecological trend in the development of the Bangkok metropolis over the last thirty years has been the growth of the middle classes and the development of their characteristic domestic habitat, the *mubanchatsan* or developer-built housing estate and the *Chumchon Kheha*, its publicly constructed equivalent. Residential functions are now the most dominant of land uses of the Bangkok Metropolitan Region's territory. The home and its principal locus, the housing estate, assumes critical importance in a study of urban culture and society because of this typicality. Notably, over the past decade or more, the greatest proportion of media advertising expenditure in Thailand has been devoted to promoting housing estates. The images flowing from these advertising campaigns were a potent force projecting images of affluence, comfort and status (Ockey 1999: 240–1). A popular genre of television family drama focusing on the lives of Thailand's rich reinforced the associated images of affluence and exclusivity (Hamilton 1992). Curiously, the housing estates of Bangkok region have received little detailed ethnographic attention by social scientists as a site of cultural reproduction.[1]

In this chapter I investigate the relationships between biography, household, social identity and the rise of neighbourhood organisation in a middle-class housing estate in the northern suburbs of Bangkok. Recent writings on urban life and landscape in Asia characterise housing estates overwhelmingly as theatres of private consumption and material display. However, to paraphrase the title of one recent Thai novel: there is another 'story' in the housing estates (Yok 1997). Notably, perceptions of place identity and a sense of control/confidence in the surrounding social environment is of considerable significance in the lives of many people who dwell in the housing estates. Interestingly, a major survey of middle-class home-purchasers in Bangkok housing estates (conducted by the Asian Institute of Technology during 1985–6) found that over half of the respondents stressed that the degree of neighbourhood friendliness was a major criterion for choosing to live in the housing estates, even above considerations of price (Thongchai, Tips and Sunanta 1986: 2). Focusing in detail on the Pratchaniwet housing estate, I argue that culturally-derived notions play an important part in the way that settlements develop into neighbourhoods. Moreover, the actual process of this neighbourhood building is of considerable importance to social memory and to the ongoing process of maintaining the public/private nexus in middle-class residential areas. To put the latter point another way, social networks and place identity may be as significant to the middle classes – although determined by a different dynamic – as they are for the slum-dwellers who have received the bulk of attention in studies of Bangkok's urban neighbourhoods.

In this chapter I explore the idioms which householders use to describe their lives, the history of their local living environment, their expectations and the degree to which public life and social networks play a role in the evolution and everyday life of this housing estate and its people. I do not apply a zero-sum definition of community, its components or prerequisites – I use it here rather to refer to relative levels of cooperation, communication and identification with the neighbourhood as a place. I aim therefore to develop an emic understanding of residents' own outlook: their understandings of their housing estate in the past and present expressed though their own Thai terms and repeated expressions. It is from their own articulations that a critically important term – *khwamsabai* (well-being, comfort) – the achievement of which gains particular prominence in their individual and collective accounts of the estate – points to the values they attach to place and neighbourhood.

The middle classes: values and the question of neighbourhood

The landscape of consumption which has risen to transform the life and appearance of the Thai metropolis – the shopping malls, condominiums, golf courses and the highways – has been noted as symbolic of the material impact of a so-called 'new' social formation – the middle class. However this new middle class, the product of 1980s affluence and economic boom (the so-called mobile-phone mob) who allegedly toppled the military regime of General Suchinda Kraprayun (in May 1992) have attracted overwhelming attention as a political variable rather than a socio-economic formation (Girling 1996; Hewison 1996; Ockey 1999). So what is the Bangkok middle class? As elsewhere in Asia, it is not a homogeneous social formation. In her pioneering work on middle-class families of Bangkok in the late 1970s, Juree Vichit-Vadakan highlighted the continuing importance of the key distinctions in lifestyle, aspirations and values between the Thai and the Sino–Thai among the lower-income ranks of this formation (Juree 1979). More recently, James Ockey argues that: ‘it is at best analytically dubious to speak of a single middle class in Thailand. There are instead diverse fragments and diverse constructions which have not as yet been conflated into a single class.’ He argues for a key distinction between the consumer middle class, many of them new rich, and the occupational (or status) middle class, with major differences in education and incomes (Ockey 1999: 245). It is the former group which has attracted most attention in recent literature, even though civil servants are still a key element in this diverse grouping. Notably, the level of civil service salaries is an index of standards of living in Thailand, and when they are raised or lowered by the government, incomes and consumer prices are immediately influenced. Joel Kahn proposes using the plural term middle classes to convey a sense of occupational and social diversity (Kahn 1998b: 87–8), a term which I will also adopt here, in addition to defining one of its subgroups as lower middle-class.

Here I deliberately employ the plural term middle classes to refer to that diverse middling socio-economic cluster between the economic elite and the poor. Thai scholars have coined the term *chon chan klang* (‘middle level group’) in their discussions of this socio-economic formation (Sungsidh and Pasuk 1992). People in the housing estate of Pratchaniwet employ the more commonly used term *pan klang* (literally average, between, or middling) to describe their socio-economic situation and status. This term is often paired with other commonly-used expressions such as *pho yu dai* (have sufficient to maintain oneself) and *mai duat ron* (literally ‘not in hot water’ – not in desperate circumstances) and *mai sung mai dam* (neither high nor low). This conveys the comparative nature of their estimate of their economic condition: they are not suffering from extreme hardship, neither do they enjoy the discretionary income of the rich. In this analysis of the people of the Pratchaniwet housing estate, I utilise the term lower middle-class to denote this *pan klang* group, both in terms of occupation and income level, and also in terms of a number of their key value orientations. Occupationally, they span the following groups: the lower and middle ranks of civil servants (among which are included primary, high school and technical teachers); workers in semi-government authorities (electricity, telephone and postal organisations); self-employed small business owners, tradesmen, and technicians; and white collar workers in private companies (accountants, clerks, bank workers and office managers). They share a number of core values which include a stress on the importance of education (both for themselves and their children), social respectability (appropriate public behaviour, particularly in social intercourse), self-improvement, and concern for a safe, secure and orderly environment for their families (for which the home is a key symbol and space).

There are other key values shared by many among this group. Principal among these is the value of organisation, orderliness and due process (*khwam mi rabiap*). This is particularly strong with those with civil service or teaching and military careers (the *kharatchakan*). I will emphasise later, however, that this value placed on organisation is operationalised selectively as occasion demands, while at other times networks (*khruakhai*, literally network) of various kinds – work-based hierarchies and informal friendship and kin connections – are used to attain benefits for the housing estate and mediate between households, neighbourhood and external bureaucratic agencies. In discussing the ways that the neighbourhood was mobilised – and in the process, constituted – I do not explain them exclusively in terms of 'class factors' deriving from the occupational subculture of the *kharatchakan* lower middle class. Although there is a discernible set of values operating in the estate which stem from shared social and occupational backgrounds of residents, they also derive from the broader Thai cultural idioms with which residents identify.

The Bangkok middle classes are a varied social formation. The housing estates in which the vast bulk of them reside are of different size, design and layout, price and management type. Nor do their homes form the only focus of the lives of the residents. As noted aptly with reference to the Singaporean middle class:

> The status of this class is itself constructed by self-identifying individuals from an aggregate of experiences and sentiments derived from different realms of daily life: work, housing environment, material consumption, recreation and family and personal affiliations, with each contributing only partly to this status.
>
> (Chua and Tan 1999: 145)

Nevertheless, the relative significance of such key symbols as the home and the consumption items within it – as well as the activities that are hosted there, which comprise collectively important capital and symbolic investment, form a key dimension in the lives of the Thai middle classes, to which other issues relate and without which an account of social formation would be incomplete (Ophan 1995). As Ken Young notes, housing estates must be regarded as 'among the strategic sites for the construction of individual and social identity' (Young 1999: 76).

But is the housing estate an appropriate site for gaining insights into patterns of social interaction and articulations of collective identity? Do the middle classes really have a 'place' in these estates in the sense that they share meaningful associations in, and identification with a space and environment of living (Massey 1995: 41–71)? Bangkok residents, whether originating from the provinces (*tang changwat*) or born in the metropolitan region (*khon muang*), are the first to say that community feeling and relationships (*khwamphukphan*) are hard to find among those with money in the city. The commonly expressed description of their disposition is *dua khrai dua man* – meaning 'everyone looks after their own interests with no concern for others'. It may be argued that it is pointless to address the local area as a site for middle-class community (a contradiction?) in the technologically-driven space of flows where the economic and private lives of the middle classes in the postmodern Thai metropolis are, arguably, sustained principally by virtual communities of the internet and cellular telephone (Castells 1989: 348–51; Lewis 1998).[2] And despite the massive investment middle-class families make into the purchase and embellishment of housing, many of their members are rarely to be found at home. But it is a mistake to assume that the luxurious and exclusive housing estates of the wealthy, bounded by security check points and high walls, are typical of Bangkok's *mubanchatsan*. Social interaction *does* take place within the housing estates of Bangkok, and particularly among that group which I have designated the lower middle class. As a site of field research, housing estates are particularly challenging for the ethnographer, given the relatively privatised nature of life. Indeed this probably explains the small number of studies so far undertaken, whether in Thailand or elsewhere.

Plate 6.1 The entrance gate of a high income *mubanchatsan*, incorporating security guard post. (Photo: Author)

However, under certain circumstances it is possible to gain access to the networks which comprise the lower middle-class estates. While the findings and interpretations of this chapter may be restricted to the lower middle-class estates (particularly those built by the National Housing Authority), they do at least provide some insights into the social dynamics of the substantial number of the estates occupied by this group.[3]

It is worth noting here that, just as solidarity and forms of collective identity are generated among the urban poor through struggles to defend survival space, so too among housing estate neighbourhoods, shared practical problems hinging around the challenges of the urban environment have formed the basis of collective action. Unlike the case of Singapore, where state intervention, social and demographic planning and ideology play a major role, in Thailand public housing does not extend to social planning and local management to anywhere near the same degree. Neighbourhoods have often been faced with practical challenges, particularly in matters such as flood prevention, infrastructure improvement and the development of facilities. It is around these issues that the Pratchaniwet housing estate in this study mobilised its social resources. In the process, an important identification with the area and its people emerged. Herbert Gans' now classic study of suburban families in Levittown, North America (1967) raised important questions which are still relevant to consider. Historically, the emergence of the suburban social landscape was driven by spatial, economic and social trends which separated homes from work places. Home and the home environment emerged as key lifestyle priorities for

Plate 6.2 Homes in a cheaper middle-class *mubanchatsan*. (Photo: Author)

the suburban dwellers whose demands and interests eventually came to dominate modern urban life. But as Gans showed, interaction and group life could still flourish in the new suburbs, built around networks of common interest, life cycle, and shared concerns (Gans 1967: 404–6). The few existing studies of group organisation and neighbourhood life in the suburban housing estates of Asian cities likewise suggest that alienation and privatised lifestyles are not a necessary consequence of suburbanisation and the advent of the housing estate. Indeed, cultural factors can play a key role in the process of locality-focused interaction and identification (see Ben-Ari 1991). Such cultural factors, in turn, may form the basis for sustainable local-level activities which also have an effect on alleviating some key problems affecting the urban community.

Pratchaniwet 2/3 and the National Housing Authority of Thailand

Much of the housing stock purchased by the lower ranks of middle-income earners in the BMA and its expanding suburbs in the 1970s and 1980s was provided, however belatedly, by state agencies. The most important of these has been the National Housing Authority (NHA), formed in 1973 from a number of pre-existing agencies and given full responsibility for the provision of public housing in Thailand. In the early 1970s Bangkok faced an alarming housing shortage. According to one report in that decade, Bangkok faced a twelve-year backlog in the supply of public housing, comprising 133,524 units (Choop and Chadsri 1978: 45). In the mid-1970s the private housing industry was producing about 50 per cent of Bangkok's housing stock, but exclusively for upper-income groups; so much so that only 16 per cent of the population could afford to purchase them (Chiu 1985: 84, 212). The housing shortage was as much a problem for the middle classes as it was for the urban poor, because the backlog in housing production was essentially a shortage in housing provision for newly established families of the city's expanding technical, bureaucratic and professional middle class. The NHA thus became responsible not only for low-income housing production, but for middle-income earners as well, especially that large group of the lower ranks of the administrative grades of the civil service.

The Pratchaniwet 2 Phase 3 estate was one of a number of estates planned in 1976 for a target income group of households earning between 3,000 and 5,000 baht per month (US $150–250 at 1976 rates). At this time 'the poor' were considered to be those households earning monthly incomes of less than 3,000 baht. Pratchaniwet was located on land purchased by the NHA from rice-farmers in Pak Kret District, Nonthaburi Province, on the northern fringes of Bangkok's rapidly expanding built-up area. Pratchaniwet 2 Phase 1 had been undertaken earlier by the BMA for low-income earners on land nearby. Designed for income group 'C' (the poorest

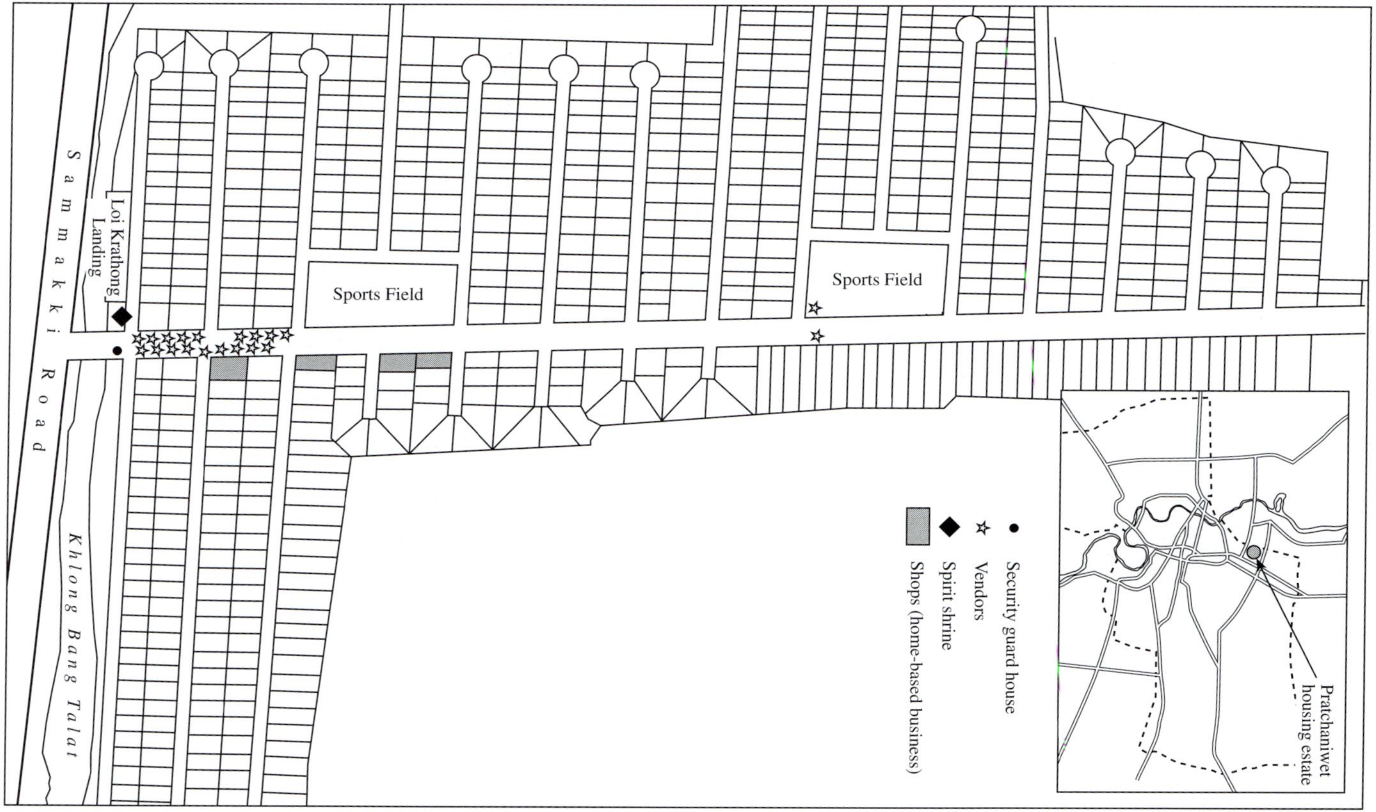

Figure 6.1 The Pratchaniwet 2/3 housing estate.

housing was allocated to 'A' designated groups), Pratchaniwet 2 Phase 3 (hereafter called simply Pratchaniwet) was an estate of 420 detached two-bedroom homes offered to lower-middle income earners for hire purchase, in contrast to the rental arrangement of lower-income projects (Chiu 1985: 118–19). Opened in 1978, Pratchaniwet estate was laid out as a roughly L-shaped block with its entrance facing an east–west tributary canal (Khlong Bang Talat) of the major north–south running Khlong Phapha, alongside of which ran Pratchachun Road, linking Nonthaburi province to the central city. House-blocks were arranged along twenty-two residential streets of varied length leading into a main *soi*, along which were two open spaces intended for development as recreation reserves (see Fig. 6.1).

The lives and housing choices of householders of the Pratchaniwet estate reflect the general trends identified by commentators on population and housing in Bangkok for that period. The larger number of the people who came to Pratchaniwet were government employees of various departments and agencies. Almost universally they were young married couples with very young children. Helen Chiu has dubbed the period from the 1940s to the 1970s in Bangkok in housing terms as a time of 'self-help and slums' because in order to meet their housing needs urban dwellers either settled in informal settlements (slums) or met their needs through family connections in shared accommodation. This is certainly the case with Pratchaniwet residents. Prior to moving to the estate, most had either lived with parents, in-laws or relatives, or been accommodated in the various types of dwellings supplied by their employers (e.g. police family quarters). The choice to move to this flood-prone and remote settlement bounded by canals and rice farms was dictated by a common concern to build a family and achieve a semblance of security. Like the burgeoning educated middle class in that period, the larger proportion of these young people had been born outside Bangkok, principally in the central region, but also with a large proportion from the southern Thai provinces; they had come to the city for their education (vocational or secondary/tertiary), having lodged with relatives in the city until they finished schooling and found work in the city, where most government jobs were centred (Thai University Research Associates 1976). Below we can see the broadly similar experience of movement, career and housing choice which these people shared.

Pratchaniwet households: a profile

Before discussing the key themes arising from interviews and observations of the Pratchaniwet estate, it is useful to note some of the key socio-economic features of the households comprising this settlement in the years 1996–7.

Place of birth and social origins

Only slightly more than a quarter of all household heads in Pratchaniwet were born in Bangkok (27 per cent), with the largest proportion from the central region (32 per cent) and significant representations from the south (15 per cent) and the northeast of Thailand (10 per cent). Given the rural childhood backgrounds of many of the householders, it is perhaps not surprising that some residents should still describe themselves as *khon ban nok* (country person or unsophisticated person) at heart.

Age cohorts and household size/composition

It is notable that the majority of household heads are aged over 45 years, with a high concentration in the 45–54 age group. This underlines the historical development of the Pratchaniwet estate and its place in the chronology of suburban development in the Bangkok region. A tiny proportion of households (6 per cent) are newly formed. The single largest group of households comprises those with four members, with a majority of the nuclear family type (parents and offspring). Nonetheless, there are a number of variations in composition, with 12 per cent of the households containing additional members who are siblings of household heads, or nephews or nieces. Other households (9 per cent) include one or two of the household heads' parents. A number of families (17 per cent) are headed by widowed adults, mainly women.

In addition, we can note the life cycle stage of most households reflected in the age profile of their members: the majority have dependent children of teen age undertaking tertiary study as well as younger children still attending secondary schools. Additionally the life cycle stage is reflected in the number of income contributors to households. Fifty-six per cent of sampled households had both male and female partners working and contributing to the household income. A further 23 per cent of households had three or more incomes, derived from grown-up children in addition to the household head and partner. This was a clear factor in differentiating households by income, with a higher proportion of two-income families enjoying incomes of over 20,000 baht per month (US $800 pre-1997 crisis exchange rate) than single-income families.

Occupations

The largest single proportion of household heads work in the civil service (29.5 per cent), with a further 13 per cent working in semi-government authorities, such as customs clearance, telecommunications, airlines, electricity, water supply and postal services. A significant proportion of household heads (17 per cent) are employed by companies in administrative, clerical or sales positions. Self-employed household heads represent

14 per cent of the total householder group, with the remaining occupations distributed between the private sector (commerce: 4 per cent, independent professionals, including journalists and doctors: 4 per cent) and the public sector (teachers: 6 per cent, military: 4 per cent). Skilled tradespeople and technicians are a relatively small group, with 7 per cent represented among the sampled household heads of Pratchaniwet.

Incomes

While most householders describe themselves as *khon thammada* (ordinary people), their household incomes, when compared to national and Bangkok scales, are quite considerable. Most of these households' incomes are far above the GNP per capita of Thailand, and match the figures for average incomes of Bangkok households at 20,000 baht (NSO 1997). Families with incomes of 20,000 baht or above comprise 82 per cent of Pratchaniwet's households. There is no doubt, however, that household expenditures are also considerable. Car purchase and home renovation are significant areas of outlay. A large proportion of families are also maintaining teenage or grown-up dependents still studying. While most families have completed house payments to the NHA and thus fully own their homes, investment in renovation has been considerable. Some families have completely rebuilt on their blocks. However, most owners have modified and added to their homes step-by-step, as necessity and finances have allowed (see Table 6.1).

Unity through adversity

When asked to identify the most significant event to have taken place in the history of the people of the estate, all original Pratchaniwet house-

Table 6.1 Home renovation by home owners, Pratchaniwet 2/3 NHA housing estate, showing cost and number of times renovated (15 per cent systematic sample survey)

Number of times	*Less than 100,000 baht*	*100,000–499,000 baht*	*500,000–999,000 baht*	*One million baht and above*	*Total*
Once	26	19	—	—	45
Twice	8	7	—		15
Three	1	6	1		8
Complete re-building	—	1	—	9	10
Not renovated	*	*	*	*	10
Not applicable	*	*	*	*	12

Note
* Renovation costs not applicable.

holders are unanimous in stressing the effects of the great floods of 1983 – for it was the collective mobilisation to protect the estate from the rising waters which galvanised householders into a self-conscious *chumchon* (community) in their eyes. I begin therefore with the theme of collective memory rather than individual's perceptions of neighbourhood and environment, because it lies at the heart of householders' conception of Prachaniwet as a place. Interestingly, to people living outside the Pakret area, the Pratchaniwet estate and its surrounding district (formerly low-lying rice fields) is associated with flooding, a perennial problem that has become more serious as the city has grown, diversified and densified. To Pratchaniwet residents – at least those household heads who experienced the floods of 1983 (approximately half of the current household heads) – these events signal the birth of the community and its capacity to organise. However, it is not organisation per se which is at issue in their assessment, but the significance of the quality of relationships, and thus of *sammakki* (friendship) and *namchai* (generosity and fellowship).

The questions of management and organisation have been present at Pratchaniwet since the beginning, because the NHA was obliged to provide assistance to residents until such time as the specified 20-year service contract with the estate (that is, the collective group of households) expired in 1999. The issue of local participation in the maintenance of NHA hire-purchase estates, while acknowledged as necessary in the literature of Thai public housing specialists, has never received concerted attention by NHA authorities beyond the functional requirements of maintenance. As elsewhere, the NHA estates of the Pratchaniwet area (including Pratchaniwet 1, 2 and 2/3) are serviced by an Area Housing Office which is responsible for the sewerage and drainage system, water supply, electricity maintenance in public areas and ironically, flood protection (see Sittichai 1978). After first arrival, most new residents made friends fairly quickly with their neighbours in nearby houses of their *soi*, but the general sense of alienation stemming from arrival in a new and strange place was enough to prompt some of the householders to advertise a meeting in order to discuss matters of common concern, and principally to assist in the process of mutual acquaintanceship.[4]

Notably, the first major project was not directed to improving infrastructure or facilities on the estate, but to the organisation of a traditional Thai seasonal ceremony (*Loi Krathong*). Those residents active in organising the first meeting were civil servants and teachers with some administrative experience. This meeting was publicised by the group through leaflets distributed dooor-to-door, and it was this group that chaired the first gathering at a nearby school hall. One of the organisers recalled that his motivation to foster some collective activity in Pratchaniwet was spurred by nostalgia for his close-knit Sino–Thai neighbourhod in the inner city, where he had lived with his parents and new wife prior to moving to Pratchaniwet. From this meeting an estate committee was elected.

In addition, representatives were elected from each *soi* of the estate to act as liaison points between residents and the committee on matters of concern. An assembly of the whole estate was planned, to be convened each year to receive the committee's annual report and to elect a new committee.

Just a few years after their initial occupancy of the estate, residents confronted a major environmental challenge and the realisation that they had to help themselves. In the monsoon season of 1983 (June to October), major flooding of this former rice-growing area was anticipated. In mobilising against the coming flood, the committee and the residents drew on both formal and informal sources of support. Although the NHA had some sandbags there was no sand, and furthermore there were insufficient sandbags to go around. A major effort had to be made to find the necessary sand and bags and to mobilise assistance to build a sandbag wall around the estate. One resident contacted her brother-in-law who was an army brigadier, and through his influence procured some soldiers and a truck. Sand was obtained from the district office (Pak Kret), although residents had to organise their own transport. People took days off work to take part in the campaign to maintain the sand bag wall and the pumps (supplied by the NHA). Women made food for the working groups who maintained twenty-four hour guard around the estate in rosters. Those who could not assist in practical ways donated money for the purchase of food or equipment. In the two weeks of serious flooding, residents found that they had saved their estate from damaging flood waters and that all the other NHA estates in the Pak Kret area had been damaged by the flood. Pratchaniwet 1 had been unable to mobilise resources. Pratchaniwet 2, an estate built for high-income senior civil servants, was seriously damaged. It appeared that the people of Pratchaniwet 2/3 had discovered an indispensable survival resource – their own organisational capacity.

This event also underlines something important about Pratchaniwet as a place of living. Environmentally it was a massive compromise. Located literally at sea level, the estate would always be prone to the danger of inundation. Householders had made a decision to invest in 15 to 20 years of house repayments for small two-bedroom bungalows – which they often described as dog kennels (*ban ma*), or chicken coops (*lao kai*) – to find that they would have to make an effort, each year, to save themselves from the most elementary and regular of Bangkok's environmental threats. Unlike Pratchaniwet 1 and 2 estates, which are only occasionally flooded, Pratchaniwet 2/3 needs constant maintenance because of its low-lying position. Flood prevention is at the core of the estate's survival as a viable settlement. By the late 1990s the basic routines for flood prevention remained the same as at the time of the settlement's first establishment. Pumps need to be maintained and monitored throughout the year, gutters and drains need to be checked for blockages, the canal at the front of the estate needs surveillance; and in the rainy season the committee members need to constantly patrol the area, looking out for changes in the water level. Defective equipment needs replacement or repair either with the assistance of the NHA, or by volunteer technicians from within the community.

In reflecting on the way that flood prevention has become integral to the organisation and survival of the estate, one might be tempted to ascribe the sociability which has developed as a tangible quality among Pratchaniwet people as solely environmentally-driven. That is partly correct, but the associated qualities of interaction which have been mobilised have reinforced what can be described as cultural competencies among residents. To argue that had the floods not occurred then there would have been no birth of community (*mi chumchon* gert *khun*, as the residents express it in Thai) obscures a number of other critical variables. These are frequently highlighted by residents themselves when they compare their experience with that of the neighbouring estates in that fateful first year of the flood. Why did the other estates not mobilise successfully? In answer to that question, residents use cultural and class categories in defining what constitutes their own 'place'. These categories lie at the heart of the cultural construction of Pratchaniwet as a locality-based community. In the case of Pratchaniwet 2, Prachaniwet 2/3 householders thought that the rich residents (mostly higher-ranked civil servants) were just too busy to give time to society (*mai mi wela hai sangkhom*), with the clear implication that such people didn't (and don't) care about their neighbours. One Pratchaniwet householder said that the Pratchaniwet 3 residents thought they could solve all problems by spending money in employing labourers to build sandbag walls and operate the water pumps for them. Referring to the other housing estates (such as the low-income Pratchaniwet 1), there was a widely shared view that they simply did not have the organising capacity and commitment (*mai mi rabiap* – no system). In this case the implied social advantage of Pratchaniwet 2/3 lies in the culture of the *kha ratchakan* (the civil servant, the soldier, the teacher – in short the educated person) and the capacity to get organised to solve immediate problems, in contrast to the relative disorganisation of a possibly more diverse – as well as poorer – neighbourhood.

These perceptions of difference and contrast need some further consideration. Several of the interviews I conducted with householders of Pratchaniwet 1 and 2 suggest that there were a number of conditions that limited their capacity for preventing the depredations of the 1983 flood. Households heads in Pratchaniwet 2 were senior civil servants whose work commitments kept them away from their homes, and whose lifestyles were orientated to networks outside their domestic and neighbourhood living environment. Although these residents knew their closest neighbours, their sociability was limited. Socio-economic factors seem to be relevant in helping to explain the relative degree of neighbourhood-based social interaction. While a large proportion of Pratchaniwet household heads admit that their main friendship connections are focused around work colleagues outside the estate, there is still a lot of networking within Pratchaniwet. The few studies which have compared levels of social interaction in high- and medium-income housing estates in the Thai metropolis suggest that high levels of contact characterise medium-income housing estate residents. This seems to be at least partly due to the role of women's networks in sustaining connections between households on an everyday basis. In high-income estates, families employ domestic servants (for shopping, childminding and housekeeping), a factor which enhances the private nature of families' lifestyles. Among medium-income families, where domestic servants are less commonly employed, women's activities bring them into frequent contact with neighbours – through the use of public transport, shopping at local markets (and vendors' stalls within the estate) and other activities (Worawan 1985). Women of the generation that founded Pratchaniwet gave up their working lives for long periods (and often permanently) in order to care for their infant and growing children. In their daily life these women's friendship networks established during critical times of the life cycle were important for mutual assistance, and are sustained even when children have grown and left the household. Residents of Pratchaniwet 1, discussing the events of 1983, point out that networks did exist in their estate, but it was difficult to coordinate activities. In this low-income estate, there were many people renting the small row-house units in addition to considerable levels of residential mobility into and away from the estate. This helps to explain the difficulties of organisation.

These points highlight the critical importance of the leadership groups in Pratchaniwet for the effective organisation against the 1983 floods. They also suggest the importance of the previous years of collective activity in establishing traditional Thai seasonal festivals in the estate. A reinforcing factor was the shared life cycle characteristics of the new families comprising the bulk of residents, and its importance in laying the foundations for *soi*-based friendships and beyond. The fact that they were overwhelmingly comprised of new homeowners (a relatively low percentage of these NHA units had been the subject of speculative purchase and resale) reinforced shared commitments to staying and surviving. The interesting point is that this is a community of individualists whose values focus on investment in their homes, occupational advancement, and the education of their children. One might suggest that it is simply enlightened self-interest that explains the effectiveness of committee–neighbourhood relations. Certainly self-interest is a crucial element in the continuing patterns of participation – notably, a factor present in Bangkok's slums as well. However, there is also a set of shared values which bring the idiom of management together with an affective idiom of community (*khwamphukpan* – togetherness) and legitimises self-interest as a public good. I will outline these central orientations below, before discussing life-course and self/community perceptions and valuations.

Competencies

A range of skills and cultural factors come into play in the organisation of the Pratchaniwet estate neighbourhood and the procurement of its resources. They derive from traditional Thai sociability as well as values and practical orientations associated with workers in the Thai bureaucracy – the *kharatchakan*, a critical occupational subculture within the broad formation we have described as the Thai middle classes (see Juree 1979). There are two interaction/communicative modes which I would delineate in the terms my interviewees described them: *chai rabiap* (use due, or correct process) and *chai khruakhai* (use one's network, or influence). It is important to note that such modes are used as a resource precisely because the community is not an affluent one, and thus needs to depend on public facilities – not only private money and influence – to gain assistance in practical matters of the estate's environmental improvement and ongoing maintenance. Thus, in dealing with the outside world, committee members of the estate use a judicious mixture of both methods and idioms. Below, I give two examples of their use and effectiveness in maintaining the estate.

Trees and rom reun *(cool shade)*

Pratchaniwet people recall that when they first arrived there in 1978, the estate was a stark, boring and barren-looking place. The houses were of identical design, and the main street and the main and subsidiary *soi* were unprotected by shade. The picture is very different today. Large and leafy *Bradulai* trees (Angsana trees) along the pavements provide shade, atmosphere and cool the streets. The effort to modify the environment of the estate was the first major environmental initiative of the members of Pratchaniwet's assembly. One member discovered that the Bangkok Metropolitan Authority had supplies of *Bradulai* trees in its nurseries which were not being used. Contacting NHA officers, he suggested that these young trees might be fruitfully used in lining the streets of Pratchaniwet. With no real bureaucratic obstacles in the way, the trees were obtained and planted in the streets with the help of NHA workers. A major factor was that the committee member himself was a civil servant, and was sufficiently confident to make the suggestion and spend time persuading the relevant officials of the feasibility of the proposed arrangement.

Repairs

In the mid-1980s a severe thunderstorm damaged the roofs of several homes in the estate. On inspection, residents discovered that the roof frames had been poorly constructed by the original building contractors. The NHA was contacted to rectify the matter, but the officials were slow in processing

Plate 6.3 The main *soi* of Pratchaniwet, shaded by Bradulai trees. (Photo: Author)

the complaints. One of the committee members happened to know the governor of the NHA and contacted him directly to come and see the damage. When the governor came to the estate he inspected the damaged homes and the roof beams of twenty additional houses. Persuaded that this was a general construction fault, he assured residents that it would be made good by the NHA. At the same time the governor was welcomed by the coffee club, an informal weekly meeting of the Pratchaniwet committee. Two modes had been used in this encounter with officialdom: *Khruakhai*, or a network of connections, together with a countervailing mode of Thai sociability which was used to soften the sense of possible confrontation with the governor as *phuyai* (big person – person of status commanding respect).

Structure of governance: sociability = solidarity

We might view the management functions of the committee as simply an enabling activity – essential boring work to maintain essential facilities, without which the privatised world of Pratchaniwet as a middle-class housing estate could not be sustained for its householders. Certainly the *raison d'être* of managing the estate is to enhance its livability. However the practicalities of managing the estate are tied to key social processes as well as the instrumental aims. When the first committee was formed in 1979 its major activity was to organise a Loi Krathong celebration, a traditional rite derived from an ancient Brahmanical ritual of floating impurities away on waterways (in the form of small decorated vessels made of banana leaves) to rededicate the soul. This seasonal rite is particularly popular among Thais because it traditionally involves family groups and reunions. According to former committee members, the cooperative activities directed to organising this first celebration helped lay the social basis for later mundane activities directed to maintaining the facilities and condition of the estate. Preparation had involved the cleaning of the canal fronting the estate (which was full of building debris from the estate's construction), the building of a landing, and hiring of a military band for the music. Then, as now, particular attention was given to keeping the children amused and contented. Thus a major focus of later activities would include the upgrading of the sports field in the estate. Estate-wide celebrations of major festivals, including New Year, Songkhran and Loi Kratong are well attended and popular at Pratchaniwet, with over 50 per cent of households attending the three principal seasonal gatherings regularly each year. Interestingly, while the longest resident households (17–18 years) register nearly 60 per cent regular attendance, the group with next-highest level of attendance is that of households resident less than five years. Length of residence does not appear to be a critical variable influencing participation in neighbourhood events.

A further emphasis on sociability was made through the establishment of a weekly coffee club, which helped to break down residents' reticence in approaching the estate committee. The informality of these gatherings meant that business was brought up amidst conversation. The matter of the roofing problems, for example, was first brought up in the coffee club among *soi* representatives, then it proceeded to a formal gathering of the estate assembly before efforts were then made to contact the NHA. A more recent innovation has been to have the coffee club meet outdoors every Sunday morning in a permanent central and accessible location (on the edge of the sports field/running track). This has made it easier for residents to directly approach committee members with problems, as opposed to having to enter a committee member's private home. Such problems include road blockages caused by carelessly-stored building materials, the high speed of cars, suspicious people entering the estate and thefts. Committee members respond individually or collectively to complaints and questions.

Above all, the coffee club breakfasts combine sociability with business. Discussion topics range from the maintenance of electricity boxes on the estate to forthcoming national elections; from recent local, national and international news items to the experiences of a neighbour on a recent holiday abroad. In short, the mode within which business takes place is that of informality and sociability. For the committee members themselves,

Plate 6.4 The virtues of informality: members of the Pratchaniwet coffee club talking to residents. (Photo: Author)

the work itself takes on the character of a hobby. Members ride around the estate on bicycles or small motorcycles, communicating to the security guard's shelter or with each other by means of walkie-talkies (purchased by a committee member on a trip overseas). As one member puts it – 'work on the committee allows me to meet people and learn things, I also enjoy it'. The role of *soi* representatives can also help to reinforce street and neighbourhood-level bonds through mutual assistance. Several members of the committee are electrical and mechanical technicians who are able to assess technical problems (the pumps for example) and attend to domestic electrical problems. These competencies, mobilised in the framework of estate maintenance, help to cement friendship ties as well as reinforce the general pattern of informality that surrounds committee activities.

This is not to say there are no personal conflicts on the estate, cliques, or misunderstandings and long-held grudges. In the early 1990s, a committee spent money on chairs for the park which were widely considered to have been overpriced. Rumours of misspent and pocketed funds swept through the estate until a formal assembly meeting and accounting took place. Former members of the managing committee at the time of that controversy still avoid talking to the new committee because of this. As one former resident (who still visits the estate) points out: 'this is a matter of *Sakdi* (honour/dignity) among some people'. Particularly in the matter of the estate maintenance funds, residents must see that their committee is putting the money to work. The maintenance funds are raised from a monthly levy of 100 baht on each household. This is a system inaugurated by the estate assembly itself, prompted by concern for the insufficient level of services offered by the NHA and the municipality. The expenditures incorporate payment of the security guards on the estate, purchase of extra water pumps and garbage collection services. Since the debacle with the old committee, a notice board has been erected on the estate's central *soi*, itemising and reporting on all committee activities, projects and expenses.

Aside from these matters, members themselves are keenly aware of the need to preserve harmony in the estate for the sake of its continued existence as a pleasant place to live. While rumours and resentments bedevil neighbourhoods and body-corporate managing committees throughout the world, it is an oft-noted characteristic of Thai society that individuals pay particular attention to maintaining and building 'face' (*raksa na*), and that particular cultural/behavioural modes of conflict avoidance have been developed to preserve harmony (see Klausner 1992). It is important to assembly representatives that people on the estate are not offended and that discord does not spread throughout the neighbourhood. There is, for example, a problem of collecting monthly dues from about forty families on the estate. Asked why the recalcitrant householders have not been directly approached, committee members say that they would rather not create hostility through direct confrontation, but rather pursuade these residents more gently by showing evidence of how these funds are used for the benefit of the estate. It is an exercise in moral suasion.

This concern and the capacity to compromise and signal various policies indirectly is illustrated by a recent car accident which involved the drunken friend of a resident's son who lost control of his car, colliding with two resident's cars and a brick wall. In an effort to publicise how excessive car speeds caused damage and disruption, the committee pasted photographs of the accident on the estate notice boards instead of chastising the family directly. Nonetheless, this was interpreted by the family as an act of denunciation. Soft words of placation were needed in order to convince the householder concerned that this was not an attack on his family's honour, but a reminder of the perils of hazardous driving in the neighbourhood. The committee, even though comprised of elected representatives at the *soi* level, has to tread softly on some issues so that it is not seen as oppressive. This is not to say that it comprises a permanent clique. In so far as my own observations during field research suggest, members of the committee occupy their positions because their neighbours want them to be there. When committee members don't have time, they will step down from office, as did one chairman during my period of research (1996). Some representatives are continually re-elected. Another feature of the current representatives is that some are very recently-arrived but have become known to neighbours through everyday patterns of social interaction.

World views, life history and neighbourhood intersections

From interviews with individual householders, committee members and former committee members, it is clear that the conscious dispositions towards cooperation in the Pratchaniwet estate grow out of the objective preconditions which have become progressively reinforced over the years. They can be summarised in the following points:

- *A similar age cohort.* The greatest proportion of householders are of the same broad age group; their families are thus experiencing the same types of changes according to life cycle phases.
- *Bonds with neighbours.* The greatest proportion of householders came to the estate at least ten years ago and have had the opportunity to form friendships, particularly among neighbours in the same *soi*. Such friendships have ramified into broader networks through the estate.
- *Similar commitments and values.* While the greater proportion of households now enjoy comfortable incomes, the experience of these families has been one of compromise. Very few interviewees were pleased when they first came to the estate. The houses were particularly unsatisfactory. Throughout the past 10–18 years these householders have gradually made improvements to their homes, as their income opportunities have allowed. They have shared similar values in their commitment to family-building as well as to education as a principal means of social improvement. Many household heads continue to study, particularly now that they have extra time.
- *Perceptions of status affinity and similarity.* While the incomes of households are now highly diversified, most householders note that they and their neighbours share the same social level – this is expressed in terms such as *radap dieowkan*. While some people have experienced greater good fortune than others, as displayed in their varied brands of cars and style of home renovation (or reconstruction in some cases), most interviewees are adamant that this in itself does not alter the fact that people in the estate grew up together – *derb do duaikan*. This is an explicit recognition that they should not be envious. It is also in keeping with an important cultural value placed on face-to-face acquaintanceship in Thai society – *kanruchakkan*.

I have used the term 'lower middle-class' in describing Pratchaniwet residents. In material terms they are distinguishable from the affluent elite of the middle classes by average incomes and financial commitments which require them to limit and prioritise their expenditures. To be *pan klang* is to be conscious of these limitations. This is reflected in the management of the estate as a whole, where certain projects require the active input of residents and the pooling of skills. In terms of individual values, there is an emphasis on self-improvement and self-help, while socially there is an emphasis on respectability combined with informality. These latter orientations are not contradictory: respectability involves politeness in interactions (neighbours always address each other by name prefaced with the respectful *khun* second person pronoun) and a reticence in concerning themselves too closely – or at least being seen and heard to be concerned – with their neighbours' personal business. But there is also an emphasis on informality and face-to-face interaction, as seen in the advent of the coffee club as the preferred way to conduct weekly business. This stems at least in part from the relatively humble social origins of most of the residents, who, although having experienced economic mobility in their careers, have nevertheless retained some of the easy familiarity that marks *khon thammada* – ordinary people – in their society.

Pan klang is also reflected in the residents' determination that Pratchaniwet will not degenerate into a 'slum', a term adapted from English that is used to imply disorganisation and environmental/social degradation in neighbourhoods. This vivid fear of degeneration through disorganisation reinforces the importance of managing the estate to maintain the desired standard. For example, the most recent project (in 1997) was the building of a market shelter to house all the food vendors who work in the estate (some of whom are residents, others outsiders, but all are well-known to residents). This is a measure designed to reduce congestion on the pavements and ease cleaning tasks. Modes of informality are important means by which Pratchaniwet's hard-won environment and security are maintained: thus residents are proud of the fact that burglaries in the estate are rare, because they all keep a watch on their neighbours' homes and look out for strangers entering the *soi*.

Conclusion

In this chapter I have advanced the interpretation that the organisation of the Pratchaniwet 2/3 NHA estate derives its character from effective patterns of association and sociability, patterns which have their basis in objective socio-economic characteristics (income levels and demographic phases) as well as the values of the *kharatchakan* lower middle class. But beyond that, what appears to make this estate work, where others have not, is the way that it has been constructed as a place through skilful

Table 6.2 Household heads' reasons for remaining at Pratchaniwet 2/3 (15 per cent systematic sample survey, 1996–7)

	*Reasons for continuing residence**	*Number*	*%*
1	Good friends in the community *(Mi phuan di, rak phuan)*	2	2
2	It's nice and shady here *(Rom Reun)*	12	13
3	Like it, it's comfortable to live here have achieved a comfortable state here *(Chop, Yu Sabai/Sabai yu laeo)*	27	29
4	Good environment *(Singwaetlom di, banyakat di)*	3	3
5	Staying for children's sake (friends, school) *(Luk rak phuan, Luk yang rian yu)*	6	6
6	Convenient to travel (to work) *(Saduak nai kandernthang)*	17	18
7	Don't know where to move to *(Mai ru cha bai nai)*	21	22
8	Planning to leave, given opportunity	4	4
9	Other	2	2
Total		94	100

Note
* Many respondents gave multiple reasons – in such cases, the first was chosen.

cultural and social mechanisms that have responded to environmental problems (in this case the 1983 floods and the continuing necessity to maintain the environment). But it is not a 'community' in the sense of the paradigms proposed by many students of the urban poor (multiplex social bonds derived from common dialect/income, social necessity, and especially defence against the state and eviction agencies). When residents are asked about why they still remain at Pratchaniwet, many emphasise the location in relation to work (even though travel times extend up to 2.5 hours), rather than factors relating to the social environment. Interestingly, very few claim to have plans to leave the estate. Some emphasise that their children are still attending school. Evidently (and not surprisingly) household heads often express the same sort of practical points that brought them to the estate in the first place. But there are also interesting variations in responses which are worth highlighting, particularly the generalised 'it's comfortable here' (*sabai yu laeo*), which outranks the more specific emphasis on commuting convenience as a reason to remain. Positive qualitative reasons (environmental and social) given for remaining in Pratchaniwet (1 to 4) amount to a majority of 54 per cent of total responses.

The Pratchaniwet estate remains distinctively middle-class, not only in terms of incomes and occupations, but also by virtue of the aspirations of its householders towards individual attainment and socio-economic improvement – value orientations which characterise the middle classes throughout all societies. Nonetheless this suburban estate has not been dissolved (at least not yet) through the process of income mobility which many households have clearly experienced. While families undergo the problems faced by their counterparts throughout the metropolis, such as brain-numbing traffic jams, the adverse health affects of air pollution, and the lack of sufficient time to commit to their families (see Ross and Pongsomlee 1996), they do nevertheless express a discernible sense of place. It is clear that the people of Pratchaniwet were able to respond creatively to the challenges facing them because of a set of preconditions (educational backgrounds, social affinities and communicative competencies among other things). But I have argued that there were also some culturally specific Thai factors at work which enabled problems to be addressed, and the processes of problem solving itself (through sociability) lent cultural legitimacy and reinforcement to these very practical objectives.

7 Fields of cultural capital

Land, livelihood and landscape transformation on the rural–urban fringe

Introduction: the ambiguous rural–urban fringe

In 1970 the province of Nonthaburi was described in a guide to Thailands' seventy-three provinces as a distinctively agricultural area. Conveniently located on the northern and northwestern boundaries of the Bangkok Municipal Area, it was recommended to weekend travellers from the city as a place famous for its Turian gardens; here they could tour a traditional landscape of placid canals and rice fields, and make merit at old and renowned temples (Supha 1970: 114–16). Above all, the province was identified by the image of its many small orchards worked by sturdy Thai gardening families (*chao suan*) (Yani 1995: 83). But within two decades of this guide's portrayal of rusticity, Nonthaburi experienced a radical transformation in its economic base and its landscape, like its counterpart metropolitan fringe provinces Pathum Thani and Samut Prakan. From the 1980s, expanding road and highway networks to the north of the BMA opened formerly inaccessible agricultural land to the burgeoning housing industry. From the early 1990s, housing estates (*mubanchatsan*) spread to the western side of the province, following the new state highway projects and bridges which cut across the river. The construction boom boosted residential land uses in Nonthaburi to 23 per cent by 1990 (compared to 12 per cent six years earlier), a figure far in excess of the other four provinces bordering the BMA (Banasopit *et al.* 1990: 34; Somkiat 1989: 40). By 1995, agriculture accounted for just 4.22 per cent of the province's Gross Provincial Product, despite the fact that agricultural activities still dominated overall land use (71 per cent). By contrast, manufacturing contributed 29 per cent and construction activity 11 per cent to the province's economy. Trade and services were Nonthaburi's principal economic sectors (Nonthaburi Province, Planning Office 1996: 12).

By the 1990s, Nonthaburi's annual population growth rate exceeded all other provinces in Thailand (Alpha Research 1994: 24). In the wake of these population changes, the Ministry of the Interior belatedly reclassified sections of former rural districts to sanitary districts (*sukhaphiban*) with the result that by 1990 40 per cent of the province's population resided in officially-designated non-rural areas (*thesaban*) (NSO 1990b).[1] In 1996, the preamble to the province's amended Master Plan noted that parts of Nonthaburi were already indistinguishable from Krung Thep. Its designated role for the future was to act as a receiving area (*rongrap*) for the people and burgeoning economic activities of an extended metropolitan space (Nonthaburi Province, Planning Office 1996: 5).

From the late 1980s, the transformation of the 'urban fringe' of Bangkok and other Asian cities has attracted the increased attention and study of policy-makers, planners, regional geographers and a variety of other social science researchers. Geographers have identified the mixed and dynamic functions of these spaces as a new regional phenomenon heralding the break down of distinctively rural and urban geographies. The mixed ecological and economic spaces formerly defined as urban fringes are now generally viewed as interacting components of new mega-urban regions of Southeast Asia – territorial formations with multiple and contrasting land uses (McGee 1989; Ginsburg 1991). Most argue that this new hybrid regional form in Southeast Asia owes its primary origins to the driving force of global investment flows following regional and global industrial restructuring and state-driven export-orientated industrial policy (Douglass 1995; Greenberg 1994). Recent research, however, shows that local as well as global investors are determining the distribution and concentration of land uses (Parnwell and Luxmon 1997). The ultimate end-point configuration of these dynamic regional spaces is unclear, and a variety of future scenarios have been sketched – from ultimate homogenisation to continuing internal diversity. Some analysts suggest that older village settlements may persist, although serving modern dormitory functions (Greenberg 1994; Webster 1995). Despite varied emphases on local or global factors producing and sustaining Bangkok's extended metropolitan region, geographers' models have told us little of the social dynamics and communities underlying this complex and dynamic space – they have focused largely on surface distributions with only passing attention to the localised socio-economic dynamics of landscape production. In contrast, the few detailed social studies conducted in these mega-urban regions of Southeast Asia show that ordinary local people play a crucial role in contributing to changing land uses and economic activities (Allen 1994; Brookfield, Hadi and Mahmud 1991). This chapter likewise approaches the study of the mega-urban region by examining the role of local agents of change – ordinary people – whose lifestyles and decision making may be seen to mediate the broader forces of change.

It is easy to portray the people of the fringe areas as victims of the incursion of the city, and the metaphor of invasion in fact dominates scholars' interpretations of change on Bangkok's rural–urban fringe (for a recent example see Anuchat and Ross 1992: 17).[2] The sheer ecological and visual change to former rice-farming and orchard areas is dramatic. Housing estates, freeways, factories, department stores and modern transport are juxtaposed dramatically with rice fields, canals and small village settlements. As one gardener of Bang Kruai District, Nonthaburi, remarked of the process: '*sangkhom muang khao ma kin mot lery*' ('urban society has come in and consumed everything'). Yet this is only part of the story. Together with his neighbours, the same gardener attended a public hearing on the new master plan for Nonthaburi (in 1996) and vehemently opposed the classification of his land as 'rural and agricultural' on the grounds that the land values of his holdings would be depressed. He vowed that his children would never work in agriculture: his eldest daughter was studying marketing at a private university and on graduation she would marry her boyfriend and live with him in a new housing estate in one of Bangkok's suburbs across the river. This highlights something about the ways in which these households and their members participate in a complex process of change and consumption. The characteristics of this process are distorted when the expanding urban frontier is used as a territorial metaphor to encompass broader processes of social change, as if the city has been imposed on an innocent and unchanging rural populace. In territorial terms, agricultural settlements may be apparently surrounded or absorbed into a new urban landscape, but fundamental changes in household strategies have contributed to such transformation long before such physical encroachment commenced.[3]

This chapter is based on ethnographic and survey research which I conducted in two subdistricts of Nonthaburi province in the period 1995–6. It investigates how agricultural smallholders perceive and act in their changing environment, both outside and within their immediate surroundings. A key theoretical approach guiding this research is that local socio-economic 'actors' play an important part in the overall process of change, responding and interacting with broader structural changes to economy, society and space (Bryant 1995; Spencer 1993). A critical area of study in this local context is land, and its function and meaning for landowners and users. It is a dimension which is at once both economic and cultural, since it is tied to the process of status accumulation, a central element in Thai cultural practice. Land represents a multivalent resource – it is alienable property (*sapsin*), a place for living (*thi yu*) a livelihood resource (*thi din*) and household inheritance (*moradok*). My central argument in this chapter is that strategies promoting household livelihood and status reproduction on the part of gardeners (*chao suan*) and rice-farmers (*chao na*) have, over the past three generations, played a critical role in the underlying transformations of these areas.

Bang Khanun and Phimonrat: settlements in transition

The two subdistricts (*tambon*) of Bang Khanun and Phimonrat are located in the districts (*amphur*) of Bang Kruai and Bang Buathong respectively, on the western side of the Chao Phraya River. They represent the diverse and complex landscape within which agricultural households pursue their livelihoods today. Bang Kruai is an old orchard area, and Bang Buathong a rice-growing district. These settlements once formed the most highly productive agricultural regions of the Chao Phraya delta, a traditional farming ecology based on rain-fed crops sustained by the seasonal inundation of natural and man-made water channels. The alluvial soils of the delta have sustained settlements for centuries. In the Bang Kruai district, in the south of the province, Thai village settlements devoted to fruit and rice cropping existed from at least the early sixteenth century (as recorded in maps, see, e.g. La Loubere 1986). As elsewhere in the delta, small villages clustered along the natural levees of the river banks and routes of canals, with their gardens and rice fields watered by the seasonal flooding of the river. The pattern of settlement here was relatively dense, and is evidenced by the large number of *wat* dating from the sixteenth century, which points to the existence of communities capable of producing a surplus to be translated into the important task of merit making. The villagers of Bang Khanun were linked into a web of economic exchange extending from small markets to the large market town of Talat Khwan, which assumed importance as an administrative centre under the name of Muang Nonthaburi from the seventeenth century (Terwiel 1989: 89, 121–2).

However, until the late nineteenth century, the regions of Nonthaburi beyond the main waterways focusing on the Chao Phraya River were unpopulated and inaccessible unless settlement was made feasible by extending canals, a process often undertaken on a modest scale by communities themselves (Tanabe 1977: 27). Areas in north and central Nonthaburi province have a varied settlement history. Mon refugees (who migrated in a series of waves in the seventeenth and eighteenth centuries) were encouraged to farm the sparsely populated districts around Pakret and Pathumthani (formerly Sam Khok). By the early nineteenth century these clusters of Mon villages had become the most substantial settlements between Muang Nonthaburi and the old capital of Ayutthaya to the north (Terwiel 1989: 122). To the west of the Chao Phraya River, settlement began to spread from the Bang Buathong canal, pioneered from the 1840s by Lao war captives and later by Malay Muslims forcibly resettled from the defeated sultanate of Pattani. The Phra Phimonrat canal – originally a small modified natural stream west of Khlong Bang Buathong – was settled first by Lao households. They were joined in later decades by larger groups of Malay families from the Pak Kret area. They built their homes on the banks of this modified natural stream, cleared the surrounding forests for rice-cropping, and established familiar religious institutions to sustain their communities.

The central provinces bore the brunt of the transformation of the Thai economy in the nineteenth century (see Chatthip 1984: 36–50; Douglass 1984). The communities of Bang Khanun and Phimonrat were enmeshed in this broader process, which saw expanding production and an increasing monetisation of the peasant economy. In the 1860s major state projects such as the new Mahasawat Canal (linking Bang Kruai to Nakhon Chaisri in the west) opened further land for settlement in the Bang Khanun area. At the turn of the century, the small stream used by the farmers of Phimonrat was widened in order to facilitate settlement and allow for the easier transportation of rice to Bangkok. The expansion of cultivation was spurred primarily by the decline of the corvée labour system and the dismantling of the precapitalist *sakdina* system of population and labour control, giving greater opportunities for peasants to search for and attain smallholdings of their own (Tanabe 1977: 61). Even before land titles were issued in the late 1890s, farmers could acquire rights to cultivate new land, which included the right to sell or mortgage holdings (Wales 1934: 121–2). Pioneer farmers eagerly embraced opportunities for proprietorship in a new market economy (Sharp and Hanks 1978: 77). In Phimonrat the first major wave of settlement and land acquisition seems to have occurred from the mid-1890s and continued into the first decade of the twentieth century. Recollections of elderly farmers of Phimonrat indicate that some of these settlers held rice-fields of up to 150 rai (60 acres, or 24 hectares).

From the later decades of the nineteenth century the livelihoods of the peasant households of Phimonrat and Bang Khanun were linked to broader markets through an expanding group of Chinese rice-trading middlemen and rice-millers. Production was almost exclusively devoted to rice among Phimonrat households, while in Bang Khanun families engaged in both market-orientated fruit growing and rice cultivation. In the latter area the growth of a metropolitan consumer market in Bangkok led to peasant households converting rice-fields to orchards to such an extent, that by the 1940s, little rice-land remained in the Bang Kruai district. Although relying increasingly on a money economy for their livelihood, households were sustained by patterns of subsistence production, using local food resources as a basis for household sustenance. In Bang Khanun, women commonly sold or bartered orchard surpluses at local canal-based markets to supplement family needs. Customary practices of labour exchange were common in both areas until well into the twentieth century. Patterns of communality were reinforced by a physical isolation imposed by slow water-borne transportation.

Old Bang Khanun residents recall that visits to Krung Thep were rare among family members as late as the 1940s, taking place once or twice a year for the purchase of essential supplies unobtainable locally (mosquito nets, for example). Phimonrat farmers rarely ventured beyond the market and district office of Bang Buathong, a journey on foot which took the best part of a day to accomplish. The years after the Second World War ushered in a period of accelerated change in both the social horizons of households and their connections to an increasingly diversified labour market and economy. The period saw a diversification of income sources among villagers into petty trade, transport and construction, as well as expanding opportunities for education and the status resources of white collar work for the children of the better-off households. As a result, the nature of the villages was changing. Some households had little to do with agriculture. New arrivals purchased small plots from farmers to build houses. Children of farmers and gardeners (who pursued occupations in government service or other non-agricultural work) built houses next to their parents, contributing to an increasing densification of village settlement. These were added to the existing house plots of farm labourers, who, although having no rice land or orchards, generally owned their homes. By the 1990s a high proportion of village homeowners could not be equated with agricultural livelihoods, despite the fact that many could claim kin connections with – and might be living next door to – agriculturalists who worked the fields and orchards beyond the canal banks.

From the 1950s motorised boats transported goods to markets and also transported increasing numbers of family members to work in Bangkok. The eastern side of the province bore the brunt of ecological transformation. During the 1960s and 1970s commercial activities, housing and industry expanded northward from central Bangkok along newly constructed road and highway networks. On the western side, including Bang Khanun and Phimonrat, radical change in the local living and working environment of agricultural households was delayed until new bridges were constructed across the Chao Phraya River from the 1970s onwards. Today, the Bang Kruai district is linked both to the metropolis and its surrounding districts by the traditional canal transportation routes and newly constructed roads. The Rama VII bridge joins Bang Kruai to the eastern side of the province. Bang Buathong (to the north of Bang Kruai) was formerly reached only by canals and a few minor roads, but has since been made accessible by the construction of the north–south Talingchan–Suphanburi Highway. In 1983 a new bridge crossing the Chao Phraya River connected the Bang Buathong district via Rattanathibet Road to the eastern side of the province and beyond. Both Ban Kruai and Bang Buathong districts are characterised by an increasingly diverse land use, with road construction that has influenced patterns of land sale and conversion to commercial or residential use.

The mid-1980s saw light manufacturing establishments locating in the vicinity of the Phimonrat villages (formerly part of Tambon Bang Buathong). In 1994 the total number of establishments in this area numbered 193, employing over 3,500 people. Most of these firms were small, with only two employing over a hundred people (Department of Town and Country Planning 1994: 110). The bulk of recent population growth and new housing development lies to the east of Tambon Phimonrat, close to the district centre (*amphur*) of Bang Buathong. But from 1992–3 land purchases in a number of villages heralded the arrival of housing estates in the immediate vicinity. By 1995 there were seven housing projects nearing completion, focusing on the land close to the north–south Talingchan–Suphanburi highway, but also scattered to the west. The westward expansion of estates was facilitated by a new road cut through the rice-fields in the early 1990s on the initiative of the local Phimonrat farmers (through the Tambon Council). In 1995 a visitor to Phimonrat would encounter a landscape of considerable diversity. Entering Tambon Phimonrat from the eight-lane Talingchan–Suphanburi highway, one first encountered huge advertisements proclaiming the modern lifestyles available in Muban Bang Buathong Phase 4 and Wirotville, the latter featuring large units in *Satai Roman* (Roman Style) for *khon mi radab* (people with class/status). Proceeding further westward, crossing a bridge over one of the small lateral canals, a less congested landscape opened out to reveal farmers ploughing their fields, some of them wedged between new *mubanchatsan*. Signs indicating the names and official numbers of the *muban* (villages) stood next to new entrance lanes (wide enough for vehicles) recently cut through to the villages lining the Phimonrat canal 50 metres distance from the road. On the canal itself, a busy commuter traffic of motorised boats plied between the villages and the market town of Bang Buathong – mainly comprising housewives going to and from the town market and school children. But the road had clearly become an alternative focus of activity, with a variety of shops and small petrol pumps servicing passers-by.

In Bang Khanun too, signs of the new wave of housing estates in 1995 were conspicuous, with three estates under construction on the *tambon*

Plate 7.1 A farmer of Tambon Phimonrat ploughs his land which is bounded by a nearly completed *mubanchatsan*. (Photo: Author)

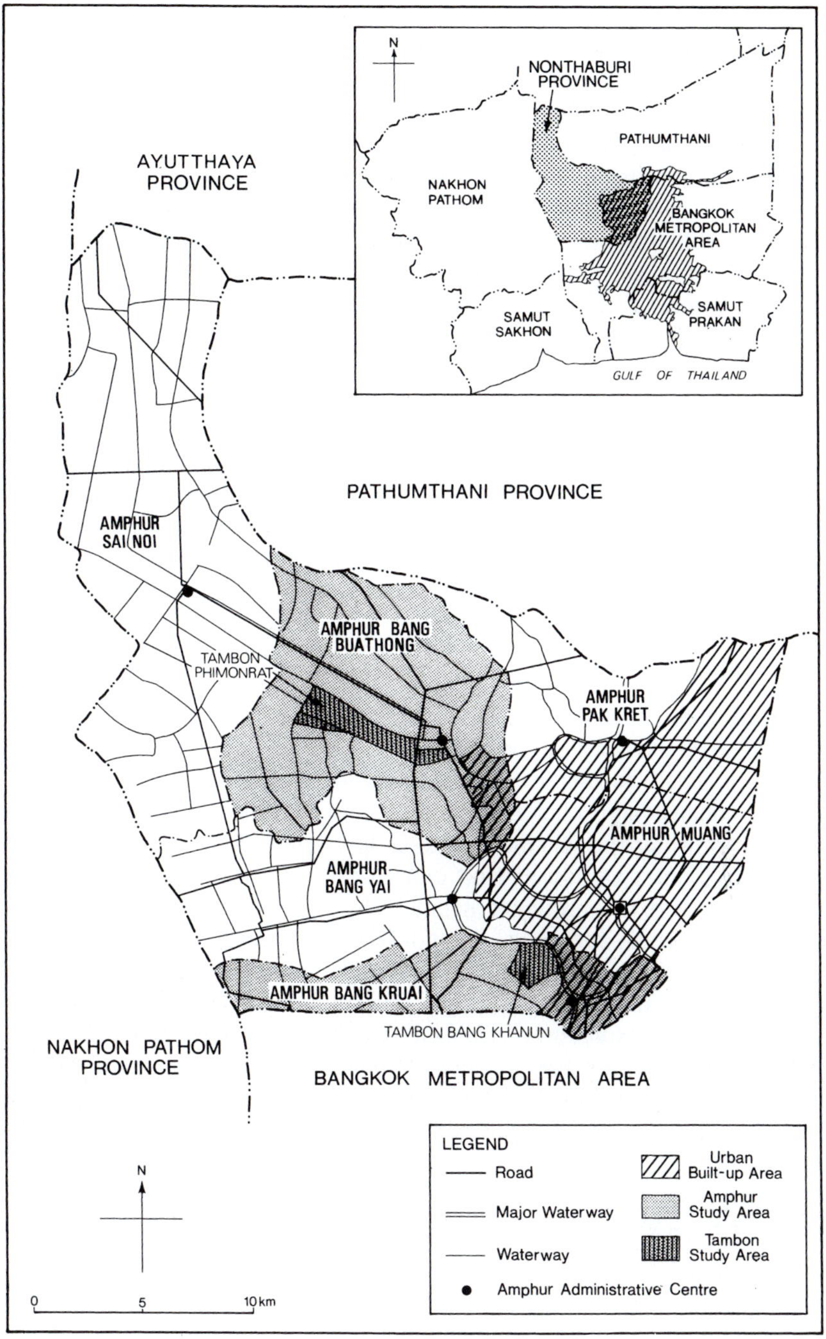

Figure 7.1 Nonthaburi province, showing Tambon Phimonrat and Bang Khanun, with metropolitan built-up area, 1996.

border, and another one inside the *tambon* boundary completed and open for inspection. With its winding entrance road yet to be widened and sealed, Bang Khanun still appeared verdant, with thick canopies of coconut palms and densely planted orchards of banana, jackfruit and mangosteens lining the narrow road. Yet hand-painted signs advertising land sales betrayed this apparent isolation. While most gardeners still lived in homes along the Bangkok Noi canal or its subsidiary streams, new white-stuccoed homes were noticeable, announcing their owners' modern lifestyles with driveways and fancy gates. As in Phimonrat, a steady commuter traffic comprising a diverse assortment of *song thaeos*, motorbikes, decrepit bicycles and Hi-Lux vans highlighted the varied incomes and livelihoods of the local people. Most strikingly symbolic of the recent orientation to the roadway was the newly-constructed gateway to Wat Bang Khanun, welcoming visitors with its shining gold, blue and red glass tiles. Next to the gleaming new *wat* gateway, a humble thatched noodle stall conducted a healthy business with elderly women merit-makers and garden labourers. The following sections of this chapter explore the emergence of these hybrid local landscapes in relation to the evolving and adaptive livelihoods, family strategies and status concerns of local households.

Land, labour and income

The gardeners of Bang Khanun practise a livelihood that seems little changed since the days of their forebears. Their densely planted orchards, seemingly small forests of coconut and betel palms, jackffuit, turian, pomelo, bananas and other fruit varieties, rely on the monsoonal rains to periodically water the channels of their low-lying plots. Many gardeners commonly plant a variety of fruit crops which ripen throughout the year, in order to assure a continuous income. This pattern of cultivation, known as *lom luk* (literally meaning 'up and down', seasonal) reflects the traditional gardener's concern to ensure household subsistence, self-reliance and flexibility. This method contrasts with tree fruit specialisation, known as *yun ton*. The cultivation of fruit orchards has always been orientated to markets, but gardening also has the advantage of producing food for daily consumption. This is one reason given by many gardeners for the fact that their lifestyle is relatively comfortable (*thamngan sabai*), involving steady work all year round, in contrast to the intense periods of seasonal labour demanded of rice-farmers.

Despite the apparent simplicity of planting practices, they reflect a keen awareness of gardeners' orientation to the market, and the fruit varieties planted by the *chao suan* have evolved accordingly. It is common to find a pattern of planting combining plants of a very old age (turian, coconut and betel palms) together with recently-planted fruit crops such as oranges, pomelo and limes, a response to the expanding demand of the metropolitan market. Another reason for the development of these crops is the increasing age of the gardeners, most of whom are now aged 50 years and above. The harvesting of tree fruit such as jackfruit (*khanun*) and turian demands considerable exertion as well as expenditure on the hiring of labour, assets which many elderly gardeners do not have, unless their children continue to work the orchards as a vocation. So changing the mix of crop types has been one adaptation to changing conditions. Yet another reason has been the replacement of fruit trees damaged by major floods, particularly that of 1983 and the most recent and most devastating flood of 1995. Traditional tree crops such as the turian take a long time – seven years – to reach full maturity. Moreover, many turian trees have died through the effects of floods, and environmental changes brought about through air and water pollution have led to a severe decline in the yield of these traditional tree crops. Today, gardeners of limited means prefer to invest in crops which will assure a quick return and yield saleable fruit throughout the year.

The average size of garden holdings is small, generally 2–4 rai (0.8–1.6 acres). Gardeners say that some twenty years ago it was possible to make a reasonable living from 2 rai but this is now no longer the case, due to increases in costs of labour, fertiliser, pesticides, food and family necessities. The size of the holdings today also reflects a progressive reduction in land plot size through family inheritance practices. In 1990, average incomes of gardening households (40,000–50,000 baht) were in fact lower than the province per capita income (62,797 baht), and substantially lower than estimated average incomes for households in the greater Bangkok region (82,764 baht) (NSO 1997). In fact, Bang Khanun gardeners' annual incomes were not much higher than those of skilled tradesmen in the same district, and substantially lower than the average incomes of government employees (70,000 baht) (Agricultural Office, Bang Kruai District 1994: 26; NRDC Data Base 1990).

Yet these average income figures can be misleading. Some gardeners can enjoy extremely high incomes through specialisation of crops, but this demands a greater investment and risk than many have the capacity or the will to take. This is one of the key distinctions between orchard operators in Bang Khanun, reflecting disparities in income and approach. The better-off gardeners comprise three subgroups. First, those who concentrate on producing tree fruits (such as oranges, turian, jackfruit, mangosteen and satorica) which enjoy higher prices in the market; second, those who grow fruit tree cuttings which are in great demand in the provinces where fruit growing has expanded; or third, those who focus on the expanding urban consumer market for flowers by growing roses or orchids. Profits from these specialised products grown on the limited holdings of 3–4 rai can yield annual incomes in excess of 100,000 baht per year, but they require considerable investment.

The characteristics of agriculture and incomes in Phimonrat contrast strikingly with those in Bang Khanun. In contrast to Bang Khanun, where the majority of gardeners own their land (82 per cent), less than half of

Plate 7.2 Lung Suphap with his jackfruit trees, a traditional *chaosuan* of Bang Khanun, growing a variety of seasonal fruits (*lom luk*) for a stable but basic income. (Photo: Author)

the households of Phimonrat own all the fields they work. Moreover, a quarter of these households own holdings of less than 10 rai, which is insufficient to produce an adequate income from rice-farming alone. Ten rai of rice-land harvested twice a year yields an estimated net income of just 22,000 baht, which is just over half the annual income of factory workers in the district. Those who work 20 rai of rice-land are not substantially better-off than full-time factory workers either (averaging 44,000 baht per year as compared to 40,000 baht). On these estimates, only a third of Phimonrat farmers (those with over 30 rai) earn incomes above the average of regularly employed wage-workers (NRDC Data Base 1990; Agricultural Office, Bang Buathong District 1994: 23–4). It is thus hardly surprising that many rice-farmers also work as hired agricultural labour or combine farming with non-agricultural occupations, particularly in the building industry. Family histories reveal a pattern of ever-reducing landholdings due to the division of land for inheritance. And, as with other

Plate 7.3 The modern *chaosuan* of Bang Khanun: Khun Somchet with the orchids he sells to middlemen for marketing to major Bangkok hotels and overseas buyers. (Photo: Author)

rice farming communities, smallholders have faced problems of increasing debt through the need to invest ever-larger amounts of money into buying or hiring machinery, paying for fertiliser and hiring labour for planting and harvesting. Increasingly, loss of land has been the result (for which see Chantana 1993: 6). There are numerous cases of rice-farmers mortgaging their holdings to the local rice-miller or to better-off farmers in the area, and eventually losing title to this land through their inability to repay debts. In one Phimonrat village, all the farmers grow rice on land which their families once owned, but now rent from the local rice-miller due to indebtedness.

From the early 1970s, many Phimonrat households turned to fruit tree cultivation to supplement their vulnerable and declining incomes. It made sense to utilise the slack period after harvest for extra money, and planting a variety of fruit crops in small sections of a farmer's holding offered the advantage of gaining supplementary income throughout the year.

Gradually, some rice-farmers in Phimonrat devoted their efforts completely to fruit cultivation, since more income could be gained from cultivating less land, even though the initial investment was higher than rice per rai. For example, from planting one rai of land with mango trees, a farmer could eventually earn an annual income of an estimated 19,200 baht, or over seventeen times the amount that could be earned from planting the same area with rice (1,100 baht) (Agricultural Office, Bang Buathong District 1994: 23). It was a rational response to the constraints imposed by small landholdings and a changing family occupational structure where fewer children (and often none) were engaged in the agricultural enterprise.

Administratively defined as rural, the two *tambon* under consideration here are grouped into wider districts (*amphur*), which comprise adjacent municipal (*thesaban*) and sanitary (*sukhapiban*) subdistricts. These classifications and boundaries primarily reflect evolving patterns of population density and the ways the state has mapped them. To highlight the specific characteristics of the households in the two *tambon*, it is useful to view occupational and workplace statistics at this district level first, since this reflects the immediate environment of the farming and gardening households – including the market towns, the housing estates with new populations, and the key transportation nodes where a diverse service industry has developed. Many households of *amphur* Bang Kruai and Bang Buathong pursue non-agricultural occupations within Nonthaburi province or further afield in the metropolitan region. In 1990, households with members solely engaged in agriculture comprised just 21.7 per cent of households in Bang Buathong and 29.6 per cent in Bang Kruai (Amyot 1994: 160). Considered at a district level, the role of agriculture as a sole income-earning activity is clearly less important than non-agricultural wage and salary earning. In Bang Buathong, factory work is an important source of income for household members, with a greater proportion of women engaged in industrial labour. In Bang Kruai, the workforce is more diverse, and in contrast to Bang Buathong where the majority of wage and salary earners find work within the district, most non-agricultural workers of Bang Kruai (79 per cent of males and 82 per cent of women) travel into the metropolitan district to work (Amyot 1994: 162).

Not surprisingly, the proportions of Phimonrat and Bang Khanun households engaged in agriculture are somewhat higher than these district averages. In Tambon Bang Khanun, families categorised by local officials in 1994–5 as 'agricultural households' represented 34 per cent of all resident families, while in Tambon Phimonrat 51 per cent were counted in this category (Agricultural Office, Nonthaburi 1995: File No. 4; Agricultural Office, Tambon Bang Buathong 1994: 19). These 'agricultural households', are officially defined as those families owning or renting farm land with household heads engaged in agriculture. But despite this designation, these families have a varied occupational structure linking members to the non-agricultural sectors of industry, commerce and government

Table 7.1 Proportion of total household income derived from agriculture, horticulture and aquaculture, households in Tambon Bang Khanun and Tambon Phimonrat, 1995

Tambon	*Proportion of household income (%)*					
	None	*< 20*	*20–49*	*50–79*	*> 80*	*Total*
Bang Khanun	50.8	11.4	8.1	6.5	22.9	70
Phimonrat	35.0	7.2	4.1	9.2	44.3	102

Source: Author's 1-in-5 household survey, 3 villages Bang Khanun, 4 villages Phimonrat, 1995.

service both in the inner metropolitan area or the immediate area. Table 7.1. shows that agricultural activity provides varied proportions of income for different families, and is the sole support of only a minority of households living in the villages of these *tambon.*

In 1995 I conducted an occupational survey of families in villages of the two *tambon.* It showed that in Phimonrat villages only 26.6 per cent of households headed by agriculturalists had all adult children following their parent's occupations, while 44 per cent of these households had no adult children in agriculture. For Bang Khanun, the proportions were 14.7 per cent and 41.1 per cent respectively. Notably, a significant proportion of these farm operator-headed families had adult children distributed across the employment sectors. In Phimonrat, 24 per cent of these households had at least one adult child sharing in their parent's enterprise, while in Bang Khanun, 44 per cent of the surveyed agricultural households had at least one adult child working the family orchard.

Clearly, families continue to engage in agriculture at a variety of levels in these villages in the context of an overall decline in rice-farming and gardening across the generations. The significance of agriculture in supporting household livelihood is determined by the capacity of households' landholdings, their access to labour and capital inputs, and the market. These patterns need to be assessed in the context of continuities and changes in the function of land as a multiple resource, and by viewing the household as a dynamic historical agent deploying resources towards the acquisition of status – i.e. cultural capital – as much as survival.

Land and status

The sale and conversion of land to new residential, industrial and commercial uses is one way of portraying the central dynamic which transforms the landscape of the urban fringe. Viewed from particular localities and family histories, it is rarely that simple, either as a process or an outcome. To comprehend patterns of land disposal, we must appreciate that landholdings have many meanings and functions. In common with peasant households in Thailand, families in Phimonrat and Bang Khanun have traditionally utilised land as a multiple resource – for survival, for profit and accumulation, and for cultural capital. While today land no longer provides the sole income for a large proportion of households – and non-agricultural work often offers individuals and families better incomes – it still constitutes the key historical foundation for economic advancement and has to a large extent determined contemporary patterns of differentiation among households.

Possession and transmission of land through inheritance has played the pre-eminent role in determining life chances and status. In both Bang Khanun and Phimonrat, local people have a keen awareness of the property holdings of their neighbours and measure their status accordingly. Traditionally, land gave wealthier families the capacity to reproduce and expand landholdings and status through further land purchase, arrangement of favourable marriages for children, and education of their offspring. In Bang Khanun, a household's capacity to afford education for sons (and later, daughters) provided them with access to work in government service (*rap ratchakan*), an occupation which still continues to be held in high esteem for its status and security benefits. Family histories in Bang Khanun show how wealthier families in the 1930s were investing in sons' education for government service, with the result that the occupational profiles of their households diversified, even though the core household remained committed to an agricultural way of life. The case of Lung Pherm (Uncle Pherm) illustrates this process. Lung Pherm was born into a gardening family which was considered to be well-off. His father and mother held land in two subdistricts, comprising 33 rai of both rice land and orchards. After his marriage at the age of twenty in 1935, his father gave him 20 rai of orchards. He and his wife later purchased a further 10 rai of orchard land in Bang Khanun, where they moved to live. On his father's death, Lung Pherm inherited a further 13 rai of orchard land, raising his total holdings to 43 rai. His wife bore eleven children. Of these, two sons followed their father's occupation as gardeners, while two entered government service, one as a military officer and another as a school teacher. Three of his daughters also received secondary and further education and entered government service. The youngest of these daughters studied to university level and entered teaching. Another daughter finished her secondary schooling, married a gardener and maintains an orchard in another district. Lung Pherm's orchard holdings clearly allowed him to generate enough income to educate his children while maintaining an adequate living – and they allowed him to distribute land to those sons and daughters who continued in agriculture.

As suggested above, the division of land for inheritance could affect the fortunes of succeeding generations engaged in gardening because landholdings were progressively reduced. In this sense the diversification of families' occupations into non-agricultural sectors might be seen as a strategy of survival as well as status acquisition and maintenance. Nonetheless, possession of larger holdings and the income derived from them ultimately framed the opportunities of children and grandchildren, helping maintain their economic status, whether in agriculture or not. The case of Lung Suthin is instructive here. Lung Suthin (68 years of age) is the retired headmaster of the local school of Wat Bang Khanun. His parents' total orchard holdings of 10 rai had generated sufficient income for them to support his and his sister's vocational education, yet they seem never to have considered abandoning gardening. On completion of his teacher training, he returned to Bang Khanun to work at the local school and in 1948 married a woman from the neighbourhood where he had grown up. He and his wife used their orchard to supplement the modest government income from his salary. They lived and worked on a holding of 5 rai of orchard land inherited from Lung Suthin's parents. He maintained a lifestyle of both gardener and *kharatchakan*, and is still highly respected in the community. Like women in the neighbouring garden families, his wife pursued the traditional role of *mae kha* (female vendor), selling the garden surplus at the nearby floating market. Given their large number of children, neither occupation on its own would have been enough to maintain their growing family. But when combined, these incomes permitted both the maintenance of the family's livelihood and the advancement of the childrens' life chances through education. They raised a large family of eleven children, and were able to support their education through secondary school and technical or commercial colleges. Only his youngest son continues the occupation of gardener on Lung Suthin's garden land. He is a chemistry graduate who made a deliberate choice to return to gardening to be with his parents and pursue a different lifestyle to his peers who work in commerce and industry. He stresses that the land is *moradok* (family inheritance), and thus should be maintained and nurtured.

Bang Khanun residents who consider themselves poor (*chon*) in comparison with their neighbours explain the origins of their condition in terms of their parents' lack of land, or the absence of inheritance. Mrs Chum (aged 37 years) emphasises that she and her two sisters and four brothers attended school for only four years, because her parents had no orchard land and could not generate enough income to pay for any further education. Until the time of her marriage she worked in the small orchard of her maternal grandmother and worked as a daily labourer on neighbours' holdings. Life improved for Mrs Chum and her husband when her grandmother died and bequeathed to her a house and orchard holdings of 2 rai. She, her husband and her sisters have divided the crops between *lom luk* and roses. They do not grow the roses in enough quantities to sell as single flowers, but rather use them to make garlands which are then sold at the large market of Pak Khlong Talat in Bangkok. The orchard produce brings them a bare income of around 3,000–4,000 baht per month. Given the limited family income, Mrs Chum does not expect her children to be educated beyond the early years of secondary school.

Similarly, among the Muslim rice-farming families of Phimonrat, fortunes have been based on transmission of and access to land, as well as the capacity of landholdings to sustain livelihood. The stories of men and women who are now without farming land indicate that the progressive reduction of landholdings and the continued uncertainties of incomes from these small farm holdings were fundamental constraints to the maintenance of livelihood and economic status. Pu Abdullah (grandfather Abdullah) is 81 years of age. His father was a large landholder of 150 rai of rice land. He was one of four children who received an inheritance of around 35 rai each. While this was a medium sized rice farm, Grandfather Abdullah became progressively indebted to the point where he lost this land to those neighbours to whom he owed money. He then worked as a farm labourer for neighbouring rice-farmers and later tried his hand as a vendor in Bangkok. With little education and no land, his seven children worked as farm labourers or vendors. For others with insufficient land, farm labouring (*rap chang*) was combined with cultivation of their own fields.

Grandfather Abdullah's situation contrasts with the fortunes of the two brothers Ibrahim and Ismael in the neighbouring village of Ban Rongsuat. Their father had inherited 30 rai of rice land from his parents and had purchased a further 24 rai from relatives in the area. Together, they inherited this total landholding of 54 rai. This farmland enabled them to maintain a standard of living which they describe as '*dikwa chon noi*' (a little better than poor) and 'better than eating salt' (*mai dong kin klua*). Yet this land represented not only a livelihood (*kan tham ha kin*) but also important cultural capital. In 1988 they sold 10 rai of this land (at 15,000 baht per rai), and with the proceeds paid off their debts to the local rice-miller and financed the costs of a pilgrimage to Mecca. They gradually converted 10 rai of rice land into orchard and rented the remaining land to farmers from a neighbouring village. Rented at 500 baht per rai, they receive a total rental income of 20,000 baht annually, in addition to at least twice that amount derived from their newly expanded fruit orchard. Both men were able to afford schooling expenses for their children to at least the level of senior secondary school. Their sons are a hairdresser, radio technician, jeweller and religious teacher. Of their daughters, one works as a nurse and another a hairdresser, while the youngest is at school.

Among the communities of the rural–urban fringe, land continues to play the fundamental role as an economic foundation for household strategies and the acquisition of cultural capital. But agriculture as such is less and less the basis of occupations. Occupational diversification has a long history – especially among Bang Khanun households – and was evident as early as the 1930s among families of means. The trend towards occupational

Table 7.2 Aspirations for children's occupations among parents in agriculture, Bang Khanun and Phimonrat, 1995

Work type	*% household preferences*	*No.*
Achieve high educational qualifications*	22.0	38
Business (self-employment)	3.4	6
Career with regular salary	13.9	24
Government service	29.0	50
Professional	2.3	4
Let children decide	29.0	50
Total	100.0	172

Source: As in Table 7.1.

Note
* These respondents did not specify occupations but stressed the importance of children achieving the highest possible qualifications as preparation.

diversity within lower-income families more recently is the result of an expansion of livelihood possibilities accompanying change in the economy generally since the 1970s. From the level of the household, it is important to acknowledge that this process is one in which households have played an active part. The households of Bang Khanun and Phimonrat are marked by a major contrast in the lifestyles between generations. While an older generation of grandparents and parents are largely wedded to agricultural vocations, many are adamant that they do not wish their children to enter agriculture. There is a general consensus among parents that there is no future in agriculture (*mai kao na*), and besides, it involves hard manual work (*tham ngan nak*). Also, an extremely important consideration among parents is to ensure security for their childrens' futures. The uncertainties of agriculture determined by the external market, fluctuating climatic conditions and disasters (especially floods), provide a fragile basis for a secure life in old age. In this they share the outlook of Thai farmers far more distant from the metropolis. In responding to a survey question about preferences for childrens' occupations, the highest proportion of household heads specifying desired occupations for their children stressed that government service was the most desirable. Government service represented comfortable work with regular income (*sabai*), and it was secure with the assurance of a pension on retirement (*man khong*) (see Table 7.2).

Thus, in considering decisions of households to dispose of land on the urban fringe, these existing orientations and expectations of farming and gardening families need to be acknowledged. Long before the asphalt met the rice fields, farming households were in transformation.

Responses to change: the uses of land

Environmental change

The destructive environmental impact of the advancing urban frontier of housing, industry and commercial activity on agricultural land has clearly played a critical role in rendering an already fragile agriculture virtually untenable as a basis for household livelihood (Banasopit *et al.* 1990: 51–2). Although fewer households now rely completely on agriculture as an income source, environmental changes have impacted negatively on the last generation of full-time farmers and gardeners. Viewed strictly from the perspective of agriculture, urban expansion is entirely negative. In Phimonrat, nearby housing development and industry have polluted canal water and brought pests (such as mice) to ravage the remaining rice fields. In the eastern half of Phimonrat – closest to the highway where housing estates have made the greatest incursion – fewer and fewer rice farms are viable. Most rice farming is practised to the west, where less land has been sold. In Bang Khanun, polluted river and canal water has had a major impact on the health of fruit trees which once flourished. Gardeners argue that the marked decline in turian yields over the past two decades is due to changes in air temperature, air pollution in the metropolis, and the continued vibrations caused by traffic using nearby roads.

But farmers and gardeners actively participated in the changes to their own environment. In Bang Khanun, gardeners had been quick to take advantage of new technology by attaching engines to their boats, a trend which added to increasing water pollution through the release of oil and petrol into the canal water. In both *tambon* over the last decade, local people have donated land for the construction of subsidiary roads to connect their settlements to the expanding road network. While adding many conveniences (allowing better access to services, markets and hospitals, for example), these initiatives opened these districts to an expanding housing industry. In describing the development of roads in their areas, agriculturalists invariably use the term progress (*khwamcharoen*) in a positive way to describe recent changes.

Moreover, the changing patterns of settlement have also been welcomed by many households. While Phimonrat farmers complain that the canals have been polluted, they also stress that the factories which opened nearby from the early 1980s afforded employment opportunities for their children close to home. In the predominantly Muslim villages of this *tambon*, the greater proportion have members working in factories. Prior to this, changes were already underway. Daughters began working in the industrialising district of Phrapadaeng (southeast of the BMA) in the 1970s. But the new factories in the Bang Buathong district allowed Muslim girls to work closer to home, which was a major advantage to parents, always concerned to protect their daughters' sexual virtue. Pa Mo (Auntie Mo) has two daughters who once worked in Prapadaeng, but now work in a nearby umbrella factory. She expresses a general view of the factories among her neighbours by noting '*diawni sabai*' ('now we are comfortable'). In one village (Ban Ronkrachom) the village headman works as a guard at a nearby factory and communicates with his assistants by mobile telephone. The advent of factories in Bang Buathong also presented new opportunities for local families to supplement their incomes by selling food to factory workers.

Alternative uses of land

From the mid-1980s an increasing demand for land for housing – increasingly accessible through an expanding road network – led to an escalation of land prices in the BMA's adjacent provinces. In Phimonrat, between 1985 and 1990, the average selling price for a rai of land rose from 30,000 baht to 70,000/100,000 baht. By 1995 prices per rai had soared to 2 million baht (3 million baht for land located close to roads). In Bang Khanun the price per rai had been around 50,000 prior to the land boom, but by the mid-1990s prices were equivalent to those in Phimonrat. One response of farmers and gardeners was simply to sell all their holdings. But in such cases householders did not necessarily abandon agriculture. Among households where agriculture was still actively practised, profits from land sale were often used to purchase land in other provinces where agricultural land was cheap.

The landscape to the east of Phimonrat may at first glance give the impression of a wholesale desertion of the area by its former occupants. However, the movement of farming families and the utilisation of land was determined by calculations concerning its most effective deployment. Notably, very large housing estates of over a hundred units are not conspicuous along the Bang Buathong–Sai Noi Road because of the difficulty faced by developers in assembling sufficient land blocks. Land for the largest housing estate near the main highway was able to be purchased easily because the whole parcel was owned by the Vietnamese Christian community at Bang Buathong. Most commonly, farmers have only disposed of sections of their landholdings. The logic of a landholder selling only part of his/her rice fields is based on a strategy of maximising the uses of assets for the household, particularly preserving sections for passing on to children and retaining still-productive or otherwise useful land. Thus Hadji Dawo planned to sell 17 rai of his holdings which were already surrounded by a housing estate. However he was preserving the remaining 8 rai for his six children to inherit. Selling sections of land in the climate of high land prices prevailing from the late 1980s to the mid-1990s offered farmers the advantage of paying their debts while preserving sections of their land for continued production, as we saw in the case of the two brothers, Ibrahim and Ismael. Lung Yaya sold 2 rai of his 11 rai holdings in 1989 at 800,000 baht per rai in order to liquidate debts incurred to a neighbour and the agricultural cooperative. With the 1 million baht remaining to him, he arranged for a pilgrimage to Mecca with his wife (50,500 baht) and made improvements to his house. He and his family continue to work the remaining land which they converted to fruit orchard.

For some Phimonrat people who had struggled all their lives to make ends meet, the chance to sell their insufficiently productive land during the land boom gave them new opportunities. Mrs Si-a had farmed 8 rai with her husband, but both had also needed to work as farm labourers to gain additional income. In 1994 they sold this 8 rai to a property developer known to their son, who was a driver for a construction company. With the proceeds of the sale (8 million baht) Mrs Si-a purchased a truck for her eldest son to establish him as an independent transport contractor, and deposited the remaining funds in the bank, with plans to later build a new house on a small plot of land inherited by her husband in a neighbouring *tambon*. Such strategies are of course not available to completely landless families, but to some extent, land sale has increased the status of some economically marginal households in Phimonrat. In Phimonrat, the partial sale of holdings over the decade to 1995 has commonly been used to repay debts, fund children's education, rebuild homes and purchase vehicles (see Table 7.3).

New income-generating activities

A more common approach to complete or partial land sale in Bang Khanun and Phimonrat has been the reorientation of income-generating activities towards the new opportunities presented by changes in these districts. More road traffic and more housing settlements with diverse populations has created an environment conducive to a range of family business activities which support overall household livelihood. On the border of Tambon Bang Khanun, where a sealed road has been upgraded to carry traffic to the *amphur* office, families have shifted the locations of their homes and opened small noodle stalls to cater to the *amphur* staff and to local people who travel to the *amphur* office and the hospital located behind it. Larger, more specialised concerns include restaurants attached to houses. Some gardeners have leased sections of their properties close to the road for outsiders to construct restaurants, but most often these are run by family members, relatives or their friends.

Some families who found themselves favourably located to new patterns of activity and traffic movement in the area have deployed their landholdings in ways that have assured complementary income sources both from outsiders and for family members. At the bridge leading to the Bang Kruai District office, one family has succeeded in attaining conspicuous success: garden land near the banks of the canal was developed for the building of a four-storey apartment block, to accommodate the increasing

Table 7.3 Use of funds from the sale of agricultural land in Tambon Phimonrat, 1985–95. Sales in villages Ban Khaisam and Ban Rongsuat

Owner's occupation	*Qty sold*	*Qty remaining*	*Use of holdings remaining*	*Reason for sale/use of funds*
Rice-farmer	11 rai	20 rai	Rice growing	Pay debts
Rice-farmer	10 rai	10 rai	Idle land	Too old to work/funds for retirement
Teacher	1 rai	House plot	Domestic use	Children's education
Agricultural labourer	200 wa	1 rai	Orchard	Building new house
Gardener	1 rai	3 rai	Orchard	Children's education/pay debts
Rice farmer/ agricultural labourer	2 rai	House plot	Domestic use	Land surrounded by housing estate*/ raise capital
Rice-farmer	30 rai	30 rai	Rice growing	Children's education/pay debts
Gardener	10 rai	5 rai	Orchard	Children's education
Rice-farmer/ gardener	10 rai	5 rai	Orchard	Pay debts/building new house/pick-up truck
Storekeeper/ gardener	2 rai	10 rai	Orchard	Children's education/pay debts
Rice-farmer (retired)	14 rai	2 rai	Given to children	Children's education/purchased house plot and built new house
Gardener	3 rai	25 rai	Orchard	Pay debts

Source: As in Table 7.1.

Note
* Sale funds were used to rent 65 rai of rice land in a more convenient location.

number of office workers employed in the western suburbs of the BMA as well as *amphur* officials. A relative from Bangkok purchased this land. The strip of land between the apartment and the canal was reserved and leased to other relatives who opened a canal-side restaurant which succeeded in attracting considerable custom. The land behind the apartment block was retained by the family, who built a new two-storey home as well as a small laundry and grocery store adjacent to the apartment block which the women of the household operate. In this case the family have completely abandoned gardening. Deeper into Bang Khanun, several families have benefited from partial land sale and built new modern brick homes. These homes have been designed to include shops facing the passing road, which are operated by the wives of the gardeners. Households and individuals with less capital have also begun to locate small noodle shops along the road leading into Bang Khanun.

In Phimonrat a similar pattern of entrepreneurial activity has developed along the Bang Buathong–Sai Noi Road. Local families enriched by land sales have completely rebuilt homes next to the road and opened stores attached to their residences. More typically, however, most local business concerns are fairly modest. For example, one family (whose old rice lands abut the road) operate a small petrol pump in addition to an eating house and general store which attracts business from both locals and the increasing number of passers-by, including building contractors, truck drivers and construction labourers. Behind the store the family have established a large pond for commercial fish breeding. Behind this fish pond they still maintain about 8 rai of rice land. These various enterprises have been developed for different members of the family to maintain. Another case of this family division of labour can be seen in the use of the brothers Ibrahim and Ismael's now-disused rice land bordering the road. They have kept the roadside land for the use of two of their married sons who formerly worked in Bangkok. One son, who works as a radio technician, has built a small wooden home incorporating a room which is used by his wife as a hairdressing shop. Another son works with his wife in the adjoining building, selling meals to Muslim neighbours.

The logic of this diversification of land uses among households in Bang Khanun and Phimonrat is to maximise the longer-term income generating potential of families, often in combination with agriculture. This is a pattern which highlights major generational differences within families, where parents and grandparents still pursue agriculture because it is the only occupation they know, while their children engage in lighter forms of work associated with petty trade and small business. The retention of family landholdings also reflects a prevailing concern of parents for their children's future. While windfall gains may be made by selling land, many parents with children who have yet to finish their education want to keep sections of their land to build homes for their children. In Phimonrat people frequently exchange tales of newly enriched neighbours who sold all their landholdings and spent the proceeds unwisely on expensive consumer items. They see these stories of misfortune as salutary lessons from which to learn more durable strategies when using their land resources. They see a major source of future income for their children in the construction of rental accommodation for the increasing population in the locality. There is a generally shared view that family landholdings must be preserved wisely, for the twin purposes of future sale for capital accumulation and sustainable income generation for their children.

The future of the village and its function

Defining 'The village'

In the context of current changes towards the so-called 'mega-urban region' configuration, we need to ask: how viable are villages as settlement forms, and how meaningful are they as cultural spaces for their inhabitants? As numerous anthropologists have argued, the use of the term 'village' is problematic in relation to studying agrarian societies in both the past and present. In Thailand, administrative boundaries of officially-designated *muban* have borne little correspondence to significant socio-economic networks and cultural practices of peasants (Kemp 1982: 102–3; Sharp and Hanks 1978: 140–1). In Phimonrat and Bang Khanun, as elsewhere in Thailand, administrative designations do not confine the relations sustained by households, economically or socially. Within any one *muban*, for example, fields and gardens have long been owned and worked by households in other *muban*, and kin networks extend well beyond such artificial geographical limits. Among the settlements of Phimonrat, relationships extend across administrative boundaries and natural features which are used as boundary markers for bureaucrats. For example, although Ban Rongsuat (Muban No. 5, Tambon Phimonrat) was divided physically into two sections by the widening of the Phra Phimonrat Canal shortly after the Second World War, the two halves of the original village were integrated by religious and kin connections. Five years ago the canal became a *tambon* boundary when Tambon Phimonrat was created. Such official namings and boundary inscriptions are of limited use in identifying the village as a meaningful space among local people.

The traditional Thai rural village gained its character because of the mutual reinforcement of overlapping social, territorial, and economic organisation. Clearly in both of the areas under study here, the economic factors binding households to village settlements are extremely weak, in the sense that common work orientations in the life paths of family members are declining. If defined in the sense of an integrated socio-economic subsystem, the villages in Phimonrat and Bang Khanun have already ceased to function in the traditional sense, as have most villages in Thailand. Such changes have resulted from transformations at both the societal and the household decision-making level, as local people have attempted to maximise income- and status-generating activities (e.g. Sharp and Hanks 1978; Tomosugi 1995). Villages no longer signify a space shared by households bound principally by a common livelihood devoted to agriculture. The diversity of sources of income, particularly in the money economy, the scale of geographical movement among household members, their consumption patterns and expectations, have so diverged from the traditional patterns that equated the village with models of the rural community and economy that the very terminology used to describe and analyse villages in the contemporary period are being seriously questioned (Rigg 1994). How then can we define the villages of Bang Khanun and Phimonrat in relation to these changes? Are they merely blandly functional dormitory settlements, a representation proposed by some regional geographers? I suggest that when these local settlements are viewed as sites of social and cultural process, a number of important changes and continuities can be observed.

Kinship and the idiom of reciprocity

The villages of Bang Khanun and Phimonrat can still be characterised as locality-based communities whose households share close affective bonds due to length of residence. This factor remains significant in determining the identity of these settlements, regardless of the occupational fragmentation of many households. In both Phimonrat and Bang Khanun, local people live with neighbours who are either direct relatives, or fictive kin (*phi-nong nap thu kan*: siblings who respect each other). Despite the decline of mutual assistance in farming (*long khaek*, or *ao raengkan*), the idiom of kinship tends to define relations between neighbours. The expression '*rak kan muan yat*' (love each other like family) is often used by residents for their neighbours, and this social system is also recognised by outside officials. A common heritage in farming or gardening and its work culture is a key foundation for this sensibility, and such bonds are most strongly felt among the older generation. Nonetheless there is also a pattern of mutuality in social practice which still reinforces and actualises this model of local society. This is most clearly seen in the ways that kinship ties link families of different economic status. In this face-to-face society, the poor and landless relate to more fortunate neighbours through idioms of reciprocity and obligation which blunt the otherwise sharp edges of inequality between groups. Thus Pa Chin (Auntie Chin), a landless widow in Bang Khanun, lives on the orchard land of an elderly teacher who lives in another district with her married son. Pa Chin has an arrangement with this owner whereby she can live on the land and work the orchard, in exchange for giving the owner half of the produce of the orchard. During the floods which ravaged the district, the district headman (*kamnan*) paid local labourers above the average rate (300 baht instead of the usual 200 baht), because, he explained, he knew all of them and felt sorry for them.

In fact, assistance to less fortunate neighbours is often also assistance to kin, since the Thai definition of *yat* (family) is extremely wide. It encompasses not only blood relations, (however distant) but close family friends. Such broad bilateral and affective linkages give the appearance of familiarity and intimacy to patterns of daily social interaction, even though individuals are always conscious of the economic status of their neighbours. Particularly among the older generation, forms of verbal address – characterised by direct and often rough speaking and jocularity – combined with the custom of most men and women of dressing in plain traditional rural clothing – might even suggest that there were few status distinctions in everyday life. This is not the case. In the following section I will focus on religious life and ritual, and suggest that status distinctions in these communities are generated through traditional practices which express both the continuity of traditional cultural capital and the appropriation of new symbols of modernity.

Religion, locality and cultural capital

In the local societies of Bang Khanun and Phimonrat, it is possible to treat religious life and practice as akin to an ethnographic prism through which one may view how new social expectations are worked out in symbolic ways. We have seen some of the ways that households have responded to economic change and environmental transformations in the long and the short term. We can view these as expressions of identity and status which affect the configuration of the local landscape in the context of wider social and economic changes in Thai society. Religious life in the close-knit local societies of Bang Khanun and Phimonrat has also contributed to transformations in the environment, for while in the ritual context it continues to affirm locality-based identities and networks, it also draws on wider influences and symbols which promote new distinctions between people and communities.

Social relations as well as existential commitments to locality are still important features of local life in Bang Khanun and Phimonrat. They have an integrative and place-making function and are reinforced strongly by religious activity. Such a process takes place among the Thai Buddhists of Bang Khanun in relation to their *wat*. In general, the connection of the individual to any particular temple is determined by relationships between the temple and his or her family. A *wat* occupies a special place in the life of a family if it is associated with the cremation of parents and grandparents. The place of cremation constitutes a significant existential space for the individual and family, even if they leave that locality in later life. On the anniversary of the deaths of parents, it is customary for the children to make merit at those *wat* where their parents were cremated. It is easy to see that in the case of well-established and continuous village settlements, this association of ancestors with descendants is reinforced in each generation. A common answer to questions about why people attended Wat Bang Khanun to make merit was '*pho-mae kert yu thini, dai yu thini*' ('My mother and father were born and died here'), or '*banphoburut kert yu thini*' ('My ancestors/forebears were born here'). So, the reinforcement of family association establishes the *wat* as a significant place. In the case of men and women aged in the late fifties and over, these associations are critical to their identity with the area. They do not feel comfortable making merit at other *wat* – '*Mai sabai chai*' – unless such activity is part of a merit-making pilgrimage (*Thot Phapha*). For males, this association is reinforced by their customary ordination at the village *wat*. Thus, at Wat Bang Khanun, the men who led the chanting every *wan phra* (Moon Day) had all been ordained at the temple as young men for the customary rains retreat period of three months (*phansa*). This form of attachment is independent of the abbot or the monks currently attached to the *wat*. In Tambon Bang Khanun and the surrounding *tambon*, each *wan phra* will see elderly and retired villagers spending the day in the *sala* following the eight precepts to make merit to improve their next life (*chat na*). The *wat* is thus a site for the reproduction of key traditions associated with place and also life cycle. At the beginning of the morning of the *wan phra* ceremony elderly women, their daughters and granddaughters, sit at the rear of the *sala* preparing food for the monks; the men will set up the mats for the monks, sweep the floor, check microphones and arrange for the collection of donations after the feeding of the monks. The senior men and young men in the congregation will take the plates of food to the monks after the initial chanting and lead the congregation in the collective chants which follow. After the departure of the abbot and monks from the *sala*, the men will distribute the food to the congregation who remain. The food at Wat Bang Khanun is prepared in traditional manner and served in dishes made from banana leaves (*bai tong*). The women are very proud of this, and claim that very few Thai *wat* will prepare food in this manner.

A key relationship between village and *wat* is thus merit-making focused on family members. Such a relationship not only connects individuals to the *wat* but establishes important horizontal links binding local households together. For key ceremonies, such as ordination, merit is made publicly. Additionally the *wat* is the site for the key rite of cremation, and cremation is a public event where social obligations are displayed and thus where the respect relation is reinforced. Cremations and the social activities preceding and concluding the activities demand a great deal of preparation – it is here that neighbours and friends honour obligations and assist in activities ranging from food preparation to organising music and the entertainments. During the time of this study Grandma Phap, an old lady of 82 years, died and was cremated at Wat Bang Khanun. Both she and her husband had been born in the district. They had eleven children and their kinship network encompassed many *tambon* in Amphur Bang Kruai. They could count at least ten families in the village as direct kin, and this encompassed probably half of the regular attenders of the *wat*. The funeral ceremony, which occupied five days, activated the relationships binding *wat*, kin and locality. Each day the food alone cost 10,000 baht, but if volunteer labour was not available this would have been much more expensive. It is at such *ngan* that villagers express the difference between themselves, *khon ban nok* – rural people, and *khon muang* – urban people, even though they live in an increasingly complex and hybrid social and economic environment. Here they make their own food, they do not hire caterers. Relatives and neighbours are mobilised to assist in activities which express key loyalties and collective values. The ceremonies attract a wide range of social groups from the local villages and there is little in the way of social exclusivity.

Despite communal appearances, the major *wat* ceremonies also involve displays of hierarchy and status. In large ceremonies such as that of Grandmother Phap, many obviously well-to-do friends and relatives attended from outside the community. Many of them were friends and associates of her children, including businessmen, military officers and local officials. But the most significant aspect of hierarchy was the expense of the ceremony and the local knowledge that Grandmother Phap had been a prominent donor of money to the temple. During her life she had paid for the bell tower and the reception building at Wat Bang Khanun. Her worldly resources had been translated into the cultural capital of temple improvement: an activity publicly recognised as symbolising her ability to gain merit and advance into the next life with advantage. It has long been recognised that the hierarchy of Buddhist merit accumulation in Thai society mirrors hierarchy in the mundane world. As Hanks pointed out: '. . . the effectiveness of a thousand baht outweighs the widow's battered coin' (Hanks 1962: 1248).

Although conspicuous merit-making by the rich has always been a feature of Thai society, its impact on the cultural geography of localities has never been so dramatic as in contemporary Thailand, and Bang Kruai is no exception. A new iconography of wealth and modernity has been translated into the religious landscape of temples, and it is marked by a concern to display modernity and affluence in architecture and decoration. No more do the *wat* of Nonthaburi contain the simple and unassuming structures which served the forebears of the *chao suan*. New buildings constructed with the donations of newly-enriched and old established families alike gleam with iridescent blues, greens and reds on their gables. Old and decrepit preaching and ordination halls often stand juxtaposed with the freshly-built products of merit-making. Families now donate newly fashionable images, such as the Chinese Bodisatva Kuan Yin, to the old temples of the district. More conspicuously, there is a concern to make the *wat* landmarks in their areas by constructing large new buildings and

Plate 7.4 The new featurist landscape: the towering Suwannahong of the new *bot* of Wat Chalo, Bang Kruai district. (Photo: Author)

images, a process notable in many parts of Bangkok and Thailand generally. While the specific projects may originally be the ideas of abbots, they channel the willing energies of merit-making residents. Some structures owe their origins to individual merit-makers, such as the spectacular new two-storey preaching hall at Wat Keao Fa (of the village of Ban Phra That), built from the money gained from a deceased gardener's recent land sale. Other efforts at merit-making may be more collective in nature, such as the project of the abbot of Wat Chalo to construct a new ordination hall (*bot*) in the form of a giant *Suwannahong*: a royal barge with a mythic swan image at the prow. This tall swan head towers over the nearby district, announcing visually the distinctiveness of the temple. The original ordination hall which holds the *wat*'s old Buddha images dates from the mid-Ayutthaya period (seventeenth century). It has been left to decay in the *wat* grounds and presents a stark contrast to the glistening spectacle of the new landmark.

Plate 7.5 The decay of the old: the humble old *bot* of Wat Chalo. (Photo: Author)

The landscape of Bang Kruai, as expressed in its temples, is developing an orientation towards featurism, a phenomenon which is consonant with the economic changes within the district. It highlights the abandonment of agriculture, the onset of consumerism among local and new residents, and a demand for conspicuous spectacle which is a version of urban sophistication and modernity. Prosperity and merit-making have reinforced each other to build a new religious landscape. However, the foundations of this process are rooted in villagers' traditions of enhancing merit. The use of wealth and cash from land sales and other sources of non-farm income are channelled by traditional impulses. While poorer gardeners may still live a simple life without many of the luxuries enjoyed by wealthier neighbours, they nevertheless participate in the creation of this new geography of consumption by sharing a collective vision of *khwam-charoen* (progress, advancement), in their aspiration towards improving their temples. For those richer residents whose new wealth from land sales is visibly signified by pick-up trucks, two-storey homes and ornamental gateways, they are ensuring a degree of merit which balances their good fortune, and in the process they are upgrading their temple's appearance to reflect their status.

In the Muslim communities of Phimonrat the twin characteristics of religious life – its tendency to reinforce communality and place identity as well as to reflect socio-economic distinctions – are also noticeable. But they express themselves in somewhat different ways to the Buddhists of Bang Khanun. The *Surao* (mosque) expresses the religious brotherhood which distinguishes these communities from the surrounding Thai Bhuddhist society. The obligatory Friday rituals of prayer are followed by virtually all households and reinforce the bonds of place identity, despite the increasing diversity of livelihoods and lifestyles. Support for the maintenance of the *surao* has long been held as an index of religious worth and social esteem among local Muslims. From the earliest history of the Muslim villages in Phimonrat, wealthier farmers donated land for religious use. At least 30 rai of the land around the *surao* in Ban Rongkrachom was in fact donated by landowners and is now used to accommodate landless households at nominal rents. These features of the local society and its intimate relation to central Islamic values encourage a sense of fellowship and communality which apparently overrides distinctions in wealth.

Yet at the same time new trends serve to emphasise distinctions in the community on the basis of religious practice. There has always been an emphasis on channelling family resources towards the religious education of males in households, and one of the sources of a family's greatest pride has been to have a son who has studied in religious schools in Pattani (southern Thailand) or Malaysia and returned to teach religion in the community. Increasingly, however, the tendency has been for families with enough means to send children – including daughters – to study overseas in the Islamic heartland of the Middle East. This is one (although not the only) source of change in religious practice, whereby wealthier families are turning towards stricter forms of Islamic practice. Many villagers now make a distinction between those households which follow strict Islamic precepts (*nap thu sasana Islam khreng khrat*) and the majority who still follow a more relaxed style, formerly common to Thai Muslims. Invariably, followers of the new fundamentalism are those who have been influenced by their own children, some of whom have returned to teach at the local religious school. These families are well-to-do by local standards. Parents' economic resources have thus been channelled into religious education which, in turn, accesses prevailing trends in the Islamic world, acting to differentiate the lifestyles – expressed particularly in the dress of womenfolk – of these wealthier households from those of their neighbours.

Conclusion

While state policy and market forces have played a critical structural role in transforming the functions and physical landscape of Bangkok's expanding mega-urban region, the process of change and its particular local and subregional configurations have also been strongly influenced by household strategies on the part of gardeners and rice-farmers. They have actively participated in the social and economic transformations of their society, and shaped their environment in the process.

The smallholding economy of Nonthaburi's agriculturalists, particularly the gardeners, has always been intimately tied to the economy of the metropolis, and their production strategies have developed in response to changing market conditions. For the last half-century rice-farming households in Phimonrat have shared with their counterparts in other central provinces the experience of major problems associated with rising costs of production, fluctuating rice prices, reduced land-holdings through inheritance patterns and debt. Well before the urban frontier of housing estates and factories encroached into formerly rural landscapes, these households had become occupationally diversified, incorporating work patterns and networks tied into the metropolitan economy.

Land is the crucial resource in the task of household reproduction, and access to new opportunities for status and livelihood have been historically tied to the accumulation, preservation and transmission of land. Increasing land prices and new settlements in these districts have been appropriated towards these ends. These livelihood strategies have been tied not only to the exigencies of survival, but also to the quest for status among neighbours and wider fields of cultural capital shared in Thai society and the metropolis. Today, in the context of an increasing commodification of symbols and conspicuous consumption characteristic of modernity, these traditional status concerns have made a significant impact on local areas in the ways that space and traditional institutions such as temples are utilised and displayed.

8 Condo land

Global forms and local ecologies

Introduction: high-rise buildings, 'globalisation' and inner-city urban forms

In Bangkok at the time of the 1997 financial crash – as elsewhere in the region – there was no more striking symbol of the apparent link between city form and global finance than unfinished skyscrapers, a visual reminder of the *hubris* of Bangkok's building entrepreneurs and the fragile foundations of Thailand's prosperity (Tasker and Prangtip 1999). The high-rise office and condominium blocks of the region's urban centres are viewed as symptomatic of the homogenisation of the Asian city and its culture by the forces of advanced transnational capitalism (Forbes 1996: 54–7). Ada Louise Huxtable has argued that high-rise buildings highlight dramatically the links between capitalism, architecture and urban space. She notes:

> Today's tall building is a puzzling and paradoxical package. Its standardized, characterless, impersonal space creates recognizable charismatic monuments and enduring images of twentieth century cities. For better or worse it is measure, parameter, or apotheosis of our consumer and corporate culture.
>
> (Huxtable 1982: 112)

The high-rise condominium and apartment block is the residential counterpart of the corporate skyscraper. It represents a quintessentially modern urban phenomenon, and its emergence in Asian cities – especially inner districts – has been rapid and synonymous with the urban property boom which was a central part of the region's much acclaimed growth to the later 1990s.

Condominiums and their associated commercial structures and precincts have attracted attention for study largely in terms of real estate investment and urban land-use functions. They have been portrayed as part of a global system of real estate financing and marketing, within which cities function as key spaces of accumulation (Haila 1997). Linked to the model of world and global cities advanced by some leading scholars (Friedmann

1986; Sassen 2000: chapter 3) the portrayal of Pacific Rim cities as part of an integrated international property market linked to flows of footloose transnational investment capital is an oversimplified one. The global real estate model was first generated when analysts attempted to interpret the spectacular wave of Japanese investment in central city properties in North America, Europe and Australia which took place in the 1980s, fuelled by surplus capital generated by pension funds (Goldberg 1995: 251–2). Closer scrutiny shows that this 'global' phenomenon (as represented even in the case of Japanese real estate investment) was actually comprised of flows of capital into specific property markets where foreign ownership regulations were the least restrictive (e.g. Australia and the USA). The property markets of Asia's major cities are in fact diverse. Variations in foreign investment controls and property laws – thus the relative openness of markets to foreign finance and investment – and different levels of economic growth, combining with inherited urban spatial patterns, histories and differing building industry dynamics are key factors behind this diversity (Seek 1995: 813–19). Real estate development certainly accompanies flows of capital and firms in the broader process of shaping the world cities – as major economic and administrative nodes – of the Pacific Rim, from Bangkok to Shanghai. This may reshape city skylines in apparently uniform ways, but their formative dynamics are shaped by a range of circumstances, both new and inherited (Wu 2000).

Notably, real estate cycles are distinctive from place to place within the Asia region, and specialists in the field acknowledge that real estate markets around the world are not fully integrated (Brown and Crocker 2001). Of course, the existence of such variety is itself an important ingredient of an international capitalist property market where opportunities are found and exploited for investors at different phases of property cycles throughout the world. However, the particular characteristics of investment patterns and the relative contribution of local and international agents in particular countries must be acknowledged (Bradbury 1995). Due to restrictions on foreign ownership of property, the role of international corporate players in direct investment in Bangkok has not been as important as the participation of individual investors from the region purchasing single units in Thai-owned blocks constructed by local companies (total foreign ownership of condominium blocks was restricted to 40 per cent) (Healy 1996).

Considered on a broad scale, changes to the landscape of the Thai metropolis were clearly a product of economic restructuring flowing from its role in the world economy and the concomitant changes in demands for industrial, commercial and residential land uses. In particular, Japanese corporations played a key role in expanding the functions of East Asian and Southeast Asian cities by establishing a wide range of branch and subsidiary service firms throughout the region. Japanese banking, construction, insurance, shipping and tourist firms were located in Hong Kong, Singapore, Kuala Lumpur and Bangkok, consolidating the Pacific Rim as a space of intense regional economic transactions, generating considerable demand for new office and residential supply in those urban centres. In 1990–5, of the thirty-five Pacific Rim urban centres where such branch businesses were established, Bangkok was ranked fourth-highest (behind Hong Kong, Singapore and Los Angeles) – with over 140 firms (Edgington 1997). In the process of rebuilding Bangkok's inner-city skyline, foreign firms – as joint venture partners, engineering and architectural consultants – were prominent. But it is also important to note that the bulk of investment in this building was local, flowing from accumulated capital derived from the export economy. Overseas direct investment in construction amounted to just 7–9 per cent of total FDI in the late 1980s, and was largely directed to infrastructure and industrial projects (*Bank of Thailand Quarterly Bulletins* 1988–9). The boom in office and high-rise condominium developments was directed towards supplying increasing demands for space both for local and overseas firms and individuals.

The symbolic economy of the global modern high-rise building form certainly played a part in driving the construction of new towers, intended as new trophies and cultural capital inscribed in the skyline for prominent companies (see Busaba, Krissana and Chiratas 1997). Yet global form needs to be distinguished from global agencies and global financial flows in the reshaping of Bangkok's inner city space. The housing sector at large was already oversupplied by the time financial markets were liberalised in Thailand (see Chapter 3). These new sources of global finance did not create Bangkok's building boom, they simply compounded an existing building bubble caused by local entrepreneurs' over-investment (Pasuk and Baker 1998: 113). The real estate sector became linked to global circuits of capital because a high proportion of the funds available through finance companies were lent for property development in an already oversupplied market. In 1996, when the Bank of Thailand restricted loans for property development and increased interest rates, the building sector's collapse had already begun (McLean 1997). The global dimension is clearly important in understanding a range of processes, including Bangkok's developing regional urban functions, architectural trends, high-rise development patterns and the cosmopolitan living styles associated with these structures. However, resort to the trope of 'global' in depicting Bangkok's building boom and the dynamics of its property market – including the transformation of key sectors of the inner city – has clear limitations if it is used to imply that construction and particular developments were determined by global actors.[1]

Superficial views of the landscapes of the Asian – particularly Southeast Asian – inner cities actually mask a complex process of urban spatial production dependent on a range of actors and inherited urban histories. This chapter provides an overview of Bangkok's inner city condominium boom, followed by a more focused discussion of the emergence of luxury condominiums in Bangkok. This residential sector is not discussed

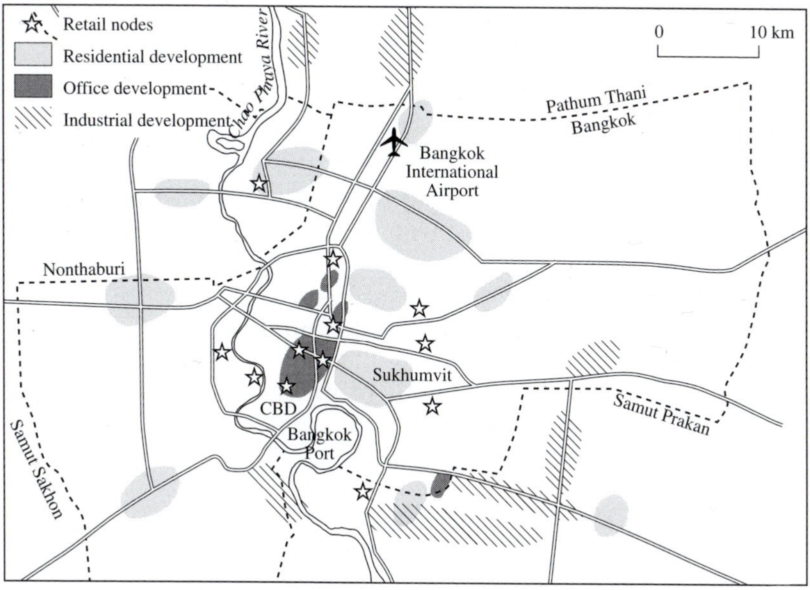

Figure 8.1 Bangkok represented as a cluster of international real-estate investment zones by the brokerage firm Richard Ellis.

Source: Based on Richard Ellis, UMI Market Profiles, 1992.

in isolation, but in the context of the history and characteristics of the spaces into which these new structures have been inserted. In the final section of the chapter I focus on the Sukhumvit district. This area was associated with affluent Thai suburbanites and western expatriates from its first emergence in the post-Second World War years, and it subsequently became a favoured site for the construction of luxury condominiums by both joint venture business concerns and family companies. Rather than inaugurating a new revolution in lifestyle for Thais in the city, the high-rise built form dominant in Sukhumvit (and Silom) has catered largely to a foreign market of expatriate executive workers, despite being financed and constructed by Thai firms. Moreover the condominiums of Sukhumvit have not obliterated alternative forms of public life: these global symbols and environments of contemporary urban life coexist with local and district-based ecologies, informed by layers of activities, shaped by the area's varied workforce, tourists and its local population of shopkeepers and service workers. The existence of this layering and its sustaining of different – but coexisting – ecologies raises the question of whether the process of gentrification and corporatisation – applied to districts in western cities such as New York – can be applicable to residential districts in inner Bangkok. Luxury condominiums have been assimilated into an inner urban landscape history, but have not extinguished it, thus exemplifying how the global has been accommodated and appropriated into more localised processes and patterns informed by history and culture (Beauregard 1995: 239–44; Douglass 1995).[2]

The condominium boom in Bangkok

Defined as a multi-storeyed apartment block, designed for the individual purchase of single apartments, and with an emphasis on providing shared recreational and consumption spaces, the luxury condominium is one of the classic building forms of the late twentieth century. Allied with the office block, condominiums have become standard features of modernising skylines and transforming inner cities.

The high-rise condominium precincts of Bangkok developed from the 1980s as a product of a number of converging trends. They include on the supply side:

1. Ever-increasing inner-city land prices responding to increasing demands for business and residential uses, leading to original landowners selling or developing their landholdings.
2. Building firms erecting higher structures on smaller blocks to maximise investments.
3. A national government which responded to the building industry by framing laws allowing foreigners partial equity in new constructions.

And on the demand side:

1. A foreign investment boom leading to demand from foreign companies for high-status and conveniently-located accommodation for expatriate employees as well as office space.
2. Worsening urban traffic congestion which, by default (and in the absence of adequate land-use zoning) reinforced a pattern of high-income office and residential proximity, attracting high-income Thai families to invest in condominiums as weekday residences.

Luxury high-rise condominiums emerged as a new element in the property market and as a new residential form in Bangkok in the late 1980s. The groundwork was laid by the Thai government in 1979 with the passing of the Condominium Act (allowing for multiple ownership titles on single land blocks). This was consolidated in 1991, with further government legislation allowing non-resident foreign investors 49 per cent of equity in condominium units and a maximum of 40 per cent of total equity in condominium blocks. Concerns were initially expressed about the extent to which the condominium concept of collective ownership and shared living would be taken up in the market. But the idea was quickly embraced by a number of firms, particularly because of the effects of increasing urban land prices. The novelty of the new condominiums was most clearly expressed in the four condominium towers that began to rise in the high-income area of Sukhumvit (Bangkok Bank 1980: 347; Meeker-Buppha 1982: 31–3). By the end of 1982, over 50 condominium projects were under way in Bangkok (20 per cent of them in the high-priced ranges) and by February 1989, 116 projects had been completed, representing nearly 80 per cent of total condominium supply in Thailand. By this time it was possible to classify clearly the range of condominiums being built and their markets. Within the group of residential condos were high-income residential units, resort units and low-income units. Notably, middle-income units were rare at this time, a key indication of the preference of the Bangkok middle classes for suburban housing estate units. High-income units sold for an average of 1.5 million baht (approximately US $60,000) with average floor areas of 120 square metres. Low-cost condominiums ranged from 20 to 40 square metres, costing on average a quarter to a third of the price of the high-cost units. The second category comprised the office condominiums which combined residential facilities. These could be up to five times the size of the high-income residential units and cost from 28,000 to 50,000 baht per square metre (US $1,120–2,000) (Manop 1989: 9). Low-cost condominiums were located in suburban areas where land prices were cheapest, in keeping with the capital of the many small construction companies and contractors entering the industry at this time (Siek 1992: 1141). In contrast, the office–condo and luxury residential condominiums, with the exception of the resort type, were built in the inner city. It was thus the built landscape of the inner city that received the full impact of this building trend.

In 1989 one expert noted:

> The condominium market in Thailand is growing rapidly and gaining popularity in the Thailand real-estate market. Since land prices are soaring exorbitantly, it seems that only development with high density use of land will be able to yield higher profit.
>
> (Manop 1989: 36)

Over the period 1985–90 rental and sale prices in the office and luxury condominium market increased by 300–400 per cent (Colliers Jardine 1994). Shortly after the Gulf crisis, which began in August 1990, Thailand's real estate market went into a slump, with the Bank of Thailand compounding developers' difficulties with tighter credit policies. In Bangkok, total high-rise office supply reached saturation point by 1991 and from this year there was a drop in property values and rentals. The downfall of the Chatichai government in the coup of February 1991 dampened investor confidence in the residential property market, particularly among foreigners, depressing prices further by an estimated 10 per cent (Richard Ellis 1992). Oversupply

Plate 8.1 The inner city as a building site: condominiums rise in a Bangkok *soi*, 1990. (Photo: Author)

was chronic by the end of 1992, when office vacancy rates increased markedly. Some projects were postponed or cancelled as a result of the decline in capital values. An even more severe glut of supply affected the middle- and high-income residential property market (Simister 1994). Many condominium projects tried to survive the market downturn by renting instead of selling units, while other firms converted condominiums to serviced apartments. As one property market commentator noted: 'The days of easy sales and quick money have all but disappeared' (Pipat and Cimi 1991).

By 1994 Bangkok had 11,590 first-class residential units, comprising 45 per cent condominiums, 40 per cent apartments and 15 per cent serviced apartments (Pinit 1994). Much of the oversupply in the residential sector stemmed from a mismatch between supply and demand, with the oversupply in the condominium market largely in the middle-priced projects, where competition for sales was fiercest. Apartments and serviced apartments fetched greater returns and enjoyed higher occupancy rates compared with condominiums at this time, however luxury serviced apartments were not familiar to most investors. Moreover, they required the maintenance of support services which they were reluctant to consider, given the fact that their interests were essentially in selling the units. Condominiums continued to remain popular with developers, with this category comprising over 90 per cent of all new high-income projects in the early 1990s (Pinit 1994). This balance of supply reflected the conservative nature of local investors and landholders. To many medium-sized developers and owner–developers, condominiums seemed to offer quick returns with minimal service and maintenance commitments following completion.

Despite the troubled years of 1991–2, economic growth boosted the income and buying power of the urban middle classes, and there was a renewed demand for residential stock. However, from 1993 it was a buyers' market and the surging prices and rentals for condominiums characteristic of the late 1980s were no longer evident (*Bangkok Post* 20 December 1993; Colliers Jardine Research 1995). As for the luxury condominium market in the inner zones, supply continued to outpace demand by 1995, and conversion to serviced apartments was common. Until 1994 international property agencies noted that there had been a general correspondence between trends in the annual increase in foreign expatriate workers and condominium building. After this year the growth rates of expatriates declined, but luxury condominium building continued its upward surge (Colliers Jardine Research 1997: 160). Continued building was at least partly due to the expectation that high- and middle-income Bangkokians would invest in inner-city condos in an effort to combat delays caused by chronic traffic jams in the city (Busrin 1996). Market research bore out these claims, as more white-collar and professional Thais were compromising long-held aspirations of living in free-standing homes in favour of the practical concerns of proximity to workplaces. However, the bulk of these buyers could not afford Sukhumvit condominiums: instead they chose developments in areas further out from the centre (e.g. north in Huai Khwang and east in Bang Na) (*Bangkok Post,* Business Post 11 October 1996: 9). Competition among developers in the inner city led to a degree of differentiation among luxury projects and an emphasis on comprehensive facilities (see below), largely to attract Japanese and Western expatriate tenants and Asian buyers from the region.

In Bangkok the new luxury condominiums were concentrated in established high-status residential and business areas, where large blocks of freehold property were available for development. In the late 1980s international property consultant firms defined four key zones of the city for high-yielding developments, with the key established clusters around Silom–Sathorn roads (72 per cent of commercial offices) and a secondary cluster grouped around Sukhumvit–Asoke roads (15 per cent). Of all new inner-city construction in 1989 these two areas accounted for 42 per cent and 24 per cent respectively. These two zones were key areas for the boom in office condominiums of the late 1980s, fetching the highest purchase and rental prices in the city. In 1989 Sukhumvit accounted for 60 per cent of all completed luxury condominium projects, with Silom having 32 per cent (Appendices to Manop 1989). By the mid-1990s, the overwhelming proportion of luxury condominiums and apartments (an estimated 70 per cent) were concentrated in the Sukhumvit district (Pinit 1994: 18; Colliers Jardine Research 1995: 191).

Notwithstanding realtors' rhetoric about the continued demand for 'quality' projects in the market, there was a serious oversupply of luxury condominiums (*Bangkok Post*, Business Post 2 August 1996: 8). On the eve of the 1997 financial crash, sales had already slowed considerably, and average vacancy rates among newly-completed projects in Sukhumvit and Silom were almost 40 per cent (Pitchon 1997: 29). The financial crash and the rise in interest rates led to credit-squeezed companies suspending building on existing projects. Average rents and values of condominiums plummeted as a consequence of the surplus supply (Krissana 1997). By the end of the decade much of the outstanding stock of luxury condominiums in the inner areas had been sold at auctions for 30–50 per cent less than asking prices. Buyers included foreign nationals (particularly from Singapore and Hong Kong) as well as Thais living overseas (*Bangkok Post*, Business Post 27 June 1998: 3; 26 September 2000: 8). The condominium boom was over in the inner city. The inner-city high-rise residential sector had stabilised into a number of discernible sub-markets lined to different tenure and investment modes. They included the rental condominium market, rented serviced apartments, owner-occupied condominiums, and leased condominiums. Owner occupancy was a relatively minor part of the market, representing an average of just 30 per cent of condominium occupancy (Pitchon 1997: 30). Aside from the effects of the financial crisis and the general economic slowdown, the limits to the spread of condominiums in the city were set by a restricted demand in the luxury residential marketplace, the constraints of foreign ownership laws, and the resistance of Thai buyers to living in condominiums (Krissana and Busrin 1996).[3] This can be characterised as a cultural phenomenon which acted to combine with other factors (income limitations chief among them) in restricting large-scale movement of Thais into inner-city condos. Moreover, by 1997–8, housing had become so much cheaper that one incentive for condominium purchase was removed. Those Thais who purchased condominiums in the inner zones were doing so for fundamentally logistical, rather than lifestyle reasons. These housing preferences distinguished them markedly from the foreigners who preferred the inner-city high-rise condominiums and apartments in areas such as Sukhumvit and Silom (Pichai 1999). A few years after the economic crisis, it was by no means evident that there had been a long-term transformation in the housing preferences of the Thai middle classes at large, nor a substantial repopulation of the inner city by this group. The luxury condominium zones remained dominated by a cosmopolitanism which drew much of its character from the long association of these areas with foreign residents.

The condominium: producing and marketing a lifestyle

Since its beginning in the 1980s, the residential condominium market has diversified and led to the production of a variety of residential subecologies, even within the same districts. At the highest end of luxury units, this diversification emerges from the new emphasis by project designers and marketers on the creation of total living environments and comprehensive facilities. This is driven both by the power of the attraction towards constructing a lifestyle environment in the inner city replete with the physical and aesthetic trappings of exclusivity, and the push factor of an urban environment which is counted as one of the worst in the world in terms of air and noise pollution.

The early luxury condominium projects offered quality building materials and fittings as their basic attractions, standard sized unit shells with optional designs, and maid's quarters with a separate entrance. Facilities shared with other residents included central laundries, lobbies and reception areas, function rooms and gymnasia. Early projects such as 'Promsuk Condominium' (opened in 1987) stressed the qualities of privacy as well as a measure of selective sociability in the features of its fourteen-storey tower block on Sukhumvit:

> A closed circuit T.V. system, of course, continually monitors goings-on at the lobby and lift halls to make sure your privacy within the sublime, homey world of Promsuk Condominium remains at all times, undisturbed.

An important attraction of the inner city condominium tower was its view of the metropolis, aiming to enhance 'The feeling of having a private individual home suspended high above Bangkok's skyline' (*Promsuk Condominium* 1987).

At 314 square metres each, the units of Promsuk Condominium were generous indeed. Few of the condominiums built after 1989 could match this size, given the escalating price of land and building costs. By 1990 the average luxury condominium would soar twenty storeys and above, with units in the higher-end projects averaging between 50 and 250 square metres and prices per unit from 3 million baht (US $120,000). But the most significant difference emerging in the 1990s was the variety of projects, among them those providing complete and virtually autonomous living environments for those who purchased or rented the units.

Those developers with sufficient land and capital backing launched major residential and leisure complexes that aimed to capture the high-income local and expatriate market through the appeal of comprehensive services, facilities and management. In the Sukhumvit area such projects included the massive President Park development, built on one of the few remaining large blocks in the area (at the southern end of *soi* 22 and 24). Hailed by its promoters as a 'self-contained luxury residential community' reflecting a 'one stop living concept', the President Park development is one of Bangkok's most exclusive luxury condominiums. It was described by one property commentator as:

> A product which is for Bangkok revolutionary in the quality of its finishes, the entrances, the podium recreation areas, and a 7,000 sq. metre club facility (with five restaurants, five swimming pools, five tennis courts, two squash courts), health facilities of the standards of other health clubs, and a range of pampering available for the eventual occupants which is comparable to Parkview in Hong Kong.
>
> (*Bangkok Post Investment and Property Supplement*, 22 November1993)

Units of this luxury complex were successfully sold to Hong Kong, Taiwanese and Singaporian investors (*Bangkok Post* 18 December 1993).

Although President Park was situated in what would seem to be an awkward cul-de-sac at the end of a shophouse-lined *soi* (lane), the advertising staff of Richard Ellis (the international brokerage form) capitalised on the proximity of its location to the newly completed Sirikit Park and the new Queen Sirikit National Convention Centre. The project featured five residential towers (between 33 and 45 storeys) housing serviced apartments that sold from 10.8 million baht. Exclusivity and privilege were the key themes in the project's promotion. The play on proximity to city facilities was as important as its detachment from Bangkok's negative attributes – 'President Park residents are ensured easy access, a crucial factor when planning where to live in Thailand's congested but vibrant city' (*Bangkok Post, Thailand Property Guide* Spring 1994: 45). The project's advertising played on the symbolic capital of its location, juxtaposing the images of its 33- and 45-storey residential towers with photographs of the iconic towers of Manhattan, the Eiffel tower and even Rome's Capitoline Hill. It was to be a cosmopolitan place. Under the connotative rubric 'It's all a matter of position', the plush advertising booklet of Richard Ellis invited purchasers to reflect upon the city and their own enhanced status: 'Look out the window of your luxurious apartment and take in the dazzling panoramic views of the metropolis. The traffic is omnipresent. But stop to consider that you are, in fact, living in an extraordinary city within a city.'

A high proportion of the new President Park complex was directly leased out to overseas companies and embassies. By 1994, only 141 of its 402 units were privately owned – with 40 per cent of these Thai owners, and the rest East Asian and European. Rather than occupying the premises themselves, the majority of Thai owners leased their units to foreign residents (Richard Ellis 1994).

The President Park Group is controlled by a Sikh family which has gradually built up its landholdings in the Sukhumvit area over several generations, and has businesses including engineering and fast food in its range of activities. The group controls at least seven other serviced apartment towers in the Sukhumvit area. Despite the size of this group's activities, it is not representative of the bulk of the owners of Sukhumvit's condominiums or apartment towers. The majority are smaller companies.[4] Nonetheless most recent luxury projects were distinguished from those of the 1980s by a meticulous attention to management, services and the maintenance of an ambience of safety, affluence and virtual autonomy from the surrounding urban scene through the provision of facilities such as putting greens, jogging tracks and sports complexes.

Inner-city shopping and entertainment spaces

The condominium boom accompanied the construction of new retail complexes in the inner city. In Bangkok the massive new suburban department store complexes to the east (Seacon Square and the Seri Centre) and to the north (Future Park Rangsit) have defined new consumption spaces in the city's sprawling middle-income housing belts. At the same time, however, the fashionable inner city received attention in the 1990s with an equivalent emphasis on 'One Stop Entertainment' centres. The downtown middle classes of Bangkok were estimated to generate a collective purchasing power of around 3 billion baht annually, so it is not surprising that new shopping complexes were being planned for this area. (Krissana 1994).

The Emporium project was started in 1993. Situated next to the now-popular Sirikit Park, it was planned to comprise a 38-storey building with a 36,000 square metre shopping centre, a 25,000 square metre amusement park, parking provision for 2,500 cars and a 350-room five-star hotel, with a prestige office tower. The project was administered by a division of the Sophonphanich family's giant Bangkok Bank, a partner and owner of the land block. The other partner is the Mall Group, a company responsible for six of Bangkok's major suburban shopping complexes, which boasted a sales turnover of 10 billion baht (approximately US $40 million) in 1993 (*Bangkok Post* 20 October 1993). One feature of the Emporium marketing strategy was its focus on Sukhumvit residents. Thus, one early project advertisement (*Bangkok Post* 22 November 1993) announced: 'All of life's needs for the Sukhumvit resident. So that 300,000 families here never need to go anywhere else'.

The publicity images mirrored the cosmopolitan identities of the key groups inhabiting the 'one-stop living' condominium complexes. The project went further towards serving consumption needs by centralising in its fashion galleries the design studios which were still scattered throughout the Sukhumvit area in small shops and converted houses. The three-level 'Fashion Venue' was planned to be divided into style and subculture sections, all focusing on women's fashions. The key image in the advertisement was a six-armed woman dressed completely in black, gazing at the viewer and holding fashion objects in four hands: the remaining two hands embrace her own body, completing of the image of self indulgence. The retro-dressed Shiva-figure projected the consuming power and multiple needs of the middle-class woman. Marketed as incorporating 'The Most Trendy and Stylish Department Store', Emporium publicity played on the consumption desires of Sukhumvit's inner-city rich condominium set.[5]

The condominium in Sukhumvit: erasure and persistence of ecologies and street life

The gentrification model and inner-city restructuring

As upper- and middle-income urban residences, condominiums have followed the office tower of the transforming downtown sectors of Pacific Rim centres, marketed almost universally in terms of their luxury, convenience and modern urbane (e.g. the global use of 'executive' as a prefix) advantages. In the inner cities of North America and Europe, change is most often typified as gentrification. For example, Carpenter and Lees identify common underlying processes and stages of gentrification within the inner cities of New York, Paris and London, the metropolitan centres from which the gentrifying characteristics became visible before their reproduction in other urban centres. They point out that 'gentrification is thus one expression of the globalisation of culture in a postmodern world' (Carpenter and Lees 1995: 288). In assuming that 'broadly similar processes are remaking and reshaping cities around the world', they describe gentrification as beginning in cycles of investment and disinvestment. In the gentrified locale, the pattern of consumption is altered, most obviously in local commerce in cuisine. Public space is altered through private investment in refashioned streetscapes and renovated or distinctively decorated buildings. Thus, the gentrified area becomes an 'exclusionary landscape'. It makes concrete the 'common elements of a globalised gentrification culture'. Gentrification revalues the centre, not only by the restored warehouse or working-class terrace house, but by the living space and the cultural demands of the condominium or apartment block (Sudjic 1993: 207).

In Asian cities, this gentrification model is not so clearly applicable. The middle classes have been less concerned to reoccupy the city centre as to indulge in the cultural capital of large houses in suburban estates. In some countries, such as Japan, researchers suggest that a near-equivalent of gentrification may be occurring in the occupation of condominiums in inner city areas (Fujitsuka 1994). In the case of Bangkok, some of the key features of the gentrification process are absent. Thus, it is notable that the key areas developed for luxury condominium complexes have long been associated with high-income groups. A large-scale wave of Thai middle-class reoccupation of the centre has not take place: rather the occupants have been largely foreign expatriates and affluent Thai families who were always located in the inner city. The other side of the process, displacement, needs acknowledgement. In Bangkok, the groups displaced were also relatively new occupants, in that they were slum-dwellers, rather than long-standing old communities. If this variant of displacement is acknowledged then perhaps some elements of the gentrification model may be applied, although not fully. A key part of the argument about universal trends towards inner city recomposition under capitalism (whether portrayed as gentrification or other variants) is that this restructuring of the inner city is pioneered by a process of creating exclusionary residential and business zones. It is to this process and its characteristics that we now turn.

The evolution of the Sukhumvit district

In Sukhumvit, the space taken up by the condominiums can easily be pictured as the locus for a new middle-class lifestyle, yet there are strong continuities linking its contemporary functions and its earlier history as one of Bangkok's first residential suburbs, which, almost from the beginning, had been associated with a western presence. Sukhumvit (a road which actually extends eastwards from Bangkok to the Cambodian border) is definable as a district (together with its tributary *soi*) extending west to east along a 5.7 kilometre length, from Ploenchit to the Phrakhanong canal. The main road, constructed in the 1930s, was formerly known simply as the Pak Nam Road, an extension of Ploenchit road, which ran eastwards from the old city (Thawee 1997: 149–50). The district surrounding this road (Tambon Bangkapi) became a key element in the spatial transformation of Bangkok from a compact city of a little more than half a million in 1947 to a sprawling metropolis of over two million by 1960. Bangkapi's rapid transformation from an area of rice fields to a residential motor car suburb began towards the close of the Second World War with land speculations undertaken by the prominent Indian Muslim businessman A.E. Nana (Brown 1994: 214–19). Residential development was facilitated by the construction of narrow *soi* in place of the small tributary canals which fed into the main canal lining Sukhumvit. Some fifty-eight *soi* now lead from north and south into the road. The long narrow land blocks formed from the subdivided rice fields and the narrow subsidiary *soi* which follow the routes of the old canals have influenced the ecology ever since.

In the late 1950s the district of Bangkapi appeared as a relatively homogeneous suburb of compound houses in a city which was otherwise comprised of multifunctional districts and neighbourhoods (Litchfield *et al.* 1960: 13). Occupation of land along Sukhumvit road and its tributary *soi* proceeded apace into the 1960s as well-off households of high-ranking officials and business families moved out of the congested older inner city to the generous land blocks of Bangkapi. The upgrading of Sukhuvit Road by the American aid agency USOM increased the area's attraction (Banchawan 1992: 89–90). The large bungalow houses of the affluent were so closely associated with Bangkapi that one geographer dubbed the type 'Bangkapi style' housing (Sternstein 1964: 154). Many owners of houses rented them to westerners or took in foreign boarders working for various international agencies to make extra income. Norman Bartlett, who worked as the press attache to the Australian Embassy and lived in Bangkapi during the 1950s described it as a quintessential modern suburb:

> Bangkapi is one of the reasons why living in Bangkok is much like living in any other modern city. Bangkapi is new and neat and suburban, tropically suburban, a garden suburb pleasant enough to live in but more like Santa Barbara or Palm Beach, without the sea, than Siam. Everybody in Bangkapi goes to the office. Cars cause peak hour traffic jams. In the cars are harried fretful people who must not be late on their way to what people do in offices nowadays in nearly every city in the world.
>
> (Bartlett 1959: 46)

The district was favoured by foreign countries for their embassies, and a number of exclusive schools (both international and Thai) were established there. In the mid-1960s Bangkapi could still be regarded as a fringe area of the city. It comprised a mixture of old and declining (mainly Thai–Muslim) neighbourhoods near the main canals (Phrakhanong and Saensaep), relatively new residential settlements of middle-class Thai, and a number of government institutions. Numerous vacant land blocks along the *soi* became the sites of rented slum settlements (Morell and Morell 1972: 5–6). Over 20 per cent of all land was still vacant in the mid-1970s (see Table 8.1). Low-density middle-class housing had resulted in a fragmented land-holding pattern which, despite the changes to the ecology of the district, still proves resistant to homogenisation of land uses and ecology, since individual family strategies determine the allocation and usage of land blocks (Interviews, John Lang Wooton, Richard Ellis, Bangkok 1993).[6]

By the early 1970s Sukhumvit road was lined with shophouses at the *soi* (lane) mouths and several hotels had been built, as well as a number of restaurants. The presence of thousands of US troops on R & R leave

Table 8.1 Land use changes, Sukhumvit Road (north), 1958–91 (% of total area)

Land use	*1958*	*1974*	*1991*
Residential	46.38	63.01	69.05
Commercial	0.31	2.25	10.73
Manufacturing	0.14	1.81	2.55
Government office	0.00	0.21	0.86
Education	2.35	3.87	4.31
Religion	0.86	1.02	1.01
Embassy/legation	0.00	0.16	0.59
Agriculture	2.52	0.00	0.00
Road surface	1.11	2.11	2.11
Vacant/unused land	36.74	25.57	8.82
Total	100.00	100.00	100.00

Source: Banchawan 1992.

accelerated this trend towards diversified functions. By the time the Americans pulled out from Thailand in the mid 1970s, Sukhumvit road was well-supplied with a tourist-orientated infrastructure of bars and hotels. From the mid-1970s the westernmost edge was being developed for the middle-eastern tourist wave which followed the oil price hikes of OPEC. The former GI hotel, the Grace, was bought by Saudi investors. The tourist mix soon diversified, with German, Swiss and English arrivals, all represented in various small-scale tourist-related ventures, from beer gardens to travel agencies and restaurants. Although by the early 1980s the main road was lined with a burgeoning mixture of shops and tourist venues, many *soi* of this main thoroughfare were still quiet tributary lanes with spacious houses on generous grounds, home to prominent members of the Thai elite as well as foreign professionals and business people. The district's role as a residential suburb had been reinforced, while it acquired additional functions relating to key activities in the expanding metropolis (see Table 8.1).

Conversion of some of the large land blocks in the *soi* of Sukhumvit to luxury apartments was taking place in the early 1970s, but they were generally no more than six storeys in height. The trend towards higher density high-rise accelerated from the early 1980s, in response to the provisions of the 1979 *Condominium Act*. Sukhumvit quickly became the area with the highest concentration of luxury condominiums in Bangkok, due to its proximity to existing business districts as well as retail and tourist amenities. High-rise residential buildings increased from sixty-five in 1987 to 163 four years later, with office towers increasing from eight to thirty and hotels from five to sixteen over the same period (Banchawan 1992: 86). In less than a decade this once low-rise district was overshadowed by towers. By the early 1990s the area took on the character of a construction site. From 1988 Sukhumvit boasted the highest number of new construction permits and area (by square metres) in the whole of the BMA. Notably,

Plate 8.2 The condominium towers of Sukhumvit. (Photo: Author)

Table 8.2 Multi-storeyed buildings in the Sukhumvit district (subareas) by type, height and construction period

Area	*Building type/function*					*Height (floors)*				*Building period*		
	Ap't	*Condo*	*Office*	*Hotel*	*Total*	*< 5*	*%*	*> 20*	*%*	*By 1986*	*1987–92*	*1993*
West	67	29	24	27	147	11	7	28	19	86	42	20
Central	171	52	39	19	281	66	23	62	22	127	105	49
East	112	7	9	0	128	109	85	8	6	47	71	10
Total	349	88	72	46	437	189	42	67	15	260	218	79

Source: Data re-aggregated from Kiat 1993.

Key: West = *Soi* 1 to 21; Central = *Soi* 21 to 63; East = *Soi* 63 to Khlong Phrakhanong.

the Sukhumvit district exhibits clear variations in its build environment, with the *soi* in its western section experiencing the most active reconstruction. Eastwards, the low-rise profile still dominated beyond the main road, indicating the persistence of older residential uses and different investment decisions (notably, low-rise rental apartment construction) by local landowners (see Table 8.2).

Metropolitanisation and homogenisation

On a macro scale, the changing land uses of the Sukhumvit district can be portrayed as evidence of a process of metropolitan expansion, whereby the various commercial, financial and retail activities of the metropolis absorb a suburb formerly dominated by low-density and low-rise residences (Kiat *et al.* 1993: 1–7). From the mid-1980s the state played a role in shaping the role of Sukhumvit within the metropolis, largely through new transport infrastructure and the redevelopment of government-owned land uses. Asoke Road was extended southward across Sukhumvit Road, cutting through low income housing to meet Rama VI Road. The new road (Ratchadaphisek) fronted the substantial property of the government Tobacco Monopoly. In 1989 the government began the construction of a major convention centre, of a size in keeping with the new regional aspirations of the government and the Thai business elite. The Queen Sirikit Convention Centre was finished in time for the 1991 World Bank Meeting, an occasion which provided an opportunity for displaying the city. The Sirikit Centre became a key site, consolidating the future direction of change in the district towards that of a commercial and administrative extension of the old CBD. This ambitious structure was erected at the expense of one of the city's major slum settlements (Duang Phitak) (*Nation* 18 June 1991; *Bangkok Post* 22 June 1991).

Further to the east, the site of the Department of Meteorology was cleared for a new public park, which opened in 1993. Both developments added value to the surrounding land and attracted a flurry of building on nearby sites, including office towers, condominiums and hotels. The Tobacco Monopoly site to the north of the Convention Centre, soon to be vacated (although as of 2002 it had not been moved) features a large artificial lake (formerly used for industrial purposes) which will become a central aspect of a new park, and has already attracted office projects nearby, claiming it as 'Lake Ratchada' (after the name of the road) (*Bangkok Post Investment and Property* 27 December 1993). On the corner of Ratchadaphisek a new stock exchange was foreshadowed. All of these developments signalled the expansion of Sukhumvit's functions as a commercial and administrative extension of the old Central Business District.

Soi-based ecologies and the limits to erasure

The changes discussed above suggest that Sukhumvit has been a key site for the homogenising impacts of an expanding urban land market hand-in-hand with state-initiated infrastructure and land redevelopment projects. A closer view shows that there has been a degree of variation in the changes occurring. The area is in fact constituted by *soi*-based ecologies, which, while being transformed in various ways, still exert an influence on urban life. By 'ecology' I mean here a system comprising the interrelations between the resources and population of an area and the distribution and mix of these elements. Built form, land uses, the layered economic base of the district and the associated activities of the Sukhumivit's population combine to shape the diverse character of its *soi*, and are in turn shaped by it. The high-rise developments, including hotels and condominiums, have impacted on – but also been assimilated within – the diverse activity system that has been formed around the *soi* configurations of Sukhumvit.

These configurations have evolved, changed and persisted in relation to the uses of the district. Sukhumvit can be conceived as an ensemble of diverse but interrelated spaces comprising various layered activities which are generated by distinguishable groups, that is the district's workforce, its tourists, its residents, and other groups which use its institutions and sites, such as school students. Sukhumvit's spaces support niches of activity and identifiable subgroups. Such activities stem from local and international influences; indeed key actors in the economy of the Sukhumvit region are dependent on international tourism and business activity for their survival, both at the top end (hotels) and at lower ends of the income generating system (taxi drivers, freelance prostitutes). Although the registered population of the municipal district (Khet Khlong Toei) which incorporates Sukhumvit is numbered at 251,431, the daytime population is in fact much larger, comprising about 25,000 people engaged in retail activities, services (such as hotels), banks and government education and embassies. In addition there are about 61,590 students and an estimated 17,500 tourists. Altogether, the daytime population is about 428,629 (Kiat *et al.* 1993: 3–11).

Viewed from the level of Sukhumvit's *soi*, the process of change over the period from the 1970s can be seen to be generated by the entry of new retail, entertainment and service activities into formerly isolated lanes (Cohen 1985). The penetration of these uses and the degree to which they displaced earlier functions have depended on a number of conditions dictated in part by inherited ecological factors in the area, including patterns of land use and the character of each *soi*. For example, the numerous dead-end *soi* have generally seen less substantial change than those that are through-ways to major roads. Where high-rise development has occurred in short *soi* it is almost entirely residential, unless focused on corner blocks. In contrast, the through-*soi* were always more diverse in their land uses, and have attracted much more new development (Bangon 1987: 30–50). At the same time, other factors have influenced the nature and pace of change. The narrower *soi* have been less suitable for redevelopment than wider routes, and the persistence of a highly dispersed landownership pattern has influenced the overall pattern of differential *soi* development. The varied intensity of change across the district has also been dictated by the pressures applied on different subareas: thus the western section of Sukhumvit, closer to the central city, received the brunt of pressures for land sales while the *soi* here underwent considerable building and transformation from the 1980s as new condominium blocks, hotels and commercial structures were introduced.

Aside from a number of *soi* in the extreme west, many of Sukhumvit's tributaries continue to exhibit multiple use patterns. The case of *Soi* 22 (*Soi* Sainamthip) is instructive here in displaying the persistence of heterogeneity in the overall context of change. Studied by Erik Cohen in 1983–4, *Soi* 22 was seen to exemplify a pattern of urbanisation he characterised as 'lateral *soi* expansion'. Running southwards between Sukhumvit and Rama IV Roads, this *soi* was marked by considerable diversity in its early landscape. It incorporated shophouse clusters, markets, apartments, compound houses and several large slum settlements. Cohen observed how new retail functions were entering this *soi*, and how the new building of duplexes and shophouses was taking place laterally along its tributary lanes (Cohen 1985). This was an essentially physical portrayal of change, indicating the changes in spatial configuration which ensued as a formerly isolated area became absorbed within an expanding metropolitan complex. The process, rather than the ultimate consequences, was the central theme of his discussion. When I studied this *soi* in 1993 and the following years, the observable changes which had taken place, although remarkable, were equally notable because a new diversity had emerged and elements of an older pattern of multifunctional *soi* use were persisting.

New developments in the *soi* from the mid-1980s all pointed to the process of metropolitan homogenisation of functions. These new functions were signified by three luxury hotels at the north end of the *soi* (near Sukhumvit Road) and a major new condominium block to its south – the huge President Park complex. In 1993 a number of further luxury condominium developments were advertised on vacant blocks which had once been the site of slums. Together with the high-rise tourist and expatriate accommodation facilities, a number of low-rise apartment blocks had been built. New shophouses – double the width of the older shophouses lining parts of the *soi* – had been constructed and occupied by tour agencies, restaurants (catering to Thai office workers and tourists) and high-class tailor's shops. Others catered to night life activities, in particular an increasing number of exclusive Japanese and Korean Karaoke bars (which increased from two to seven between 1992 and 1999).

While these changes were conspicuous – as was the increased traffic congestion associated with it – just as clear was the notable diversity of the people and their activities in this *soi* and its connected lanes. Older shophouse clusters in the numerous lateral lanes leading off the *soi* continued to function as residences for Sino–Thai families, even though these families had often ceased doing business from these buildings. Other old shophouses hosted small-scale service and retail activities, including motorcycle repair shops and small cheap hairdressing establishments. A major shophouse cluster had been built by a local Thai landowner to the south, on the site of an earlier rental slum and banana grove. In 1985 this had been reported by Cohen as a new development. Comprising two *soi* (known as *Soi* Setthi 1 and 2), by the 1990s this cluster housing over 500 people had become a multifunctional and small manufacturing area with associated cheap rental residential uses for wage workers in the Rama IV Road area and the Sukhumvit district generally. As the name of this private development suggested (*setthi* means wealth) it brought the local Butsabong family considerable income in leases and rents. Three landowners at the north end of the *soi* constructed cheap apartments in the small lateral lanes, and many more small apartments were constructed near the *Soi* Setthi shophouse precinct by local Thai landowners. Notably many shophouse businesses lining *Soi* 22 (including the newly built larger styles) subdivided and rented the upper floors to workers in the service industries surrounding the area. At least 50 rooms are used for this purpose in the northern section of the *soi* alone. Rooms are rented for between 1,200 and 1,500 baht per month. Those renting included women working in the nearby expatriate bars as well as motorcycle taxi drivers and hotel workers. Changes in the *soi* had not emptied it of people, in fact the process was quite the reverse, given the existence of a varied employment market in services in the immediate and surrounding districts. The *soi* also hosts considerable informal sector activity, focusing on food and transport, and catering to different income groups, from office workers to hotel employees. In the mornings, some fifty motorcycle riders work in the *soi*, transporting people to and from work (and to each end of the *soi*) while over twenty food vendors sell soup and morning meals. In the evenings the number of food and transport providers in the informal sector increases. If the area considered as the overall activity zone of the *soi* includes *Soi* Setthi and its many connected lanes, the total number of informal sector workers numbers at least 120 people in the mornings and more in the evening hours) (author's field notes).

Clearly, *Soi* 22 has undergone considerable change in the fifteen years since Cohen's innovative study of *soi* ecology and expansion, and many features associated with his concept of 'metropolitan invasion' are indeed applicable to portraying its transformation. However, the small-scale businesses which once dominated local trading activity have not been displaced in the *soi*: rather, they have adapted to the changing economic opportunities that came with new functions in the area. This is notable particularly with respect to tourists. Thus, while most of the smaller shophouse businesses catered for a local Thai clientele until around 1990, there has been a discernible shift towards catering for tourists from the new hotels, with small concerns converting to become air-conditioned restaurants and souvenir shops. Trends evident in the city at large are reflected in *Soi* 22, notably with the introduction of minimarts, which, in the northern sector of the *soi*, attract more foreign tourist, expatriate and

Thai clientele than the smaller stores. So far, however, there is still a measure of coexistence between types of businesses in the *soi*.

The persistence of small-scale business concerns in the midst of corporatised enterprises (such as the large hotels and food retail chains) is explained largely by the way that landowners' decisions and the continuing diversity of activities and demand in the area intersect. Unlike the extreme west of the Sukhumvit area, where land and redevelopment was substantial, triggering an exodus of earlier Thai land owners – particularly homeowners – the area of *Soi* 22 (which falls within the area of central Sukhumvit, see Table 8.2) has seen substantial retention of holdings by small owners. There are still older compound houses and bungalows which local Thai owners have refused to sell, despite tempting offers made by development companies during Bangkok's boom years. The choice to

Plate 8.3 Local life in a tributary lane off *Soi* 22: kick-boxers practising. (Photo: Author)

invest in small, family-run apartment blocks is indicative of what may be described as the *habitus* of small Thai property owners, who prefer to hold on to land and run enterprises themselves at a steady income. This is reinforced by the proliferation of small land blocks in the lateral lanes of Sukhumvit. Broader forces in the city at large have obviously played a part in allowing for the persistence of this diversity of ownership. The slump in the property market from 1994 led to an easing of pressure on land purchase and the suspension of the three large condominium projects foreshadowed in the *soi*, as elsewhere in Sukhumvit. Had the land boom continued, it is possible that price offers for land in this *soi* would have increased further, allowing developers to assemble large land blocks by buying from the small owners in the lateral *soi*. Further, a new building code introduced by the BMA in 1992 imposed stricter regulations on high-rise building developments in narrow *soi* (enforcing setback guidelines with floor area ratios) made it considerably more expensive for developers to build large complexes in lateral lanes.

In Sukhumvit, condominium developers never acknowledge the street economy of motorcycle taxis, hairdressing and tailoring establishments and many of the other shophouses which cluster around the condominium. In inner Bangkok, as exemplified in Sukhumvit, patterns of local shophouse-based businesses and associated informal sector production can persist at the level of the *soi*. The district surrounding the President Park complex is a case in point, where the Butsabong family's shophouse cluster sustains small manufacturing, with a casual labour force utilising adjacent building stock converted for use as dormitories and rented rooms. As well as a mixed residential population of low-income renters (comprising labourers, freelance sex workers, go-go dancers and service workers) there is also demand for informal sector and small-scale services from the daily office-working population. The persistence of the urban informal sector in sustaining what one researcher has designated an 'urban foodscape' in Bangkok is worth stressing: cheap, freshly cooked snacks and meals remain an important feature of urban existence, especially in a city where many people have no time to prepare their own evening meals (Yasmeen 1995).

There are layers of labour markets and uses in the economies and ecologies of the *soi* which operate with relative autonomy from the luxury condominium inhabitants. These include services for people working and living locally, such as dressmakers, hairdressers, laundries, motorcycle repair shops and motorcycle washing businesses. Businesses associated with other layers of the district's economy include the cutting shops which supply the plush tailors' shops of Sukhumvit, catering mainly to international tourists. An important group in the *soi* economy linked to the wider urban service infrastructure is the motorcycle taxi riders: these may live locally or at a distance from the *soi*. They occupy a place of con-

Plate 8.4 Food vendor and local customers at the mouth of a lane off Sukhumvit *Soi* 22. (Photo: Author)

siderable importance in the transportation system of the city, not only relatively cheap, but necessary for quick movement in a city clogged with traffic jams.

Not all *soi* maintain equal diversity, movement flows or layers of activity: this depends on the length of the *soi* and whether it is connected to other streets in a communication network. Short, dead-end *soi* may be completely empty of activity. Nonetheless, a large number of the condominium locations coexist with multilayered *soi* and district-based activity nodes and networks. Displacement of such functions is only evident in completely built-over *soi*, which are rare, given the nature of landownership and its uses. Notably new developments in the vicinity of *Soi* 22, such as the Emporium shopping/entertainment complex discussed earlier generate unforeseen informal uses. After the complex closes at around 10 pm female department-store workers gather in the nearby park and the *soi* with friends and boyfriends (who arrive on motorcycles to collect them) to eat, drink and socialise around the food stalls of nearby *soi* (including *Soi* 22): these social activities help to perpetuate the informal economy and multi-use patterns which pre-dated the new modern shopping space. The life of the district does not close down with the offices, nor do the streets empty because executives in Sukhumvit's offices have returned to their fully serviced 'one stop living' condominiums.

Conclusion

I have used *Soi* 22 as an indicative example of the diversity existing in the Sukhumvit Road area, and while this analysis may not be entirely applicable to some of the *soi* in its western sections, it does suggest that there are limits to portraying the reconstruction of Sukhumvit during the condominium boom as a comprehensive transformation of the local ecology. Property analysts, brokers and the maps which they formulate to inscribe new spaces in the metropolis carve the city into marketing spaces. In their advertisements which universally depict luxury and exclusivity, they rarely acknowledge the diversity of the locales into which they insert their set piece condominium, office and entertainment complexes. This is a key aspect of the symbolic economy which has accompanied metropolitan restructuring according to global forms: it constitutes one important representation of space, or, in Sharon Zukin's terms, a 'landscape of power' dominated by the imperatives of capitalist markets (Zukin 1991: 3–23). At the street level and scale of local ecology it is never that simple. In Sukhumvit, the condominiums have not erased the diversity of activities and the practices of street life, even if broader forces are informing the character of that diversity. In this district, and Bangkok generally, the street mix may be altered by the condominium, yet local traders and landowners have often proved resilient in adapting to change. They are adept at responding to the demands of neighbouring residential and working groups regardless of income. The shopping strip is a localised market more flexible and adaptable than that for condominium apartments, and even if the restaurants and boutique clothing stores oust older land users, the dominant mix of shops may be refigured but often survives.

It is generally assumed that the central business and residential districts of Pacific Rim cities reflect a fairly straightforward process of assimilation to global urban forms associated with the economic and cultural integration characteristic of advanced world capitalism. High-rise office, hotel and condominium developments are the conspicuous architectural symbols of this assimilation. But closer study does not support this simplistic portrayal. These inner city spaces are neither undifferentiated terrains of singular economic processes nor passive recipients of a globally determined property market.

9 Sex workers in Bangkok

Refashioning female identities in the global pleasure space

Introduction: representations of Bangkok as sex capital

On the global map of tourism and travel, Thailand, and particularly Bangkok, stands out as a key space of sexual pleasure and consumption. In western print media, and in TV broadcasting, programmes on Patpong night life featuring the evocative term 'sex tourism', often linked with HIV–AIDS issues, are always sure of a wide viewing and listening audience. The persistent popular western stereotype of Bangkok as a world centre of sexual pleasure for foreign men (e.g. 'the sexual supermarket of Asia') developed during the 1970s in the wake of its use as a Rest and Recreation (R & R) place for US servicemen (e.g. *Washington Post* 11 August 1978). In the decade 1975–85 the ratio of male to female foreign tourists entering Thailand increased from 2:1 to 3:1, and there is little doubt that the increasing number of tourist-orientated sex venues in Bangkok and Thailand's resort towns (both for heterosexual and homosexual men) was a principal attraction (Meyer 1988: 256). In 1984, one of the most famous hit songs was 'One Night in Bangkok' (written, ironically, to mark a chess tournament held in the city). Its lyrics show how strongly the image of the city and its tourist red-light districts had merged in the western imaginary:

> One night in Bangkok and the world's your oyster,
> the bars are temples, but the girls ain't free,
> You'll find a God in every Golden Oyster,
> and if you're lucky then the God's a She,
> I can feel an Angel slidin' next to me.[1]

The strength of this global media-driven image of Bangkok was impressed upon the Thai public in 1993 when *Time Magazine* reporting on world prostitution, featured a front cover picture showing a Bangkok bar girl sitting in the lap of a western male customer. Interestingly, very little of the feature article dealt with Bangkok or Thailand, but the icon of Bangkok was a key image for the sale of this issue (Hornblower 1993). In the same year the *Longman's World Dictionary* featured a controversial entry referring to Thailand as a 'place of prostitutes', which created justifiable outrage among government leaders. The *Bangkok Post* commented on the *Time Magazine* issue, noting:

> When we talk about perfume we think France. When we talk about rugs we think Persia. As for Thailand, an image or product with which most people associate used to be teak, rice or the easy smile. But gauging from the international media's coverage during the past several years, that easy Thai smile has now been replaced by scantily-clad young girls – prostitutes, to be direct.
>
> (*Bangkok Post* 9 July 1993)

Despite the efforts of the Thai government to counter these global stereotypes (for example, by promoting family tourism) the stereotyping of Bangkok as global sex capital persists, underlining the ways that both images and global economies reinforce each other. Interestingly, the well-known haunts of commercialised sex in western countries (Times Square in New York and the red-light district of Amsterdam, for example) have received much less publicity in the world press. As Richard Parker notes: 'Much like race, sexuality . . . has been neatly packaged as an especially important figure in the range of images used to distinguish North from South, the First World from the Third World, the developed nations from the developing countries' (Parker 1999: 1). The ways in which images of Thai female sexuality have been generated in various forms (literature and film) by western 'orientalism' – the western fascination with the exotic 'other' of Asia – have received increasing attention by scholars (Hamilton 1998; Manderson 1998). Significantly, however, much of this western scholarship on prostitution in Thailand and other countries of Southeast Asia (such as the Philippines) has adopted its own version of the global media stereotypes, underlined by theoretical assumptions which posit the victimisation and passiveness of 'Asia' in the global economy of sexual pleasure. New feminist approaches to sex work in the west have emphasised that women can exercise agency through assertive displays of their sexuality and desire (Zatz 1997). However, with only rare exceptions (see Odzer 1994) Asian sex workers remain consigned to victimhood status in western feminist accounts of prostitution (e.g. LeMoncheck 1997: 110–11). The image of passivity and powerlessness extends to the portrayal of Bangkok's landscape: thus, we find one American scholar describing 'the whole city' as 'an erotic theme park' an essentially passive space for tourist consumption (Robinson 1993). In one sense, such statements simply point to the most conspicuous element in Bangkok's function as an international tourist city – but the caricature also betrays the continuing orientalism of much western scholarship, which disregards the reality that the multiple exploitative power of global consumption industries – such as sex-orientated tourism – may be subject to mediation, appropriation and contestation at the local level by the Thai women and men engaged in the sex trade (for discussion on this point see Ryan 2000). Like other large cities of the world and the Asian region, the sexual life and economy of Bangkok has its own history, shaped both by changes in society and their intersection with broader cultural and economic processes (see e.g. Barmé 1997; Ong-at 1990 for Bangkok; de Manila 1980; Hershatter 1997 for Manila and Shanghai). Notably, the Thai metropolis is the site for the formation of a variety of sexual cultures (lesbian, transsexual and gay) which are part of a complex of global sexual cultures and identity formation (Altman 2001: Chapter 6). These have ramified into the worlds of local and tourist-orientated prostitution in the city (Anand 1997; Storer 1999). Here I focus on Thai women sex workers.[2]

In this chapter, I suggest that Bangkok's red-light districts – often seen as a constructed pleasure space of the tourist-orientated sex trade, are as much made, sustained and manipulated by women sex workers themselves as by the infrastructure and foreign clientele of commercialised sex services. Through studying the life narratives and practices of women as they engage and disengage with prostitution and the Thai metropolis, it is possible to develop an alternative perspective of how Bangkok is used and constituted. I re-examine and re-contextualise the practices of prostitution in terms of the interacting spatial/sociocultural fields within which women engage as they strategise towards accumulating survival and status resources. I treat women sex workers here not as complete 'victims' of an unequal Thai sex–gender order and global political economy of sexual exploitation, but as agents with the capacity to transform their lives. They do so in the micro-spaces of their interaction with foreign men and through the deployment of cultural capital as they move between key spheres of their lives, between lovers, peers and families.

Thai prostitution and the tourist-orientated sex trade – dominant approaches and alternatives

The macro-processes of east–west global tourism, the political economy of the Thai tourism industry and the patterns of regional and socio-economic inequalities which underlie the gendered nature of poverty, in addition to the Buddhist religious norms which relegate women to a lesser moral status, have all been well-treated in the literature pertaining to prostitution in Thailand (Enloe 1989; Keyes 1984; Muecke 1992; Pasuk 1982; Truong 1990). The structural conditions underlying the rise of foreign-orientated prostitution and the much larger phenomenon of domestic prostitution both overlap and depart from each other. Regional inequalities have been exacerbated by a Bangkok-centred process of development, which led to the metropolis drawing on the rural communities as a surplus labour pool. Rural men, and increasingly women, were drawn into the urban formal and informal labour market, prostitution being one of the submarkets (Pasuk and Baker 1995: 186–9). The commercialised domestic sex trade focusing on brothels, massage parlours, hotels and entertainment venues emerged with expanding incomes which supported an expanding clientele for sexual services in Thailand from the late 1950s. This expansion was unrelated to foreign tourism (Sukanya 1983). The structural changes underlying the growth of tourist-orientated prostitution by the 1980s were clear. The foreign-orientated sex trade followed the expansion in the tourism sector generally from the mid-1970s and was given the blessing (indirectly) of the state through tourism promotion. Tourism expanded dramatically to form a significant foreign currency-earner for the Thai economy whose fortunes had become bound to the global marketplace, not just in resources, but in services (Pasuk and Baker 1995: 148–9).

The structural demographic and labour market shifts and their links with Thailand's open economy are the undeniable macrocontexts within which we must comprehend the experiences of ordinary Thais, among them women entering prostitution as a survival strategy. Nonetheless, in relation to foreign-orientated prostitution at least, the dominance of this perspective has tended to overshadow a number of key dimensions of the practice of commercial sex itself and the contexts of this practice. Prostitution is not just another form of 'off-farm labour'; it bespeaks a range of transformations that extend beyond the simple tradition/modernisation dichotomies which posit collapsing village societies and alienating urban labour markets. Women's experiences are not just an effort to shore up the disintegrating village social structure through dutifully remitting money to their families – their identities are tied into wider sociospatial transformations where they are redefining themselves in Thai society. This gap in understanding is expressed well in the reluctance of the Marxist–feminist scholar Than-Dam Truong to explore women's motivations and consciousness in her structural study of the political economy of sex and tourism in Southeast Asia. Truong devotes only one paragraph to the 'world view' of female sex workers, cursorily remarking that it is 'rather complex', largely perhaps because from the vantage point of Marxist–feminism, while large numbers of sex workers are engaged in a form of labour (through commodification of their sexuality), they are not conscious of themselves as a class 'for-itself': rather, they interpret their situations individually and often seek solutions in relationships with customers/lovers (Truong 1990: 187).

This begs a whole range of questions about just what sexual labour involves, both in terms of womens' approach to it as paid work and other dimensions, such as their experiences of such labour – treated in terms of movement, changing contexts of work and relationships. Much recently published work on the tourist-orientated sex trade (in Thailand and elsewhere) basically repeats the truisms of earlier political economy scholars, implying a monolithic sex industry, coordinated sex tourism and third world/first world dualities of power (e.g. Bishop and Robinson 1998; Thiesmeyer 1999). So too, the complicated realities underlying sex-trafficking are often oversimplified to construct a uniform stereotype of Thai women's victimhood, despite key differences within and between domestic and tourist-orientated prostitution (note the critique by Lisa Law 1999). However, studies by anthropologists are beginning to show that a far more complex process than previously acknowledged is at play (e.g. Lyttleton 1994). It is perhaps unsurprising that these more sophisticated perspectives have been developed through detailed ethnographic research – the best of it conducted in the native language of the informants (unlike western political economy-based studies). A recent ethnographic study by one adventurous young Thai women academic (who disguised herself as a bar worker for her research in Chiang Mai bars) strongly supports the argument that women in tourist-orientated prostitution are active, assertive and skilled agents in the interactions that take place in the red-light districts (Mukdawan 2000).

This chapter focuses on the Sukhumvit Road area, which hosts one of the key tourist red-light zones of Bangkok. It is based on an ethnographic study of women sex workers in beer bars, restaurants, expatriate bars and go-go bars. Bangkok is by no means the only place of tourist–prostitute encounters, but this area focus brings into relief some important interactions of spatial and social practices which in turn relate to some more general processes occurring in Thai society, particularly among women of rural origin.[3]

Concepts towards a spatial anthropology of tourist-orientated sex work

A number of key concepts used in the following discussion should first be outlined. I treat women as 'agents' having the capacity to devise projects and act on them, following Sherry Ortner's useful definition as 'the capacity of social beings to interpret and morally evaluate the situation to formulate projects and try to enact them' (Ortner 1995: 185). At the same time such agency is mobilised in a set of strategies based on a set of value-orientations which, while not derived from an unchanging cultural base, are nevertheless grounded in a set of dispositions (or *habitus*, following Bourdieu 1977: 78–87) towards achieving certain key cultural capital. I use this framework of 'practice', much as I have done in earlier chapters of this book, to illuminate the significance of cultural patterns in contemporary Thai society and the metropolis. Such key cultural capital is expressed in status markers which are connected to identity formation. Yet it should be noted there that women engaged in various forms of sex work, like their sisters in other walks of life, construct their identities in multiple ways. Selfhood, as a constructed and dynamic site of 'being-in-the-world' (for which see Kondo 1990: 31–48), is expressed and constituted in a number of fields, including the domestic (family), the peer group (friends) and the sexual (lovers/partners). I will argue that prostitution is a project in the recovery of selfhood, and is directed to achieving material and emotional gains following the trauma and disillusion which forms the background for many women's entry into the commercialised sex world. This focus does not discount the broad structural dimensions of inequality (the economic, gendered and religious frameworks) within which women enter and practise prostitution, but it reorientates our attention to the ways women negotiate and make choices (albeit constrained choices) within a range of contexts.

It is important to conceive of Thai women sex workers' practices as simultaneously social, temporal and spatial. Drawing on the propositions of the feminist geographer Linda McDowell, I suggest here that the ongoing construction of these women's identity takes place through a series of cross-cutting locations in which the different aspects of the self vary. Moreover, these women actively 'construct' space through material, social, performative and symbolic activity (McDowell 1996: 41). I draw on these insights in using the terms 'oscillation', 'place' and 'arena' to encompass the dynamic spatial dimensions of women sex workers' practices in Bangkok and beyond. The term oscillation refers to womens' irregular patterns of circulation between the country and city. It is distinct from migration because of this irregularity and frequency and unpredictability (see Chant and Radcliffe 1992: 11–12). More than simply geographical movement between points, oscillation also describes women's movement between spaces of significance in their lives. It may be expressed in terms such as the engagement of women in the modernity of the city and the tradition of rural society (Mills 1997), but it is more complex than this, because the level of transformation in Thai society and economy is such that the consumption patterns and expectations associated with modernity are present in villages as well as urban areas (Rigg 1994, 1997). For women sex workers, 'rural' and 'urban' are in fact overlapping fields of economic and social significance in their lives, and they share multiple engagements with such fields with other Thai women.

Utilising Allan Pred's idea of 'practiced place' identities (see Pred 1984), I suggest that women's encounters in the work/entertainment sites that constitute Bangkok's sex tourist zones can be read as practices of appropriation (and thus transformation) of spaces through interpersonal encounters and renegotiation of their identities. Apprehension of this process needs to take into account not only the performative contexts of commercialised sex work, but the framework of role perceptions acted out in relationships across the tourist zones and beyond, and, importantly, the way that prostitution is an episode in, to use Pred's expression, 'biography formation'. Women use the sites – the infrastructure as-it-were – to develop, as much as possible, personalised relations which then ramify beyond the bars themselves into a set of significant spheres for identity building. In the red-light zones and beyond, women pursue strategies (a broad set of objectives). Strategies may have multiple goals: for such women it can include revenge on Thai ex-husbands, support for family members and collective projects, rebuilding material and moral prestige in the public arena (through consumption goods and lucrative partnerships with foreigners), and emotional/sexual security. Encounters with customers (*khaek*) – who are often transmuted into lovers (*faen*) in these encounters – occur across a range of sites in the city which are utlised as arenas of action where women skillfully act in engaging foreign men in romantic dramas and relationships.

Building a city of women: the infrastructure of commercial sex

Prostitution in Thailand is founded on long-standing patterns of structured economic and gender inequality, supported by a value system which marginalises women in terms of moral worth and power, yet impels them to assume key economic and social responsibilities. Foreign tourism has played a minor role in its overall growth (Sukanya 1983: 30). Nonetheless the women engaged in various forms of tourist-orientated prostitution today are a most conspicuous group, because of their high visibility in venues located in the established and modernised downtown areas of the metropolis and resort centres (such as Pattaya and Phuket) (Wathini and Guest 1994: 16). Bangkok's local underworld of prostitution was established from the mid-nineteenth century and its growth was directly linked to the expansion of demand for sexual services generated by the Chinese male immigrant workforce of the city. The Chinese quarter of Sampheng was the acknowledged centre of the city's brothels (often located near gambling dens and markets) and the larger number of prostitutes were indentured Chinese and Japanese women trafficked into Siam (Skinner 1957: 126). The involvement of Thai women in this trade appears to have been minimal at this time. Among the Thai, the prevalence of polygamy and slavery (largely debt slavery) allowed many men the privileges of sexual access to women without the need for prostitutes. So established was Sampheng as the city's red-light area that well into the twentieth century the term *Sao Sampheng* (Sampheng Girl) was widely used as a euphemism for prostitute, even after Thai women began entering the trade in large numbers from the 1950s. In the nineteenth century, the hotels and drinking houses along Charoen Krung Road patronised by foreigners (particularly seamen) featured prostitutes from Russia and other western countries. In 1928 there were 203 licensed brothels with 974 prostitutes in Bangkok, although there were at least a further 2000 non-registered prostitutes working in the city (Meyer 1988: 315). Thai women began entering the sex trade of the city in large numbers only from the 1950s, when Chinese immigration flows were stemmed. By this time, modes and venues of commercialised sex had diversified. The standard brothel venue persisted in Sampheng, but also expanded to the Thewet district along Wisut Kasat Road. Massage parlours – popularised by the Japanese military during the occupation years of the 1940s – were reintroduced and included sexual services. The cosmopolitan clubs at venues such as the Trocadero (Surawong Road) included dancing clubs where patrons (Thai and foreign) could negotiate the price of sex with the women who worked as hired dancers. Other sex workers included 'Taxi Girls' who arranged with clients to meet in their hotels or homes – they were popular among the increasing numbers of foreign men working in Bangkok (Krull and Melcher 1966: 38–9). Although prostitution was declared illegal in 1960, prostitution flourished in a disguised form (in hairdressing salons, for example), or through the simple expedient of payments to police. Hotels were a common venue for small massage parlours or brothels. In the 1970s, one western researcher studying Bangkok's potential tourist accommodation noted with surprise that most of the city's second-class hotels (largely Chinese-owned and managed) were little more than camouflaged brothels (Donner 1978: 834). By this time 'short-time' motels and hotels (*Rongraem Chuakhrao*) had become part of the city's diverse landscape of sexual liaison: they were the places where married men could meet mistresses, young men could have sex with sweethearts and both groups could hire prostitutes in secret.

Bangkok's foreign-orientated sex trade (like that in Manila) was stimulated from the mid-1960s by the surge in demand accompanying the US military Rest and Recreation (R & R) programme, which brought thousands of servicemen to the metropolis. The R & R programme quickly stimulated the development of a commercial foreign-orientated sex service infrastructure. The entertainment demands of US servicemen helped transform Bangkok's premier middle-class district of Sukhumvit (and nearby Phetchaburi Road) into an entertainment strip, comprising bars and hotels. But it was the expanding expatriate civilian population of these years (albeit nourished by Vietnam-related money flows) that laid the basis for Bangkok's best-known red-light district, Patpong Road (Dawson 1988: 39–41). Go-go dancing was first introduced into Patpong in 1969, and helped to stimulate a growth period in that precinct. By the late 1970s Bangkok's red-light district of Patpong was already famous, and the Sukhumvit area was also well-known. However the period of commercialisation and large-scale investment began only in 1982, when small shophouse bars were enlarged to become glamorous and slick venues. Live shows and sex acts were introduced in Patpong from 1984 (Dawson 1988: 95). By this time there had been a dispersal of the night life infrastructure. '*Soi* Cowboy' in the Sukhumvit area (named after the first bar-owner, an ex US airman) was developed in the early 1980s featuring a largely expatriate clientele and small shophouse bars. By 1985 there were 50 bars in that small street. Like Patpong, *Soi* Cowboy changed character from 1986, when new German bar owners expanded the size of their venues to fit more customers and glamourise surroundings. An extra street of night clubs opened in Patpong to serve an exclusively Japanese clientele. By the mid-1980s a new area of expatriate bars had emerged in the vicinity of the newly-built Washington Cinema. The first of these bars had transferred from Patpong under the pressure of rising costs of rent and competition with Chinese syndicates. In the same period the Nana Entertainment Plaza, a three-level court of twenty go-go bars – opened in the Sukhumvit district to take advantage of the expansion of tourist hotels in that area. Old GI hotels had been converted to short-time hotels for freelance prostitutes and their customers; alternatively, like the Grace Hotel (formerly a US officers' R & R hotel) some opened coffee shops as meeting places. The wave of German tourists of the mid-1980s caused a boom in open air *Beergarten*, which were open to freelance prostitutes. A range of taverns and small open-air beer bars and late-night coffee lounges (notably those of the 'Therme' turkish baths and the Malaysia Hotel) were also operating. This variety of venues characterises the zone today (see Fig. 9.1)

We should note a number of features of the emergent sex-trade infrastructure in Bangkok. First, tourism in general was not well promoted by the state until the mid-1980s; rather, the initiatives stemmed from private sector investment. Despite the significance of the statistic that tourism revenues surpassed those from the export of rice in 1982, official investment in Thai tourism infrastructure was low and belated. Linda Richter (1989: 81–3) has noted the fragmented and uncoordinated development of tourism infrastructure and the considerable diversity of modes of tourism. In such a framework it is difficult to see how sex tourism could have been so well coordinated by different business interests within Thailand. Truong's work attempts to find links between key actors in government, capital and tourism sectors, but finds little direct match. While there was some articulation between officialdom and business in the forging of the R & R contracts, supplying accommodation and sex services to American service personal, the militarisation metaphor weakens when the period after US withdrawal is considered. Truong also provides some statistics about the small-scale investment in massage parlours, tea houses and go-go bars in the late 1970s, but is unable to unravel tourist-related and local prostitution markets. Acknowledging the diversity of levels of services in the sex trade infrastructure, she establishes linkages on a general level only, and implies that imbalances in hotel investment favouring large establishments constrained smaller ventures to find ways of attracting group tours, which apparently bore fruit in sex tours. The evidence for these causal changes is minimal (Truong 1990: 170–1).

The persistent use of the terms sex industry and sex tourism by researchers implies a monolithic system: in reality it is multilayered and disarticulated. It is united (but not coordinated) only through the concentration of complementary venues – coffee shops, bars, hotels, night clubs

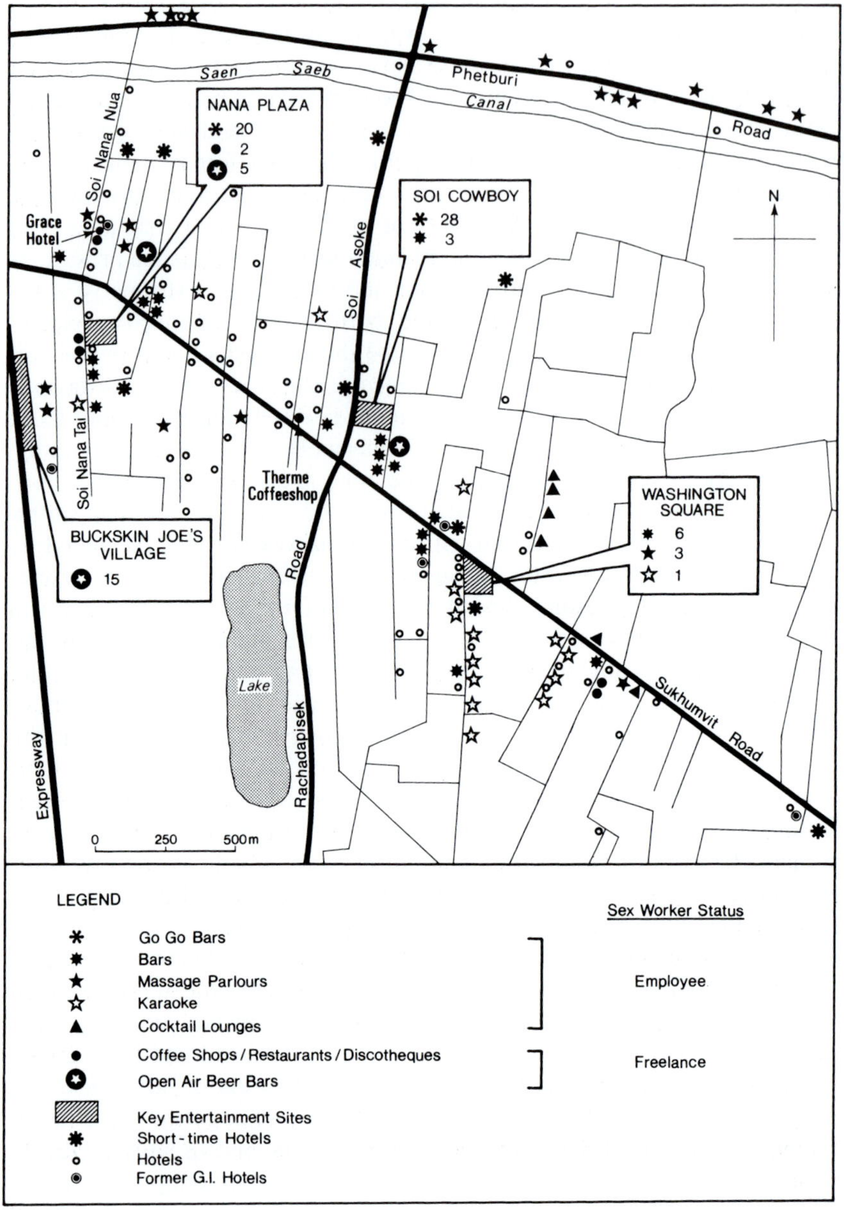

Figure 9.1 Sex trade-related sites in the Sukhumvit area, 1996.

in several key locations, the component venues of which gain from the agglomeration economies of proximity, but whose ownership patterns and workers are diverse. Hence in the districts of Patpong and Sukhumvit we find not only standard three star hotels, but short-time hotels and motels (otherwise known as curtain hotels), outdoor bars, indoor bars, massage parlours and discotheques as well as karaoke clubs and restaurants. These districts provide venues which act as sites for a variety of markets to operate simultaneously in the same space. To impute monopolies of ownership from such spatial concentrations is highly questionable. Similarly, the highly-publicised organised sex tours (which gave birth to the term sex tourism) to Thailand from Germany and Japan flourished for only a brief period in the early 1980s, before being publicly denounced both in the countries of origin and Thailand. Some western academics still imply that coordinated sex tours still exist; in fact they are not necessary for the purposes of foreign men in search of sex in Thailand. As early as 1982 over 50 per cent of foreign tourists to Thailand (70 per cent male) were return visitors (Economist Intelligence Unit 1984: 24). They knew where to go and where to stay without the aid of promotion agencies.

By 1987, a year the Thai government promoted as 'Visit Thailand Year', there were well-established concentrations of sex-related entertainment venues in Bangkok, as well as the burgeoning beach resorts of Pattaya and Phuket. Young rural women boosted the tourism subsector of the city that was entertaining ever greater numbers of foreigners. In 1987 foreign visitors numbered 3.5 million, an increase of 24 per cent over the previous year (Bangkok Bank 1988: 35). Of these tourists to Thailand the majority were males, representing an average of 65 per cent of all western tourists. Among foreign tourists from the Asian region there was an even higher imbalance in favour of men. This disproportionate figure could not be explained by business trips by males, since over 85 per cent of western, Middle Eastern and Asian tourists came for the expressly declared purpose of holidays. In particular the West German and Japanese tourists were dominated by males (65 per cent and 75 per cent respectively). These were the very groups who were having a major impact in the refashioning of sex entertainment venues in Bangkok. Official reports about the success of national tourism policy waxed lyrical about the attractions of Thailand's rich culture and natural settings. This was only part of the story, and local people knew it. In 1991, despite the AIDS pandemic, males still represented 65 per cent of foreign tourists entering Thailand (*Bangkok Post* 21 February 1993).

Modes of prostitution: worksites and employment regimes

Tourist-orientated prostitution is a form of prostitution undertaken by a minority of women in this highly differentiated industry – an estimated

2 per cent of the women engaged in sex work (Forsyth 1990). It is but a subsector of a larger Thai commercial sex trade, which is estimated to comprise between 150,000 to 800,000 women, depending on whether the estimate is provided by government or NGO sources respectively (*Bangkok Post* 31 December 1996). The interpretations I offer thus apply to a subset of Thai women engaged in sex work, a group who experience a wide variety of work situations (for which see Wathini and Guest 1994: 39–49).

Precisely because of the variability of its forms in Thailand, prostitution as a transaction between men and women has variable meanings and entails a wide range of experiences for women. For women within the Thai system there are significant differences in work situation, remuneration and clientele. In the low-priced brothels in both city and country towns, Thai men obtain strictly short-term sex services. Large and well-appointed massage parlours, which proliferated from the 1970s, serve a more well-heeled clientele. In Thailand the sale of sex services has for a long time been associated with entertainment. Thus at traditional dance and entertainment venues women are employed as companions for men. Restaurants featuring female singers (*Sao Nakrong*) also provide this service. Commonly the singers will be paid for sitting with guests and will receive garlands and tips as recognition of their singing prowess. Often they will be asked to have sex with the patron and will be paid accordingly. The recent popularity of karaoke nightclubs has expanded the number of venues for women working as companions and singers (Lyttleton 1994). During the boom years 'member clubs' multiplied for businessmen, while the western model of go-go bars was also introduced (with a notable concentration in the Saphan Khwai area in the northern suburbs). Streetwalking prostitution takes place in a range of settings. Sanam Luang (near the Royal Palace) has long been a site for women who walk the streets in search of customers. The large coffee shops of some well-known hotels serve as meeting places for freelance prostitutes and Thai men. Around Hualamphong railway station a disguised system of casual prostitution operates among some female food vendors as a means to supplement their incomes (*Bangkok Post* 22 February 1999).

Among female sex workers who deal with westerners in districts such as Sukhumvit, there are a broad range of venues and hence work situations and remuneration. They include the massage parlours, escort services, go-go bars, outdoor beer bars and coffee shops and restaurants. In addition there are expensive cocktail lounges, member clubs, karaoke clubs and member clubs exclusively for Japanese patrons, where women can be taken away for sex for a fee. Most of these forms of venue emerged during the 1960s as a result of increasing western and foreign presence in Thailand and Bangkok, both of expatriate workers and of military personnel. A distinction needs to be drawn between those establishments where women are employed directly and those where they are free to visit and work freelance. In addition, there are bars where women employees' involvement

Plate 9.1 Women at work in a go-go bar, Nana Plaza. (Photo: Author)

with customers is entirely optional: that is to say, the business of the establishment is not principally to offer sex services, but women can make arrangements with customers if they wish.[4] With conventional work options (such as factory work), offering monthly wages of between 2,000 and 3,000 baht,[5] work in foreign-orientated prostitution offers the possibility of earning between 10,000 and 50,000 baht per month, although there are in fact wide variations in incomes. Whether in freelance work or go-go bars, these earning levels are far superior to the rates earned by women in Thai brothels. None of the women I interviewed had ever considered entering the local sex trade, both because of the low rates and their aversion to Thai clientele. For them, working in a Thai brothel carried a stigma far greater than that associated with tourist-orientated work.

The conditions of work vary considerably. Thus in go-go bars and many hostess bars, women typically receive a nominal salary which they supplement with earnings from sex with customers. Over the last five years, with an apparent reduction in the numbers of women entering the work-force, and an increase in competition among bars in the go-go venues, some bar owners now offer daily rates for dancers. At Patpong and Nana Plaza, women also earn different rates of salary according to whether they dance naked, partly-naked or with swimming costumes. In addition they receive a share of the tips gained at the bar on each evening of their shift. In these bars a series of fines are usually applied to women for various infringements – smoking cigarettes on the job, arriving late for work, etc. Indeed some women have little of this nominal salary left at the end of the month due to numerous fines imposed by managers. On the other hand those with the skill or good fortune to gain regular or frequent customers will offset these losses a hundred-fold with earnings gained through their sexual services. In these bars women cannot leave during their work shift unless the customers pay 'bar fines' to take them out of the work venue. Women working freelance do not share these conditions: they can arrive at the venues whenever they want, and do not need to deal with any onerous rules or regulations. However, these freelance workers need to rely far more on their interpersonal skills in attracting customers, since these bars generally attract large numbers of women (a sex worker/customer ratio of about 3:1) who compete for the clientele.

There are a number of important characteristics about the 'workforce' in this diverse industry. Very few women regard their work in the beer bar and go-go scene as permanent. Work in a go-go bar may involve six months or two, perhaps even four years, depending on circumstances.[6] Change of jobs is also constant as women seek places with better patrons or better employers, or have problems with fellow workers. Other women return to the provinces to find work near their homes and children. Some return from villages to work in Bangkok. Others never return, having given up on the prospect of earning much money, or having made enough money to buy land or invest in a small business. Others marry foreigners and also disappear from the bar scene. At any one time in Bangkok, women working with foreigners will be at different stages of their encounter. Of the women I interviewed, some had just begun work in bars while some came to a bar and returned home after just two or three days; some had accumulated money and others had not; some had long-term boyfriends who sent money regularly, others only experienced short-term encounters with foreign men; some were about to marry and to leave Thailand; others had just returned from holidays overseas. Bar owners in Bangkok, whether Thai or foreign, constantly complain about the difficulty of attracting and keeping women as workers. Notably, one of the major reasons for reduction in numbers of women in any work venue, particularly go-go bars, is the frequency with which women leave work after finding a 'boyfriend' among customers. The nature of the workforce in this industry is thus highly volatile, highlighting the fact that the women are essentially individualistic opportunists and entrepreneurial, often at the expense of bar owner's principal business interests.[7]

The ages of the fifty women studied here ranged from nineteen to forty-two years, with the majority (almost two-thirds) aged between twenty-one and twenty-five. Grouping these women by their work places is somewhat difficult since there is a high degree of movement between modes of sex work (for example, shifts between go-go dancing to hostess work in beer bars). At the time of my first meetings with the women in this group, the distribution of work sites and modes was 42 per cent hostesses in expatriate bars; 35 per cent dancers in go-go bars; and 23 per cent freelance sex workers attending coffee shops and beer bars. Of regional origins the majority were from the northeast (68 per cent) – the common origin of most women in the foreign-orientated sex trade – with women from the north, east and central regions sharing equal proportions (10 per cent) and a very small number (2 per cent) from Bangkok. It should be noted here that not all women in the sex trade are of peasant origin or lack education. The group, while predominantly of rural origin, includes women who have studied at tertiary institutions but discontinued for various reasons, and many who have lived in the metropolis for extended periods.

Khai dua (selling sex): the meaning of prostitution

Kanprachot chiwit

Why do Thai women become involved in western/foreign-orientated prostitution? To understand the nature of cross-cultural encounters and expectations of customer-cum-lovers, this question is of considerable importance. Much has already been researched and written about rural poverty and the importance of women's role as dutiful daughters in supporting parents and family (Khin 1980; Pasuk 1982; Muecke 1992). These factors are important in understanding key elements of women's identity construction – that is, who they are. But what should be emphasised is the way that conditions in the life courses of these women have framed their decisions to become involved in selling sex to foreign tourists and expatriates in Bangkok and other areas of Thailand.

From information gained from interviews conducted with women across a number of different working contexts, I suggest that poverty itself is not a sufficient condition for women to enter sex work related to foreigners. Women enter the business of selling sex to foreigners with hesitation, with anger, with hate, with resignation and with abandon, never calmly or without fear. A key factor framing many decisions has been emotional crisis in the breakdown of a relationship with a Thai partner. Or at least, such an event has led to a temporary or permanent experiment in changing lifestyle following such an emotional crisis. This may or may not lead to total rejection of Thai males as potential future partners. Walter

Meyer, one of the few researchers to seriously comment on this recurrent theme in women's life stories, described the process of entry into prostitution (aside from cases in domestic prostitution, where women have often been forced into such work by traffickers) as 'adjustment to perceived deprivation' in social and economic terms (Meyer 1988: 321). If the information from my research (based on a study of over fifty women) is any guide, then it would appear that a high proportion of workers in tourist-orientated go-go bars and beer bars tend to enter prostitution at an older age than those women entering work in the Thai brothels, and research suggests that their immediate motivations may also be distinctive, in that relationship breakdown is cited as a minor cause of the latters' entry into sex work (Wathini and Guest 1994: 56–7; Pasuk 1982: 14–16).

Women entering freelance prostitution, beer bar and go-go bar work, often have an impulse towards either *kanprachot chiwit* (literally life-spiting, or self-punishment) or a less anger-infused attitude of *seng chiwit* (frustration with life). Such a disposition impels women to gravitate to places of difference and danger, and the well-known night spots and bars of Bangkok where foreigners congregate are well-established destinations. Of over fifty women I studied, 80 per cent had children, and about 80 per cent of this group had broken marriages from a combination of male partner's infidelity, gambling/drinking habits or financial instability. An important factor in the entry of women into tourist-orientated prostitution is that involvement with foreigners represents a new and exciting, even frightening experience, which initially at least, forms part of the aim of *kanprachot chiwit* – the act of spiting one's life. Some women may not carry through their attempted escape into another world – I have spoken to women who have worked in expatriate bars for one or two days and then left for home, unprepared to commit themselves. Others have come to the freelance beer bars with friends or siblings, having argued or broken-up with husbands up-country and decided to find out for themselves what the strange bar scene was like. Such an adventure acts as 'time-out' from domestic affairs, but it does not preclude an experiment with prostitution which may lead to some longer term involvement with a foreigner.[8]

Used on its own, the term *prachot* means sarcasm, but in terms of actions, it can refer to the direction of frustration or anger towards a substitute object (see Klausner 1992: 57–8, who describes it as 'projected vilification'). A common example of such behaviour in Thai society is the act of kicking one's dog in lieu of one's boss, if he has displeased you; another is to indirectly punish someone but not clearly reveal the reason; thus the object of resentment may or may not be aware of the meaning of the action. In both examples, direct confrontation is avoided, a state consonant with dominant behavioural values which stress restraint in revealing strong negative emotions.[9] *Kanprachot chiwit* is also consistent with a recognised form of female anger which is expressed by their running away from husband, family or home at times of conflict (see Phillips 1965: 26). *Kanprachot chiwit* can take the form of self punishment of oneself in lieu of the person who has been the cause of the problem. In the case of women it appears to occur at times of great disappointment, when a familiar world has been shattered or sorely tested. This often comes in the form of betrayal by husbands when they have affairs or take minor wives (mistresses). Some women recalled this strong reaction of anger and disappointment, which impelled them to run away from their familiar milieu and confront a completely different environment. Noi (aged 27, waitress at the Honey Beer Bar), emphasised that in addition to her feeling of rejection, she felt determined to experience a degree of the sexual freedom in which her unfaithful husband had clearly indulged.

Loss of face (*na sia*, *na daek*) is also an important part of the emotional content of the *kanprachot chiwit* reaction. For example, Phon's world was shattered when her husband, a policeman, brought his mistress home and informed her that this woman would also be living in the house with Phon and her daughter. Already upset by knowledge of her husband's lover, Phon saw this move as a complete insult, and left the home with her child. But she explained her entry into bar work not in terms of punishment towards her husband, but in terms of her need to support her child as well as her disillusion with Thai men. Working in an expatriate bar was the closest approximation to a complete change of life for her. Women can express anger and frustration with a former situation without wanting to pay back former lovers: their common outlook is one of resignation or determination to escape into another world. Tip (Gunslinger Bar, *Soi* Washington) said that in her case *prachot chiwit* meant not compromising or holding onto hope in her familiar world any more, because of disappointments with her marriage and financial status: '*Chang man, chiwit chan sia laeo, tham hai sia sut-sut loei*' ('To hell with it, life is spoilt anyway, why not spoil it completely!'). Within the general mode of *kanprachot chiwit*, some women never conceal their anger towards their Thai partners: Nom (Umbrella Bar, *Soi* Cowboy) hit back at her drunken husband when he beat her: to Nom his beating her signalled his breaching of trust and devotion as a partner and she never went back to him. Tip had been frustrated with her marriage (arranged by her father) for a number of years and tried to escape by changing her factory jobs frequently – her husband always followed her, and she often confronted him to allow a divorce. Unhappy with life and in desperation, she followed a friend's suggestion and went to an expatriate bar in Washington Square.

Seng chiwit

Seng chiwit is often mentioned by women as the basis of their entry into prostitution. This expression refers to a range of emotional states, from profound disillusionment with life circumstances to boredom. It is often generated by a combination of financial difficulties and frustration with relationships with families, Thai husbands, or interpersonal conflicts. Thus Nit – a nineteen-year-old Isan woman, formerly a factory worker in Bangkok – expressed her motivation to enter work in a go-go bar in *Soi* Cowboy in terms of the tedium of her work ('*mai mi issara*', no freedom) and its low pay, together with the attractions of a lifestyle where she could engage in night life with friends of her own age and purchase the sorts of clothes she had always wanted to wear. She added: 'I had already lost my virginity to a Thai boy, so why not make money from my body with the *farang* (western foreigners)?' This expresses well the combined motivations of many younger women who enter work as hostesses or dancers in the tourist-orientated red-light districts of Bangkok. Young women's engagement with modernity is expressed through consumption patterns and a more open assertion of sexuality which challenge norms of female respectability. These explorations are also accompanied by involvement in commercialised sexual encounters, among women in Thailand and also throughout the developing world (Murray 1991; Talle 1998). Chim, a go-go dancer from a nearby bar in the same area, volunteered a classification of the motivations of the women working in *Soi* Cowboy bars (a total of 500 to 700 women): some 10 per cent came for the lifestyle and for fun (*phuying ha sanuk*), 30 per cent came purely to make money, regardless of their personal circumstances (*phuying ha ngun yang dieo*), while 60 per cent were women with a combination of personal and financial motivations (*phuying thi mi banha*, women with problems). She had formed this view after living and working in the area for over two years, and I would suggest that her interpretation is more valid than any estimate that could be produced by academic researchers or NGO workers through formal surveys.

Fear and risk

The world of prostitution is both alien (in terms of direct experience) and yet also familiar to women entering sex work in Bangkok. Isan girls have been brought up in villages with stories of an earlier generation of women who worked in bars and lived with GIs as *mia chao* (rented wives) – this early generation of women may have been morally condemned by villagers, but stories also abound of women enriched by entry into a morally forbidden occupation. While most bar dancers, hostesses and freelance prostitutes share peasant origins, they are rarely strangers to the city as such. Before entering the trade, most worked in the metropolis – many as factory workers, others in low-paid service or labouring occupations (such as domestic service or construction work) the informal sector or small-scale vending. Notably, most women were introduced to sex work directly through friends or with information from acquaintances. Through them, the once unknown territory of the red-light zones of the metropolis – places they had once only heard about – are directly experienced.

Plate 9.2 The comfort of friends: hostesses at an expat bar taking a snack. (Photo: Author)

Women almost universally begin the work of prostitution with fear and trepidation – the psychological and behavioural adjustments are often traumatic. Not only do these women have to become accustomed to routinely engaging in the most intimate of physical acts with strangers of other races and cultures, but the work demands adjustments in their public persona which go against many of the gendered behavioural norms which have constructed their identity as women. Attracting *farang* customers (whether from a distance across a bar or from the dance floor) requires an explicit presentation of the body and sexuality which is largely alien to their experience. For example, behaviours such as direct eye contact – commonly considered a sign of brazenness and rudeness among Thais – have to be cultivated as a technique to attract attention. Women often do make determined decisions about the types of sex work they enter. Many of those who work as hostesses in expatriate bars or coffee shops shun the idea of dancing and exposing their flesh to strangers. They have been brought up to believe that being brazen (*na dan*) is hateful and that modesty and shyness (*khwamai*) are essential female virtues. However, the imperatives which led to their entry often encourage a fatalism and practicality which can overcome deeply felt moral constraints. Phin, a go-go dancer in a Nana Plaza bar related how she sought work in her bar initially as a waitress (*dek serp* – literally girl drink-server) but these positions were all full at the time. She was offered a job as a dancer instead, and she accepted because, as she explained: 'I came this far, so I might as well go all the way'. Phim's work friend, on overhearing our conversation, assertively expressed her own attitude to go-go bar work with the idiomatic Thai expression: '*Dan dai ai ot*' ('I'm shameless and beyond modesty').

The critical facilitator of women's transition into the world of sex work is the subculture formed around women's friendship networks, collective coping strategies and mutual socialisation. While women clearly have to cope with adjustments and problems alone, both at the individual psychological level and an interpersonal level with customers, it is critical that we appreciate the collective dimension of prostitution as a woman's world. Women commonly advise newcomers about the explicit and cheeky forms of behaviour required of their work. Women literally learn to *perform* the trade in the company of other women: they learn how to make body contact, to wink seductively, and to speak a smattering of English. More experienced women often introduce their neophyte friends to male customers whom they know and trust as *farang chai di* (foreigner with good heart) or *farang nissai di* (foreigner with good character). If women have been able to meet the manifold challenges of their encounters within the world of selling sex, and if they remain in the work for between six months to a year, they often experience and display a radical change in behaviour and outlook. When I met Mem a year after she had first began work as a timid hostess in an expatriate bar she admitted: 'I can't believe how I've changed, I used to be so shy, but now I can say anything and do anything.' The changes in sex workers' presentation of their bodies through make-up, hairstyling and tight and revealing clothing not only signals an adaptation to a standard style for the occupation of prostitution; in fact, these presentations of their bodies are often consonant with the fashions considered 'sexy' or modern (*than samai*) among women of the same generation in the city at large. Younger women in the go-go bars in particular find a shared space for indulgence in a hyperactive youth culture shaped around discos (which they often attend together after work) and common global fashion markers, such as the wearing of tattoos.

One critical condition allowing for women's ease of entry into sex work in Bangkok is the ecological configuration of the city itself and the distance between women's families and their workplaces. The red-light zones are well-defined precincts, and they thus allow women to engage in sex work with anonymity, beyond the disapproving gaze of Thai neighbours and their families. Even when they are walking hand-in-hand with their customers in the streets, they are doing so in a setting where other women are doing the same thing. They work in what might be described as the 'toleration zones' of the city. Because sex work is almost universally night work, the sexualised nature of initial encounters with customers in public (even in open-air beer bars) is rendered further distant from the daylight world of the metropolis. Even when women move outside the red-light districts in the company of customers (or with boyfriends on outings), they do not encounter explicit disapproval, because of the customary reticence of fellow Thais. A large proportion of women sex workers keep their work a secret from their parents, whether their parents live up-country or in the city. This is made easier by the collusion of friends and siblings in maintaining the fictions that they are working in restaurants or factories in the city. But rural parents' tendency not to press their daughters for details of their work in Bangkok makes it easier for the dissimulation to succeed. This in itself suggests that many parents do in fact have their suspicions, but prefer not to make them explicit, since they often rely on their daughters' cash remittances. Notably, when women take customers to parental villages, they usually present them as boyfriends (*faen*) whom they have met in the city. Women's entry into prostitution is often associated with the experience of shame and moral desperation, but this does not mean that women consider themselves beyond the pale of ordinary Thai life and values. Scholars relying on representations of prostitutes in Thai literature conclude that these women can never be redeemed (such characters often die in tragic circumstance before bearing children); however, studies of popular attitudes to female prostitution indicate quite the opposite (see Harrison 1996; Peracca, Knodel and Chanpen 1998). Keeping their work a secret from families highlights the importance to many women of keeping up appearances and showing respect for parents.

From the late 1980s the danger of HIV/AIDS infection became a major fear among women in the tourist-orientated sex trade. It did not, however, restrict the flow of women into prostitution in its many guises. Rather, more women became conscious of the necessity of insisting on customers using condoms. So too, employers (in go-go bars and other venues) enforced government requirements that women have regular STD and AIDS tests at clinics. One NGO focusing specifically on sex workers (EMPOWER) also played an important role in regularly distributing condoms throughout Pat Pong and other commercial sex districts. But women's understanding of HIV/AIDS and precautions against it remain varied and often simplistic. In evaluating whether or not to sell sex to customers, women often judge men by their appearance and behaviour – if men appear dirty and dress poorly, they are judged as a greater risk than men who seem to be clean and neatly dressed (*riap roi*). Some women prefer having fewer, but regular, customers for sexual transactions, assuming that this will minimise risks of infection. Many women confess to having refused sex to a customer who did not agree to using a condom, but other women are less insistent if they are in dire need of money. Among the population of customers themselves, attitudes also vary on the necessity of contraceptive protection, despite increasing publicity advocating its use. When involvements take on a more long-term character, contraceptives are almost invariably dispensed with. Often signifying an increasing trust and intimacy between the woman and her partner (associated with the processes outlined below), it also leads to the additional risks of pregnancy.

Moving between sites and generating arenas

Bangkok bars and hotels, and the major tourist resorts in Thailand, are key sites where stories are played out in relationships between men and women across cultures. These sites, enabled by the technologies and inequalities of advanced capitalism and supported by mass tourism and global flows of capital, have created permanent spaces for such interaction and cross-cultural engagements. But the meetings and interactions which take place cannot be reduced to the over-determination of the conditions imposed by employers (if they are hostesses or dancers) and the venues themselves – these sites, considered collectively, are a dynamically produced 'practised place', as mentioned above. The red-light district of Sukhumvit, studied in this chapter, is a space defined not only by its physical infrastructure and commercial sex-related businesses, but a place generated by the continued practices of women using the space in their engagement with the varied sites of sex work.

The conditions and settings within which women meet foreigners are not identical. Women themselves will identify submarkets among customers and gravitate towards particular venues. In the process of their work, women may move between a range of sites with customers. The bar itself is only one of these sites. The linkages between these sites are activated by women's creative generation of arenas through their manoeuvring with customers. For example, a common movement takes place between the bar and the customers' hotel. As noted in other studies (Cohen 1982, 1993; Askew 1999b), women aim to maximise their economic rewards through a number of manoeuvres which include accumulating regular customers or focusing on the acquisition of principal partners. The active generation of arenas is a key sociospatial dynamic underlying this work. Thus the departure area of an airport terminal becomes an arena through a woman's manoeuvring in the construction of a farewell scene with a customer, which may be hilarious or tearful, depending on her 'reading' of the situation and her customer/lover's reactions and dispositions. To describe this as a construction does not necessarily mean that the interaction is entirely staged (as opposed to being authentic). For example, Phim accompanied Hank (with whom she had spent a week) to the airport with a work friend, Meao. On returning to her bar she was forced to admit (in the face of Meao's laughing taunts) that she had been crying, although she at first tried to give the impression to her work friends that she was indifferent. Manoeuvring may well depend on knowledge gained through repeated performative engagements across the tourist/leisure sites. The building of knowledge and skills through engagement in the varied sites of encounters with foreign men is of considerable importance in women's manoeuvring, since they need to evaluate the dispositions of their clients, balancing these with their own needs. If women become emotionally involved with customers (as many do), they have to weigh up the emotional costs incurred by long distance relationships, where there is the ever-present danger that their lovers may not return to Thailand. Through economic and emotional necessity, women need to frame their encounters with foreign men in such a way as to ensure both commitments and rewards. One experienced bar worker could classify the varied dispositions and wants of foreign men thus: 'Some people holiday. Some people work in Thailand and want girl long time. Some say, "Want to stay with Thai girl all my life". Some take holiday say "I don't care about the girl, I want make love"' (Walker and Erlich 1992: 82–3).

Different workplaces offer varied possibilities and constraints for women. Thus go-go bars are sites of explicit sexuality where attention is overwhelmingly focused on the women. Here, skills in managing verbal communication in another language are not so important in engaging customer's attention as body language. Smaller expatriate bars are quieter places where conversation skills in English are generally required, unless the western customers can speak Thai. These bars (perhaps more accurately described as expatriate enclaves) are patronised by a core group of men with long-standing friendships. The women who work as hostesses are rarely the sole centre of attention (see Beaumont 1994). Here, the bars' profits are made from selling drinks, not bar fines. Women are rarely pressured by management to go with a customer, and indeed many women make a steady basic income from tips alone, without the need to solicit customers for sex. In this environment they often build, over time, an easy familiarity with patrons as they serve drinks, food, swap jokes and listen to the conversation of the regulars.

In both of these different environments certain relationships develop with customers which are often transformed from pure economic transactions into something else. Thus, men who frequent bars as regular customers (named by women as *khaek pracham*) may, with time, become classified as friends (*phuan*), a status which engenders more complex roles, obligations and treatment than first-time customers. These men may function as confidantes (*thi rabai*), buy extra drinks for women, or even pay bar fines so that women can go home if they are ill or menstruating. Those men who have become the regular sexual customers of women in particular bars usually find themselves being treated by their favourite women's workmates as her sole sexual possession, despite these men's own ultimate intentions. This, of course, might be regarded more as an efficient way to allocate customers and minimise competition in a collective working environment, than an indication of client–sex worker bonding in the bar environment. Notably, however, women express this system in terms which

Plate 9.3 Noi, a beer-bar hostess, with a regular customer. (Photo: Author)

combine their work with other key issues of pride and reputation among workmates within the bar. Despite the bar-owners' principal concern with maintaining profits regardless of customers' preferences or promiscuity, the women themselves treat men who breach their tacit 'one-customer-one-girl' rule with disdain.

The ability of a woman to capture a customer's attention and engage his interests depends on a range of factors which include not only her own appearance, but also the customer's own preferences, her language abilities, and her capacity to read the situation as its develops. From regular encounters in a bar there is often a phase in relationships between bar workers and their clients/lovers when the spatial span of the relationship moves beyond the bar venue itself to other leisure/tourist sites. It may extend to outings to movie theatres, restaurants, shopping and other excursions. In many cases bar women will stay for the duration of their 'boyfriend's' holiday in his hotel. These sites are arenas of women's presentation of self (a consciously-constructed role), and actively develop the bonds (whether sexual, emotional or both) between them and their clients.[10] The written correspondence of foreign men with their Thai girlfriends highlights the significance of these sites in the pattern of the sexual/emotional encounter: men who have returned home often envision the relationship as an ensemble of key memories and events (see Cohen 1982; Walker and Erlich 1992). Such events are generated through the interactive moments embodied in arenas. Arenas are generated on beaches during holidays, in hotel rooms, restaurants, streets, and in departure and arrival points in airports. The holiday – a trip to a resort or popular destinations in the provinces – is a standard expectation of short-term tourists and bar women alike. Western men are charmed by the prospect of extended holidays with the Thai women they meet. On the woman's part, from a purely mercenary viewpoint, an extended holiday allows her a predictable flow of income in an unstable economic world.[11]

The following example helps to highlight the ways that an involvement can develop unexpectedly from a casual transaction to a friendship to a romance. George, an electrical contractor from Canada, a man with considerable experience of the bar scene in Bangkok, met Pun, a woman newly arrived at an expatriate bar in Washington Square as a hostess. George, who was suffering the after-effects of a difficult divorce, was not in search of a romantic involvement with a bar-worker. His friend Rick, an expatriate of long standing, introduced him to Pun because he thought George might like the company of a polite and well-spoken Thai woman. For her part, Pun had left her home in Nakhon Sri Thammarat after the death of her husband and subsequent disputes with his family over an inheritance. What began as a companionable exchange of information on their first meeting soon developed further into a friendship based on mutual sympathy (George could speak Thai, Pun spoke no English). First restricted to the bar, they began meeting at restaurants and finally in George's hotel room, where they spent most of the time quietly watching television and eating snacks. For his part, one might suggest that George was disguising an essentially economic transaction by clothing it with the appearance of a friendship. For her part, Pun confessed to me that she was initially simply acting in the hostess role and 'taking care of a customer' (*du lae khaek*). But over the space of a month, with constant meetings and outings, this relationship took on the character of a romance, with both parties confessing to feelings of intimacy. The bar management expected Pun to do her job – which meant entertaining customers and sleeping with them if requested: she did this without telling George, who understood in any case. Pun's expression of intimacy and discrimination was not in technically staying sexually faithful, but in allowing George to have sex with her without using a condom (this is a common signifier of trust and intimacy among sex workers, despite the obvious risks). George never visited Pun's home, but he took Pun to meet many of his expatriate *farang* friends in Bangkok. The intimacy was reinforced when Pun accompanied George to the airport on his departure. Although George had been paying Pun's bar fines, he has not been required to pay Pun on each of her encounters. Rather, he paid her a lump sum of money at the time of his departure. To Pun, this represented an acceptable statement of commitment on the part of her *faen*, and it was recognised as such by her coworkers in the bar.

An extension and variation on the holiday experience for the foreign male is a visit to his girlfriend's village or home to meet her parents. This is an arena of considerable importance because it will often have a major impact on him. It will often accelerate his engagement in the woman's life, through friendship with her family, and will draw him into a web of financial/moral obligations which are calculated to extend the relationship with the woman. For the women, this return to the village also articulates her small-scale movements within the red-light zone with her wider spatial practice of oscillation between city and country and significant fields of valued cultural capital, providing the opportunity to generate a key arena of self-presentation for parents and family.

In terms of women's presentation of self, the bar is a site of arenas generated not only for clients, but for peers, who are one of the three key reference groups (or spheres) towards which women fashion identity. Just as most women enter the various types of prostitution on the advice and suggestions of women friends, so too their work of meeting and relating to foreign men takes place in the presence of other women. Work companions help to establish a collective framework to reinforce confidence and in certain cases resistance. For example, to ease their own boredom on occasions, when supervisors are not watching, go-go dancers in *Soi* Cowboy bars will laughingly parody the lesbian sex shows famous in Patpong. Such arenas mock the entire enterprise of sex work in a shared moment of hilarity among working peers. Particularly in the go-go bars, women form a strong peer group which reinforces the culture of prostitution by celebrating their bodies and sensuality. In an important contribution to the literature on sex worker–client encounters and identity-construction, Lisa Law has proposed that dancing bars in the Cebu (Philippines) operate as a third space for women: that is, they are a space beyond the constructed dualisms of oppressor/victim which so much of the literature and NGO discourse imputes to the sex worker–client encounter (Law 1997b: 114–15).

Arenas, as mentioned above, are generated not only through the manoeuvrings made necessary in the pursuit of income from sex work. They are generated in periodic encounters with family and siblings in the frequent oscillation between the 'place' of work (the red-light district) and the 'place' of the village, both of which represent the key fields of cultural capital towards which women strategise. The enactment of valued and expected roles (of committed mother to children and loyal daughter to parents) takes place in social encounters which punctuate women's movements. Assisting families at times of emergency, attending important religious rituals (funerals, new year celebrations, ordination of brothers into the monkhood) all enact important elements of selfhood in the network of relations and obligations which comprise the place of the household and its village setting.

Plate 9.4 The boyfriend: Geoff, with Et (left) and her sister on a visit to the village (Chiang Mai). (Photo: Courtesy Geoff Stanton)

Different arenas may be played out simultaneously. This is seen in the following example of Geoff's trip to Et's home in Chiang Mai Province. Et, a freelance bar worker, had known Geoff (an expatriate American English teacher) as a regular customer for several months. Lacking enough money to return home to Chiang Mai in sufficient style during the important *Khao Phansa* festival period, she invited him to go to her village. In paying for the beer and alcohol, as well as much of the food consumed during the family's domestic entertainment, Geoff served the purpose of supporting Et's material and social role as eldest daughter in the family. In addition, the visit also served to consolidate the relationship between them, even though this didn't appear to be Et's original intention. Geoff got to know members of Et's family, participated in celebrations and rituals, and tried his hand at rice planting. Et pleased her parents and younger sisters by bringing money (Geoff's) to help with their school fees and presenting a man who appeared to be a good candidate for a permanent partner and patron, at least in the eyes of her parents. Following their return to Bangkok, Et moved into Geoff's apartment. Knowing the members of the family, Geoff continued to participate in supporting the family's status in their community, and Et stopped working.

Cultural capital

Cultural capital comprises status markers in those broad domains of values called 'fields'. While these domains transcend particular places of engagement, the cultural capital (converted from economic gain) assumes value precisely because it is recognised as such by the key groups in women's lives who mediate these fields of value. There are at least three broad and overlapping spheres where women channel the material resources of their work (and the relationships which often ensue) into cultural capital (status resources). One sphere centres on parents and family and is manifested in material contributions to efforts at house building, economic projects, and various consumer goods or material needs (paying off debts, school fees of siblings, motor vehicles, etc.). The sphere of peers relates to those goods and resources that help affirm her identity to networks of friends in the workplace and elsewhere in the city. Cultural capital in this sphere comprises a woman's status as a girlfriend being taken care of and supported by a foreign boyfriend (thus not having to engage in sex work, temporarily or permanently), and in many cases a 'modern woman' of style – the status markers supporting this identity include clothes, jewellery, fees for language lessons and other projects such as holidays. Such status markers may be accumulated through monogamous attachments or more casual engagements with a multitude of customers. However, the generally accepted preference is that women find a single man. The achievement of visible status through material possessions and emotional security (expressed in the ways that women often change their public personas from promiscuous and hedonistic bar dancers to faithful wives – *mia*) encourages both admiration and jealousy in women's workplaces. The sphere of the lover is perhaps more variable, since it centres on the ways individual women relate to their partners in daily life and in terms of emotional affirmation.

The relationships between foreign males and Thai prostitutes involve both pecuniary and emotional dimensions because of the cultural models employed by the women and the idioms they adopt in the relationship. Long-term relationships, whether of cohabitation or of serial visiting and sojourn in Thailand on the part of foreign men, arise in part from them adopting a patron role in a patron–client relationship not necessarily of their own making. Anthropologists have argued that reciprocity of protector and loyal client is a predominant indigenous model in Thai relations (Hanks 1975). But, just as importantly, it is a fundamental dimension of male–female relations in marriage and partnerships in Thai society, especially peasant society (Hanks 1962: 1257). In this understanding of the meaning and value of the compact, the reciprocal exchange of care and welfare needs both parties to comply (Phillips 1965: 32–3). 'Love' is a term played with in the bars and beds of Bangkok, but ultimately as an explanation of the bonds and compacts in partnerships as they evolve among Thai women and western men, love is a complex of exchanges (Cohen 1987). When commercialised sexual encounters between customers and bar women become personalised and ongoing, the understanding of exchange itself becomes more generalised, and not tied to payment for specific sex acts. To women, material well-being is a symbol of a lover's regard – of conferring face (*na*) and honour (*kiat*). The reciprocity which is negotiated in ongoing relations entangles men in a constant effort to prove the value (*khun kha*) of their partners through assisting various projects, explicit or implicit, of women's self-fashioning.[12]

The meaning of relationships between *farang* men and Thai women, the translation of material into emotional bonds, is best seen by appreciating the signifying importance of gold, and more specifically, gold chains. In Thai society the possession and display of gold ornaments and chains in particular is of crucial significance. Gold betokens assets and solidity/ security – in other words, it gives the wearer face (*na*). In strictly practical terms gold can be encashed or pawned in times of need. Beyond social status and encashment potentiality, gold chains are significant in symbolising key relationships and compacts. Unlike the customary cash payment made to a bride's parents, the gold given by a woman's betrothed stays in her possession. Among sweethearts, even prior to marriage, the giving of a gold chain signifies the commitment and strength of regard of the lover. Similarly, *farang* suitors are expected to at some stage show the depth of their regard by giving gold chains.

While *farang* men themselves have no role in the production of the meaning of gold as a status marker, they are involved in its symbolic economy. We see more clearly the ways that gold serves emotional and transactional uses in the following example of Chai's gold chains. When Chai broke up with her American boyfriend the special meaning she attached to her gold chain as a gift/bond of love and commitment was broken. She had no regrets in selling the expensive chain to pay for her mother's hospital fees. But her mother (living in Prachinburi province) did not know that she had broken up with her *farang* lover (who had visited the family home), and on Chai's visit to the hospital she asked where her chain had gone. This affected Chai deeply, because, as she said: 'I didn't want my mother to know that things were starting to get difficult for me financially, or that something had gone wrong'. The gold chain symbolised her important relationship with the American, it showed her family that she had some material capacity – particularly significant because of her experience of financial dependence on her family after her Thai husband had deserted her. She had resolved never again to express such dependence and moral vulnerability in the face of her family. Thus when a new customer, Brian, got to know Chai a little better, he was concerned to see Chai crying, and learned that it was about the matter of the chain. As an expression of his increasing affection, Brian bought Chai a new gold chain, symbolically cementing their relationship as special, and giving Chai the confidence to face her parents at an important village funeral which she was expected to attend. The story and the life of the chain does not end here. Brian returned to Hong Kong and his wife, but kept contact with Chai and promised to send her money regularly. Within a few months Chai was facing financial problems, having left the Comanche go-go bar after Brian had left Thailand. With financial commitments mounting (support for her daughter and doctors bills) she was compelled to pawn her new chain to raise cash, but she did not sell it, as she had the American's gold chain. She asked Brian to send more money, because she wanted to redeem the gold chain. Rather than selling the chain, she wanted to keep it to affirm the compact with Brian. This example shows how the materiality of the gold chain became transmuted into a status marker in the domestic arena for Chai, and how its additional value as an emotional marker of her compact with her *faen* was affirmed in her reluctance to sell it for cash. At the same time, Brian's sending of some cash to help her redeem this chain affirmed his importance to her as a lover with a stake in her life. He was a person to be relied upon (*thi pung*). There are certainly many cases where women have sold their gold with no compunction whatever, but they were cases where no compact had been made. Gold, perhaps a quintessential item of congealed labour value for sex workers (after Marx), can also be transformed into another link in the entangled material–emotional compacts of Thai and *farang*.

Western customers-cum-boyfriends become sources for a wide range of status-conferring commodities whereby women can display a modern, 'sexy' identity. While relatively few women in the sex trade may achieve long-lasting material security through the economic rewards of their work, those that do succeed, even temporarily, visibly subvert the moral order of the urban Thai middle class by virtue of attaining the cultural capital of modernity through engaging in stigmatised work.

Oscillating through fields

Oscillation – the irregular movement between urban and rural places and the simultaneous engagement in key fields of cultural capital – is a pattern generated both by the nature of sex work and (more importantly) the necessities of womens' multiple commitments which drive their strategies. Very few women regard their bar work as long-term. This derives from their motive for entry, their own self-perception, and other obligations. In fact, a large number of women come to the bars only when short of money or when there is free time. For some rural women such free time comes when the harvest is over up-country. For others, need and opportunity dictate their movement into and out of the work. The work experience is temporary even among most of the women who come to the go-go bars and coffee shops, expatriate bars and night clubs and work for longer periods in the red-light zone. Work in a go-go bar may involve a short spell of six months or a longer period of two to four years, depending on circumstances. Of the group of women studied in this research, 45 per cent had worked for a year or less, 29 per cent for two to three years, and 26 per cent between three and seven years.

Women return to the provinces for varying periods to find work near their homes and children. Many return to work in Bangkok after spells of village sojourn, citing boredom or lack of money as key factors. Others never return to Bangkok, having given up on the prospect of earning much money, or having made enough money to buy land or invest in a small business. Others marry foreigners and disappear from the bar scene altogether. Of the fifty women studied here, ten married foreign customers during the period of my research (1994–8), while another ten left sex work to cohabit with foreign expatriate boyfriends or to be permanently supported by tourists who had returned to their own countries pending marriage arrangements. Of the others, most admitted to having had at least one intense emotional involvement with a customer, during which time they had been supported financially.

Women encounter foreign men in the context of experiencing Bangkok and new places in their lives. Erik Cohen has argued that the dominant form of prostitution engaged in by Thai women with foreign men should be described as open-ended, since it is not acknowledged as a full time occupation by the women (he argues that such prostitution is 'incompletely professionalised') and it generally entails more than just an exchange of sex for cash (Cohen 1993: 159–61). Understanding such patterns as practised strategies of self-recovery is important. Such self-recovery requires transgression of normative cultural sanctions (explicit use of the body as sexual instrument, open sexuality and promiscuity) and necessitates movement between specialised sites of the sex-industry infrastructure and public areas of the city. Regardless of the variable length of time invested in this work, these womens' encounter with prostitution in Bangkok can be interpreted from a life-course perspective as an experiment in life style change stemming largely from personal crises and disappointments. Moreover it is a conscious choice to defy normative constraints on their behaviour as women in pursuit of cultural capital. It is part of the broader story of the negotiation of meaning in a time of major impacts on women's roles and status from wide-ranging social and economic change (Richter 1992; Yot 1992). However, we should not impute to their movements the goal of eventually restoring a village mode of existence once destroyed. These women are not of the generation which saw the city as hostile and threatening – in fact, many have engaged in urban work prior to entry into prostitution. The city itself is part of a broader field of modernity and style of life in which women actively participate and fashion their identities.

Conclusion

The encounters between foreign men and Thai women sex workers can be characterised by the complementary impulses of the males' desire for radical simplicity and the woman's experimentation leading to normalisation of her life (in terms of income, role and status). Women's lived narratives intersect with those of foreign men and help to shape the nature of key sites of cross-cultural encounter in Bangkok. Sex workers meet foreign men and manage these encounters in the micro-settings of beer bars, go-go bars, karaoke clubs and coffee shops where the consumption and commodification of women's bodies is an integral element in the ecology of interaction. While the victimhood of women has been the dominant motif in the literature on sex tourism (for exceptions see Law 1997a and Odzer 1994), I have argued here that women, at the level of their own life courses, in their work environments and with their customers, are agents, not victims, despite their position in a socio-economic formation which disadvantages them. Through their sociospatial practices across the many sites of encounters with foreign men – the bars, resorts, hotels and streets – women generate the arenas which help shape the meaning and benefits of transactions, material and emotional.

With respect to the stereotyping of Bangkok – and of Thailand generally – as a sexual playground for foreign men, we need to acknowledge the global nature of the sex trade. In fact, there are more Thai sex workers working in Japan and European cities (such as Amsterdam) than in the tourist zones of Bangkok (Watanabe 1998). Until recently, there has been far more attention given to the issue of global trafficking than the equally significant reality that Thai women sex workers are intensely entrepreneurial, and voluntarily work offshore in considerable numbers (Murray 1998; Platt 2001). Nonetheless Bangkok remains a key space in the economy of foreign expatriate and tourist pleasure. Bangkok has grown as a world city, with its role founded on the New Industrial Division of Labour and, arguably, the 'New International Sexual Division of Labour' – the latter term arguably incorporating an acknowledgement of its female-dominated industrial labour force as well as its tourist-orientated sex workers (see, e.g. Ong 1985; Mills 1999). In terms of its role in sex-orientated tourism, Bangkok can be portrayed as both a pleasure space for foreign men and a working space for Thai women sex workers. This space (actually a complex of sites and zones within the metropolis) is not only a product of unequal economic development and dependency, but also of cross-cultural interactions and fantasy. In an important essay on theorising local–global interactions in world cities, Robert Beauregard (1995: 242) asks the question 'what if the global is constituted by the local?' Here I have argued that the Bangkok of the tourist and foreign (expatriate) male is simultaneously a space of women's (most of them rural women) strategising – it is not simply a pleasure space constructed by foreign male desire. From the perspective suggested here – that of women's narratives, practices and identities – 'Bangkok' is a series of sites where women engage in strategies to entangle their customers in relationships and transform them into lovers with obligations towards a range of status-enhancing ends.

10 Contesting urbanisms

Constructing the past and remaking the present

Introduction: history, culture and the remaking of Krung Thep

During the 1980s and 1990s, the landscape of Bangkok became part of a contested terrain where contrasting and conflicting ideals and representations of urban life and its organisation were debated. Centring on the fate of old inner-city communities, state heritage conservation policy priorities and urban redevelopment projects, these conflicts engage with wider debates on the life and history of the city – what it is becoming, what it could be, and for whom. These debates and contestations in public forums are unprecedented in the life of the Thai metropolis. Their advent parallels the broad emergence of new advocacy groups, ideologies and structures of organisation among the middle classes and key intellectuals which began during the political ferment of the 1970s and after. Just as significant, the conflicts over the meaning of the spaces of Bangkok show how reflection on – and reconstructions of – the past and history are a central ingredient of modernity and social change itself. This chapter departs from the ethnographic approach of most of the earlier chapters in this book, focusing on the importance of representations in shaping the metropolis, and how public debate over the past has brought issues of contesting urbanisms into far greater focus in Bangkok than ever before.

During the 1970s, a broad policy of promoting Thai culture, religion and historical consciousness emerged in response to social and economic changes evident by this second decade of national development policy. The conservation of the old royal centre of Bangkok (Rattanakosin Island) became part of this official promotion of Thainess, founded upon an historical narrative of cultural, territorial and royal dynastic continuity. The conservation of Rattanakosin Island from the early 1980s was a successful response (in technical terms at least) to urban change and owes this success to the force of accumulated associations between monarchy and national identity which draw on an older – but nevertheless pervasive – image of the old city as the sacred centre of the polity and social order. In a notoriously ill-planned city, the Rattanakosin zoning provisions were enforcible due to two key factors – the land of the palace precinct was largely owned by the crown or government ministries and the prestige of the monarchy – as in other realms of policy implementation – was critical in engineering unanimity among normally fractious and competing bureaucrats. The Rattanakosin project aimed towards creating a visual showpiece of cultural monuments and aesthetically pleasing vistas. Thai culture and its royal dispensation were to be presented essentially as things of beauty. Increasingly, policy towards preserving and modifying the old centre and associated royal pageants have also been directed towards attracting overseas tourists, whose spending is of central importance to the contemporary Thai economy. Beginning in the mid-1990s the BMA inaugurated new policies of promoting a more vibrant city lifestyle. Its programmes incorporated street festivals and weekend walking streets, fusing the formal conservation planning objectives of the state's conservation agencies with the need for reviving Bangkok as a recreation space for tourists and middle-class Bangkokians alike. In its aims, the BMA shared with Rattanakosin Plan administrators a concern to clean up street vistas (which incorporated the eviction of vendors and the demolition of shops and houses deemed unsympathetic to conservation objectives) in order to make old inner-city pedestrian areas attractive. The BMA programmes reflected the influence of western trends in regenerating inner cities through festivals and transforming areas into boutique zones for middle-class consumption. However they complemented the overall plans of Rattanakosin bureaucrats in their quest for building a space of visual spectacle and recreation. Until protests and publicity occurred, little attention was given to the fact that ordinary people lived and worked in Rattanakosin.

The state's promotion of Rattanakosin as a showpiece precinct of royal urbanism succeeded at the expense of a formerly un-voiced popular urbanism – patterns of life sustained and reproduced by local neighbourhoods and popular activity zones in the city. Recent events and conflicts over urban space in Bangkok show how the state-promoted focus on royal heritage, increasingly linked to the marketing of *Moradok Thai* (Thai heritage) for international tourism and national cohesion, has ignored a heritage of popular urbanism reflected in the *yan* of the old city. Local urban pasts and places which were neither obviously royal, nor part of a national narrative, simply were not heritage within this discourse. Recently, among some vocal planners, academics and communities, attention to the 'little traditions' of life in localities has raised awareness of urban traditions whose physical legacy may be less tangible or coherent in the city, but which are nevertheless potent claims on both the past and present. Traditionally, Bangkok was a space of coexistence between the great and little traditions of urban life, reflected spatially in the coexistence between the royal citadel and its surrounding *yan*, or urban villages (see Chapter 1). Much of the socio-economic base which supported the existence of the old *yan* has been transformed, yet official exclusion of what may be described as a heritage of coexistence threatens to destroy the central characteristics of indigenous Thai urbanism which have a legacy in the everyday life of people in the inner city. Whether this pattern of coexistence is relevant to modern suburban Bangkokians who have participated in the spatial and cultural transformation of the metropolis is a critical question. Yet there has been a discernible revival of interest in the question of the quality of urban life generally, and in the communities and neighbourhoods of the old inner city in particular. Notably, the most recent efforts to promote this locally orientated urbanism have been spearheaded by middle-class activists under the rubric of making Bangkok a liveable city, harnessing distinctively contemporary methods of publicity to promote a consciousness of urban life based not merely on materialist consumption, but acceptance of difference pasts and their value.

Krung Thep and Thai heritage: from royal project to national policy

From its inception as the seat of the Chakkri dynasty, the royal capital of Krung Thep was the pre-eminent focus of the monarchy's legitimising symbols and rituals. As we have seen, the *krung* defined the *muang* and its claims to power and continuity (see Chapter 1). Throughout the first four reigns of the dynasty, this 'text' was reproduced and embellished towards reinforcing its pre-eminence. By the reign of King Chulalongkorn, the appearance of Rattanakosin began to change as the monarchy embraced the new icons of modern European architecture and elements of urban form. Chulalongkorn appropriated western architecture and monarchical rituals, adding modernity to the royal dispensation. It has been argued that two contrasting forms of urbanism, indigenous and western, fractured the spaces of colonial cities in Asia, marking the external imposition of modernity onto traditional societies (King 1990). In the Thai case, both elements were assimilated by Chulalongkorn into the symbolic capital represented by Krung Thep.

King Chulalongkorn's efforts to reshape Bangkok as the capital of a modern absolutist state through architecture, planning and new state rituals was paralleled by initiatives towards defining Siam as a territorial nation state with a discernible and continuous history. The construction of Thai identity is distinctively modern, in the sense that it can be traced to the efforts of Chulalongkorn's father (King Mongkut – Rama IV) to collect and identify artefacts of the past and display them to foreign dignitaries in order to establish the antiquity of Siam and the legitimacy of his own dynasty in the eyes of western powers (Cary 1994: 54–65; Thongchai 1994). During the reign of King Chulalongkorn and his successor Vajiravudh the connection between history and monarchy was reinforced through a number of institutions, including the National Museum (established in 1887) and the Fine Arts Department (established in 1916), as well as the latter's promotion of the triad of Thai loyalties: nation, religion and king (Vella 1978: 31). An archaeological service was established in 1924 and its major efforts were devoted to excavations at the sites of the old royal centres of Lopburi and Ayutthaya.

Following the coup which toppled the absolute monarchy in 1932, national heritage was emphasised at the expense of dynastic glory. Following the abdication of King Prajadhipok in 1935, and particularly from 1938 after Phibul Songkhram's assumption of dictatorial powers, the status of the Thai monarchy and its symbolic apparatus were downplayed in favour of nationalism and militarism (Keyes 1987: 65–6). Royal spectacles such as the ploughing ceremony and royal barge procession (customary during Kathin celebrations) disappeared from the public calendar of the state. The monuments erected in Bangkok during Phibul's first and second periods in office (1935–45, 1946–57) emphasised the achievements of Thailand's military men. Significantly, it was during Phibul's second term of office that the monument to King Taksin was erected to symbolise the achievements of a non-Chakkri king in building the nation through war and maintaining national independence. The traditional royal symbolism of Krung Thep held little meaning for Phibun and his supporters. Although the institution of monarchy was sidelined by the nationalist regime, the dramatic and literary works of Luang Wichit Wathakan laid a firm ideological base for an official interpretation of built heritage as a legacy of wise and valiant national leaders (Barmé 1993). In 1935 the first legislation was enacted for the preservation of monuments and sites. Throughout the 1950s, during Phibun's rule, the Fine Arts Department continued to focus principally on the ancient city sites of Sukhothai and elsewhere, while in Rattanakosin, individual monuments were registered under general monuments legislation.

Suppressed by the nationalist-ruled state for two decades, the links between Krung Thep and the institution of monarchy were re-established after Field Marshall Sarit Thanarat assumed power in 1957. Sarit's aim was to forge national unity around the goals of economic development and anti-communism, with common loyalty to the king assuring stability and order (Thak 1974: 402–4). The new King Bhumibhol was actively encouraged by Sarit to develop a more conspicuous role as a national figurehead. The traditional royal barge procession associated with the royal *kathin* (distribution of monks' robes), centring on Chao Phraya River and the royal temples of Bangkok, was re-established. The ploughing ceremony was revived, focusing attention once again on Rattanakosin Island and the old palace/temple complex as a ceremonial site (Thak 1974: 410–13). The king served Sarit's purposes well, while King Bhumibhol used this opportunity to advance and consolidate the reputation of his dynasty in his complementary roles as exemplar of national traditions and a modern serving monarch committed to the public welfare and socio-economic development. By the 1970s, King Bhumibhol proved himself indispensable to the Thai polity through judicious intervention in times of political and ideological conflict (Hewison 1997: 61–3). In a period of unprecedented social and economic change, he crafted his kingship to represent an essential feature of cultural continuity and Thai identity. Already the centre of national narratives as taught in schools and published in popular histories (Mulder 1997: 26–114; Reynolds 1984), the king and his dynastic forebears were also to be the centre of a developing state cultural policy which linked the benefits of an increasingly important urban heritage conservation policy to economic imperatives, particularly tourism.

By the early 1970s, a decade of state-promoted economic restructuring had led to what leaders in education and the Buddhist monkhood saw as a disturbing trend towards materialism, individualism and westernisation. The Fourth National Economic and Social Development Plan (1977–81) emphasised the need to 'cultivate the love for Thai traditional art and culture' through preserving 'national art and culture treasures' (NESDB 1977: 284). The state move to promote a unitary consciousness of identity was also driven by political considerations. The 1970s was a decade of political crisis and legitimacy, marked by the student uprising of 1973, fears of communism, and militant separatist movements among the Muslims of the southern provinces. In 1979 the National Culture Commission was founded to coordinate the efforts of various bureaucratic agencies in promoting national culture and the distinctive characteristics of nationhood. This was followed by the establishment, in 1981, of the National Identity Board, charged with the responsibility of producing publications and media programmes on various aspects of Thai culture (Reynolds 1991a: 14–15).

By this time, scholars in the Fine Arts Department were responding to world conservation trends and beginning to advocate the importance of conservation areas, as opposed to specific monuments. UNESCO began to lend support to the excavation and interpretation of the old site of Sukhothai from the late 1970s (Vira 1987). There was a trend towards a convergence of interests on the part of the state and specialists in conservation fields, with the state having a major interest in promoting historic sites for education as well as tourism. From this period the term *moradok* (inheritance, or patrimony) came into official use to describe monuments, sites and artefacts of national heritage, a reflection of the widespread promotion of the term 'heritage' in world conservation circles, and a complement to the expanding lexicon of state-promoted cultural policy terms (including *ekkalak Thai* – Thai identity; and *watthanatham khong chat* – national culture). This prevailing official definition of Thai heritage (*Moradok Chat*) is dominated by an historical narrative which is both nationalist and royal-centred. Artefacts, monuments and now urban precincts derive their significance in official discourse in terms of a history which locates the Thai kings in pre-eminent roles as national leaders and protectors of a distinctive Thai identity. The policy adopted to redevelop and plan the old royal precinct of Rattanakosin embodied this idea of *Moradok Chat*.

The Rattanakosin conservation project – Krung Thep revived

For Bangkok, the convergence of state, specialist and royal interests on conservation and the city was most clearly seen in the events staged to mark the two-hundredth anniversary of the Chakkri dynasty in 1982 and the conservation programme which accompanied the preparations. The first coordinated efforts to develop a policy for conserving and renovating the Rattanakosin district began in the 1970s with the initiative of a number of committed professional architects and other professionals, including Dr Sumet Jumsai, who had earlier been active in researching and publicising the importance of conserving the old site of Ayutthaya, and Sirichai Narumit-Rekhakan, another architect with conservation and historical interests. Both the Conservation Group of the Association of Siamese Architects and a new voluntary body, the Environment Protection Association, played an important role in promoting these ideas. Their proposals to coordinate efforts to protect the inner district from unsympathetic building developments were recognised by the Thai cabinet in the formation of a formal committee to develop area conservation proposals. Significantly, this recognition was spurred by the need for preparing the celebrations of the two-hundredth anniversary of the founding of Krung Thep in 1782. Individual renovation efforts (of major temples, the surviving forts and fragments of the old city walls) were completed

Plate 10.1 The new Rattanakosin: view of *Phukhao Thong*, with new monument (to the right) constructed in place of the old Charoen Krung Theatre. (Photo: Author)

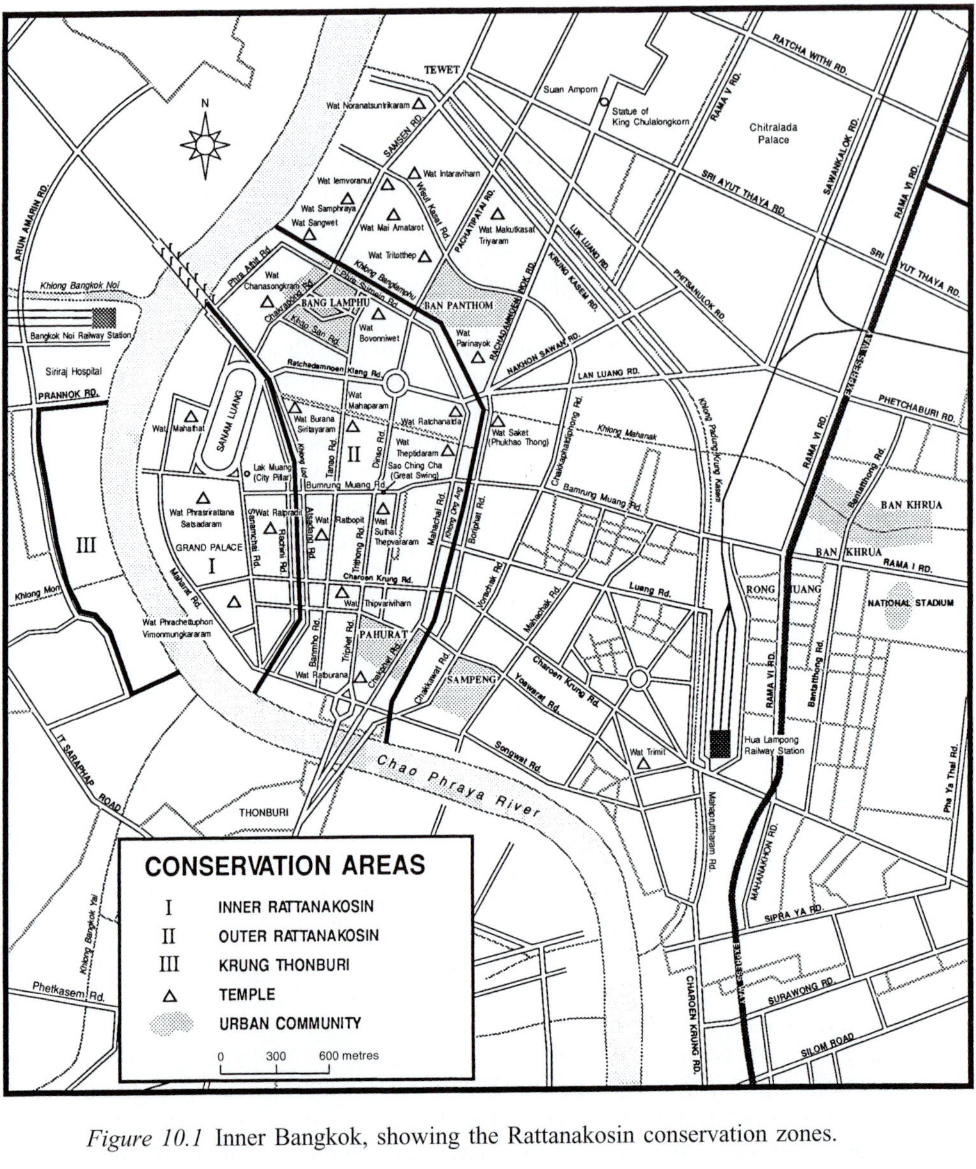

Figure 10.1 Inner Bangkok, showing the Rattanakosin conservation zones.

for the celebration year of 1982. Two years later, the Interior Ministry issued a decree on land-use regulation of the 'Inner Rattanakosin' zone, prohibiting industry and setting building height guidelines. In 1987, a decree for 'Outer Rattanakosin' (the area between the inner canal surrounding the palace area and the outer canal of Padung Krung Kasem) imposed land-use and height restrictions. In 1992 a third district was gazetted for conservation zoning on the opposite bank of the Chao Phraya River, around the site of the old capital of Thonburi, largely because private developers were constructing tall hotels which interrupted the vista of the royal centre (see Fig. 10.1).

While much of the symbolic force of the project to restore Rattanakosin rested on an evocation of traditional Thai royal urbanism, the aesthetic thinking behind the plan idea (essentially framed by architects and art historians) also generated a representation of space resembling the dominant western urban heritage paradigm, portrayed by Christine Boyer as an abstract, decontextualised arrangement of visual decor and ambience (Boyer 1994: 2–3). Symbolised in the conservation master plan when released in 1995, 'historic' Rattanakosin was to be a tableau of objects expressing in architectonic and visual form the authorised memory of the city.

Alternative views of the city: Bangkok vs Krung Thep

In preparation for the bicentennial celebrations, scholars and other writers had generated a range of publications which had collectively advanced knowledge about the historical sites and structures of Bangkok. In fact, the years surrounding the Rattanakosin bicentennial mark a watershed in the quality and quantity of information about the city. Detailed accounts of the Royal Palace and temple architecture, arts and crafts turned attention to an urban past seemingly forgotten over the previous thirty years in the race for modernity and economic development. General Prem himself chaired a committee which reviewed and approved all publications marking the bicentennial.

Yet there were other publications which extended far beyond antiquarian accounts and celebrations of the old royal city. Some Thai scholars took the opportunity to provide more detailed, and even critical, analysis of urban change (Piyanat *et al.* 1982; Pussadee 1982; Sternstein 1982). The Thai language art and culture journal *Sinlapa Watthanatham* ran a series of articles exploring the old areas of Bangkok as well as the economic role of the capital in the transformation of the Thai economy. Some publications delved more critically into the past of the metropolis, deliberately focusing on its early name of *Bang-kok*, or the place of the *yan* of ordinary people (Srisaka and Suchit 1982). Since 1982, publications about Bangkok – whether they be memoirs, novels, biographies and occasionally the study of particular districts – have multiplied, seemingly in pace with the speed at which the face of the city has been transformed by condominiums, office towers and elevated expressways. The expansion of a market for such publications arguably points to a growing readership among the Bangkok middle classes, although perhaps not necessarily to a more critical viewing of the nature of change as such. In fact, a large number of such publications focus upon the history of the palaces of royal or aristocratic families and particularly on King Chulalongkorn, widely revered as both the saviour of Thailand and the great legitimiser of modernity and those cosmopolitan patterns of life so much desired by the contemporary Thai urban middle classes (Peleggi 1997: 9).

But in addition to this popular nostalgia for the past (expressed in films and advertising as much as popular literature) there has been an emergence of critical voices among professionals and a variety of activists and communities. Thai publications such as *Sinlapa Watthanatham* (*Art and Culture Journal*) and *Muang Boran* (*Ancient City Journal*) – in addition to Thai and English language newspapers – publicised increasingly events and problems bearing on urban development, conservation and its consequences for ordinary city people. The conflicts that have emerged around these questions are a conflict between readings of the city itself – between 'Krung Thep', the aestheticised abstract heritage paradigm, as against 'Bangkok', a city of the *yan* and common people. In addition there is an important and powerful 'representation of space' (I use this term following Henri Lefebvre 1991: 38–9) which articulates with the state-promoted royal paradigm and authorises it: that is, the planned, modern, segmented metropolis. It is around these claims to urban space and its meaning that conflict has emerged, generating a counter narrative of Bangkok's urbanism.

The Rattanakosin Plan and the Bangkok Plan – heritage for monuments and leisure

One of the tasks of the Rattanakosin Committee after its first establishment was to mount a design competition for a master plan for the conservation planning of the inner area, incorporating traffic management, architecture and open spaces. In 1995, the plan was presented at a public hearing, which revealed the full dimensions of the planning concepts at play. A number of prominent planners from Chulalongkorn University opposed the overall concept which appeared calculated to remove the 'liveliness and soul' from the inner city (*Bangkok Post* 20 April 1995). In summary, the plan was driven by the principle of creating visual vistas and new recreational open spaces at the expense of uses deemed unsympathetic to the aesthetic paradigm for the heritage district. Detailed plans involved clearing shophouses and other businesses from the Chao Phraya waterfront, establishing parks and paths along the precinct's canals to allow for local and foreign tourists to circulate through the zone, and restoring those structures deemed to be architecturally of note (*Khanakammakan Khrongkan Krung Rattanakosin* 1995). The implementation of this plan depended on a longer term process of negotiation with various ministries controlling land, government investment, and the termination and lapsing of leaseholds on crown properties. Although it was not published until 1995, the master plan's objectives had been set by the late 1980s. Individual elements were to be implemented as opportunity allowed, with the cumulative result aimed for being an inner city of historic vistas. The scenario

Figure 10.2 An aestheticised Bangkok: planners' vision for the reconstruction of Tha Tian area, Rattanakosin Island.

Source: Rattanakosin Master Plan 1995.

for the Inner Rattanakosin zone made no provision to allow for the continued residence of the people who still lived and worked there.[1]

A year after the public release of the Rattanakosin Plan, the Bangkok Metropolitan Administration, under Governor Krissada, published its Bangkok Plan, devised by a team of consultants from Massachusetts Institute of Technology. Within this plan, 'heritage' issues were an important consideration. The Bangkok Plan offered an alternative view of conservation objectives, emphasising the complementarity of tourism considerations as well as local heritage significance. It focused on Rattanakosin as one of the heritage areas, but emphasised the development of strategies for enhancing the character of other key districts of the old city, including parts of Bangkok Noi and Bangkok Yai (canal-side districts on the western side of the river) as well as Samphantawong (the old Chinese quarter of Sampheng/Yawarat) (BMA Department of City Planning and MIT Consulting Team 1996: 162). A greater emphasis was placed on 'conserving and improving cultural activities' which were deemed to be an integral component of Thai heritage such as traditional markets, crafts and informal street life. Such themes reflected the background of the western consultants' heritage frameworks, which emphasised cultural resources more than cultural artefacts; an emphasis on public participation and local needs, rather than aesthetics as such. It was proposed that the management and coordination of these heritage resources was to be placed in the hands of a special Heritage Division of the BMA (BMA Department of City Planning and MIT Consulting Team 1996: 165). The Bangkok Plan, as published, was never implemented, although elements survive in some individual programmes of the BMA. While a reading of the heritage components of this plan offers a contrasting approach to the Rattanakosin Plan paradigm, it is difficult to escape the suspicion that the model being aimed at was the 'street theatre/festival' approach to inner city revival popular in the USA and other western cities under the planning buzzword of 'New Urbanism'. The plan was generated during the last period of the economic boom, when there was a confidence that the Bangkok Metropolitan Region could be forged into an engine of growth and efficiency for a modernising economy. But when Governor Krissada Arunwongse failed to gain re-election in 1996, the plan was sidelined by the incoming administration.

Tha Phrachan and Thammasat University: conflicts over the meaning of heritage space

As mentioned, the Rattanakosin committee had a long-held plan to eventually clear the old precinct of activities deemed to interfere with its streamlined heritage concept. In 1993 the committee resolved to ban the large group of mobile street vendors (*hap re phaeng loi*) from trading in the areas of Tha Chang, Tha Tian and Tha Phrachan, the riverside areas which were the main sites of activity in the Rattanakosin area. These *tha* are old boat landings which have hosted such activities for decades. In pre-modern Bangkok, dominated by water transportation, the *tha* were the original foci of trading, population movement and social activity. The clearance of over 1,000 hawkers took place at the close of February 1995 by the BMA working in cooperation with the Rattanakosin Committee, just two months before the public release of the master plan which revealed the full extent of the tranformations intended for the district. While the move provoked vocal protest from academics from the neighbouring Thammasat and Sinlapakon universities, the plan went ahead. What is important to note is how this event helped to crystallise an already existing opposition to the planning paradigm of the Rattanakosin committee and other state-promoted planning which had been threatening older neighbourhoods of Bangkok.[2] A forum was held at Sinlapakon University by the leading archaeologist Srisak Vallibhotama, and articles of protest were published in the journal *Sinlapa Watthanatham*. Long-held criticisms of the Rattanakosin paradigm were brought out into the open: the question was whether the efforts to preserve Rattanakosin and inner Bangkok were preserving sites and vistas at the expense of the real stuff of Thai urban life – its variety and the juxtaposition of different lifestyles (Phuwadon 1995). The fate of the street vendors was symbolic of this trend. This was an argument from the perspective of urban culture, not aesthetics; a view of historical value as based on social processes, not static images. Clearing Tha Phrachan had been justified on the grounds of easing traffic and footpath congestion, but critics argued that it was the first step in creating a dead city centre. The clearance of vendors coincided with a restructuring of the covered selling areas on the waterfront, which now featured more tourist-orientated goods than local items as formerly sold. The question as to whom the changes were being made for – tourists or Bangkokians? – was raised. The clearing of Tha Phrachan had, curiously, not included the banning of traffic, so that one prominent academic could note with irony that the area had simply become a car park in place of a popular selling place (*Phuchatkan Raiwan* 12 July 1996).

Opposition to the Rattanakosin Master Plan did not end with the protests over Tha Phrachan. Increasingly vocal opposition would reveal how alternative meanings of inner Bangkok had been generated by the political events of 1992. In the late 1990s a coalition of groups associated with Thammasat University initiated commemoration ceremonies and tours of inner Bangkok (including the university and the democracy monument) to highlight the significance of the university's founder (Pridi Banomyong) and its students in the ongoing movement towards democratisation (Anjira 1997a). In May 2001 the senate of Thammasat University revealed plans to relocate the undergraduate programmes of the institution to its new Rangsit campus in the city's northern suburbs of Pathum Thani Province. Led by the prominent Thammasat historian Charnvit Kasetsiri, a movement began to oppose this plan. Relocation was deemed not only to be an administrative measure driven by the University's concern over facilities, but part of a coordinated scheme linked to the Rattanakosin Committee's plans to renovate the old inner city and empty it of its people, its popular heritage and its political history. Protesters argued that the Rattankosin Committee aimed to demolish the National Theatre (located near Thammasat's Tha Phrachan campus) and completely remodel the precinct into a sterile Disney-style history park. The protest drew support from a range of democracy activists as well as local people (formed into the Rattanakosin Island Protection Group) who had been earmarked for eventual eviction under the Pattanakosin Master Plan (Sirikul 2001). By late 2001, the future of undergraduate life at the old inner city campus of Thammasat was still unclear, but the issue of relocation and its consequences has publicised and exposed as never before the contested meanings of old Krung Thep.

The *yan* fights back: Ban Khrua and the Expressway Authority

In contemporary Bangkok, we have noted that place-making has been expressed in a range of ordinary *yan* throughout the city, places which still survive – albeit transformed – in the inner city (see Chapter 4). Some of these have received a high level of publicity in their efforts to fend off development activities of the state, and in doing so have asserted alternative meanings of city living and place values. They illustrate that there are differing, and conflicting, readings of significance in the urban landscape based on fundamentally different frameworks of what urban life is about, frameworks which draw on the past in different ways.

The clearing of the Tha Phrachan vendors from the aestheticised Rattanakosin landscape was occurring at the same time as an ongoing conflict between state agencies and the old inner neighborhood of Ban Khrua was escalating. While the issue of the Tha Phrachan vendors was one which focused on the 'right to the city' of small traders in their customary space, the Ban Khrua issue involved the question of a community's identity which derived both from historical links and religious identification with a place of living. This conflict emerged in the early 1990s over the proposed displacement of this Muslim settlement to make way for an exit ramp of a new highway entering the inner city.

The neighbourhood of Ban Khrua, located on the Saen Saep canal, originated from the settlement of a group of Cham Muslims taken prisoner during the war between Siam and Cambodia in the early nineteenth century and granted settlement rights by King Rama I in exchange for the loyalty and service of its menfolk in the Siamese navy. Ban Khrua's core of identity lies in its ethnic ancestry and its religion. Its economic identity as a *yan* was once partly based on silk weaving (a tradition practised by Ban Khrua women until recently), which was revived during the 1950s and 1960s by the entrepreneur Jim Thompson. In later years the coherence of its occupational base declined through diversification, and newcomers of Buddhist background began to dilute its ethnic and religious composition. However, Ban Khrua's ethno-religious character remained predominantly Muslim, with community leadership drawn from its long-term Muslim families and its key focal points remaining the mosque and cemetery (Saoapha, Phonthip and Duangphon 1989; Charuwan and Baffie 1992).

Prior to the fall of the Chatichai government in the military coup of 1991, Ban Khrua leaders had been able to stave off efforts of the Expressway and Rapid Transit Authority (ETA) to expropriate sections of its land by appealing to the Prime Minister on the basis of the historical rights of the community to settle under the endowment of King Rama I (r. 1782–1809). However by 1992, plans to implement the expressway ramp scheme were revived by ETA officials. The response among community leaders was twofold: (1) to promote solidarity within the neighbourhood based on the continuity of Islamic identity and the close association of people with their mosque and cemetery; and (2) to publicise the plight of the community throughout Bangkok, utilising the media and public forums to elicit support from groups active in resisting slum eviction and promoting alternative planning models. Officials were barred by local people from entering the community and strict guard was maintained by neighbourhood youths for fear of arson attempts by thugs in the pay of the ETA. One report feared that the determination of the Ban Khrua Moslems was so great that there was a threat of religious war (*songkhram sasana*) (Anon 1992: 62). After a brief respite following the turbulent political period of 1992, a new government again moved to implement the ETA plan. In response, neighbourhood members demanded cancellation of the project and staged prayer meetings outside parliament, gaining considerable press coverage (*Bangkok Post* 18 April 1994; Nilubon and Chanyaporn 1994).

The chairman of the neighbourhood's defence committee, Sarot Puksamli, argued that the mosque was not like a Thai spirit house, which could be moved: the mosque was the heart of identity at Ban Khrua. He maintained that the state's proposals to remove four hundred homes and relocate residents would threaten the life of the mosque, which was tantamount to an attack on religion and the viability of the community (Author's interview with Sarot Puksamli, August 1997). Resistance to the dismemberment of the settlement was successful largely due to support from sympathetic academics and urban activists. Public hearings (held during 1993–4) were able to expose the reality that the traffic statistics of the highways department were inflated and the ramps would not substantially ease traffic flow and congestion in the inner city (see Ockey 1997: 13–17). Combined with the chronic political instability which saw governments fall in rapid succession, the process of decision-making on the project was stalled for a further five years. But despite the findings that the exit ramp was not necessary, cabinets supported the measure. The prominent historian and columnist Nithi Aeuosrivongse argued that the cabinet's decision contradicted the results of the public hearings, and exposed the continuing realities of centralised power and its quest for symbolic urban efficiency against the interests of community wellbeing (Nithi 1995a). By 1997 some compromise was inevitable, and Ban Khrua leaders were resigned to losing a section of the neighbourhood, despite their public determination to preserve the whole of the settlement space. The economic crisis of mid-1997 delayed the process somewhat, but in April 2000 the ETA announced it was ready to proceed with a land expropriation plan involving the displacement of 200 local families. By August Ban Khrua residents were still blocking the entry of ETA surveyors into the area (Supoj 2000; Vasana 2000: 44). Ban Khrua's dogged resistance to the ETA exposed an increasing tension between a state discourse of urban efficiency and a popular urbanism claiming coexistence and relationship to place as fundamental.

Against the claims of the state that the infrastructure needs of the metropolis were supreme, the Ban Khrua protest articulated an alternative valuation of urban space, a popular urbanism which asserted that culture, religion and popular memory underpinned the quality of urban life for common people in the city. Richard O'Connor's argument about the homogenising tendencies of the modern bureaucratic centre and the

Plate 10.2 Sarot Puksamli addresses a neighbourhood meeting at Ban Khrua. (Photo: Courtesy Siam Araya)

differences between the state and popular model of Bangkok is worth recalling here (O'Connor 1990: 62–7). Additionally, however, we should note how the popular model (or 'popular urbanism' as I call it) has been actively promoted through distinctively modern and reflexive ways in the contemporary period. Traditional popular urbanism was never proclaimed – it just *was*, in the sense that it emerged through practice and a structure of power which accommodated it through social networks of decentralised dependency. But in the contemporary period, popular tradition is itself manufactured through the necessity of formulating an ideological resistance against a power structure and urban regime which can no longer tolerate the variety and coexistence of differing settlement patterns and local economies. Notably, the cause of popular urbanism in modern Bangkok has gained its strongest support from the educated middle classes – professionals, academics and NGO activists. It has relied on the ability of local community leaders to mobilise strategic networks (in government, among academics, NGOs and local communities) and most importantly, harnessed the power and support of the contemporary mass media in pressuring the government and publicising issues. This articulated popular urbanism which promotes place identity and collective memory is the urban equivalent of the model of rural community culture and local wisdom promoted among Thai NGOs and academics to counter modern development paradigms. Thus, even popular tradition itself (as a counter-ideology) requires explicit delineation of the past, often in nostalgic and standardised forms.

Humanising Bangkok: promoting differences in the city

The BMA and the revival of the city

In 1996, the new Bangkok administration under governor Pichit Rattakul inaugurated a system of policy formulation based on groups of advisers drawn from the professional and public world of Bangkok. Pichit's success in gaining election that year was in fact largely due to these groups, whose advice he sought in planning his gubernatorial election campaign. The campaign focused on enhancing the quality of life of Bangkok residents. It was a broad electoral platform ranging from environmental improvement and public transport programmes to reviving the city centre. From their beginning in the mid-1980s, BMA gubernatorial elections had always been fought over questions of addressing the manifold problems of the city. Pichit's campaign was distinctive in that he emphasised the participation of specialists from outside the municipal bureaucracy. This struck a chord with the middle classes, who formed the majority of the electorate which turned out to vote. The advisory system was a new step in BMA administration which created the possibility for groups with alternative perspectives to contribute to ideas about improving the city. Among them were a number of academics, western-trained Thai academics and professionals, who had been attempting – in their professional work and through NGOs – to implement more innovative and responsive schemes. Pichit Rattakul's new regime gave them an opportunity to voice their ideas. One of these ideas was to implement weekend 'walking streets' in the inner city. Combined with this was an effort to encourage local level input into such events. This was easier said than done, given that district-level urban administration has followed a centralised model in Bangkok, with elected assemblies playing a minor role in key decision-making of urban districts. Another idea was that of a *Pratchakhom Muang* (urban civic group), linked to a plan to utilise nominated schools as assembly places for elected district representatives to gather with community groups to discuss local issues. The proposal was consistent with the provisions of the new national constitution, which embodies the principle of decentralisation of political power. It was a direct consequence of the efflorescence of new demands for participatory government generated by the 1992 democracy movement. This model represented a departure from a long tradition of bureaucratic top-down metropolitan administration at the district (*khet*) level. It offered at least the possibility that people of the city at the local level could have an input into urban affairs. While the idea was publicised with great enthusiasm, its actual implementation has been slow.

The policies promoted under Pichit's governorship are not original – many of the ideas had been raised before and proposed during the previous administration – but they were distinctive because they aimed towards integrating a variety of goals – conservation and tourism, for example – and propose to allow local groups a voice in defining the city as a place. The emphasis on the distinctiveness of localities in inner Bangkok is particularly important in this context. In an interview for a Thai tourist magazine Pichit stressed:

> Bangkok is a city of villages, fifty different districts in all, and most of them are very different from one another. We are not just about temples and reclining Buddhas and street markets, there is much more. Some areas are renowned for crafts, some for special traditions, some from a very distinct heritage going back many generations, some for certain kinds of foods. So we are trying to bring out the best of each area. We are rehabilitating areas and working with these old communities. So we are trying to present Bangkok as a multi-dimensional city, not a city with problems.
>
> (BTO 1998: 18)

Notably, Pichit's promotion of urban difference in Bangkok focused as much on generating foreign tourist arrivals in Bangkok as developing local neighbourhood resources.

The vision expressed in the declaration above actually reflects the influence and initiatives of groups active outside his administration, especially the NGO network, the Bangkok Forum. In 1998 this found expression in the declaration of the project 'Humanise Bangkok', which comprised a set of ongoing locally based projects within the Rattanakosin area (incorporating the officially designated zones 1 and 2). Supported by the World Heritage Centre of UNESCO and the French Embassy, the BMA project was in fact an alternative to the earlier Rattanakosin conservation approach. While there was an emphasis on civic beautification, 'Humanise Bangkok' proposed cooperation among existing communities within the area and officialdom, together with a focus on localities and a commitment to the idea of sustainable urban development through local initiatives. For the first time in any officially endorsed inner-city conservation programme, people were counted as central to the character of Rattanakosin (*Chiwit Sisan* Krung Thep 1998).

The Bangkok Forum

Perhaps the most significant development in the urban conservation scene has been the advent of the lobby group Bangkok Forum. Following the political turmoil of May 1992 in Thailand, the Bangkok Forum was established by the Thai activist Chaiwat Thirapantu, who had studied and worked in Germany for many years. Its objectives were to enhance the quality of urban life by providing a focus for alternative views on environmental management and problem-solving, covering issues including urban heritage and urban spaces. The Bangkok Forum was not intended to be a permanent group of advocates so much as a network which could draw on individuals as the occasion arose, to offer alternative ideas as well as to mobilise and help focus public opinion on the varied issues of urban living. Using the dynamic and flexible networking of the Forum as a catalyst, Chaiwat aimed to promote positive images of Bangkok through sponsoring activities as well as protesting negative effects of developments. Much of its force is gained through media publicity, and it is no coincidence that Chaiwat's background was not as a planner, but in business administration and marketing. He enjoyed an extensive network among progressive journalists, academics, NGOs and local communities. When heritage issues are raised by the Bangkok Forum, they are addressed in terms of the broad objectives of enhancing the overall quality of urban life, driven by the principal goal of fostering a commitment to the city as a shared living place. This was an entirely novel development among conservation groups in Bangkok. Certainly there are associations which have drawn attention to important and valued aspects of the city (for example, the Association of Siamese Architects, the Society of Friends of Bangkok Canals, the Siam Society), but the Bangkok Forum offered a more inclusive approach to conceiving of Bangkok. By the mid-1990s, this group had gained acceptance by the BMA as one of the key opinion-makers in the city.

A critical contribution of the Bangkok Forum in encouraging a broadly-based pattern of conservation in localities was the promotion of the study of the district of Banglamphu (in the northern area of Rattanakosin) and assistance with publicity regarding the history and nature of this old inner city area. One of the early *yan* of Bangkok, this district reflects much of the early urbanism of the pre-modern city. Clustered around the temples and a number of early Muslim mosques are a variety of neighbourhoods which are distinctive by virtue of ethnic and religious continuity and length of residence (see Chapter 6). Phra Athit Road (parallel with the Chao Phraya River) features a number of the early palaces of the nobility (now converted for use as official buildings of international agencies). In addition, an echo of the city's early morphology is found in its shophouses, behind which cluster wooden Thai houses. Some of the noble families of the palaces of Phra Athit Road were closely associated with early music and dancing troupes in the capital, and the neighbourhood around Wat Sangwet is still well known for the residence of the Duriapanit family of musicians, which functions as a music school (Askew 1993; Chaiwat 1998).

From 1997, the Bangkok Forum began working with a number of local people to promote an alternative type of street festival along Phra Athit Road, one which was organised not by the BMA, but from the neighbourhood itself. The catalyst was the forthcoming centenary of the Duriapanit Music School and the discovery of a surviving Lamphu tree by students involved in a history project at the Wat Sangwet school. The Lamphu tree was significant because the district (Banglamphu) was identified with this once prolific tree species in the area (Sombong 1997). The street festival emerged as the first public project of a new civic group which comprised not only local traders and prominent local figures, but people connected with the nearby Sinlapakon University. Coordinated by the Bangkok Forum, the street festival drew attention to small-scale, locally focused activities, as opposed to centrally organised street events which have become part of the BMA's urban improvement programme. Chaiwat argued:

> The success of a walking street festival . . . should not be determined by the size of the crowd or the decibel level. One thing remains a concern: participation of the communities in the vicinity of these temporary walking streets. Can the communities initiate their own festival or should the authorities give orders?
>
> (Chaiwat 1998)

Staged in January 1998, the street festival was also designed to bring attention to an issue central to the BMA's *Pratchakhom Muang* policy of local citizens' participation in planning. It focused on the fate of the old Teachers' Council (*Khurusapha*) Printing Warehouse, a nondescript building in danger of demolition at the corner of Phra Athit Road. Owned by the treasury department, this disused building was scheduled for demolition to make way for a public park. This was consistent with the official Rattanakosin conservation plan policy for civic beautification. However, the Phra Athit Civic Group, with the Bangkok Forum as its public advocate, argued that the building should be used as a cultural centre for a wide variety of activities for the locality, a function clearly consistent with the Bangkok governor's model of *Pratchakhom Muang*: the active involvement of localities in creating a liveable city (Anchalee 1998). The widespread media publicity surrounding the question of the building's imminent demolition exposed the complexity of heritage significance issues in the city. Here was a building dating back no earlier than the 1930s, with no pretensions to architectural beauty; nonetheless it was a key focus of an affirmation among a variety of Banglamphu residents and groups that it could become a centre for reviving local identity – not only to recover the past, but to forge new links among the different generations now inhabiting the area. To the Treasury Department, the building had no inherent historical or aesthetic significance. A Thammasat University lecturer argued that although the building was not registered with the Fine Arts Department, it nevertheless should be subject to an assessment because it was within the Rattanakosin precinct. Students from Sinlapakon University

Plate 10.3 The *Khurusapha* building (right) in Phra Sumen Road, repainted and preserved. (Photo: Author)

staged a media exhibition to highlight the early functions of the building and publicise the potential of the structure as multifunctional centre. In May a meeting between civic group representatives, academics and other supporters resolved to petition Governor Pichit to delay demolition (Patharawadee 1998; *Siang Chak Futbat* 1998). Local advocates' presentation of the case for preservation transcended narrow arguments about the preservation of the physical past *per se*: they extended into the broader claim of local networks to create a future for urban localities based on both past historic identities and present social and cultural needs. In late 1998 the arguments of these networks were forceful enough to persuade the Head of the Treasury Department to cancel plans for demolition of the structure. The building was to be set aside as a multifunctional facility, incorporating a library for local youth, a coffee shop and venue for musical performances (Author's interview with Chaiwat Thirapantu, August 2000).

The 'Humanise Bangkok' project showed that the BMA administration was capable of incorporating local initiatives into its overall planning, and that this orientation – unlike the Rattanakosin conservation project – encouraged a degree of local participation with broader objectives than simply creating aesthetic vistas. There is indeed some convergence between local and municipal interests in the upgrading of streets and public areas, focusing on drawing tourists into the area to maintain businesses and incomes. However there is potential conflict. The increasing efforts of the BMA to renovate and enliven the inner city and its nearby river banks are related to a downturn in the economy and a corresponding focus on drawing the overseas tourist dollar. In 1996–7 the Fine Arts Department undertook restoration work on the Phrasumen Fort at the mouth of the Banglamphu canal. At the same time, an old lumber yard which had formerly obscured the river view along Phra Athit Road was demolished in line with Rattanakosin plans. In its place a boat-landing was constructed to commemorate King Bhumibhol's fiftieth year on the throne. These changes drew some criticism for their attention to tourism and grand spectacle in contrast to local needs. Congestion caused by tourist buses and cultural shows staged by outside groups at the expense of local traders and performance groups were identified as possible consequences, as well as the removal of a popular local shrine. Hence, the compatibility of tourism and locally supported conservation in the city may not be as smooth as Governor Pichit's rhetoric allowed. Within a short time, Phra Athit Road, with its small restaurants and student bars, was being touted in tourist magazines as 'Bangkok's Left Bank', a possible harbinger of transformation in this locality flowing from clearance and monument upgrading (Piprell 2000).

Conclusion

Among the numerous struggles and debates surrounding urban space in contemporary Bangkok, the question of urban and architectural conservation has become increasingly prominent over the last decade. The conflicts which have emerged have raised critical questions about the character of the city, its future, and the authority of the state to determine the cultural significance of place and intervene in the landscape. I have pointed out how the valorisation of historical space in Bangkok has been strongly informed by a paradigm of significance drawn from sacred, royal space in the guise of the Rattanakosin Conservation Project, which aims to symbolically fuse the monarchy, historical precinct and nation in a grand narrative of national heritage (*moradok chat*). This narrative has tended to marginalise alternative meanings, exemplified in the common spaces occupied by ordinary people in the city – through its excluding power it reduces their significance and claims to preservation or protection. This is not to suggest that the old palace area and its surrounding temples and other structures do not retain considerable symbolic importance. Indeed, the monarchy commands perhaps more veneration among Thais than it ever has in the past half-century, and areas of Rattanakosin are frequently the sites of key royal rituals, processions and celebrations (royal birthdays, cremations, parades). In this respect the old symbolic 'text' of the city remains preserved within the wider modern metropolis – embraced and accepted by ordinary Thai people living within and outside the metropolis.

Nonetheless, the implementation of a modern zonal-planning concept to the preservation of the Rattanakosin area had a considerable impact on groups of ordinary people in the immediate vicinity. This plan, together with other efforts of state agencies to rationalise inner city space, ultimately generated strong resistance, giving rise to an alternative view of Bangkok. The affected groups, neighbourhoods and their supporters articulated a 'popular urbanism' which was hitherto unarticulated because it was simply an aspect of everyday life. At the heart of this popular urbanism is the acceptance – indeed necessity – of coexistence of different functions and uses in the city's spaces, particularly at the street level. As with the NGO/slum networks which have mobilised around the issue of the right to stay and the importance of *khwamben chumchon* (being a community), the patterns of mobilisation which have grown around preservation of places is supported by assertions and claims to space which are essentially new, supported by a broad ideology of group solidarity and alternative development. Likewise, the recent trend towards popular heritage preservation takes distinctively modern forms, based on networking, committees, lobbying and media publicity. A powerful rhetoric formerly monopolised by state agencies (such as *watthanatham* – culture, and *moradok* – heritage) have now been appropriated by activists and local neighbourhoods to argue for a 'place' in the city and an urbanism based on an acceptance of coexistence.

Notes

Introduction

1 It is notable that the scholarly study of Bangkok has been largely monopolised by technical and economic disciplines, while the question of the relation between Bangkok and the broader Thai sociocultural system has been less well attended. Rudiger Korff (1989a, 1989b) and Richard O'Connor (1978, 1990) remain notable exceptions in dealing with this question. An important essay by Herbert Rubin (1974) on this topic, although dated, is still well worth consideration.

2 I refer to Michel de Certeau in this context not because I have embraced his distinctive approach to the study of 'the practice of everyday life' (see note 3) but because his writings do emphasise the dynamic nature of peoples' activity in the city and their production of meaning through movement and use of space. He even employs the expression 'practiced place' to refer to the generation of meaning in cities and space generally. However, his use of the term 'place' is somewhat ambiguous. His theorising about movement and urban peoples' 'tactics' emphasises their individualised movement and resistance to totalising and oppressive places, defined as spaces endowed with pre-given characteristics and meanings. Yet he also defines place as the product of visualisation not only by powerful agencies, but as the outcomes of the practices of ordinary urban dwellers (Certeau 1984: 117–22).

3 Bourdieu's theory of practice has been criticised as being ultimately deterministic by other theorists, particularly de Certeau (Certeau 1984: 50–60). Michel de Certeau's postmodernist conception of 'the practice of everyday life' emphasises the multiplicity of elusive tactics (making do) whereby people in the contemporary capitalist world (he defines them as consumers) resist various forms of power and control imposed by the market and the state (34–42). In my view, de Certeau's portrayal of people's agency largely as resistance is based on a polarised conception of urban society as comprising a simple contest between the powerless and the monolithic state and market. This schema continues to underline most social studies of urban life which focus (in detailed studies at least) almost exclusively on the urban poor, thus overlooking a wide range of other actors in the city. Eurocentric in his view of the city and society, de Certeau marginalises the significance of cultural idioms in informing people's action. I employ Bourdieu's framework of *habitus* because, despite its defects, it allows for an understanding of people's agency as a set of affirming and creative repertoires (or strategies) which draw on cultural resources and understandings to actualise goals which are meaningful.

1 Cosmology, accumulation and the state

1 The god Indra, who resided in his palace atop the central pillar of the universe (Mount Meru, in both Hindu and Buddhist myths of the origins of the universe) had been accorded the role of symbolically authorising Thai royal cities since the time of Sukhothai in the thirteenth century (Gosling 1990: 64).

2 The tacit support given by the Chakkri kings to animism and popular spirit beliefs throws doubt on the suggestion that there was a trend towards a thorough-going 'rationality' in the outlook of the monarchs throughout the nineteenth century (see Johnson 1997).

3 Thus the location of the chedi tower *Phukhao Thong* (completed in the fourth reign, 1851–68) was outside the walls to the east of the palace, and not the north west, as in Ayutthaya. The *wang lang* was located across the river, in Thonburi, and not in the precinct of the walled city, as in Ayutthaya. The design of new temples named after Ayutthayan prototypes departed from them in numerous ways, and it is difficult to see similarities in construction and alignment, despite the efforts of some scholars to find such correspondence (e.g. Woodward 1984).

4 The history of this ancient image was associated with a cult of veneration inaugurated by the kings of Chiang Mai which affirmed the image's powers as a guardian of prosperity and fertility for the kingdom, a cult which affirmed the connection between the image and the functions of the god Indra, and between Buddhist sacredness and royalty. The latter connection was signified in the custom whereby the Emerald Buddha was fitted out in royal regalia (Reynolds 1978: 182–3).

5 The French cleric Nicholas Gervaise, who worked in Ayutthaya as a missionary from 1683–6, noted that the site of Bangkok, which had first been fortified during that time, was 'the chief key to the Kingdom of Siam' (Gervaise 1989: 235).

6 The influential noble families did have important regional bases and networks. A conspicuous example is the Bunnag family with their stronghold in Ratchaburi Province. However, such provincial bases were ultimately a reflection of access to patronage in court circles (see Rujaya 1984: 179–203).

7 In the Ayutthayan period this had the cumulative effect of expanding the population, to the extent that by the seventeenth century the capital and its immediate surrounds hosted the largest population of the Tai region, with an estimated 150,000–200,000 people (Reid 1993: 71–3).

8 Rama III and IV attempted to compensate for technological disadvantages by commissioning the construction of square-rigged vessels for their own use as trading vessels. However, this could not counteract the growing dominance of the European trading fleets in international and long-distance transport of trade goods.

9 He was recorded as saying: 'Their countries had roads that made every village and town look orderly, pleasant and clean. Our country was greatly overgrown with grass or climbers; our pathways were but small or blind alleys; our larger pathways were dirty, muddy, or soiled, and unpleasant to look at, causing us to be ashamed in front of foreigners from all countries' (Thiphakhorawong 1966, vol. II: 260).

10 Notably, the new roads built during the fourth reign were given names which signified secular change and progress, such as *Fuang Nakhon* (Revive the City) and *Bamrung Muang* (Improve the City).

11 The influence of these landholding patterns and their function as a basis of elite wealth has continued to this day: the Crown Property Bureau (successor to the Privy Purse) is the largest owner of land in Bangkok, and descendants of old elite families still control considerable holdings of rented land in both Bangkok and the central provinces (Hewison 1989: 130–1).

12 Rural population growth rates rose from the turn of the century, but were absorbed by the availability of land. As long as rural land and incomes were sufficient, Bangkok's growth dynamics and population composition remained distinctive from the agrarian economy over which the city presided. These conditions were progressively eroded in the central plains and exposed by the depression of the 1930s, which stimulated the first noticeable wave of rural immigration to the city, but they were not to fully impact on the capital until the post-Second World War years.

13 Among the palaces passing into the hands of the state after 1932 were Bangkhunphrom Palace (Samsen Road) and Ban Maliwan. The demise of the princely palace households had begun earlier in the century, largely as a result of the financial difficulties of aristocratic households. In this context, the official confiscations after 1932 accelerated the existing trend towards the domestic dispersal of the traditional elite families and the demise of their once-conspicuous presence in the city.

14 He later claimed that this was part of a plan to use Petchabun as a base to overthrow Japanese forces (Wyatt 1982: 259).

2 The transformation of Krung Thep

1 I advance this approach to overcome the distinctions which have developed between structural models of the Thai state and interactional models of culture. In this and the following chapter I will argue that 'culture' is embedded (structured) in institutions and is articulated in relations between groups at all levels. Rather than abandoning the insights of the early scholars of Thai culture (especially the north Americans) as marginal to structural explanations of power, I suggest that they are an essential element to its operation and negotiation at all levels, from the ministerial board room to the street. Notably, contemporary studies of Thai administrative and political behaviour still find it necessary to explain key problems in terms of a constellation of persisting practices that can only be explained as structured through inherited 'cultural' modes – such as the notion of institutionalised anarchy and the weak Thai state advanced by Chai-anan Samudavanija (1995). In adopting this approach, I draw on arguments for incorporating the dimension of power into the concept of culture in urban anthropology (e.g. Horn 1989).

2 The surge in demand for imported luxury goods in Bangkok following the Second World War is described by Alexander MacDonald from the perspective of a newspaper proprietor in search of advertising business at this time (MacDonald 1949: 12).

3 For example, among the numerous national level agencies whose activities impacted on the capital were: The Metropolitan Electrical Authority, The Metropolitan Waterworks Authority, the Telephone Organisation of Thailand, the National Housing Authority, the Expressway and Rapid Transit Authority, the Port Authority of Thailand, the State Railway Authority of Thailand and the Industrial Estates Authority of Thailand. In the 1980s the Bangkok Metropolitan Administration controlled only one-seventh of the total government budget allocation for expenditures and projects relating to the Bangkok metropolis.

4 In 1986–9, two-thirds of all Japanese FDI in Southeast Asia went to Thailand (see ADB 1991).

5 The Thai Development Research Institute employed a number of prestigious academics to study new options for directing growth of the metropolitan region in the late 1990s. They recommended establishing a powerful committee to oversee and coordinate growth. It was admitted, however, that prospects of

efficient and decisive management were 'remote' and that 'slow and indecisive' government would continue (Mehdi 1996: 329).

6 There are varied views about the coherence and character of the Thai urban working class, focusing on ideological, political and industrial characteristics. For an orthodox Marxist interpretation, see Ji Ungpakorn (1995).

7 According to Pasuk and Pradit's research on two districts in Bangkok, an overall proportion of 34 per cent of workers for self-employed entrepreneurs were unpaid family workers. In food vending the proportion was 88 per cent (Pasuk *et al.* 1988: 12).

3 The 1990s – a global city in a global age

1 Flood control measures, incorporating the use of a lock system for canals and the building of dykes, had been implemented after the inundation shock of 1983. By the time the 1995 floods ravaged the capital, these measures were proven to be effective in protecting the high-valued inner business and government precincts of Bangkok, but only at the expense of the fringe agricultural, residential and industrial areas in the BMR, which suffered severe damage.

2 Pasuk and Baker rightly stress that the advent of civilian government administrations, beginning with Chatichai Choonhavan's government in 1988, spelt the 'provincial takeover of parliament and cabinet' (Pasuk and Baker 1997: 26).

3 A related portrayal of the evil city is generated by rural NGOs and their supporters who assert the virtues of the rural community over the corrupting, materialistic city and the modernity which it stands for (see, e.g. essays in Sanitsuda 1990).

4 Banglamphu: change and persistence in the *yan*

1 Some hotel and shopping zones in Bangkok – Silom and Sukhumvit, for example – host tourists of different nationalities such as Japanese and Western visitors, while other key hotel zones exhibit distinctive concentrations, such as the Yawarat area, where hotels attract a predominantly Chinese clientele from mainland China and Southeast Asia. Since the 1970s the area of north *Soi* Nana off Sukhumvit evolved as a distinctive niche accommodating Muslim visitors from the Middle East and Africa. Predominantly western tourists who frequent the sex-entertainment venues of western Sukhumvit tend to cluster in hotels around *Soi* Nana south.

2 This included the large weekend market at Sanam Luang, which in 1982 was relocated to the northern suburbs in Chatuchak. However, the concentration of markets in inner Bangkok is still significant.

3 This is purely a matter of expediency in order to present official *khet* data, because actually it should encompass the area between the Chao Phraya River and Samsen Road northwards beyond Wat Sangwet. Unfortunately this area has been included in an administrative unit encompassing a larger region, making it impossible to capture statistically the precise settlement space. Moreover, the area covered by Khwaeng Bowoniwet is larger than the area under consideration (encompassing part of the Saochingcha area), and ignores the physical boundary presented by the wide Ratchadamnoen Avenue.

4 The Muslims of Bangkok are a heterogeneous group with varied histories of settlement. Thonburi was an early settlement of Iranian and Turkish Muslims even before the Chakkri dynasty was founded. Others were of Indian origin. The only two Muslim settlements in Phranakhon district are located in the Banglamphu area, while the majority of the twenty-six inner-city Muslim communities, focused on the mosques, are in the Yannawa District. See Bajunid

(1992: 21–37) for an account of the distribution of Muslim settlements in contemporary Bangkok, their origins and characteristics.

5 Talat Nana was located on the northern side of the Khlong Banglamphu, opposite Talat Yot.

6 Estimates are derived from a total survey sample of 300 people across six neighbourhoods, conducted in 1991–2.

5 Genealogy of the slum

1 Nopadon Sahachaisaeree maintains that the popular or communal form of land allocation prevalent in Bangkok's slums is one which does not share the market and price fluctuations of the capitalist form of allocation (Nopadon 1995: 294). This is a mistaken interpretation. In both rental and squatter settlements the prices of housing rights and rents (for both rooms and houses) do indeed change in response to changing conditions of supply and demand. In large established settlements located close to sources of work, such as Khlong Toei, prices have been continually increasing. Similarly, rentals are subject to change. One of the reasons given by slum-dwellers for moving to vacant plots in the inner city and relocation sites has been that rental prices charged by houseowners in the established slums are far too high (see *The Nation* 11 March 1989; Askew 1998: 37). In cases where slum housing has been damaged or destroyed by fire, slum landlords have commonly increased rents for their rebuilt homes (Askew 1998: 35).

2 At the Rom Klao relocation settlement which was opened by the NHA in the outer suburb of Lat Krabang in 1985, over half of the original 224 eligible occupants either sold their rights to others or rented their land plots and moved to other slums in the city, closer to their places of work (Bijl *et al.*1992: 17).

3 Land-sharing was only possible when residents could afford repayments for repurchased land through the establishment of cooperatives, and generally it was only government landowners (such as the Crown Property Bureau) that were prepared to sell land blocks at below-market prices. Two western academics who participated in the Sengkhi project argued that community participation and reliance on decision by consensus should be limited due to the differences in interests among residents as to choices of land plot sizes and locations (Yap and Angel 1992: 59–66).

4 By 1992, the HSF had helped at least ten slum groups successfully negotiate purchase of alternative land and resettlement by these methods (Bijl 1992: 41–3).

5 As Berner notes, this practical emphasis of the urban poor has disappointed Marxist-inspired scholars who have labelled slum people's values as petit bourgeois (Berner 1997: 188).

6 Interestingly Kamon, as leader of Lock 9, had been one of the outspoken opponents of the project to move the people to Prachinburi Province in 1989. Kamon is a general trader and is said to have made a great profit from selling building materials to the families at the new settlement at Watcharaphon. He does not, however, appear to have been involved in drug dealing or gambling dens, although he may well have been in Olarn's entourage, said to have received regular payments from the Port Authority. The leader of Lock 11 community is known to have received two land plots (Author's interview with new committee of Locks 9–12, 16 September 1996).

7 Prateep's prominent role in the pro-democracy demonstrations of 1992 and the Confederation for Democracy are detailed in Hata (1996: 172ff) and McCargo (1997: 255–7). Reflecting her widespread popularity in the broader community, in March 2000 Prateep was elected to the Senate in the first elections conducted under the provisions of the new constitution.

8 In 1985, when NGO leaders were celebrating Khlong Toei's first land-sharing achievement, a representative of the smaller slums of Bangkok pointed out in a public forum that the Khlong Toei experience could not be replicated elsewhere. He gave three reasons for this: (1) the sheer size of the slum population and its capacity to protest eviction; (2) it was represented by Prateep Ungsongtham who was famous and well respected; and (3) its many development projects and improvements were due to the assistance of international funds and NGOs (Thawisak 1986).

9 Notably, it was Prateep's status as 'mother' to many people in Khlong Toei that Orlan and his supporters targeted and attempted to undermine in their public reaction to her charges that they were behind the major gambling dens and drug gangs (*Phuchatkan* 28 January 1997).

6 A place in the suburbs

1 Technical studies dealing with residential satisfaction are numerous for housing developments in Bangkok (especially the NHA estates), but they tell us little of the lifestyles and nothing of social life and activities in these housing estates (see, e.g. Thongchai, Tips and Sunanta 1986).

2 'The space of flows' is a term coined by the sociologist Manuel Castells to characterise the telecommunication-linked networks connecting and sustaining groups, individuals and institutions that appear increasingly to be dominating advanced urban regions, contrasted with 'place-based community spaces', largely of the poor and marginalised (see Castells 1989: 348–51).

3 A number of problems face the researcher of the middle classes, particularly those adopting ethnographic interviews and observation: (1) the essentially privatised nature of middle-class life itself which places major obstacles in the way of ethnographers in developing participant observation opportunities and networks of informants; and (2) the time-consuming nature of the research. I enjoyed an advantage in gaining an introduction into the Pratchaniwet estate through a committee member who is now a senior-ranking official in the Thai development bureaucracy. This may well have biased the findings, particularly since Pratchaniwet is clearly a success story. Aside from this, the hoary old question of the comparability of individual case studies needs to be acknowledged. I here admit that the findings must be limited, perhaps no more limiting than the massive questionnaire surveys which ignore elements of social process and interaction styles in favour of box-ticking on standard indicators.

4 Some residents claim that an estate committee was already founded by the NHA at an early stage of the estate's history, but one of the original assembly promoters emphasises that the idea was not an NHA plan. The NHA itself maintains no records of the early foundation years of the Pratchaniwet estate; moreover, issues of committee establishment do not feature in NHA literature or publicity dealing with the advantages of such estates. In the absence of any reports or research on this, one can only assume that the matter of estate, or community, committees is generally not given priority.

7 Fields of cultural capital

1 According to local government guidelines prevailing until the restructuring of local administration under the 1997 constitution, sanitary districts could be formed when a place contained a population of no less than 1,500 people or 100 dwelling units within a 5 square kilometre area. Municipalities (aside from cities) required settlements of over 10,000 with a population density of at least 3,000

people per square kilometre. There are cases of sanitary districts which are extremely large and municipalities which are quite small in terms of total population – thus the sanitary district of Pakret contains a population of over 116,000, representing 75 per cent of the *amphur's* population, and covering 48 per cent of its total area (42 square kilometres). By contrast, the municipality of Bang Buathong comprises a population of just over 10,000, representing only 15 per cent of its *amphur* population. In the absence of any official statistical measure denoting urban areas in Thailand, demographers and urban researchers generally consider that both of these administrative units should be counted as urban. Using these criteria the urban populations of the component districts of Nonthaburi range from a high in the east of the province of 89 per cent (*Amphur Muang*) to lower levels in the west (e.g. Bang Kruai 41 per cent; Bang Buathong 15 per cent) (Leman Group 1994: 11–13).

2 The metaphor of invasion and the theme of encroachment as a principal cause of agricultural decline is clear in the following judgement by Anuchat and Ross (1992: 7): 'It is apparent that urban expansion in Bangkok will result in the loss of most of the fertile agricultural lands, as farmers are forced to give up their farms and sell their lands to more profitable urban projects'. A more balanced interpretation of the processes underlying land conversion on the rural–urban fringe in the BMR is offered by Banasopit *et al.* (1990: 40–66). They note that while the destruction of agricultural land through negative urban environmental impacts is the most visible cause of land conversion, the fundamental cause lies in the fact that prices to be gained from selling land are far in excess of the returns farmers can expect from farming, particularly rice growing. Low agricultural incomes are thus a key factor.

3 Anthropological studies of people on the rural–urban fringe tend to perpetuate the image of a passive and vulnerable rural world, transformed by external forces. Thiravet's study of farming families in the Pakret district of eastern Nonthaburi in the late 1970s succeeded in showing something of the ways that people exploited the possibilities of urban expansion through diversifying occupations and selling the topsoil of their rice fields to building contractors. Even so, it is notable that their strategies are portrayed as essentially defensive tactics, and their practices are described as an 'adaptation' to new conditions, as if the process of urbanisation was externally driven, and not tied into broader patterns of social change (Thirawet 1979). The recent rise of concern for endangered communities and traditional culture in Thailand has also contributed towards the conceptual bifurcation of urban and rural cultures, adding nostalgia to the persistent sociological myth of the integrated, spatially bounded village (Yani 1995).

8 Condo land

1 Pasuk and Baker have noted how global capital and markets were linked to only a small range of sectors in the Thai economy, and that the boom was essentially focused on the drive to profit from domestic demand. This tended to characterise most of the property sector (Pasuk and Baker 1998: 56–7).

2 Robert Beauregard has argued that much of the theorising which sees global forms as initiated in a handful of 'world-cities' and then exported to the second-league centres, is an oversimplification. He argues that theories which view the 'local mediating the global', misrepresent the relationships of actors who create cities and, by emphasising scale as an organising concept, they devalue the manner in which global actors might have local communities. He emphasises that the global–local polarisation (a dichotomy of spatial scales) misrepresents the multitude of spatial scales and actors involved in contemporary urban change (1995: 239–40). In a similar spirit, while not addressing urban form as such,

Mike Douglass has argued for attention to be paid to 'the localisation of culture' in the context of world capitalism and its effects in East Asia, and for acknowledgment that: 'There will . . . be many types of cultural transformations emanating from global–local interaction' (Douglass 1995: vii).

3 These limits were exposed clearly in the debates which took place over changes to foreign property ownership legislation in 1996–7. The severe housing glut which confounded Bangkok's housing industry in 1996 led to a desperate search for measures to soak up the surplus housing stock and inject necessary money into the market. One suggestion, pushed by the building industry and supported by the Prime Minister – Banhan Silpa-Acha – was to amend the Condominium Act to allow foreign nationals ownership of 100 per cent of condominium developments (up from the 40 per cent established under the Act). Despite a cabinet resolution supporting this measure there was considerable opposition, and the idea eventually lapsed. The case against increase of foreign ownership rights spanned arguments about the nature of the market to the question of national sovereignty, and appeals to the cause of national interest ultimately buried the idea (Amarin 1997).

4 An example of a smaller enterprise is that of the Pitchitsingh family business, whose capital base was founded originally on the import and export of textiles prior to expansion into building and managing of apartments. The firm's second deluxe apartments, Hawaii Tower, was completed on Sukhumvit *Soi* 23 in 1993.

5 Notably, many of these extra features were not included in the complex when it was opened in 1996.

6 Only in the 1990s were some of the largest blocks on the prime area lining western Sukhumvit being sold and developed into retail/business complexes.

9 Sex workers in Bangkok

1 *One Night in Bangkok*, lyrics by Tim Rice, The CHESS company, RCA VICTOR, New York, 1988. From the Broadway musical *Chess*.

2 I need to emphasise the relatively limited scope of this discussion: it concerns heterosexual relations between Thai female sex workers and western males within the contexts of their working and personal lives and their own key understandings of sexuality, of relationships and actions. I do not address the gay scene in Bangkok, which is of considerable significance in the overall study of 'the body' of Bangkok and Thailand and the global topography of desire. Nor do I deal at any length with the Asian customers/lovers (Japanese, Taiwanese, Korean, Malaysian), who form a much larger group of heterosexual consumers of sex services than do westerners in Thailand.

3 The information used in this chapter is derived from field notes compiled from meetings and unstructured interviews mainly conducted in *in situ* work venues in the Sukhumvit district of Bangkok between the years 1993–6, and supplemented by the author in further interviews and observation in 1997, 1998 and 2000. For further discussion on methodology, see an earlier essay (Askew 1999b). The names of all informants have been disguised to preserve confidentiality.

4 The variety of sites and work regimes in the infrastructure of the sex trade of Bangkok is very similar to the situation prevailing in the sex-trade zones of the Philippines (see Chant and McIlwaine 1995: 214–16).

5 For example, the minimum wage for factory workers in late 1996 was 145 baht per day, but many employers pay less than this.

6 This high level of movement into and out of sex work characterises both tourist-orientated and domestic sectors. Thus, one study finds average length of employment in sex work in Thailand is between eighteen months and two years (see Wathini and Guest 1998: 162).

7 For a more detailed discussion of this topic, see Askew (1999b).

8 Anna Lowenhaupt Tsing has given an account of similar motivations for women in a different part of Southeast Asia (Tsing 1993: 215).

9 While *prachot* in the village context, according to Klausner, may be 'a ruse used to express grievances without causing disruptive forces to hold sway in the field of human relationships', *kanprachot chiwit* is a recognition by women that relations have indeed been disrupted.

10 I use this now well-known term, coined by Erving Goffman, to depict role-play in social situations (Goffman 1969).

11 Agreements are usually reached before holidays for the man to pay a daily sum or a lump sum of money to the woman.

12 I have noted the interconnected idioms of reciprocity and compensation in relation to women (particularly rural women) in an earlier discussion (Askew 1999a: 17). The practice of bride-price payments and increasing levels of commoditisation in Thai peasant society are discussed in an interesting paper by Andrea Whittaker (1999).

10 Contesting urbanisms

1 It should be emphasised that the area demarcated as Inner Rattanakosin, the principal focus of architectural restoration and vista-production in the plan, was a diverse settlement from the beginning. Aside from the large community within the royal palace and the dependants in the associated princely palaces, various communities of people associated with the functions of the court (elephant keepers, for example) were settled on the river banks. By the period of Chulalongkorn in the last quarter of the nineteenth century, shophouses were constructed along Maharat Road between the palace walls and the Chao Phraya River. By the end of the century, what had once been floating markets of vendors had moved onto the old boat landing areas (*tha*) and established markets. This aspect of Rattanakosin's history was ignored in the plan in favour of a sanitised and decontextualised representation.

2 Khwansuwong Athipo (of Chulalongkorn University) is a good example of the most articulate and active of a small group of planners who advocated what he described as an indigenous Thai-style urban model for Bangkok which embraced a diversity of livelihoods and settlements (see Khwansuwong 1991).

Bibliography

Abu-Lughod, L. (1991) 'Writing against culture', in R.G. Fox (ed.) *Recapturing Anthropology*, Santa Fe: School of American Research Press.

Achara Deboonme (1994) 'A diet of fast food and wine', in Pana Janwiroj (ed.) *The Rise of the Thai Middle Classes. The Nation Year-end Report*, Bangkok: The Nation Publishing Group.

ADB (1991) *Asian Development Outlook*, Manila: Asian Development Bank.

Agricultural Office, Bang Buathong District (1994) *Naeothang Kanphatthana Kankaset Radap Tambon* [Trends in Agricultural Development at the Tambon Level], Nonthaburi: Agricultural Extension Office, Ministry of Agriculture.

Agricultural Office, Bang Kruai District (1994) *Naeothang Kanphatthana Kankaset Radab Tambon* [Trends in Agricultural Development at the Tambon Level], Nonthaburi: Agricultural Extension Office, Ministry of Agriculture.

Agricultural Office, Nonthaburi (1995) *Annual Tambon Data*. Typescript files.

Akin Rabibhadana (1969) *The Organization of Thai Society in the Early Bangkok Period 1782–1873*, Ithaca, NY: Southeast Asia Programme, Cornell University.

—— (1975) 'Bangkok slum: aspects of social organization', Ph.D Dissertation, Cornell University.

—— (1978) *Rise and Fall of a Bangkok Slum*, Bangkok: Thai Khadi Research Institute, Thammasat University.

—— (1983) 'Persistence within change: Thai society in the nineteenth and twentieth centuries', in Narong Phuangphit and Phongsak Chirikraisiri (eds) *Sangkhom Thai Nai 200 Pi* [Thai Society Over 200 Years], Bangkok: Chao Phraya Press.

—— (1991) 'Muang Sawan Mai Mi Slum – Ru?' [In the Heavenly City there are no slums – are there?], unpublished paper.

—— (1999) *Chumchon Ae-at: Onkkhwamru kap khwampenching* [Slums: Knowledge and Reality], Bangkok: Office of the Department for Research Support.

Allen, A. (1994) 'Environmental transformation on the rural–urban fringe: Yogyakarta, Indonesia', paper presented to the Asian Studies Association of Australia Biennial Conference, Perth, Western Australia, 13–16 July.

Alpha Research (1994) *Thailand in Figures*, Bangkok: Alpha Research.

Altman, D. (2001) *Global Sex*, Chicago: Chicago University Press.

Amara Phongsapich (1990) 'Politico-economic development impacting on society and traditional values', paper presented to the USIS ASAT Conference, 'Societies on the Move: Changing Values', Suan Nong Nooch, 15–16 June.

Amarin Khoman (1997) 'Thailand is not for sale', *Bangkok Post* 2 February.

Amnuay Viravan (1998) 'The great Asian crisis: danger and opportunity', in *Can Asia Recover its Vitality? Globalization and the Roles of Japanese and U.S.*

Corporations. JETRO–IDE Joint Symposium, March 1998, Tokyo: Institute of Developing Economies.

Amornrat Mahitirook (1997) 'Port agency moves to clear slum', *Bangkok Post* 25 February.

Ampha Santimetanedol (1996) 'Community leaders fall out over drug problem', *Bangkok Post* 30 September.

Amporn Jirattikorn (1999) 'Women, modernity and sexuality in the contemporary Luktoong song genre in Thailand', Masters Thesis, Southeast Asian Studies, National University of Singapore.

Amyot, J. (1994) *The Structure of Employment of the Rural Population of the Central Region of Thailand*, Bangkok: Chulalongkorn University Social Research Institute.

Anand Nawilai (1997) 'Phuchai khai dua hai ke nai Krung Thep' [Gay prostitution in Bangkok], paper presented to the seminar 'Urban Culture: Community, City and Change in Bangkok', 7–8 July, Bangkok, Sinlapakon University.

Anchalee Chaiworaporn and Varaporn Chamsanit (1994) 'The lexicon of impatience', in Pana Janwiroj (ed.) *The Rise of the Thai Middle Classes, The Nation Year-end Report*, Bangkok: Nation Publishing Group.

Anchalee Kongrut (1998) 'Residents try to save building', *Bangkok Post* 10 March.

Anderson, B. (1977) 'Withdrawal symptoms: social and cultural aspects of the October 6 coup', *Bulletin of Concerned Asian Scholars*, 9, 3: 13–30.

—— (1978) 'Studies of the Thai state: the state of Thai studies', in E.B. Ayal (ed.) *The Study of Thailand: Analysis of Knowledge, Approaches and Prospects in Anthropology, Art History, Economics, History and Political Science*, Athens, OH: Ohio University Center for International Studies, Southeast Asia Programme.

Anek Laothamatas (1996) 'A tale of two democracies: conflicting perceptions of elections and democracy in Thailand', in R.H. Taylor (ed.) *The Politics of Elections in Southeast Asia*, New York: Woodrow Wilson Center Press and Cambridge University Press.

Anjira Assavanonda (1997a) 'Activists stage tour of "historical sites"', *Bangkok Post* 19 May.

—— (1997b) 'Fewer northern girls enter flesh trade', *Bangkok Post* 1 August.

Anon (1992) *Muban Islam 200 pi. Ro wan sun salai bai kap khwam charoen* [Two hundred-year-old Islamic village awaits destruction through progress], *Siam Araya* 1, 1: 57–64.

Anuchat Poungsomlee and Ross, H. (1992) *Impacts of Modernization and Urbanization in Bangkok. An Integrative Bio-social Study*, Nakhon Pathom: Institute for Population and Social Research, Mahidol University.

Aphar Phamorabut (1982) *The History of Bangkok. Summary of Political and Cultural Events from the Age of Establishment to the Present*, Bangkok: Duang Kamol.

Apichat Chamratrithirong *et al.* (1993) 'Report on the rate and modes of internal migration in Thailand, from the national study on internal migration in Thailand. Progress report', presented at the Conference, 'New Findings from the Study of Internal Migration in Thailand', Centre for Population and Social Research, Mahidol University, 2 November.

Arsa Sarasin and Chira Hongladarom (1999) 'A back to basics view is required', *Bangkok Post* 30 April.

Asian-Pacific Center (1996) *Industrialization and Changes of Thai Society. The Effect of Japanese Corporations on Thailand*, Fukuoka: Asian-Pacific Center.

Askew, M. (1993) *The Banglamphu District. A Portrait of Change in Inner Bangkok*, Bangkok: Thailand Development Research Institute.
—— and Paritta Ko-Anantakul (1992) 'Bangkok: the evolving urban landscape', in Amara Phongsapich, M.C. Howard and J. Amyot (eds) *Regional Development and Change in Southeast Asia in the 1990s*, Bangkok: Chulalongkorn University Social Research Institute.
—— (1994) 'Bangkok: transformation of the Thai city', in M. Askew and W.S. Logan (eds) *Cultural Identity and Urban Change in Southeast Asia. Interpretative Essays*, Geelong: Deakin University Press.
—— (1998) 'Khlong Toei community structure study: an assessment of social and settlement characteristics, economy and attitudes to change', report of research supported by the LIFE programme (UNDP), presented to the Bangkok Metropolitan Administration and Grass Roots Development Foundation. Unpublished manuscript.
—— (1999a) 'Labor, love and entanglement: Bangkok bar workers and the negotiation of selfhood', *Crossroads: an Interdisciplinary Journal of Southeast Asian Studies* 13, 2: 1–28.
—— (1999b) 'Strangers and lovers: Thai women sex workers and Western men in the "pleasure space" of Bangkok', in J. Forshee and C. Fink (eds) *Converging Interests: Traders, Travelers and Tourists in Southeast Asia*, Berkeley: Center for Southeast Asia Studies, University of California.
Atiya Achakulwisut (1997) 'Bailout? Whose bailout?' *Bangkok Post* 22 August.
Atthachak Satayanurak (1995) *Kanplianplaeng Lokathat Khong Chonchan Phunam Thai Tangtae Ratchakan Thi 4 – P.S. 2475* [Changing Worldview among the Thai Elite From the Fourth Reign to 1932], Bangkok: Chulalongkorn University Press.
Auge, M. (1995) *Non-places. Introduction to the Anthropology of Supermodernity*, London: Verso.
Aurapin Bunnag (1978) 'A study of land use and socio-economic and demographic change in the suburban areas of Bangkok', in R.D. Hill and J.M. Bray (eds) *Geography and Environment in Southeast Asia*, Hong Kong: Oxford University Press.
Bajunid, O.F. (1992) 'The other side of Bangkok: a survey of Muslim presence in Buddhist Thailand's capital city', in Yoshihiro Tsubouchi (ed.) *The Formation of Urban Civilization in Southeast Asia. Supplement*, Kyoto: Center for Southeast Asian Studies, Kyoto University.
Baker, C. (1999) 'Assembly of the poor: the new drama of village, city and state', *Thai Development Newsletter* 37: 15–21.
Banasopit Mekvichai *et al.* (1990) *Urbanization and the Environment: Managing the Conflict*, Bangkok: Thailand Development Research Institute.
Banchawan Khongsawang (1992) '*Kansuksa Kanplianplaeng Rupbaep Kanchai Thidin Pu Yu Asai Yan Sukhumvit: Krung Thep Mahanakhon*' [A Study of Changes in Residential Landuse Patterns in the Sukhumvit District: Bangkok], Master of Urban and Regional Planning Dissertation, Chulalongkorn University.
Bandit Rajavatanadhanin and Dharani Kothandapani (1995) 'Chavalit wants new site for second airport', *Bangkok Post* 11 September.
Bangkok Bank (1980) 'Condominiums', *Bangkok Bank Monthly Review* 21, 10: 346–7.
—— (1983) 'Fast foods – a new business mini-boom', *Bangkok Bank Monthly Review* 24, 10: 410–13.

—— (1988) 'Another boom year ahead' *Thailand Business* 12, 1/2: 34–45.
—— (1985–9) *Monthly Bulletins*.
Bangkok Post Various issues (no authors given).
Bangkok Postal Department (1883) *Sarabanchi Chu Ratchaton nai Changwat Thanon lae Trok Samrap Chaophanakngan Krom Praisani Krung Thep Mahanakhon* [List of Persons in the Province, Streets and Lanes for Use of the Officers of the Postal Department in Bangkok], vols 1 and 2, Bangkok: By Royal Command.
Bangon Chomchampi (1987) '*Kansuksa Kanchai Punthi Nai Soi Sukhumvit 3–63 Chak Thanon Sukhumvit Chot Khlong Saensaep*' [A Study of Landuse in Soi Sukhumvit 3–6 from Sukhumvit Road to the Saensaep Canal], Masters Degree Thesis, Srinakariwirot University.
Bank of Thailand (1988–9) *Quarterly Bulletins*.
—— (1994) *Economic Performance in 1994 and Outlook for 1995*, Bangkok: Bank of Thailand.
Barmé, S. (1993) *Luang Wichit Wattakan and the Creation of a Thai National Identity*, Singapore: Institute for Southeast Asian Studies.
—— (1997) 'Towards a social history of Bangkok: gender, class and popular culture in the Siamese capital – 1905–1940', Ph.D Dissertation, Australian National University.
Barnes, T. and Duncan, J.S. (1992) *Writing Worlds. Discourse, Text and Metaphor in the Representation of Landscape*, London: Routledge.
Bartlett, N. (1959) *Land of the Lotus Eaters. A Book Mostly about Siam*, London: Jarrolds.
Batson, B.A. (1984) *The End of the Absolute Monarchy in Siam*, Oxford: Oxford University Press.
Beaumont, R. (1994) 'Bangkok, Texas', *Metro Magazine* (Bangkok) 3 (October): 34–7.
Beauregard, R.A. (1995) 'Theorizing the global-local connection', in P.L. Knox and P.J. Taylor (eds) *World Cities in a World System*, Cambridge: Cambridge University Press.
Beck, U. (2000) *What is Globalization?*, London: Polity Press.
Bell, P. (1997) 'Thailand's economic miracle: built on the backs of women', in Virada Somsawasdi and S. Theobald (eds) *Women, Gender Relations and Development in Thai Society*, Chiang Mai: Women's Studies Centre, Chiang Mai University.
Bello, W., Cunningham, S. and Li Kheng Poh (1998) *A Siamese Tragedy. Development and Disintegration in Modern Thailand*, London: Zed Books.
Ben-Ari, E. (1991) *Changing Japanese Suburbia. A Study of Two Present-day Localities*, London: Kegan Paul.
Berman, M. (1988) *All That is Solid Melts into Air. The Experience of Modernity*, reprint with new preface, originally publ. 1982, New York: Simon & Schuster.
Berner, E. (1997) *Defending a Place in the City. Localities and the Struggle for Urban Land in Metro Manila*, Quezon City: Ateneo de Manila University Press.
—— and Korff, R. (1995) 'Globalization and local resistance: the creation of localities in Manila and Bangkok', *International Journal of Urban and Regional Research* 19, 2: 208–22.
Bijl, J. *et al.* (1992) 'The resettlement of slums in Bangkok', unpublished discussion paper presented to the National Housing Authority of Thailand.

Bishop, R. and Robinson, L.S. (1998) *Night Market. Sexual Cultures and the Thai Economic Miracle*, New York: Routledge.

BMA (n.d.) *Bangkok New International Business District*. Bangkok: Bangkok Metropolitan Administration.

—— (1991) *Statistical Profile of BMA*, Bangkok: Bangkok Metropolitan Administration.

—— (1993) *Statistical Profile of BMA*. Bangkok: Bangkok Metropolitan Administration.

BMA, Department of City Planning and MIT Consulting Team (1996) *The Bangkok Plan. A Vision for the Bangkok Metropolitan Administration Area 1995–2005. Discussion Draft*, Bangkok: Bangkok Metropolitan Administration.

BMA, Planning Division (1986) *Phaenthi Sadaeng Kanchai Thidin Rai Khet Khong Krung Thep Mahanakhon* [Landuse Map of the Districts of the Bangkok Metropolis], Bangkok: Bangkok Metropolitan Administration.

Boonkong Hungchangsith (1974) 'Economic impact of the US military presence in Thailand, 1960–72', Ph.D. Dissertation, Claremont College.

Borisut Kasinphilr and Chantharaphen Wiwatthanasukseri (1995) *Bangkok Laent – Laent aen Hao* [Bangkok Land and Land and House], Bangkok: Matichon.

Borisut *et al.* (1990) *Pha Thurakit Mubanchatsan Lae Khondominiam* [Finding Your Way Through the Housing Estate and Condominium Business], Bangkok: Samit Publishing.

Bourdieu, P. (1977) *Outline of a Theory of Practice*, London: Cambridge University Press.

—— (1990) *In Other Words. Essays towards a Reflexive Sociology*, Stanford, CA: Stanford University Press.

Bowring, J. (Sir) (1857) *The Kingdom and People of Siam*, 2 vols, London: John W. Parker and Son.

Boyer, C. (1994) *The City of Collective Memory*, Cambridge, MA.: MIT Press.

Bradbury, N. (1995) 'Every market tells a story', in *Building the Cities of the Future. A Survey of Property Companies in Asia* (Supplement to *Euromoney*), September: 4–5.

Brookfield, H., Hadi, A.S. and Mahmud, Z. (1991) *The City in the Village. The* in-situ *Urbanization of Villages, Villagers and their Land around Kuala Lumpur*, Kuala Lumpur: Oxford University Press.

Brown, R.A. (1994) *Capital and Entrepreneurship in Southeast Asia*, London: Macmillan.

Brown, S.J. and Crocker, H.L. (2001) *A Global Perspective on Real Estate Cycles*, New York: Kluwer Academic Publishers.

Brummelhuis, H.T.(1984) 'Abundance and avoidance: an interpretation of Thai individualism', in H.T. Brummelhuis and J.H. Kemp (eds) *Strategies and Structures in Thai Society*, Amsterdam: Anthropological-Sociological Centre, University of Amsterdam.

Bryant, C. (1995) 'The role of local actors in transforming the urban fringe', *Journal of Rural Studies* 11, 3: 255–67.

BTO (1998) 'So who's running this town anyway?' [Interview with Pichit Rattakul], *Bangkok Timeout Magazine*, 4, November: 18–19.

Bundit Chulasai (1983) 'L'evolution des lodgements urbains a Bangkok – Thailande', Ph.D Dissertation, Unite Pedagogique D'Architecture No. 1, (Paris).

Buphanard Suvanamas (1982) *Bangkok: Urban Functional Structure 1782–1982*, Bangkok: Thai Khadi Research Institute.
Bureau of Crown Property (1991) *The Urban Poor and Alternative for a Decent Place to Live*. Committee of Policy Formulation, Slum Improvement and Reconstruction Programme. Bangkok: The Bureau of Crown Property.
Busaba Sivasomboon, Krissana Parnsoonthorn and Chiratas Nivatpumin (1997) 'Making modern monuments', *Bangkok Post* 31 March.
Busrin Treerapongpichit (1996) 'Mapping future trends', *Bangkok Post. Thailand Property Guide*, Bangkok: Post Publishing: 55–6.
Bussarawan Teerawichitchainan (1997) 'For sale: Burmese Virgins', *Bangkok Post* 13 June.
Caoili, M.A. (1988) *The Origins of Metropolitan Manila: A Political and Social Analysis*, Quezon City: New Day Publishers.
Carpenter, J. and Lees, L. (1995) 'Gentrification in New York, London and Paris: an International Comparison', *International Journal of Urban and Regional Research* 19, 2: 286–304.
Cary, Caverlee (1994). 'Triple gems and double meanings: contested spaces in the National Museum of Bangkok', Ph.D. Dissertation, Cornell University.
Castells, M. (1983) *The City and the Grassroots*, London: Edward Arnold.
—— (1989) *The Informational City*, Oxford: Blackwell.
—— (1997) *The Information Age. Economy Society and Culture. Volume II. The Power of Identity*, Oxford: Blackwell.
Cate, S. (1999) 'Cars-stuck-together: tourism and the Bangkok traffic jam', in J. Forshee, C. Fink and S. Cate (eds) *Converging Interests. Traders, Travelers and Tourists in Southeast Asia*, Berkeley: Center for Southeast Asia Studies, University of California.
Chai-anan Samudavanija (1990) *Rat Kap Sangkhom* [State and Society], Bangkok: Chulalongkorn University Press.
—— (1995) 'Economic development and democracy', in Mehdi Krongkaew (ed.) *Thailand's Industrialization and its Consequences*, New York: St Martin's Press.
Chaiwat Thirapantu (1998) 'Phra Athit street festival ... rekindling community spirits', typescript press release, Bangkok Forum.
Chaloeylakana Wongtrangan (1988) 'Thai elite struggle in the 1932 revolution', Ph.D Dissertation, Johns Hopkins University.
Chalongphob Sussangkan (1987) *The Thai Labor Market. A Study of Seasonality and Segmentation*, Bangkok: Thailand Development Research Institute.
Chant, S. and McIlwaine, C. (1995) *Women of a Lesser Cost. Female Labour, Foreign Exchange and Philippine Development*, Manila: Ateneo de Manila University Press.
Chant, S. and Radcliffe, S.A. (1992) 'Migration and development: the importance of gender', in S. Chant (ed.) *Gender and Migration in Developing Countries*, London: Belhaven Press.
Chantana Banpasirichote (1993) *Community Integration into Regional Industrial Development. A Case Study of Klong Ban Po, Chachoengsao*, Bangkok: Thailand Development Research Institute.
Charit Dingsapat (1993) 'The economy of Bangkok', in *Report of a Research Seminar of Mahidol University. Case Study of Krung Thep R.S. 211: Directions and Research Networks*, Institute for Population and Social Research, Mahidol University Salaya, Nakhon Pathom.

Charit *et al.* (1986) *Employment and Economic Activity within the Bangkok Metropolitan Region. Final Report*, Bangkok: NESDB.

Charuwan Lowira and Baffie, J. (1992) 'Ban Khrua. Adit an Rungrot ru Anakhot cha Dap Sun?' [Ban Khrua. A brilliant past – or will the future wipe it out?], *Sinlapa Watthanatham* (October): 176–86.

Chatchai Pongprayoon (1984) 'Decision making on industrial location in the Bangkok metropolis', International Conference on Thai Studies, Bangkok, 22–24 August.

Chatchai Sittikul (1986) 'Suksa thi tang Khong Chumchon Ae-at nai Krung Thep Mahanakhon' [A study in settlement patterns of slum areas in Bangkok], M.A. Dissertation, Department of Urban and Regional Planning, Chulalongkorn University, Bangkok.

Chatrudee Theparat and Amornrat Maitruk (1998) 'Cabinet restores momentum to Nong Ngu Hao', *Bangkok Post* 27 January.

Chatrudee Theparat and Krissana Parnsoonthorn (2000) 'Two executives sent to sidelines', *Bangkok Post* 12 April.

Chatthip Nartsupha (1968) *Foreign Trade, Foreign Finance and the Economic Development of Thailand, 1956–1965*, Bangkok: Prae Pittaya Ltd.

—— (1984) *Setthakit Muban Thai Nai Adit* [The Economy of the Thai Village in the Past], Bangkok: Srang San.

Cheang, W.S. (1988) 'Duang Prateep: ten years on', *Bangkok Post* 21 August.

Chet Boonpratuang, Jones, G.W. and Chanpen Taesrikul (1996) 'Dispelling some myths about urbanization in Thailand', *Journal of Demography* [Chulalongkorn University] 12, 1: 21–36.

Chintana Noppan (1986) *Suksa Kanwangphaen kanchai thidin prayot nai Khet Bangkapi* [A study for residential land use planning in Bangkapi District], M.A. dissertation, Department of Urban and Regional Planning, Chulalongkorn University, Bangkok.

Chira Hongladarom. *et al.* (1986) *Urban Food Market in Bangkok*, Bangkok: Human Resources Institute, Faculty of Economics, Bangkok: Thammasat University.

Chira Sakornpan *et al.* (1971) *Klong Toey. A Social Work Survey of a Squatter Slum*, Bangkok: Faculty of Social Administration, Thammasat University.

Chit Phumisak (1976) *Khwambenma khong kham Siam, Thai, Lao lae Khom lae Laksana thang Sangkhom khong Chu Chonchat* [The Origins of the words Siam, Thai, Lao and Khom, and the social characteristics of national names], Bangkok: Siam Publishing.

Chitraporn Vanaspong (1996) 'Lay-off crisis', *Bangkok Post* 17 November.

Chiu, Helen L. (1985) *Thai Housing Policy 1940–1978*, Bangkok: Chulalongkorn University Social Research Institute.

Chiwit Sisan Krung Thep [Humanise Bangkok] (1998) Publicity pamphlet, Bangkok: Bangkok Metropolitan Administration.

Chomlada Lorprayoon (1991) 'Vending activity in Bangkok', Master of Economics Thesis, English Language Programme, Thammasat University.

Choop Kanjanaprakorn and Chadsri Bunnag (1978) 'Administration of housing', in Nathalang Wadanyu (ed.) *Housing in Thailand. Southeast Asian Low-cost Housing Study*, Bangkok: Applied Scientific Research Corporation of Thailand.

Christensen, S.R. (1991) 'The politics of democratization in Thailand', background paper for the 2010 Project, Thailand Development Research Institute.

—— (1993) *Democracy without Equity? The Institutions and Political Consequences of Bangkok-based Development*, Bangkok: Thailand Development Research Institute.

Chua Beng Huat and Tan Choo Ean (1999) 'Singapore: where the new middle class sets the standard', in M. Pinches (ed.) *Culture and Privilege in Capitalist Asia*, London: Routledge.

Chumchon Thai: pua chiwit dikwa pua meuang thi dikwa. [Thai Community: for a better life and a better city] (1993) *Newsletter of the Society of Thai Town Planners*, vol. 1, October.

Clad, J. (1989) *Behind the Myth. Business, Money and Power in Southeast Asia*, London: Unwin Hyman.

Cohen, E. (1982) 'Thai girls and Farang men: the edge of ambiguity', *Annals of Tourism Research* 9: 403–28.

—— (1985) 'A *Soi* in Bangkok – the dynamics of lateral urban expansion', *Journal of the Siam Society* 73, 1/2: 1–35.

—— (1986) 'Lovelorn Farangs: the correspondence between foreign men and Thai girls', *Anthropological Quarterly* 59, 3: 115–28.

—— (1987) 'Sensuality and venality in Bangkok: the dynamics of cross-cultural mapping of prostitution', *Deviant Behaviour* 8: 223–34.

—— (1991) *Thai Society in Comparative Perspective. Collected Essays*, Bangkok: White Lotus.

—— (1993) 'Open-ended prostitution as a skilful game of luck: opportunity, risk and security among tourist-orientated prostitutes in a Bangkok *Soi*', in M. Hitchcock, V.T. King and M.J.G. Parnwell (eds) *Tourism in Southeast Asia*, London: Routledge.

—— (1995) 'Golf in Thailand: from sport to business', *Southeast Asian Journal of Social Science* 23, 2: 1–17.

—— (1996) *Thai Tourism. Hill Tribes, Islands and Open-ended Prostitution*, Bangkok: White Lotus.

Colliers Jardine (1994) 'Survive the slump with prime space', *Bangkok Post Thailand Property Guide*, Spring, Bangkok: Post Publishing.

Colliers Jardine Research (1995) *Asia-Pacific Property Trends, Conditions and Forecasts, July 1995*, Sydney: McGraw Hill.

—— (1997) *Asia Pacific Property Trends. Conditions and Forecasts, January 1997*, Sydney: McGraw Hill.

Community Development Office, BMA (1994) *Sarup khomun chumchon Krungthep Mahanakhon* [Summary data on communities in Bangkok], Bangkok: Bangkok Metropolitan Administration/UNICEF.

Cook, N.M.(1991) 'Thai identity in the astrological tradition', In C.J. Reynolds (ed.) *National Identity and its Defenders. Thailand, 1939–1989*, Clayton: Monash Papers on Southeast Asia, No. 25.

Courtine, P. (1995) 'The most integrated Indian community in Thailand: the Sikhs of Bangkok Chinatown', *Guru Nanak Journal of Sociology* 16, 2: 83–94.

Crispin, S.W. (2000) 'Lessons from the fall', *Far Eastern Economic Review* 163, 48: 82.

—— and Goad, G.P. (1999) 'Bangkok renaissance: tourism officials polish city's appeal to encourage longer stays', *Far Eastern Economic Review* 162, 39: 62.

—— and Wang Nokgaew (1999) 'Cycle of despair', *Far Eastern Economic Review* 23 September (Internet edition).

Cummings, J. (1987) *Thailand – a Travel Survival Kit*, South Yarra, Victoria: Lonely Planet.

—— (1997) *Bangkok. A Lonely Planet City Guide*, Hawthorn, Victoria: Lonely Planet.

Cushman, J.W. (1993) *Fields from the sea. Chinese Junk Trade with Siam during the Late Eighteenth and Early Nineteenth Centuries*, Ithaca, NY: Southeast Asia Programme, Cornell University.

CUSRI (1991) *Socioeconomic Analysis of Eastern Seaboard and Upper Gulf Region. Executive Summary. Submitted to the Office of the National Environment Board*, Bangkok: Chulalongkorn University Social Research Institute.

Darling, F.C. (1965) *Thailand and the United States*, Washington DC: Public Affairs Press.

Dawson, A. (1988) *Patpong. Bangkok's Big Little Street*, Bangkok: Alan Dawson Publishing.

de Certeau, M. (1984) *The Practice of Everyday Life*, Berkeley: University of California Press.

De Manila, Q. (1980) *Manila: Sin City? And Other Chronicles*, Manila: National Book Store Publishers.

Department of Fine Arts (n.d.) *Raingan Kansamruat Boransathan nai Krung Rattanakosin* [Report on the Inspection of Ancient Sites in Rattanakosin], Bangkok: Division of Archaeology, Department of Fine Arts.

—— (1963) *Inao. Chabap Hosamut Haeng Chat* [Inao. National Library Edition], Bangkok: Khlangwithaya.

—— (1991) *Chiwit Lae Ngan Khong Sunthon Phu* [The Life and Works of Suthon Phu], Bangkok: Khurusapha Printing.

Department of Town and Country Planning (1994) *Raingan Wichai Phua Kanwang Lae Chat Tham Phangmuang Ruam Muang Nonthaburi. Prap-prung Thi 1.* [Research Report for the Comprehensive Town Planning of Nonthaburi. First Revision] Bangkok: Department of Town and Country Planning, Ministry of the Interior.

De Wandeler, K. and Areepan Khanaiklang (1992) 'Low-income rental and rent-free housing', in K.S. Yap (ed.) *Low-income Housing in Bangkok. A Review of Some Housing Sub-Markets*, Bangkok: Asian Institute of Technology.

Dhani Nivat (1969) 'The city of Thawarawadi Sri Ayudhya', in *Collected Articles by H.H. Prince Dhani Nivat*, Bangkok: Siam Society.

Dhiravat na Pombejra (1990) 'Crown trade and Court politics in Ayutthaya during the reign of King Narai (1656–88)', in J. Kathirathamby-Wells and J. Villiers (eds) *The Southeast Asian Port and Polity. Rise and Demise*, Singapore: Singapore University Press.

Donner, W. (1978) *The Five Faces of Thailand. An Economic Geography*, St. Lucia, Queensland: University of Queensland Press.

Douglass, M. (1984) *Regional Integration on the Capitalist Periphery. The Central Plains of Thailand*, The Hague: Institute of Social Studies.

—— (1995) 'Global interdependence and urbanization: planning for the Bangkok mega-urban region', in T.G. McGee and I.M. Robinson (eds) *The Mega-Urban Regions of Southeast Asia*, Vancouver: UBC Press.

—— (1997) 'Urbanization and social transformations in East Asia', in W.B. Kim, M. Douglass, S-C. Choe and K.C. Ho (eds) *Culture and the City in East Asia*, Oxford: Clarendon Press.

—— (1998) 'World city formation on the Asia Pacific rim: poverty, "everyday" forms of civil society and environmental management', in M. Douglass and J. Friedmann (eds) *Cities for Citizens. Planning and the Rise of Civil Society in a Global Age*, Chichester: John Wiley & Sons.

—— and Zoghlin, M. (1994) 'Sustaining cities at the grass roots: livelihood and social networks in Suan Phlu, Bangkok', *Third World Planning Review* 16, 2: 171–200.

Dowall, D.E. (1989) 'Bangkok: a profile of an efficiently performing housing market', *Urban Studies* 26, 3: 327–9.

Drakakis-Smith, D. (1981) *Urbanisation, Housing and the Development Process*, London: Croom Helm.

Drucker, D. (1987) 'A time to listen to the people', *Bangkok Post* 22 February.

Duncan, J. (1990) *The City as Text. The Politics of Landscape Interpretation in the Kandyan Kingdom*, Cambridge: Cambridge University Press.

Durand-Lasserve, A. (1980) 'Speculation on urban land, land development and housing development in Bangkok: historical process and social function 1950–1980', paper presented to the Thai-European Seminar on Social Change in Contemporary Thailand, 28–30 May.

Economist Intelligence Unit (1974) 'National report no. 16 – Thailand', *International Tourism Quarterly* 2: 13–29.

—— (1984) 'National report no. 92 – Thailand', *International Tourism Quarterly* 2: 12–30.

Edgington, D. (1997) 'Japanese service firms and the hierarchy of Pacific rim cities', research paper presented to the Centre for Advanced Studies and Department of Geography, National University of Singapore, 24 October.

Edler, M. (1996) 'Society, space and shopping: a geographical examination of Bangkok's retailing revolution', Honours Thesis, Department of Geography, University of Sydney.

EIT (Engineering Institute of Thailand) (1993) *Traffic Problems. Causes and Solutions. The Symposium on Traffic Problems 9–10 November, 1992*, Bangkok: Engineering Institute of Thailand.

Emon Niranrat (1996) *Thatsana Thang Sangkhom Nai Nowaniyai Thai Samai Ratchakan Thi 7* [Social attitudes in Thai novels during the Seventh Reign], Bangkok: Ton Or Grammy.

Enloe, C. (1989) *Bananas, Beaches and Bases. Making Feminist Sense of International Politics*, Berkeley: University of California Press.

ESCAP (1988) *Trends in Migration and Urbanization in Selected ESCAP Countries*, Bangkok: United Nations.

—— (1993) *Urbanization in Asia and the Pacific*, New York: Economic and Social Commission for Asia and the Pacific.

Evers, H.-D. and Korff, R. (1982) 'Urban subsistence production in Bangkok', Working Paper No. 25, Bielefeld University.

Evers, H.-D. and Silcock, T.H. (1967) 'Elites and selection', in T.H. Silcock (ed.) *Thailand. Social and Economic Studies in Development*, Canberra: Australian National University Press.

Evers, H.-D., Korff, R. and Suparb Pas-Ong (1987) 'Trade and state formation: Siam in the early Bangkok period', *Modern Asian Studies* 21, 4: 751–71.

Forbes, D. (1996) *Asian Metropolis. Urbanisation and the Southeast Asian City*, Melbourne: Oxford University Press.

—— (1997) 'Metropolis and mega-urban region in Pacific Asia', *Tijdschrift voor Economische en Sociale Geografie* 88, 5: 457–68.

Forsyth, T. (1990) 'Anger in the land of smiles', *Independent* 23 June.

Friedmann, J. (1986) 'The world city hypothesis', *Development and Change* 17: 69–83.

Frisby, D. (1986) *Fragments of Modernity*, Cambridge, MA: MIT Press.

Fuchs, R.L. and Pernia, E.M. (1987) 'External economic forces and national spatial development: Japanese direct investment in Pacific Asia', in R.J. Fuchs, G.W. Jones and E.M. Pernia (eds) *Urbanization and Urban Policies in Pacific Asia*, Boulder, Co: Westview Press.

Fujitsuka, Y. (1994) 'Gentrification: a review of research in western countries and future research on Japanese cities', *Jimbun Chiri* [*Human Geography*] (Kyoto), 46, 5: 496–514.

Fuller, T., Peerasit Kamnuansilpa and Lightfoot, P. (1990) 'Urban ties of rural Thais', *International Migration Review* 24, 3: 534–62.

Gans, H. (1967) *The Levittowners. Ways of Life and Politics in a New Suburban Community*, New York: Vintage Books.

Gervaise, N. (1989) *The Natural and Political History of the Kingdom of Siam*, trans. John Villiers, Bangkok: White Lotus.

Ginsburg, N. (1991) 'Extended metropolitan regions in Asia: a new spatial paradigm', in N. Ginsburg, B. Koppel and T.G. McGee (eds) *The Extended Metropolis. Settlement Transition in Asia*, Honolulu: Hawaii University Press.

Girling, J. (1981) *Thailand. Society and Politics*, Ithaca, NY: Cornell University Press.

—— (1996) *Interpreting Development. Capitalism, Democracy, and the Middle Class in Thailand*, Ithaca, NY: Southeast Asia Programme, Cornell University.

Goffman, E. (1969) *The Presentation of Self in Everyday Life*, Harmondsworth: Penguin.

Goldberg, M. (1995) 'World cities and local property markets: producers and products of the new global economy', in OECD and the Australian Government, *Cities and the New Global Economy. Conference Proceedings. Volume 1*, Canberra: Australian Government Printing Service.

Goldstein, S. (1971) *The Demography of Bangkok. A Case Study of Differentials between Big City and Rural Populations*, Bangkok: Institute of Population Studies, Chulalongkorn University.

Gosling, B. (1990) *Sukhothai. Its History, Culture and Art*, Oxford: Oxford University Press.

Green, P.J. (1990) 'Psychological impacts of slum eviction: women in Bangkok', Master of Social Science (Psychology) Dissertation, University of Waikato, NZ.

Greenberg, C. (1994) 'Region-based urbanisation in Bangkok's extended periphery', Ph.D Dissertation, University of British Columbia.

Gregory, S. (1995) 'Airline industry to fly high in 1995', *Asian Business Review* (January): 98.

Haila, A. (1997) 'The neglected builder of global cities', in O. Kalltorp *et al.* (eds) *Cities in Transformation – Transformation in Cities: Social and Symbolic Change of Urban Space*, Aldershot: Avebury.

Halcrow Fox and Associates (1991) *SPURT. Seventh Plan Urban and Regional Transport. Executive Report*, Bangkok: Office of the National Economic and Social Development Board.

Hamilton, A. (1992) 'Family dramas: film and modernity in Thailand', *Screen* 33, 3: 259–73.

—— (1994) 'Dizzy development in Hua Hin: the effects of tourism on a Thai seaside town', in M. Askew and W.S. Logan (eds) *Cultural Identity and Urban Change in Southeast Asia*, Geelong: Deakin University Press.

—— (1998) 'Primal dream: Masculinism, sin and salvation in Thailand's sex trade', in L. Manderson and M. Jolley (eds) *Sites of Desire, Economies of Pleasure: Sexualities in Asia and the Pacific*, Chicago: University of Chicago Press.

Hanks, L. (1962) 'Merit and power in the Thai social order,' *American Anthropologist* 64: 1247–59.

—— (1975) 'The Thai social order as entourage and circle', in G.W. Skinner and A.T. Kirsch (eds) *Change and Persistence in Thai Society*, Ithaca, NY: Cornell University Press.

Hannerz, U. (1996) *Transnational Connections: Culture, People, Places*, London: Routledge.

Harrison, R. (1996) 'The good, the bad and the pregnant. Why the Thai prostitute as literary heroine cannot be seen to give birth', conference proceedings of the Sixth Annual Conference of Thai Studies, Chiang Mai, 14–17 October.

Hata, T. (1996) *Bangkok in the Balance*, Bangkok: Duang Prateep Foundation.

Healy, T. (1996) 'Home away from home: how to invest in foreign property – and survive', *Asiaweek* (August) (Internet Edition).

Hershatter, G. (1997) *Dangerous Pleasures. Prostitution and Modernity in Twentieth-century Shanghai*, Berkeley: University of California Press.

Hewison, K. (1989) *Bankers and Bureaucrats. Capital and the Role of the State in Thailand*, New Haven, CT: Yale University Southeast Asian Studies.

—— (1993) 'Of regimes, State and pluralities: Thai politics enters the 1990s', in K. Hewison, R. Robison and G. Rodan (eds) *Southeast Asia in the 1990s. Authoritarianism, Democracy and Capitalism*, St. Leonards, NSW: Allen and Unwin.

—— (1996) 'Emerging social forces in Thailand. New political and economic roles', in R. Robison and D.G. Goodman (eds) *The New Rich in Asia. Mobile Phones, McDonald's and the Middle-class Revolution*, London: Routledge.

—— (1997) 'The monarchy and democratisation', in K. Hewison (ed.) *Political Change in Thailand. Democracy and Participation*, London: Routledge.

Hobbs, C. (1992) 'Bad feelings on Khao San', *The Nation* 12 March.

Hong, L. (1984) *Thailand in the Nineteenth Century. Evolution of the Economy and Society*, Singapore: Institute of Southeast Asian Studies.

Horn, D. (1989) 'Culture and Power in Urban Anthropology', *Dialectical Anthropology* 13: 189–98.

Hornblower, M. (1993) 'The skin trade', *Time* 141: 25; 21 June:14–25.

Huxtable, A.L. (1982) *The Tall Building Artistically Reconsidered – The Search for a Skyscraper Style*, New York: Pantheon.

ILO-ARTEP (1991) *A Policy Agenda for the Informal Sector in Thailand*, Bangkok: International Labour Organisation.

Igel, B. (1992) *The Economy of Survival in the Slums of Bangkok*, Bangkok: Division of Human Settlements: Asian Institute of Technology.

Ingram, J.C. (1971) *Economic Change in Thailand 1850–1970*, Stanford, CA: Stanford University Press.

Jackson, P. (1989) *Buddhism, Legitimation and Conflict. The Political Functions of Urban Buddhism*, Singapore: Institute of Southeast Asian Studies.

—— (1999) 'Royal spirits, Chinese gods, and magic monks: Thailand's boom-time religions of prosperity', *Southeast Asia Research* 7, 3: 245–320.

Jacobs, N. (1971) *Modernization without Development. Thailand as an Asian Case Study*, New York: Praeger.

Jamnong Jitniratana (1987) 'Violence in slum eviction', *Thai Development Newsletter* 13: 12–15.

Janssen, P. (1988) 'A slower but surer Asian Tiger', *Asian Business* 24, 6: 72–5.

Jensen, L. (1989a) 'Compromising positions', *The Nation* 21 February.

—— (1989b) 'A Thai alternative to slum clearance', *World Development* 2, 1: 14–17.

Ji Ungpakorn (1995) 'The tradition of urban working class struggle in Thailand', *Journal of Contemporary Asia* 25, 1: 366–79.

Jocano, F.L. (1975) *Slum as a Way of Life*, Quezon City: University of the Philippines Press.

Johnson, P.C. (1997) '"Rationality" in the biography of a Buddhist king: Mongkut, King of Siam (r. 1851–1868)', in J. Schober (ed.) *Sacred Biography in the Buddhist Traditions of South and Southeast Asia*, Honolulu: University of Hawaii Press.

Johnston, D.B. (1975) 'Rural society and the rice economy in Thailand, 1880–1930', Ph.D Dissertation, Yale University.

Juree Namsirichai Vichit-Vadakan (1979) '"Not too high and not too low": a comparative study of Thai and Chinese middle class in Bangkok', Ph.D Dissertation, University of California, Berkeley.

Kahn, J.S. (1998a) 'Southeast Asian identities', in J.S. Kahn (ed.) *Southeast Asian Identities. Culture and the Politics of Representation in Indonesia, Malaysia, Singapore and Thailand*, Singapore: Institute of Southeast Asian Studies.

—— (1998b) 'Class, culture and Malay modernity', in J.D. Schmidt *et al.* (eds) *Social Change in Southeast Asia*, Harlow: Addison Wesley Longman.

Kammeier, H. Detlef (1984) *A Review of the Development and Land Use Problem in Bangkok. HSD Working Paper No. 13.* Bangkok: Human Settlements Division, Asian Institute of Technology: Bangkok.

—— (1992) 'The Thai-Chinese shophouse: a living history in the contemporary townscape', *Trialog* 35, 4: 14–17.

Kanchada Poonpanich (1989) 'The making of third world workers: a cultural analysis of the labour movement in Thailand, 1920s–1950s', Ph.D Dissertation, Bielefeld University.

Kanchanakhaphan (1977) *Mua Wanni . . . Krung Thep Chetsip Pi Kon* [Yesterday . . . Bangkok Seventy Years Ago], Bangkok: Ruangsin Publishing House.

Kanithar Pisitkasem (1991) 'The competitive behaviour of department stores in the Bangkok Metropolitan Area', Master of Economics Thesis, English Language Programme, Thammasat University.

Kanok Wongtrangan (1988) 'Thai bureaucratic behaviour: the impact of dual values on public policies', in L.T. Ghee (ed.) *Reflections on Development in Southeast Asia*, Singapore: Institute of Southeast Asian Studies.

Kasian Tejapira (1991) 'Pigtail: a pre-history of Chineseness in Siam', *Sojourn* 7, 1: 95–122.

Kemp, J.H. (1982) 'Kinship and locality in Hua Kok', *Journal of the Siam Society* 70, 1 & 2: 101–13.

—— (1984) 'The manipulation of personal relations: from kinship to patron–clientage', in H.T. Brummelhuis and J.H. Kemp (eds) *Strategies and Structures in Thai Society*, Amsterdam: Anthropological–Sociological Centre, University of Amsterdam.

Keyes, C.F. (1984) 'Mother or mistress but never a monk: Buddhist notions of female gender in Rural Thailand', *American Ethnologist* 11 (May): 223–41.

Keyes, C. (1987) *Thailand. Buddhist Kingdom as Modern Nation-State*, Boulder, CO: Westview Press.

Khanakammakan Khrongkan Krung Rattanakosin [Rattanakosin Project Committee] (1995) *Khrongkan Krung Rattanakosin* [The Rattanakosin Project], Bangkok: Office for Environmental Policy and Planning, Ministry of Science, Technology and Environment.

Khin Thitsa (1980) *Providence and Prostitution. Women in Buddhist Thailand*, London: Change International reports.

Khlong Toei Slum Federation (1993) *Kanprachum yai pracham pi* [Proceedings of the tenth Annual General Conference], Pattaya, 6–8 August. Unpublished typescript.

Khwansuwong Athipo (1991) *Khli Krung Thep* [Unfolding Bangkok], special issue of *Watthanatham Thai* [Thai Culture], 30.

Kiat Chivakul *et al.* (1982) *Talat Nai Krung Thep: Kankhayai lae Kanplianplaeng* [Markets in Bangkok. Growth and Change] Bangkok: Chulalongkorn University Press.

—— (1993) *Kansuksa Pu Chatthamphaen lae Phang Phatthana Khet Khlong Toei* [A Study for Planning the Development of Khlong Toei District] Bangkok: Department of Urban and Regional Planning, Chulalongkorn University.

Kidokoro, T. (1992) 'Strategies for urban development and transport systems in Asian metropolises, focusing on Bangkok Metropolitan Area', *Regional Development Dialogue* 13, 3: 74–86.

King, A.D. (1990) *Urbanism, Colonialism, and the World-Economy. Cultural and Spatial Foundations of the World Urban System*, London: Routledge.

—— (1996) 'Introduction: cities, texts and paradigms', in A.D. King (ed.) *Re-Presenting the City*, London: Macmillan.

Kitthiphongsa Wirotthanathamakul (n.d.) *Chiwit nai Wang Bangkhunphrom* [Life in Bankhunphrom Palace], Bangkok: Namfon Publishing.

Kitti Banchongrattanangan (1994) 'Kansuksa Kanyai Ban Asai Nai Khet Samphanthawong' [A study of residential mobility in Samphanthawong District], Masters Thesis, Department of Housing, Chulalongkorn University.

Klausner, W. (1992) *Reflections on Thai Culture*, Bangkok: Siam Society.

Kobkua Suwannathat-Pian (1995) *Thailand's Durable Premier. Phibun through Three Decades 1932–1957*, Kuala Lumpur: Oxford University Press.

Koisumi, Junko (1992) 'The commutation of *Suai* from northeast Siam in the middle of the nineteenth century', *Journal of Southeast Asian Studies* 23, 2: 276–307.

Kondo, D. (1990) *Crafting Selves. Power, Gender and Discourses of Identity in a Japanese Workplace*, Chicago: University of Chicago Press.

Korff, R. (1986a) *Bangkok: Urban System and Everyday Life*, Saabrucken: Verlag Breitenbach.

—— (1986b) 'Who has power in Bangkok? An approach towards the analysis of strategic group and class formation in an Asian primate city', *International Journal of Urban and Regional Research* 10, 3: 330–50.

—— (1989a) *Bangkok and Modernity*, Bangkok: Chulalongkorn University Social Research Institute.

—— (1989b) ‘Urban or agrarian? The modern Thai State’, *Sojourn* 4, 1: 45–53.
—— (1993) ‘Bangkok as a symbol? Ideology and everyday life constructions of Bangkok’, in P.J.M. Nas (ed.) *Urban Symbolism*, Leiden: E.J. Brill.
—— (1996) ‘Global and local spheres: the diversity of Southeast Asian urbanism’, *Sojourn* 11, 2: 288–313.
Krissana Parnsoonthorn (1994) ‘Moving downtown’, *Bangkok Post. Thailand Property Guide,* Spring, Bangkok: Post Publishing: 10–11.
—— (1997) ‘No end to woes this year or next’, *Bangkok Post* 17 October.
—— and Busrin Treerapongpichit (1996) ‘Views differ on more foreign ownership’, *Bangkok Post* 5 July.
—— and Peerawat Jariyasombat (1999) ‘US Starwood agrees to buy 51% Stake in Sansiri’, *Bangkok Post* 5 March.
Kritaya Archavanitkul (1988) *Migration and Urbanisation in Thailand, 1980: the urban-rural continuum analysis*, Saraya: Institute for Population and Social Research, Mahidol University.
Krull, G. and Melcher, D. (1966) *Tales from Siam*, London: Robert Hale.
Kumut Chandruang (1996) *My Boyhood in Siam*, Bangkok: Sangdad Publishing.
La Loubere, S. de (1986) *The Kingdom of Siam*, Singapore: Oxford University Press.
Lee, Y.-S. (1998) ‘Intermediary institutions, community organizations, and urban environmental management: the case of three Bangkok slums’, *World Development* 26, 6: 993–1011.
Lefebvre, H. (1991) *The Production of Space*, Oxford: Blackwell.
Law, L. (1997a) ‘Dancing on the bar: sex, money and the uneasy politics of third space’, in S. Pile and M. Keith (eds) *Geographies of Resistance*, London: Routledge.
—— (1997b) ‘A matter of “choice”: discourses on prostitution in the Philippines’, in L. Manderson and M. Jolly (eds) *Sites of Desire, Economies of Pleasure: Sexualities in Asia and the Pacific*, Chicago: University of Chicago Press.
—— (1999) ‘Review of Siriporn Skrobanek, Nattaya Boonpakdi and Chutima Janthakeero, *The Traffic in Women. Human Realities of the International Sex Trade* (London: Zed Books, 1997)’, *Journal of Southeast Asian Studies* 30, 2: 409–10.
Leeds, A. (1994) ‘Locality power in relation to supralocal power institutions’, in R. Sanjek (ed.) *Cities, Classes and the Social Order*, Ithaca, NY: Cornell University Press.
Leman Group (1994) *Metropolitan Regional Structure Study. Sectoral Study No. 2: Population*, Bangkok: Local Consultants.
LeMoncheck, L. (1997) *Loose Women, Lecherous Men: A Feminist Philosophy of Sex*, New York: Oxford University Press.
Lewis, G. (1996) ‘Communications internationalisation and regionalism in Thailand’, *The Journal of International Communication,* 3, 2: 7–18.
—— (1998) ‘Capital of desire: Bangkok as a regional media metropolis’, *Social Semiotics* 8, 2&3: 239–54.
Ling Silaporn (2000) ‘Bangkok angel’, *Lookeast* 30, 5: 15–31.
Litchfield, Whiting, Bowne and Associates (1960) *Greater Bangkok Plan 2533*, Bangkok: Litchfield, Whiting, Bowne and Associates.
Lockard, G.A. (1998) *Dance of Life: Popular Music and Politics in Southeast Asia*, Honolulu: Hawaii University Press.
London, B. (1980) *Metropolis and Nation in Thailand. The Political Economy of Uneven Development*, Boulder, CO: Westview Press.

Lubeigt, G. (1994) 'Traditional and recent aspects of urban development of Chiang Mai, Thailand', in M. Askew and W.S. Logan (eds) *Cultural Identity and Urban Change in Southeast Asia*, Geelong: Deakin University Press.

Lyttleton, C. (1994) 'The good people of Isan: commercial sex in northeast Thailand', *The Australian Journal of Anthropology* 5, 3: 257–79.

McCargo, D. (1997) *Chamlong Srimuang and the New Thai Politics*, New York: St Martin's Press.

—— (2000) *Politics and the Press in Thailand. Media Machinations*, London: Routledge.

McDowell, L. (1996) 'Spatializing feminism. Geographical perspectives', in Nancy Duncan (ed.) *Body Space. Destabilizing Geographies of Gender and Sexuality*, London: Routledge.

MacDonald, A. (1949) *Bangkok Editor*, New York: Macmillan.

McGee, T.G. (1977) 'The persistence of the proto-proletariat: occupational structures and planning of the future of third world cities', in J. Abu-Lughod and R. Hay (eds) *Third World Urbanization*, Chicago: Maaroufa Press.

—— (1989) 'Urbanisasi or Kotadesasi? Evolving patterns of urbanization in Asia', in F.J. Costa *et al.* (eds) *Urbanization in Asia. Spatial Dimensions and Policy Issues*, Honolulu: Hawaii University Press.

MacIntyre, A.J. (1993) 'Indonesia, Thailand and the northeast Asian connection', in R. Higgot L. Leaver and J. Ravenhill (eds) *Pacific Economic Relations in the 1990s. Cooperation or Conflict?*, St Leonards, NSW: Allen and Unwin.

McLean, J. (1997) 'Thai property heading down but not out', *Bangkok Post* 25 March.

Maier, J. (1993) 'Living day-to-day can be slaughter in Klong Toey', *Bangkok Post* 19 December.

Malik, G.J. (1993) 'Indians in Thailand', in J.K. Motwani, M. Gosine and J. Barot-Motwani (eds) *Global Indian Diaspora. Yesterday, Today and Tomorrow*, New York: Global Organization of People of Indian Origin.

Malee Traisawadichai (1990) 'Food, and today's urban lifestyle', *Bangkok Post* 30 July.

Manderson, L (1998) 'Parables of imperialism and fantasies of the exotic: western representations of Thailand – place and sex', in L. Manderson and M. Jolley (eds) *Sites of Desire, Economies of Pleasure. Sexualities in Asia and the Pacific*, Chicago: University of Chicago Press.

Manop Bongsadadt (1973) *The Analysis of Bangkok and Thonburi Transportation*, Bangkok: Theera Press.

—— (1985) 'Urban transport and city planning of Bangkok', in *Proceedings of the National Symposium on Urban Traffic and the Environment*, Bangkok, 16–18 October, Bangkok: Office of the National Environment Board.

—— (1989) 'Condominium market: measures to enhance investment potential and protect buyers', paper presented at the Symposium on the Real Estate Situation in Thailand, Bangkok.

Marcus, G.E. (1998) *Ethnography through Thick and Thin*, Princeton, NJ: Princeton University Press.

Massey, D. (1995) 'The conceptualization of place', in D. Massey and P. Jess (eds) *A Place in the World? Places, Cultures and Globalization*, Milton Keynes: The Open University Press.

Matichon Raiwan Various issues (no authors given).

Maugham, S. W. (1995) *The Gentleman in the Parlour* (first published 1930), Bangkok: White Orchid Press.

Medhi Krongkaew (1996) 'The changing urban system in a fast-growing city and economy: the case of Thailand', in Fu-Chen Lo and Yue-Man Yeung (eds) *Emerging World Cities in Pacific Asia*, Tokyo: United Nations University Press.

Meeker-Buppha (1982) 'The great divide', *ASEAN Investor* 1, 6: 30–8.

Mehotra, S. (1999) 'Mitigating the social impact of the economic crisis: a review of the Royal Thai Government's responses', United Nations System in Thailand (Internet edition).

Meyer, W. (1988) *Behind the Mask. Toward a Transdisciplinary Approach of Selected Social Problems Related to the Evolution and Context of International Tourism in Thailand*, Saarbrucken: Verlag Breitenbach.

Mills, M. B. (1997) 'Contesting the margins of modernity: women, migration and consumption in Thailand', *American Ethnologist* 24, 1: 37–61.

—— (1999) *Thai Women in the Global Labor Force. Consuming Desires, Contested Selves*, New Brunswick: Rutgers University Press.

MIT Consulting Team (1996) *The Bangkok Plan. A Vision for the Metropolitan Administration Area 1995–2005*, Bangkok: BMA Department of City Planning.

Moffat, A.L. (1961) *Mongut, the King of Siam*, Ithaca, NY: Cornell University Press.

Mongkol Bangprapa (1997) 'Squatters rally behind Prateep', *Bangkok Post* 4 March.

Montes, M.F. (1998) *The Currency Crisis in Southeast Asia*, Singapore: ISEAS.

Morell, D. and Chai-aan Saudavanija (1981) *Political Conflict in Thailand. Reform, Reaction and Revolution*, Cambridge, MA: Oegeschlader, Gunn and Hain Publishers.

Morell, S. and Morell, D. (1972) *Six Slums in Bangkok. Problems of Life and Options for Action*, Bangkok: UNICEF.

Mounier, A. (1996) 'Is there a labour concept in Thai culture?', *Chulalongkorn Journal of Economics* 8, 2: 231–62.

Muecke, M. (1992) 'Mother sold food, daughter sells her body: the cultural continuity of prostitution', *Social Science and Medicine* 35, 891–901.

Mukdawan Sakboon (2000) 'Research challenges sex workers' "victim" label', *The Nation* 26 November.

Mulder, N. (1997) *Thai Images. The Culture of the Public World*, Chiang Mai: Silk Worm.

Muqbil, I. (1994) 'Reality bursts room boom bubble', *Bangkok Post. Mid-year Economic Review*, Bangkok: Post Publishing: 38–41.

Mullins, P. (1999) 'International tourism and the cities of Southeast Asia', in D.R. Judd and S.S. Fainstein (eds) *The Tourist City*, New Haven, CT: Yale University Press.

Murray, A. (1991) *No Money No Honey. A Study of Street Traders and Prostitutes in Jakarta*, Oxford: Oxford University Press.

—— (1998) 'Debt-bondage and trafficking: don't believe the hype', in K. Kempadoo and J. Doezema (eds) *Global Sex Workers. Rights, Resistance, and Redefinition*, New York: Routledge.

Muscat, R.J. (1990) *Thailand and the United States. Development, Security and Foreign Aid*, New York: Columbia University Press.

—— (1994) *The Fifth Tiger. A Study of Thai Development Policy*, Tokyo: United Nations University Press.

Mydans, S. (1999) 'In debris of economic crash: Thailand's faith in authority', *New York Times* 10 August.

—— (2001) 'Bit of trekkers' exotica, looking more like home', *New York Times* 12 May.

Naengnoi Saksri (Mom Chao) *et al.* (1991) *Krung Rattanakosin. Ongprakop Thang Kayaphap* [The City of Rattanakosin. Physical Elements], Bangkok: Chulalongkorn University Press.

Nalini Khumsupha (1998) 'Naithang Kanmuang khong Anusaowari Pratchatipatai Nai Sangkhom Thai' [The political meaning of the Democracy Monument in Thai society] Masters Thesis in Political Science, Thammasat University.

Nalini Tanthuwanit *et al.* (1998) *Wiwatthanakan chumchon ae-at lae onkon chumchon ae-at nai muang. Koronisuksa Krungthep Mahanakhon* [The development of crowded communities and community organisations in the city. Case study of Bangkok], Research project on the development of urban crowded communities, Bangkok: Office of Urban Community Development. Unpublished report.

Nanak Kakwani and Medhi Krongkaew (1996) 'Big Reduction in poverty', in *Year-end 1996 Economic Review*, Bangkok: Bangkok Post.

Nangsuphim Nisit Naksuka (1993) [The Students' Newspaper]. Published irregularly by the Duang Prateep Foundation.

Nanthana Vachiraphol (1991) 'The making of the northeastern entrepreneurs in Bangkok', Master of Economics Thesis (English Language Programme) Thammasat University.

The Nation Various issues (no authors given).

Nattaporn Nupirod (1998) 'The social production of news relating to AIDS, prostitution and tourism in Thai newspapers 1987–1992', M.A. Thesis, School of Social Work, University of Melbourne.

Nenthaphis Nakavachara (1993) 'Indian communities in Bangkok: Pahurat and Ban-Kaek', in K.S. Sandhu and A. Mani (eds) *Indian Communities in Southeast Asia*, Singapore: ISEAS.

NESDB (1975) *Economic and Social Indicators*, Bangkok: National Economic and Social Development Board, Office of the Prime Minister.

—— (1977) *The Fourth National Economic and Social Development Plan (1977–1981)*, Bangkok: National Economic and Social Development Board, Office of the Prime Minister.

—— (1986) *Bangkok Metropolitan Regional Development Proposals. Recommended Development Strategies and Investment Programme for the Sixth Plan (1987–1991)*, Bangkok: NESDB/IBRD/USAID/AIDAB.

NHA (1990) *Kanprap-prung chumchon ae-at doi kankheha haeng chat* [Upgrading of crowded communities by the National Housing Authority], Bangkok: National Housing Authority.

Nibhon Debavalya *et al.* (1983) *A Study of Four Improved Congested Areas in Bangkok*, Bangkok: Institute of Population Studies, Chulalongkorn University.

NIDA (1967) *A Note on the Economic Development of Thailand under the First National Economic Development Plan*, Bangkok: National Institute of Development Administration.

Nilubon Pongpitagan and Chanyaporn Chanjaraen (1994) 'A community's show of strength', *Bangkok Post* 27 April.

Nims, C. (1963) *City Planning in Thailand*, Bangkok: City Planning Office, Ministry of the Interior.

Nipan Vichiennoi (1982) 'Urban housing in developing countries: a case study of the socio-economic status of housing purchasers of new housing estates in Bangkok, Thailand, 1969–79', Ph.D Dissertation, Oxford Polytechnic.

Nithet Tinnakul (1987) 'The slum neighbourhood: "community saved", a literature review', *Journal of Development Administration* 27, 1: 170–9.

Nithi Aeuosrivongse (1984) *Pakkai Lae Bai Rue. Khwamruang Wa Duai Wannakam Lae Prawatisat Ton Rattanakosin* [Pen and Sail: Studies of Literature and History in the early Rattanakosin Period], Bangkok: Amarin Printing.

—— (1993) *Latthi Pithi Ro 5* [The Cult of King Rama V], Bangkok: Matichon.

—— (1995a) 'Ban Khrua', *Matichon Raiwan* [Matichon Daily] 10 March.

—— (1995b) '*Songkhram Anusaowari Kap Rat Thai*' [The War of Monuments and the Thai State], in Nithi Aeusriwongse, *Chat Thai, Muang Thai: Baeprian lae Anusawari* [Thai Nation, Muang Thai: Lessons and Monuments], Bangkok: Matichon.

—— (1999) 'The "otherness" of the poor', *Thai Development Newsletter* 37: 23–4.

Nonthaburi Province, Planning Office (1996) *Phangmuang Ruam Nonthaburi. Prapprung Thi 1.* [Comprehensive Plan for Nonthaburi Province. 1st Revision], Bangkok: Department of Town and Country Planning, Ministry of the Interior.

Nopadon Sahachaisaeree (1995) 'The political economy of land and housing for the urban poor in Bangkok: a case study in Klong Toey and Wat Chonglom settlement', Ph.D Dissertation, University of Hawaii.

Nopakhun Limsamarnphun (1993) 'Out of the stranglehold', in Duangkamol Chotana and Pana Janviroj (eds) *Thailand 2010. Which Way do We Grow?*, Bangkok: The Nation Publishing Group.

Nopporn Ruangskul (ed.) (1992) *Wan Wan . . . Kap Wanni Khong Thanon Silom* [Silom Road . . . Yesterday and Today], Bangkok: Thai Danu Bank.

NRDC Data Base (1990) Household, income and landholding data from the National Rural Village Survey (Ko Cho Cho 2 Kho). Kindly re-tabulated at the tambon level for Nonthaburi province for the author by Dr Jacques Amyot, Chulalonkorn University Social Research Institute.

NSO (1970, 1980, 1990a) *Population and Housing Census. Bangkok Metropolis*, Bangkok: National Statistical Office, Office of the Prime Minister.

—— (1981) *Report of the 1981 Socio-Economic Survey. Whole Kingdom*, Bangkok: National Statistical Office, Office of the Prime Minister.

—— (1988) *Report of the 1988 Household Socio-Economic Survey*, Bangkok: National Statistical Office, Office of the Prime Minister.

—— (1990b) *Housing and Population Census for 1990, Nonthaburi Province.* Bangkok: National Statistical Office, Office of the Prime Minister.

Ockey, J. (1996) Eviction and changing patterns of leadership in Bangkok slum communities', *Bulletin of Concerned Asian Scholars* 20, 2: 46–61.

—— (1997) 'Weapons of the urban weak: democracy and resistance to eviction in Bangkok slum communities', *Sojourn* 12, 1: 1–25.

—— (1998) 'Crime, society and politics in Thailand', in C.A. Trocki (ed.) *Gangsters, Democracy, and the State in Southeast Asia*, Ithaca, NY: Southeast Asia Programme, Cornell University.

—— (1999) 'Creating the Thai middle class', in M. Pinches (ed.) *Culture and Privilege in Capitalist Asia*, London: Routledge.

O'Connor, R. (1978) 'Urbanism and religion: community, hierarchy and sanctity in urban Thai Buddhist temples', Ph.D Dissertation, Cornell University.

—— (1983) *A Theory of Indigenous Southeast Asian Urbanism*, Singapore: Institute of Southeast Asian Studies.

—— (1986) 'Merit and the market: Thai symbolizations of self-interest', *Journal of the Siam Society* 74: 62–82.

—— (1990) 'Place, power and discourse in the Thai image of Bangkok', *Journal of the Siam Society* 78, 2: 61–73.

—— (1993) 'Interpreting Thai religious change: temples, Sangha reform and social change', *Journal of Southeast Asian Studies* 24, 2: 330–9.

Odhnoff, J., McFarlane, B. and Limqueco, P. (1983) *Industrialization and the Labour Process in Thailand*, Goteborg: Swedish Centre for Working Life.

Odzer, C. (1994) *Patpong Sisters: An American Woman's View of the Bangkok Sex World*, New York: Blue Moon Books.

O'Flahertie, S. (1995) 'Mega projects and undercutting galore on Asia's high seas', *Asian Business Review* (January): 95–7.

OECD (1999) *Foreign Direct Investment and Recovery in Southeast Asia*, Paris: OECD.

Ong, A. (1985) 'Industrialization and prostitution in Southeast Asia', *Southeast Asia Chronicle* 96: 2–6.

Ong-at Rungchantharachai (1990) *Sopheni Khu Lok: Slok Haeng Chiwit Mut* [Eternal Prostitutes: Odyssey of Dark Lives], Bangkok: Matichon.

Onnucha Hutasingh (1997a) 'Intensifying conflict threatens to undermine 50 years of work', *Bangkok Post* 11 March.

—— (1997b) 'Rival slum factions trade barbs', *Bangkok Post* 11 March.

Ophan Khamdi (1995) '*Ban: Kanplianplaeng, Baepphaen Kanboriphok Banyakat*' [Home: The Changing Environment of Consumption], in Suriphon Sombun Burana (ed.) *Watthanatham Kanboriphok: Naewkhit lae Kanwikhro* [Consumer Culture: Concepts and Analysis], Bangkok: Krek University.

Orathai Ard-am and Kusol Soonthorndhada (1994) 'Household economy and environmental management in Bangkok: the cases of Wat Chonglom and Yen-ar-kard', *Asian Journal of Environmental Management* 2, 1: 37–48.

Ortner, S. (1995) 'Resistance and the problem of ethnographic refusal', *Comparative Studies in Society and History* 37, 1: 173–93.

Oudin, X. (1992) 'Relevance of the "informal sector" in Thailand', *Journal of Social Research* (Chulalongkorn University Social Research Institute) 15, 2: 91–100.

PADCO (1987) *Bangkok Land Management Study. 2 vols*, Bangkok: National Housing Authority of Thailand and Asian Development Bank.

Paitoon Cruangeo (1962) 'Changing Thai society: a study of the impact of urban cultural traits and behaviour upon rural Thailand', Ph.D Dissertation, Cornell University.

Papineau, A.J.G. (1980) *Papineau's Guide to ASEAN Lands*, Singapore: Andre Publications.

Paritta Chalermpow Koanantakool (1999) 'Community and identity of vow-fulfilment dance practitioners', paper presented to the seventh International Conference on Thai Studies, Amsterdam, 4–8 July.

—— and Askew, M. (1993) *Urban Life and Urban People in Transition. Synthesis Reports Vol. II, for the 1993 Year-end Conference: Who Gets What and How? Challenges for the Future*, Bangkok: Thai Development Research Institute.

Parker, R. (1999) *Beneath the Equator. Cultures of Desire, Male Homosexuality, and Emerging Gay Communities in Brazil*, New York: Routledge.

Parnwell, M. and Luxmon Wongsuphasawat (1997) 'Between the global and the local: extended metropolitanisation and industrial decision making in Thailand', *Third World Planning Review* 19, 2: 119–38.

Pasuk Phongpaichit (1980) *Economic and Social Transformation in Thailand 1957–1973*, Bangkok: Chulalongkorn University Social Research Institute.

—— (1982) *From Peasant Girls to Bangkok Masseuses*, Geneva: International Labour Office.

—— and Baker, C. (1995) *Thailand. Economy and Society*, Kuala Lumpur: Oxford University Press.

—— and Baker, C. (1997) 'Power in transition. Thailand in the 1990s', in K. Hewison (ed.) *Political Change in Thailand. Democracy and Participation*, London: Routledge.

—— and Baker, C. (1998) *Thailand's Boom and Bust*, Chiang Mai: Silkworm Books.

—— and Samart Chiasakul (1993) 'Services', in P. Warr (ed.) *The Thai Economy in Transition*, Cambridge: Cambridge University Press.

—— and Sungsidh Piriyarangsan (1994) *Corruption and Democracy in Thailand*, Chiang Mai: Silkworm Books.

——, Sungsidh Piriyarangsan and Nualnoi Treerat (1998) *Guns, Girls, Gambling, Ganja. Thailand's Illegal Economy and Public Policy*, Chiang Mai: Silkworm Books.

—— *et al.* (1988) *Urban Self-Employment in Thailand. A Study of Two Districts in Bangkok*, New Delhi: International Labour Organisation.

Patarawadee Phataranawik (1998) 'Fighting for heritage', *The Nation* 11 May.

Patcharee Siroros and Haller, K.J. (1994) '"Thai-style" contractual relationships: two case studies', *Contemporary Southeast Asia*, 16, 3: 317–41.

Pathomawan Netraphukkana (1996) *Kanwikhro Thi Yu Asai Nai Cherng Setthakit Sangkhom Doi Chai Su* [The socio-economic context of housing through media analysis], Master of Economics Thesis, Chulalongkorn University.

Pawadee Tonguthai (1987) 'Implicit policies affecting urbanization in Thailand', in R.J. Fuchs, G.W. Jones and E.M. Pernia (eds) *Urbanization and Urban Policies in Pacific Asia*, Boulder, CO: Westview Press.

Peleggi, M. (1997) 'The making of the Siamese monarchy's public image', Ph.D Dissertation, Australian National University.

Peracca, S., Knodel, J. and Chanpen Saengtienchai (1998) 'Can prostitutes marry? Thai attitudes towards female sex workers', *Social Science and Medicine* 47, 2: 255–67.

Phillips, H.M. (1965) *Thai Peasant Personality*, Berkeley: University of California Press.

Phisit Pakkasem (1988) *Leading Issues in Thailand's Development Transformation 1960–1990*, Bangkok: National Economic and Social Development Board.

Phuchatkan Raiwan [The Manager, Daily Edition] Various editions (no authors given).

Phuwadon Suwanadi (1995) '*Het kert thi Tha Prachan: Aosan Talat Boran Haeng Rattanakosin*' [The events at Tha Prachan: end of an ancient market of Rattanakosin] *Sinlapa Watthanatham*, 16, 7: 65–9.

Pichai Chuensuksawadi (1999) 'High-rise living has its low points', *Bangkok Post* 25 January.

Pilger, J. (1992) *Distant Voices*, London: Vintage.

Pimpaka Towira (2000) 'Locals move on tourist hub', *The Nation* 17 April.

Pinches, M. (1991) 'The working class experience of shame, inequality, and people power in Tatalon, Manila', in B.J. Kerkvliet and R. Mojares (eds) *From Marcos to Aquino. Local perspectives on political transition in the Philippines*, Honolulu: University of Hawaii Press.

Pinit Ngarpring (1994) 'The big condo wave', *Thailand Property Guide*, Spring, Bangkok: Post Publishing.

Pipat Lertkittisuk and Cimi Suchontan (1991) 'Waking up to the 1990 crash', *Bangkok Post Residential Property Guide 1991*, Bangkok: Post Publishing.

Piprell, C. (2000) 'Exploring Phra Athit Road', *Sawasdee* 29, 11: 33.

Pitch Pongsawat (1995) 'Urban land expropriation policy in Thailand: a case study of Bangkok', postgraduate research report in Land Economy, Cambridge University.

Pitchon, J. (1997) 'Report from Thailand', *Property Link. Real Estate News in the Asia-Pacific Region* (Singapore) 3, 1: 27–30.

Piyanat Bunnak *et al.* (1982) *Khlong nai Krung Thep: Prawatisat, Kanplianplaeng lae Phonkrathop PS. 2325–2525* [Canals in Bangkok: History, Changes and their Impact 1782 AD – 1982 AD], Bangkok: Chulalongkorn University Press.

Platt, L. (2001) 'Regulating the global brothel', *The American Prospect* 12, 12 (Internet edition).

Poona Antaseeda (2000) 'Order to leave Bangkok puts Mahouts on the offensive', *Bangkok Post* 7 March.

Porphant Ouyyanont (1994) 'Bangkok and Thai economic development: aspects of change, 1820–1970', Ph.D Dissertation, University of New England, NSW.

Pradai Viriyabun (1979) *Nam Thieo Muang Boran* [Around the Ancient City], Bangkok: Muang Boran.

Prapapat Niyom (1984) 'Facts and figures of slum eviction in Bangkok 1983', Paper presented at the seminar 'The right to stay: The poor, the land and the law in Asian cities', Bangkok, 20–26 January.

Prapasri Chitpatanapaibul (1993) '*Kan hai Thi phak samrap Khon Raengan nai Khet Utsahakam. Koroni Suksa Khong Khet Phrapadaeng*' [The provision of labour housing in the industrial zone. A case study of Phrapradaeng district, Samut Prakan province], Master of Housing Dissertation, Chulalongkorn University.

Prasert Yamklinfung (1987) 'Thailand: reflections on changing social structure', in *Proceedings of the International Conference on Thai Studies*, 3–7 July, Canberra Australian National University: 283–98.

Prateep Ungsongtham (1986) 'Settlement of the urban poor in Bangkok', *Housing and Human Settlements Journal* 31, 1: 38–45.

Pratt, J.H. (1993) 'Participatory evaluation of urban poor NGOs in Thailand', unpublished M.A. Dissertation, University of British Columbia.

Pravit Rojaphruk and Patcharee Luenguthai (1994) 'Who they are and how they came about', in Pana Janwiroj (ed.) *The Rise of the Thai Middle Classes, The Nation Year-end Report*, Bangkok: Nation Publishing Group.

Pred, A. (1984) 'Place as historically contingent process: structuration and the time-geography of becoming places', *Annals of the Association of American Geographers* 74, 2: 279–97.

Prema-Chandra-Athukorala and Manning, C. (1999) *Structural Change and International Migration in East Asia. Adjusting to Labour Scarcity*, South Melbourne: Oxford University Press.

Promsuk Condominium (1987) Publicity lift-out, *Bangkok Post*.

Pussadee Tiptus (1982) *Ban nai Krung Thep. Laksana lae Kanplienplaeng Song Roi Pi PS. 2325–2525* [Houses in Bangkok. Character and Changes During the last 200 years 1782 AD–1982 AD], Bangkok: Chulalongkorn University.

Quigley, K.F.F. (1996) 'Environmental organizations and democratic consolidation in Thailand', *Crossroads: an Interdisciplinary Journal of Southeast Asian Studies* 9, 2: 1–29.

Reid, A. (1993) *Southeast Asia in the Age of Commerce. 1450–1680. Volume Two: Expansion and Crisis*, New Haven, CT: Yale University Press.

Reynolds, C.J. (1984) 'The plot of Thai history', in *Papers of the International Conference on Thai Studies, Bangkok 22–24 August*, Bangkok: Chulalongkorn University.

—— (1991a) 'Introduction: national identity and its defenders', in C.J. Reynolds (ed.) *National Identity and its Defenders. Thailand, 1939–1989*, Clayton: Monash Papers on Southeast Asia, No. 25.

—— (1991b) 'Tycoons and warlords: modern Thai social formations and Chinese historical romance', in A. Reid (ed.), *Sojourners and Settlers. Histories of Southeast Asia and the Chinese*, Sydney: Asian Studies Association of Australia in association with Allen and Unwin.

—— (1998) 'Globalization and cultural nationalism in modern Thailand', in J.S. Kahn (ed.) *Southeast Asian Identities. Culture and the Politics of Representation in Indonesia, Malaysia, Singapore and Thailand*, Singapore: ISEAS.

Reynolds, F.E. (1978) 'The holy emerald jewel: some aspects of Buddhist symbolism and political legitimation in Thailand and Laos', in B.L. Smith (ed.) *Religion and Legitimation of Power in Thailand, Laos and Burma*, Chambersburg: Anima Books.

Richard Ellis (Thailand) (1992) 'Bangkok, Thailand, metropolitan area', in UMI Market Profiles.

Richard Ellis (1994) 'President Park occupancy schedule, June 1994', computer printout.

Richter, K. (1992) 'Role strain deprivation and conflict', in B. Yoddumnern *et al.* (eds) *Changing Roles and Statuses of Women in Thailand. A Documentary Assessment*, Nakhon Pathom: Institute for Population and Social Research, Mahidol University.

Richter, L.K. (1989) *The Politics of Tourism in Asia*, Honolulu: University of Hawaii Press.

Rigg, J. (1994) 'Redefining the village and rural life: lessons from Southeast Asia', *Geographical Journal* 160, 2: 123–35.

—— (1996) 'Agricultural transformation in Thailand: from rice-farm to non-farm', *Proceedings of the Sixth International Conference on Thai Studies*, Chiang Mai, Thailand, 14–17 October.

—— (1997) *Southeast Asia. The Human Landscape of Modernization and Development*, London: Routledge.

Rimmer P.J. (1995) 'Urbanization problems in Thailand's rapidly industrializing economy', in Medhi Krongkaew (ed.) *Thailand's Industrialization and its Consequences*, New York: St Martin's Press.

Robinson, L. (1993) 'Touring Thailand's sex industry', *The Nation* 1 November.

Romijn, H.B. (1993) *Dynamism in the Informal Sector in a Fast Growing Economy: The Case of Bangkok*, New Delhi: ARTEP-International Labour Organisation.

Roovers, H. *et al.* (1989) 'Alternatives to eviction of Klong Settlements in Bangkok', *Third World Planning Review*, 11 (2): 151–74.

Ross, H. and Anuchat Pongsomlee (1995) 'Environmental and social impact of urbanization in Bangkok', in J. Rigg (ed.) *Counting the Costs. Economic Growth and Environmental Change in Thailand*, Singapore: Institute of Southeast Asian Studies.

—— and Suwattana Thadaniti (1995) 'The environmental costs of industrialization', in Mehdi Krongkaew (ed.) *Thailand's Industrialization and its Consequences*, New York: St Martin's Press.

Rubin, H.J. (1974) 'The city and its relation to the Thai sociocultural system: a research perspective', in R.L. Krannich *et al.* (eds) *Urbanization in Thailand*, De Kalb: Northern Illinois University, Center for Southeast Asian Studies, Occasional Papers No. 2.

Ruland, J. and Bhansoon Ladavalya (1996) 'Managing metropolitan Bangkok: power contest or public service?', in J. Ruland (ed.) *The Dynamics of Metropolitan Management in Southeast Asia*, Singapore: ISEAS.

Rujaya Abhakorn (1984) 'Ratburi, an inner province: local government and central politics in Siam, 1868–1892', Ph.D Dissertation, Cornell University.

Ryan, C. (2000) 'Sex tourism: paradigms of confusion?', in S. Clift and S. Carter (eds) *Tourism and Sex: Culture, Commerce and Coercion*, London: Pinter.

Sakchai Kirinpanu (1993) 'Housing development in the Bangkok Metropolitan Region', paper presented at the International Workshop on Metropolitan/Regional Development, Tongji University, Shanghai, 11–14 October, unpublished typescript.

Sangad Issarathip (1986) '*Kansuksa thang Sangkhom-prawatisat khong Kanplian-plaeng Kanchai Thidin thiyu assai nai Krung Thep Mahanakhon*' [A social-historical study of change in residential landuse in the Bangkok metropolis], MA Thesis, Department of Urban and Regional Planning, Chulalongkorn University.

Sanit Samakhonkan (1996) *Mi Ngun Ko Nap wa Nong, Mi Thong Ko Nap wa Phi: Rabop Khropkhrua lae khruayat khong Thai* [*Nong* is silver and *phi* is gold: the Thai family system], Bangkok: National Institute of Development Administration.

Sanitsuda Ekachai (1987) 'Big-city slum problems: society on the edge of a knife', *Bangkok Post* 3 October.

—— (1990) *Behind the Smile. Voices of Thailand*, Bangkok: Thai Development Support Committee.

—— (1996) 'In the end, it is better to give', *Bangkok Post* 26 December.

—— (1997) 'Sale of amulets is not so charming', *Bangkok Post* 26 November.

—— (1998) 'A life of hard labour', *Bangkok Post* 15 April.

Santi Chantawilatwong (1978) '*Suksa Laksanna Khong Satthabatayakam Khong Tuk Theao*' [A study of some aspects of shop-house architecture], M. Arch. Dissertation, Chulalongkorn University.

Sao-apha Phonsiripong, Phonthip Utsupharat and Duangphon Khamnunwat (1989) *Kansuksa Buangton Kiawkap Ban Khrua Neua* [Preliminary Research on North Ban Khrua Village], Nakhon Pathom: Research Institute for Language and Culture, Mahidol University.

Sarasin Viraphol (1977) *Tribute and Profit. Sino-Siamese Trade, 1652–1853*, Cambridge, MA: Council on East Asian Studies, Harvard University.

Sassen, S. (2000) 'The State and the new geography of power', in D. Kalb *et al.* (2000) *The Ends of Globalization. Bringing Society Back In*, Lanham: Rowman and Littlefield.

Sassen-Koob, S. (1986) 'New York city: economic restructuring and immigration', *Development and Change* 17: 85–119.

Scroggins, H. (1992) 'Quiet on the SET', *Manager (Thailand)* 47 (November): 71–5.

Scupin, R. (1981) 'The socio-economic status of Muslims in central and north Thailand', *Journal of the Institute of Muslim Minority Affairs* 3, 2: 162–89.

—— (1998) 'Muslim accommodation in Thai society', *Journal of Islamic Studies* 9, 2: 229–58.

Seek, Ngee-Huat (1995) 'Risks and opportunities in changing Asia-Pacific property markets', in OECD and the Australian Government, *Cities and the New Global Economy. Conference Proceedings. Volume 3*, Canberra: Australian Government Printing Service.

Seidenfaden, E. (1928) *Guide to Bangkok. With Notes on Siam*, Bangkok: Royal State Railways of Siam.

Seksan Prasertkul (1989) 'The transformation of the Thai State and economic change (1855–1945)', Ph.D Dissertation, Cornell University.

Sermsin Soma-Lapha (1997) '"*Kha Khong Khon" Nai Sangkhom Muang*' [The 'value of people' in urban society], *Phuchatkan Raiwan* [The Manager, Daily Edition] 19 December.

Setchell, C. (1991) 'The emerging crisis in Bangkok: Thailand's next "boom"', background paper for the 2010 Project, Bangkok: Thailand Development Research Institute.

—— (1995) 'The growing environmental crisis in the world's mega-cities: the case of Bangkok', *Third World Planning Review* 17, 1: 1–18.

Sethiyon Chantimathon (1987) *Thonarachan. Chin Sophonpanich* [King of the Bank: Chin Sophonpanich], Bangkok: Matichon.

Sharhand, A., Tekie, M. and Weber, K. (1986) *The Role of Women in Slum Improvement. A Comparative Study of the Squatter Settlements at Klong Toey and Wat Yai Sri Suphan in Bangkok, Thailand*, Bangkok: Division of Human Settlements Development, Asian Institute of Technology.

Sharp, J.P. *et al.* (2000) *Entanglements of Power. Geographies of Domination/Resistance*, London: Routledge.

Sharp, L. and Hanks, L. (1978) *Bang Chan. Social History of a Rural Community in Thailand*, Ithaca, NY: Cornell University Press.

Shields, R. (1996) 'A guide to urban representation and what to do about it: alternative traditions of urban theory', in A.D. King (ed.) *Re-Presenting the City*, London: Macmillan.

Siam Rath Various issues (no authors given).

Siang Chak Futbat (1998) [Voice from the Footpath] Newsletter of the Bangkok Forum, 4, 2.

Sidhijai Tanphiphat (1993) 'Housing finance in Thailand: prospects for the 1990s', paper presented to the International Symposium on Urban Housing, Chulalongkorn University, Bangkok, 24–27 November.

Siek, Foo Tuan (1992) 'The provision of low-cost housing by private developers in Bangkok, 1987–89: the result of an efficient market?', *Urban Studies* 29, 7: 1137–46.

Siffin, W.J. (1966) *The Thai Bureaucracy. Institutional Change and Development*, Honolulu: East-West Center Press.

Silber, I.F. (1995) 'Space, fields, boundaries: the rise of spatial metaphors in contemporary sociological theory', *Social Research* 62, 2: 323–55.

Simister, D. (1994) 'Bangkok rides the new boom', *Bangkok Post. Thailand Property Guide*, Spring, Bangkok: Post Publishing: 13–14.

Simon, J.C. (1996) 'The Thai manufacturing sector: new patterns of expansion', in M. Parnwell (ed.) *Uneven Development in Thailand*, Aldershot: Avebury Press.

Siphanom Singthong (1962) *Phraratchaphithi khong Kasat Thai* [Royal Ceremonies of Thai Kings], Bangkok: Odeon.

Sirichai Narumit (1977) *Old Bridges of Bangkok*, Bangkok: Siam Society.

Sirikul Bunnag (2001) 'Campus plan spurs march', *Bangkok Post* 20 June.

Sirilaksana Khoman (2000) 'The Asian financial crisis and prospects for trade and business with Thailand', in Tran Van Hoa and C. Harvie (eds) *The Causes and Consequences of the Asian Financial Crisis*, New York: St Martin's Press.

Sirinya Wattanasukchai (2000) 'It happened on Khaosan Road', *The Nation* 7 April.

Sittichai Singhasakares(1978) 'Housing estate management', in Nathalang Wadayu (ed.) *Housing in Thailand. Southeast Asian Low-cost Housing Study*, Bangkok: Applied Scientific Research Corporation of Thailand.

Skinner, G.W. (1957) *Chinese Society in Thailand. An Analytical History*, Ithaca, NY: Cornell University Press.

Smarn Sudto and McAuley, A. (1997) *Thailand's Fifty-one Business Leaders*, Bangkok: Post Publishing.

Smart, A. (1986) 'Invisible real estate: investigations into the squatter property market', *International Journal of Urban and Regional Research* 10, 1: 29–45.

Smith, J. and Anusorn Sakseree (1999) 'Culture shock Bangkok', *Bangkok Post* 10 September.

Smith, M. (1982) *A Physician at the Court of Siam*, Kuala Lumpur: Oxford University Press.

Smith, N. (1996) *The New Urban Frontier. Gentrification and the Revanchist City*, London: Routledge.

So Plainoi (1960) *Lao Ruang Bangkok* [Stories of Bangkok], Bangkok: Ruamsan.

Soja, E. (1996) *Thirdspace. Journeys to Los Angeles and other Real-and-Imagined Places*, Oxford: Blackwell.

Somchai Chuaykliang (1987) 'Non-governmental organizations working in the slums', *Thai Development Newsletter* 13: 30–4.

—— (1997) Project notes. '*Sarup laksana nisai khong khon slum thi pen upasak to thamngan phatthana*'[A summary of personality characteristics of slum people which are an obstacle to development work], unpublished notes.

Somerville, M. (1897) *Siam on the Meinam. From the Gulf to Ayuthia*, London: Sampson, Low, Marston and Co.

Somkiat Sunthonchai (1989) '*Kansuksa Phua Kamnot Naeothang Kanwangphaenphatthana Phunthi Thetsaban Muang Nonthaburi*' [A Study to Establish Planning Guidelines for the Development of Nonthaburi Municipal Area], Masters of Urban Planning Dissertation, Chulalongkorn University.

Somphong Chitradap (1997) *Watthanatham Dek Re-ron Nai Thong Thanon* [The Culture of Itinerant Street Children], Bangkok: Chulalongkorn University Press.

Sombong Duangsawai (1997) *Lamphu. Sanyalak Prawatisat Khong Banglamphu* [Lamphu: A Historical Symbol of Banglamphu], Bangkok: Charoenwitthaya.

Sompong Patbui (1986) *Ekkasan Prasopkan Khlong Toei* [Documents on the Khlong Toey experience], Bangkok: Grassroots Development Institute.

—— and Woodthipan Rathantharee (1991) 'Slum-dwellers fight for a home', in Vitoon Panyakul (ed.) *People Centered Development. The People Forum 1991*, Bangkok: Local Development Institute.

Sompop Manarungsan (1989) *Economic Development of Thailand, 1850–1950. Response to the Challenge of the World Economy*, Bangkok: Institute of Asian Studies, Chulalongkorn University.

Somsook Boonyabancha (1983) 'Causes and effects of slum eviction in Bangkok', in S. Angel *et al.* (eds) *Land for Housing the Poor*, Singapore: Select Books.

Somsook Boonyabancha *et al.* (1988) *Struggle to Stay. A Case Study of People in Slum Klong Toey Fighting for their Home*, Bangkok: Duang Prateep Foundation.

Sopon Ongkara (1992) *Facing the Unknown. The Nation Yearbook 1991/92*, Bangkok: Nation Publishing Group.

Sopon Pornchokchai (1985) *1020 (Bangkok Slums)*, Bangkok: Japanese Volunteer Centre in Thailand, School of Urban Research and Action.

—— (1987) 'Slum growth: migration is not the culprit', *Bangkok Post* 6 December.

—— (1992) *Bangkok Slums. Review and Recommendations*, Bangkok: School of Urban Community Research and Action, Agency for Real Estate Affairs.

Soraj Hongladarom (1998) 'Global culture, local cultures and the Internet: the Thai example', *Electronic Journal of Communication* 8, 3 & 4 (Internet journal).

Spencer, D. (1993) *Landowners and the Urbanising Countryside: A Structure and Agency Approach*, Reading: University of Reading.

Sprague, J. (2000) 'As the world gets tight', *Asiaweek* 26, 6: 4.

Srisaka Vallibhotama (1987) '*Kansrang Khwamsaksit Samrap Phra Nakhon Nai Ratchakan Thi 1*' [The Establishment of Sacredness in Bangkok during the Reign of King Rama I], *Muang Boran* 13, 2: 29–41.

—— and Suchit Wongtet (1982) *Krung Thep Ma Chak Nai?* [Where did Khrung Thep Come From?] Bangkok: Chao Phraya Publishers.

Stanton, E.F. (1956) *Brief Authority*, New York: Harper and Brothers.

Sternstein, L. (1964) 'Settlement in Thailand: patterns of development', Ph.D Dissertation, Australian National University.

—— (1966) 'The distribution of Thai centres at mid-nineteenth century', *Journal of Southeast Asian History* 7, 1: 66–72.

—— (1971) *Greater Bangkok Metropolitan Area. Population Growth and Movement 1956–1960*, Bangkok: Institute of Population Studies, Chulalongkorn University.

—— (1976) *Thailand. The Environment of Modernisation*, Sydney: McGraw Hill.

—— (1982) *Portrait of Bangkok*, Bangkok: Bangkok Metropolitan Administration.

Sthirakoses [Phraya Anuman Ratchaton] (1992) *Looking Back. Book One*, Bangkok: Chulalongkorn University Press.

—— (1996) *Looking Back. Book Two*, Bangkok: Chulalongkorn University Press.

Storer, G. (1999) 'Bar talk: Thai male sex workers and their customers', in P. Aggleton (ed.) *Men Who Sell Sex – International Perspectives on Male Sex Work and HIV/AIDS*, London: UCL Press.

Suchit Wongthet (1996) *Maenam Lamkhlong: Sai Prawatisat* [River and Canal: Route of History], Bangkok: Matichon.

Suchitra Punyaratabandhu-Bhakti (1985) 'Structural problems in the governance of Bangkok', *Crossroads: An Interdisciplinary Journal of Southeast Asian Studies* 2, 2: 113–27.

Sudjic, D. (1993) *The 100 Mile City*, New York: Flamingo.

Suehiro, A. (1989) *Capital Accumulation in Thailand 1855–1985*, Tokyo: Centre for East Asian Cultural Studies.

Sukanya Hantrakul (1983) *Prostitution in Thailand*, Clayton, Victoria: Monash University, Centre for Southeast Asian Studies.

Sulak Sivaraksa (1990) *Siam in Crisis*, 2nd edn, Bangkok: Inter-Religious Commission for Development.

Sunait Chutintaranond (1998) 'Old Bangkok in Myanmar military map', paper presented to the conference 'Myanmar Culture and Society', Chulalongkorn University, 23–24 July.

Sungsidh Phiriyarangsan and Pasuk Phongpaichit (eds) (1992) *Chonchan Klang Bon Krasae Pratchathipatai Thai* [The Middle Class and Democratisation in Thailand], Bangkok: Political Economy Centre, Chulalongkorn University and Freideric Ebert Foundation.

—— and Somchai Chuaykliang (1996) '*Witthi Chiwit Thang Setthakit Khong Slum Nai Krung Thep Mahanakhon Kap Kansongserm Kanmi Ngan Tham*' [Ways of Life and the Economy of Slums in Bangkok and Support for Employment], unpublished research report, Bangkok: Chulalongkorn University.

Supha Lusri (1970) *Chetsip Sam Changwat. Lem 4* [Seventy-three Provinces, vol. 4] Bangkok: Thai Watthanaphich Press.

Suphadradis Diskul (Mom Chao) (1982) 'Phraphuttharup Samkhan Samai Rattanakosin' [Important Buddha Images in the Rattanakosin Period], *Sinlapa Wattanatham* 4, 1: 22–34.

Supoj Wancharoen (2000) 'ETA intent on acquiring Ban Khrua: further resistance likely from residents', *Bangkok Post* 24 April.

Surath Jinakul (1999) 'Cracking down on Khaosan Road', *Bangkok Post* 9 May.

Suthy Prasartset (1995) 'The rise of NGOs as critical social movement in Thailand', in Jaturong Boonyarattanasoonthorn and Gawin Chutima (eds) *Thai NGOs. The Continuing Struggle for Democracy*, Bangkok: Thai NGO Support Group.

Tadiar, N.X.M. (1995) 'Manila's new metropolitan form', in V.L. Rafael (ed.) *Discrepant Histories. Translocal Essays on Filipino Cultures*, Philadelphia, PA Temple University Press.

Talle, A. (1998) 'Sex for leisure: modernity among female bar workers in Tanzania', in S. Abram and J. Waldren (eds) *Anthropological Perspectives on Local Development*, London: Routledge.

Tambiah, S.J. (1976) *World Conqueror and World Renouncer. A Study of Buddhism and Polity in Thailand against a Historical Background*, Cambridge: Cambridge University Press.

Tanabe, S. (1977) 'Historical geography of the canal system in the Chao Phraya river delta', *Journal of the Siam Society* 65, 2: 23–72.

Tasker, R. and Prangtip Daorueng (1999) 'Concrete action', *Far Eastern Economic Review* 162, 6: 46.

TAT (Tourism Authority of Thailand) (1990) *Thailand Tourism Statistical Report*, Bangkok: Tourism Authority of Thailand.

—— (1991) 'Preliminary survey on international tourists staying in Banglamphu guest houses. January 1991', internal report, Bangkok: Tourism Authority of Thailand [in Thai].

TDRI (1991) *Managing the Urban Informal Sector in Thailand. A Search for Practical Policies Based on the Basic Needs Approach*, Bangkok: National Economic and Social Development Board.

Teera and Yaruma Ashakul (1989) *BMA Study: Urban Poor*, Bangkok: NESDB, Working Paper.

Terwiel, B.J. (1978) 'The origin and meaning of the Thai "city pillar"', *Journal of the Siam Society* 66, 2: 159–71.

—— (1983) *A History of Modern Thailand 1767–1942*, St Lucia: Queensland University Press.

—— (1989) *Through Travellers' Eyes. An Approach to Early Nineteenth Century Thai History*, Bangkok: Duang Kamol.

Textor, R. (1961) *From Peasant to Pedicab Driver*, New Haven, CT: Yale University Southeast Asia Studies.

Thai Farmers Bank (1997) 'Rising unemployment: urgent problems', *Thai Farmers Research Report* 25 December (Internet edition).

—— (1998) 'Workers return to the provinces as recession dries up urban employment', *Thai Farmers Research Report* 20 November (Internet edition).

Thai University Research Associates (1976) *Urbanisation in the Bangkok Central Region*, Bangkok: The Social Science Association of Thailand.

Thak Chaloemtiarana (1974) 'The Sarit regime, 1957–1963: the formative years of modern Thai politics', Ph.D dissertation, Cornell University.

—— (1979) *Thailand: The Politics of Despotic Paternalism*, Bangkok: Social Science Association of Thailand.

Thaksina Khaikaew (1997) 'Anti-drugs campaign runs despite threats', *Bangkok Post* 2 March.

Thawee Watngam (1997) *Thanon Kao Nai Muang Krung* [Old Roads of the Capital], Bangkok: Ton Or Grammy.

Thawisak Phuaksom (1997) 'Kan Grap Dua Thang Khwamru Khwamching Lae Amnat Khong Chonchannam Siam Pho So 2325–2411' [The Readjustment of Knowledge, Truth and Power of the Elites in Siam, 1782–1868] M.A. Dissertation, Faculty of Arts, Chulalongkorn University.

Thawisak Saeng-arthit (1986) '*Kanaphiphrai khong nai Thawisak Saeng-athit*' [Discussion of Mr Thawisak Saeng-athit], in *Naeothang nai kan kae panha khong chumchon ae-at: prasopkan chak Klong Toei* [Directions for solving slum problems. Experiences from Khlong Toei], seminar sponsored by the Canadian Embassy, Bangkok, 9 November.

Thiesmeyer, L. (1999) 'The West's "comfort women" and discourses of seduction', in S.G. Lim, L.E. Smith and W. Dissanayake (eds) *Transnational Asia Pacific. Gender, Culture and the Public Sphere*, Urbana, IL: Illinois University Press.

Thinapan Nakata (1990) 'The role of the National Social and Economic Development Board (NESDB) in assisting government', in Suchart Prasith-Rathsint (ed.) *Thailand on the Move. Stumbling Blocks and Breakthroughs*, Bangkok: Thai University Research Association and Canadian International Development Agency.

Thiphakhorawong (Chao Phraya) (1966) *The Dynastic Chronicles. Bangkok Era. The Fourth Reign (AD 1851–1868)*, 5 vols, trans. C.K. Flood, Tokyo: Center for East Asian Cultural Studies.

Thiravet Pramuanratkarn (1979) 'Impact of urbanization on a peripheral area of Bangkok, Thailand', Ph.D Dissertation, University of Washington.

Thitinan Pongsudhiruk and Fahn, J. (1993) 'Visit Thailand – please!!!', in Thepchai Yong (ed.) Thailand 2010: which way do we grow?', *The Nation. Midyear Report, July 1993*, Bangkok: The Nation Publishing Group.

Thompson, P.A. (1996) *Siam. An Account of the Country and the People* (first published 1910), Bangkok: White Lotus.
Thongchai Savasdisara, Tips, W.E.J. and Sunanta Suwannodom (1986) *An Evaluation of Private Housing Estates in Greater Bangkok*, Bangkok: Division of Human Settlements, Asian Institute of Technology and Institute of Population Studies, Chulalongkorn University.
Thongchai Winichakul (1994) *Siam Mapped. A History of the Geo-body of a Nation*, Honolulu: Hawaii University Press.
—— (2000) 'The quest for "Siwilai": a geographical discourse of civilizational thinking in late nineteenth and early twentieth century Siam', *Journal of Asian Studies*, 59, 3: 528–49.
Thorbeck, S. (1987) *Voices from the City. Women of Bangkok*, London: Zed Books.
Thrift, N. (1989) 'The geography of international economic disorder', in R.J. Johnston and P.J. Taylor (eds) *A World in Crisis*, Oxford: Blackwell.
Tomosugi, T. (1993) *Reminiscences of Old Bangkok. Memory and Identification of a Changing Society*, Tokyo: The Institute of Oriental Culture.
—— (1995) *Changing Features of a Rice-growing Village in Central Thailand. A Fixed-point Study from 1967 to 1993*, Tokyo: Centre for East Asian Cultural Studies for UNESCO.
Truong, T-D. (1990) *Sex, Money and Morality. Prostitution and Tourism in Southeast Asia*, London: Zed Books.
Tsing, A.L. (1993) *In the Realm of the Diamond Queen*, Princeton, NJ: Princeton University Press.
Tsukasa, I. (1992) 'A future projection of building volume control in Bangkok', paper presented to the workshop on Methodology for Land and Building Use Controls, Chulalongkorn University, Bangkok.
Tunya Sukpanich (1996) 'Begging business', *Bangkok Post* 22 September.
Unger, D. (1998) *Building Social Capital in Thailand*, Cambridge: Cambridge University Press.
United Nations (1991) *World Urbanization Prospects*, New York: United Nations.
Utis Kaothien (1995) 'The Bangkok Metropolitan Region: policies and issues in the Seventh Plan', in T.G. McGee and I.M. Robinson (eds) *The Mega-Urban Regions of Southeast Asia*, Vancouver: UBC Press.
Van Esterik, P. (2000) *Materializing Thailand*, Oxford: Berg.
Vaid, K.N. (1982) 'Indians in Thailand', in I.J.B. Singh (ed.) *Indians in Southeast Asia*, New Delhi: Sterling Publishers.
Vasana Chinvarakorn (2000) 'The on-going case of Ban Khrua. The road to nowhere', *Thai Development Newsletter* 38 and 39: 39–45.
Vatikiotis, M. (1995) 'Urban dreams: city dwellers want leaders who "get things done"', *Far Eastern Economic Review* 158, 26: 18–19.
Vella, W.F. (1957) *Siam Under Rama III*, Locust Valley, NY: Augustin.
—— (1978) *Chaiyo! King Vajiravudh and the Development of Thai Nationalism*, Honolulu: Hawaii University Press.
Vira Rojpojchanarat (1987) 'The conservation of monuments in Thailand', in *Final Report. Workshop on Community-based Conservation and Maintenance of Historic Buildings/Living Monuments August 23–30*, Bangkok: SEAMEO Regional Centre for Archaeology and Fine Arts.
Vitoon Panyakul (ed.) (1991) *People Centered Development. The People Forum 1991*, Bangkok: Local Development Institute

Voravidh Charoenloet (1991) 'Thailand in the process of becoming a NIC: myth or reality?', *Journal of Contemporary Asia*, 21, 1: 31–41.
Wales, Q.H.G. (1931) *Siamese State Ceremonies*, London: B. Quaritch.
—— (1934) *Ancient Siamese Government and Administration*, London: B. Quaritch.
Walker, D. and Erlich, R. (1992) *Hello My Big Big Honey. Love Letters from Bangkok Bar Girls*, Bangkok: Dragon Dance Publications.
Wanich Jarunggidanan (1985) *Muang Luang* [The Capital], Bangkok: Chulalongkorn University Translation Centre.
Warr, P.G. (1993) 'The Thai economy', in P.G. Warr (ed.) *The Thai Economy in Transition*, Cambridge: Cambridge University Press.
—— (1998) 'The Thai economy. From boom to gloom?', *Southeast Asian Affairs 1997,* Singapore: ISEAS.
Watenabe, S. (1998) 'From Thailand to Japan: migrant sex workers as autonomous subjects', in K. Kempadoo and J. Doezema (eds) *Global Sex Workers. Rights, Resistance, and Redefinition*, New York: Routledge.
Wathini Boonchalaksi and Guest, P. (1994) *Prostitution in Thailand*, Nakhon Pathom: Institute for Population and Social Research, Mahidol University.
—— (1998) 'Prostitution in Thailand', in L.L. Lim (ed.) *The Sex Sector. The Economic and Social Bases of Prostitution in Southeast Asia*, Geneva: International Labour Office.
Watson, S. and Gibson, K. (1995) 'Postmodern cities, spaces and politics', in S. Watson and K. Gibson (eds) *Postmodern Cities and Spaces*, Oxford: Blackwell.
Webster, D. (1995) 'Mega-urbanization in ASEAN: new phenomenon or transitional phase to the "Los Angeles" world city?', in T.G. McGee and I.M. Robinson (eds) *The Mega-Urban Regions of Southeast Asia*, Vancouver: UBC Press.
Wenk, K. (1968) *The Restoration of Thailand under Rama I*, Tucson: University of Arizona Press.
Westwood, S. and Williams, J. (1997) 'Imagining cities', in S. Westwood and J. Williams (eds) *Imagining Cities. Scripts, Signs, Memory*, London: Routledge.
Whittaker, A. (1999) 'Women and capitalist transformation in a northeastern Thai village', in P.A. Jackson and N. Cook (eds) *Genders and Sexualities in Modern Thailand*, Chiang Mai: Silkworm.
Wichai Naraphaibun (1997) '*Klum Sahakonraengan Yan Rangsit Chat Dern Ronarong Phonkrathop Chak Settakhit Thodtoi*' [Rangsit trade union organises campaign against the impacts of the economic depression], *Raengan Porithat* [Labour Review] 11, 10: 21.
Wilai Rangsiwong (1991) '*Suksa Laksana Lae Thi Tang Samphan Khong Ket Hao Nai Khet Krung Thep Mahanakhon*' [A study of the relationship between characteristics and locations of guest houses in Bangkok], M.Ed. Thesis (Geography), Srinakarinwirot University, Bangkok.
Williams, R. (1973) *The Country and the City*, London: Chatto and Windus.
Wilson, C.M. (1970) 'State and society in the reign of Mongkut, 1851–1868: Thailand on the eve of modernization', Ph.D Dissertation, Cornell University.
—— (1980) 'Nineteenth-century Thai administration: are our models adequate?', *Contributions to Asian Studies* 15: 29–40.
—— (1989) 'Bangkok in 1883: an economic and social profile', *Journal of the Siam Society* 77, 2: 49–58.
—— (1990) 'Economic activities of women in Bangkok, 1883', *Journal of the Siam Society* 78, 1: 84–7.

Wood, W.A.R. (1965) *Consul in Paradise. Sixty-nine Years in Siam*, London: Souvenir Press.

Worawan Wetchasat (1985) '*Kansuksa Priapthiap Ithiphon Khong Konkai Duam-uang to Baep phaen Kandamneonkan Chiwit Nai Khet Chanmuang Krungthep Mahanakhon*' [The influence of urbanisation: a comparative study of ways of life in the suburbs of Bangkok] Masters Thesis, Faculty of Sociology and Anthropology, Thammasat University.

World Bank (1993) *The East Asian Miracle. Economic Growth and Public Policy*, New York: Oxford University Press.

Wu, F. (2000) 'The global and local dimensions of place-making: remaking Shanghai as a world city', *Urban Studies* 37, 8: 1359–77.

Wyatt, D.K. (1982a) 'The 'subtle revolution' of King Rama I of Siam', in D.K. Wyatt and A. Woodside (eds) *Moral Order and the Question of Change*, New Haven, CT: Yale University Southeast Asian Studies.

—— (1982b) *Thailand. A Short History*, New Haven, CT: Yale University Press.

—— (1994a) 'The Buddhist monkhood as an avenue of social mobility in traditional Thai society', in D.K. Wyatt, *Studies in Thai History. Collected Articles*, Chiang Mai: Silkworm Books.

—— (1994b) 'Education and the modernization of Thai society', in D.K. Wyatt, *Studies in Thai History. Collected Articles*, Chiang Mai: Silkworm Books.

—— (1994c) 'Family politics in seventeenth- and eighteenth-century Siam', in D.K. Wyatt, *Studies in Thai History. Collected Articles*, Chiang Mai: Silkworm Books.

Yani Sonpraphai (1995) '*Kansupnuang Kanplianplaeng Thang Sangkhom Lae Watthanatham Chao Suan Changwat Nonthaburi*' [Continuity and sociocultural change of gardeners in Nonthaburi], M.A. Dissertation, Sinlapakon University.

Yap, K.S. (1992) 'The slums of Bangkok', in Yap Kioe Sheng (ed.) *Low-Income Housing in Bangkok. A Review of Some Housing Sub-Markets*, Bangkok: Asian Institute of Technology.

—— and Angel, S. (1992) 'Land-sharing: the Sengkhi project', in Yap Kioe Sheng (ed.) *Low-Income Housing in Bangkok. A Review of Some Housing Sub-Markets*, Bangkok: Asian Institute of Technology.

Yasmeen, G. (1995) 'Exploring a foodscape: the case of Bangkok', *Malaysian Journal of Tropical Geography* 26, 1: 1–11.

Yeung, Y-M. and Lo, F-C. (1996) 'Global restructuring and emerging urban corridors in Pacific Asia', in Fu-Chen Lo and Yue-Man Yeung (eds) *Emerging World Cities in Pacific Asia*, Tokyo: United Nations University Press.

Yok Burapha (1997) *Nai Mubananchatsan Mi . . . Niyai* [In the Housing Estate There is . . . a Story], Bangkok: Book Bank.

Yongthanit Pimonsathaen (1989) 'Towards a commercial area upgrading in a conservation district: the case of Banglamphu, Bangkok, Thailand', M.Sc Thesis, Division of Human Settlements, Asian Institute of Technology.

Yot Santasombat (1992) *Maeying Si Khai Tua: Chumchon Lae Kankha Praweni Nai Sangkhom Thai* [Women Will Sell their Bodies: Community and Prostitution in Thai Society], Bangkok: Local Community Development Institute.

Young, K. (1999) 'Consumption, social differentiation and self-definition of the new rich in industrialising Southeast Asia', in M. Pinches (ed.) *Culture and Privilege in Capitalist Asia*, London: Routledge.

Zatz, N.D. (1997) 'Sex work/sex act: law, labor and desire in constructions of prostitution', *Signs* 22, 2: 277–309.

Zukin, S. (1991) *Landscapes of Power: From Detroit to Disney World*, Berkeley: University of California Press.

—— (1996) 'Space and symbols in an age of decline', in A.D. King (ed.) *Re-Presenting the City. Ethnicity, Capital and Culture in the Twenty-First Century Metropolis*, Houndmills, Basingstoke: Macmillan.

Index